Applied Psychology: putting theory into practice

Applied Psychology: putting theory into practice

D.A. Bekerian and A.B. Levey

OXFORD

UNIVERSITY PRESS

OXFORD
UNIVERSITY PRESS

Great Clarendon Street, Oxford OX2 6DP

Oxford University Press is a department of the University of Oxford.
It furthers the University's objective of excellence in research, scholarship,
and education by publishing worldwide in

Oxford New York

Auckland Cape Town Dar es Salaam Hong Kong Karachi
Kuala Lumpur Madrid Melbourne Mexico City Nairobi
New Delhi Shanghai Taipei Toronto

With offices in

Argentina Austria Brazil Chile Czech Republic France Greece
Guatemala Hungary Italy Japan Poland Portugal Singapore
South Korea Switzerland Thailand Turkey Ukraine Vietnam

Oxford is a registered trademark of Oxford University Press
in the UK and in certain other countries

Published in the United States
by Oxford University Press Inc., New York

© D.A. Bekerian and A.B. Levey, 2005

The moral rights of the author have been asserted
Database right Oxford University Press (maker)

British Library Cataloguing in Publication Data

Data available

Library of Congress Cataloging in Publication Data
Bekerian, Debra Anne.
  Applied psychology : putting theory into practice / D.A. Bekerian and A.B. Levey.
    p. cm.
  Includes bibliographical references and index.
  ISBN-13: 978-0-19-926037-9
  ISBN-10: 0-19-926037-0
 1. Psychology, Applied. I. Levey, A. B. II. Title.
  BF636.B375 2005
  158—dc22

                                                        2005015936

Typeset by Laserwords Private Limited, Chennai, India
Printed in Great Britain on acid-free paper by
Ashford Colour Press Limited, Gosport, Hampshire

ISBN 0-19-926037-0   978-0-19-926037-9

10 9 8 7 6 5 4 3 2

■ OUTLINE CONTENTS

■ DETAILED CONTENTS

■ PREFACE

The general aim of this book is to provide the reader with a good understanding of how applied psychologists go about *being* applied psychologists. We adopt the view, as do many other people, that in order to do good applied psychology, the psychologist must ground all interventions firmly in theory. There must be a specific theoretical explanation as to why psychologists do what they do, suggest what they suggest, and intervene in the way that they intervene. For these reasons, we make sure that the reader is introduced not only to the theoretical concepts that are specific to the applied problem, but also to the more general psychological concepts that are likely to be relevant. In this regard, this book shares common features with other texts on applied psychology. However, the departure for this book is in its organization. We use real-world contexts, rather than the specific training of the psychologist, to introduce the reader to different ways in which psychologists can apply theory. We refer to these general classes of world context as rooms, each having different activities, goals, and, consequently, problems that arise. For example, rather than talk about forensic psychology, we talk about the Crime Room and the Court Room. We believe that this has the advantage of focusing the reader's attention on the most important determinant of applied psychology—namely the real-world problem that the psychologist is being asked to address. It is the real-world situation that determines what skills and expertise are most helpful, not the psychologist's training. Each room can be used as a mnemonic for helping the reader to link mainstream theoretical issues and findings with practical problems; and each chapter follows the same format, highlighting important aspects of the applied problem and showing how psychologists have translated theoretical concepts into practice. We also introduce our readers to questions that encourage them to consider the broader implications of the applied work. The book is largely about demonstrating the impact of theory on application, rather than focusing on the impact that applied work has had on theory. That would be the topic for a different book! Nonetheless, we stress that applications of psychology direct us to the *inadequacies* of theories—their conceptual gaps and where they fail to consider important features. There is no doubt that through good applied psychology, we are better able to construct theories that help us to explain and predict human behaviour.

D.A.B.

A.B.L.

Cambridge, January 2005

Acknowledgements

The preparation of these chapters would not have been possible without the help of a number of friends and colleagues, whose contributions we gratefully acknowledge. At the top of the list is our editor, Jonathan Crowe, whose expert advice and patient support proved essential to the project from the beginning. Two anonymous reviewers provided valuable comments on an earlier version, for which we now thank them. Dr. Susan Levey kindly brought to bear her very considerable critical acumen on several of the chapters and thereby helped us to improve the whole. Barbara Alderton generously offered skilled secretarial assistance at a time when it was most needed. We thank them both. Kevin Symonds, the librarian at the Medical Research Council's Cognition and Brain Sciences Unit—formerly the Applied Psychology Unit—in Cambridge, gave freely of his time in helping us to track down obscure references. We are most grateful to him for his generosity. And to Dr. Susan Goodrich, who joined us in many helpful discussions during the planning stages of the book, we offer our special thanks. Finally, we wish to record our gratitude to three generations of students who were enrolled in the courses in Applied Psychology (DB) on which the book is based. Their contributions, in terms of lively arguments, constructive discussions, and occasional misunderstandings, largely determined the form and content of the book. It is our fond hope that some of them may eventually find rewarding careers in applied psychology!

NOTE TO THE READER

Key concepts—those terms essential to the understanding of the material—are highlighted throughout the text in either italics or bold type. Those terms that are defined in the text, or whose meaning is clear from the context, are set in italics. Important terms that are not defined in the text are set in bold type and will be found in the Glossary at the end of the book. In the text we have made occasional reference to websites on the Internet. However, websites tend to be unstable and a more effective way of accessing the abundance of information on the Internet is by using well-chosen search terms. The terms that are highlighted in the text can be used for this purpose. At the end of each scenario we provide two questions, which are designed to encourage the reader to consider other and potentially wider implications of the work that is discussed. Boxes are included throughout the text. Some are used to expand details; others to introduce additional material of interest. Finally, the Bibliography contains all the references cited in the text. It also lists other books and articles that we consider to be important in understanding the field of applied psychology and we recommend them to the reader interested in pursuing the subject further.

■ FOREWORD BY PROFESSOR ALAN BADDELEY, FRS

For most of its 150 years or so of active life, experimental psychology has largely confined itself to the laboratory, where it was possible to control the environment in order to obtain reliable and robust results. However, as Bartlett pointed out many years ago, this creates the problem of whether such findings have any relevance for the less-sheltered world outside the laboratory. Happily, in recent years the subject has developed to a point at which it not only can be shown to generalize, but also can play an active part in helping people and society. This book is a tribute to that development and I am delighted to see it produced by two of my friends who were my colleagues at the Medical Research Council's Applied Psychology Unit in Cambridge, a research centre that had as its remit the application of psychological theory to practical problems. Debra Bekerian and Archie Levey have worked on both theoretical and practical problems and are well placed to write this book. The format of the book, which involves moving from one room to another, is very appropriately based on the classic method of enhancing memory by associating ideas with locations. It covers a range of important applications, presenting the considerable advances that have made psychology so rich, and interesting contexts that link theory with its practical application.

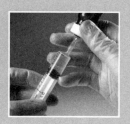

PART ONE

The Transition from Theory to Practice

1

About this book

Psychology is the study of the behaviour of animate beings, and, fittingly, it is a living, evolving discipline. No matter what you do for a living or what your interests might be, psychology and psychologists have made an impact on your life, and will continue to do so. While there are vast numbers of written references on most of the specific academic topics in psychology, much less is written on the application of psychology to people's everyday lives. There are many individual, published papers on specific applied problems, but there are far fewer books that summarize themes in applied research (see Coolican et al. 1996).

Applied research

Applied research has a long history, particularly in the UK, in which theoretical or academic psychology is applied to real-world situations. The single element that probably defines outstanding applied research from more mediocre attempts is the extent to which the researcher *successfully* maps the mainstream, academic literature onto the real-world problem. Good applied psychology is based on working hypotheses that evolve directly from mainstream psychological research. We define a working hypothesis as a preliminary description of the nature of the problems, and potential underlying factors that are based on initial observations. Sometimes the underlying factors are easy to identify, and other times they are more difficult. Once these potential factors are identified, the psychologist then reviews the available literature, which may include empirical evidence, in order to identify which theoretical concepts are most helpful in establishing how to proceed. Importantly, the working hypothesis changes as the psychologist gathers more knowledge and evidence about the problem. As we shall see, sometimes the psychologist discovers that their initial working hypothesis was wrong.

Working hypotheses

Working hypotheses should not be confused with informal conjectures or hunches. In fact, our personal conjectures or hunches about what might be important to consider are not usually helpful. While personal conjecture—based on sound experience—is unquestionably important, at least for the person, these hunches do not translate easily into explanations that can be generalized to different individuals and across different situations. While we may all have hunches, they do not necessarily link to domains of experimental literature, or bodies of independently accrued knowledge. Working hypotheses are thus more than hunches; they have clear theoretical arguments motivate them and they link those arguments directly to critical features of the real-world problem. As this distinction is essential, we provide an illustration.

The role of theory

Suppose a psychologist is asked to comment on the best way or ways in which to interview a witness to a crime. There are four ways in which mainstream, theoretical concepts can direct the working hypotheses with which the psychologist proceeds. First, theoretical concepts help to inform the psychologist about the variables in the interview situation that should be considered. In this example, any number of variables could be examined: the colour of the room, seating arrangement, and general environmental comfort; the inter-personal dynamics between the interviewer and the interviewee; the interview techniques used by the interviewer. Any one of these might influence behaviour. What is important is that the psychologist has sound theoretical concepts that would help to explain *why* any one of these factors can influence behaviour. Selecting those with a theoretical basis provides the psychologist with some rationale for choosing the variables in the first place. We do not mean to imply that the applied situation cannot inform theory, simply that the decision to use theory generally leads to more efficient research.

Second, theoretical concepts inform the psychologist on how to address the variables that have been selected. Roughly speaking, the concepts determine the framework for considering the variables in a particular manner. In our example, a psychologist could rely on concepts derived from cognitive psychology, and focus on how a witness' confidence in her memory for details of a crime can be influenced by the interview strategy. Alternatively, the psychologist could rely on concepts derived from studies of individual differences, and consider whether certain interview strategies are beneficial or harmful for individuals who have anxious personalities. While the specific choice of the theoretical concepts may be unimportant, it is essential that the concepts are well constructed and based on sound evidence.

Third, theoretical concepts identify for the psychologist the various ways to measure the variables that they have selected. For example, the psychologist might want to know whether the interview strategy was beneficial by asking the interviewer and witness how comfortable each felt during the interview. Alternatively, the psychologist might use physiological measures like the **galvanic skin response** to determine whether the witness' levels of stress increase or decrease. It is essential that the method of measurement is relevant to the issues the psychologist wishes to address. Most often this is assured by using measurements that are common within the literature, given the applied problem. The work runs the risk of being useless, or highly controversial, if no one else agrees on the measurement.

Fourth, mainstream concepts help inform the psychologist about the range of interpretations that might be placed on behavioural evidence. For example, they may conclude that when a witness' stress levels decrease this is better for the outcome of the interview. Alternatively, it may be concluded that lowered stress levels are harmful for the outcome of the interview because the witness is not sufficiently motivated. If there are no other references in the literature to the interpretation, there is no way that the psychologist can integrate their findings into the literature. Without such integration, there is little hope for the results to have any impact. They will be too novel to interpret outside of the specific situation in which the psychologist has operated and cannot be generalized to any other, related work that may have preceded it.

The nature of theories

We need to make an important point. Although we advocate theoretically driven research, we do not wish to imply that 'any old theory will do'. As we have already said, theoretical concepts are usually drawn from existing theories, not from hunches or conjectures. A central aspect of science consists of competition between theories, and this has been particularly true of the life sciences, including psychology. How can we determine that a theory is valid? Does it give a correct description of events and facts? Can it predict new events and facts? A considerable body of thought has been devoted to these questions. The extensive literature that it has generated need not concern us here, but there are two general approaches that should be considered for our purposes.

The first approach focuses on the ways in which a theory can be *disconfirmed*; that is, how a theory can be proven false by facts. The critical element in this approach is that a theory is only valid if it is *capable* of being proven false. For obvious reasons, theories do not, in general, fly in the face of reality. So, simply to show that a given theory fits the facts does not necessarily mean that it is true. Rather, there must be some logical mechanism in the theory, or some body of fact to which it refers, that makes it possible to show that it its false. This is a delicate point. Of course, we do not seek to disprove the theory in order to show that it was not valid in the first place; that would be silly. However, the theory must not be protected from disconfirmation and only theories that lend themselves to being tested, and proven correct, are valid.

Several interesting consequences flow from this approach. It implies that a particular theory may need to be tested again and again as new facts emerge. It also implies that in comparing two competing theories we should look for a special set of facts that will disqualify one of them but not the other. We must set up a so-called crucial experiment, an experiment for which the two theories make different or opposite predictions. Surprisingly, this is very difficult to do and the fields of psychology are littered with the broken remnants of crucial experiments that turned out not to be crucial! The reasons why such difficulties arise lie beyond the scope of this book. If you are interested you can consult a text on the scientific method (e.g. Agnew and Pyke 2004).

An absurd example

In order to demonstrate how difficult it may be to devise an experiment to prove that one of two competing theories is correct, let us give a rather absurd example. Remember that the point is that while it might be easy to show a theory to be true, it may be very difficult to prove, indisputably, that it is false.

One of the authors (AL) has come to believe that the electrical equipment in his house is operated by elves. They are small, invisible, good-natured, silent, and helpful. An Elf King rules them. AL communicates with the Elf King, exclusively, by a number of switches and buttons. If, for example, AL wants light in his study, he simply flicks a switch on the wall and the Elf King orders his subjects to run swiftly down a long copper wire leading to a light bulb. If AL wants music he 'turns on' the radio and the Elf King sends his helpers down the wires leading to the loudspeaker.

Now, the other author (DB) has a competing theory. DB's theory is based on notions of electrons and electrical currents—which are as equally invisible and helpful as AL's elves. Ask yourself: how can DB *prove* that AL's theory is invalid? Flick the light switch and the light comes on; AL's theory is confirmed. Turn on the electric 'oven and it rapidly heats; theory confirmed. Whatever DB does can be 'explained' by AL's theory of the elves. It is no use telling AL about electrons, the small, invisible, helpful entities that DB believes in. Their presence and activity can only be determined by observing the consequences of the actions you take. What is needed is a crucial experiment. But at this level the only crucial experiment would have to involve tests that *prove* that AL's invisible elves do not exist. But how? Obviously, there is no feasible way.

An alternative approach

Because of this difficulty, and other more formal reasons, many psychologists prefer to adopt a second approach to the question of what makes a good theory. The second approach argues that a theory is valid if it is useful. This is the Pragmatist position, so named by Alan Baddeley in his chapter in the 2001 volume *Psychology in Britain* (Baddeley 2001). The pragmatic approach says that a theory can be regarded as true for practical purposes if it gives an accurate description of the available facts. This approach may seem simplistic at first but it has a number of advantages. It enables us to isolate theoretical concepts that can be applied to a particular problem, even if parts of the theory are not universally true. We can call this the principle of local application and it is an important point to stress. The task of applied psychology is not to test the validity of theories, but to use them. While it is obviously important that the theoretical concepts have some empirical integrity, the comprehensive testing of any theory is the domain of the experimental and theoretical psychologist, not the applied psychologist. Because of this the pragmatic approach has been the usual practice in applied settings, and this choice is well justified.

Let us illustrate this with our witness example. Suppose a theory says that people who are generally anxious will be poorer at reporting details when a certain interview strategy is used. The theory also predicts that people who are depressed will be *better* if this same strategy is used. Now, one of our colleagues who is an experimental psychologist conducts an empirical study and finds that the prediction about anxious people was confirmed, but that the prediction about depressed people was not confirmed. The theory is obviously only partially supported. However we, as applied psychologists, might still want to consider whether to use the strategy or not, when asked to work on a case with an anxious witness. As we can see, the principle of local application allows us to use what is relevant, and discard what is irrelevant, for the applied problem.

The concepts underlying the issues just reviewed are complex indeed, and our treatment of them has been intentionally simple. What the reader should remember is that there are two ways to decide whether a theory is useful for a real-world problem. One way is whether a theory has been preferentially confirmed by empirical evidence; the other is whether some aspect of the theory can be used successfully to describe critical features of the problem. More often than not the applied psychologist will consider those components of a theory that are really needed, and pay little or no attention to those that are not relevant to the applied situation.

While applied research was prominent in the latter half of the twentieth century, it appears that it has lost its appeal as of late. As psychologists spend less time writing about the ways in which psychology can be applied, the importance of psychology to real-world problems seems to be growing rather than diminishing. This book intends to redress this apparent imbalance by giving the reader some idea of how Psychology is and can be regularly applied to real-world problems.

The structure of this book

This book identifies everyday problems in which psychologists could or have been asked to help. We intend to provide the reader with a good idea of who might use a psychologist, how a psychologist decides what theoretical concepts are relevant, and what a psychologist does in applying these concepts. We also show how the psychologist's input was assessed, in terms of whether their input helped, hindered, or had no impact on the applied problem. A significant point of departure from other books is that we contend that it is the problem rather than the psychologist that determines the professional roles that are adopted. Thus, the book is not structured around the training or academic background of the psychologist, but rather the real-world situation that the psychologist operates within.

We provide the reader with examples of applied settings that reflect major themes in mainstream psychological research. In what follows, individual chapters introduce general real-world settings where psychologists can be used. These real-world settings are depicted as rooms. A room provides us with a way of identifying applied problems in terms of more general real-world settings. So, for example, we have a chapter that is entitled 'The court room' (Chapter 5). In this chapter, the court room is the general class of settings, or real-world situations, where psychologists apply their skills and knowledge.

It is not our aim to explore or describe the settings as such; neither is it to define all of the possible roles that a psychologist can play in that setting. Instead we consider specific problems that arise in the real-world room, and explore how the psychologist intervened.

The structure of the rooms

Each chapter has a general introduction that provides a brief summary of the many ways in which psychologists might be or have been involved in the particular real-world room. We intend these introductions to be a review of the more traditional psychological concepts, and psychologists, that are associated with the particular room. So, for example, the court room is traditionally associated with topics falling under the heading of forensic psychology, and is traditionally the domain of the forensic and clinical psychologist. While it is *not* our approach to define the court room in terms of one specific domain or professional training, we do want the reader to have this general information about the room. However, once the room has been introduced, we then provide two specific scenarios of how a psychologist has been used that might diverge from the traditional trend. As you are introduced to each of these rooms, make a note of your own spontaneous visual imagery. The court room, for example, may suggest dark, wooden panelling, and an atmosphere of gravity, enhanced by the wigs and robes of the officials. You will find that these images help you to remember the material.

Five basic questions

We pose the same series of five questions for each scenario we provide. First we ask, *what is the problem?* This is an obvious question, as without a clear and comprehensive description of the problem, any subsequent action that is taken is likely to be incorrect. The second question, *why was the psychologist involved?*, considers why the psychologist was approached by the client. The question effectively defines why the client turned to the psychologist for assistance. For example, the psychologist may have been asked to remedy a problem that was already known to exist. Alternatively, the psychologist may be involved so as to anticipate where problems might arise. The specific reasons behind the psychologist's involvement can have serious consequences. For example, a client may ask a psychologist to address a particular problem, only for the psychologist to discover that there is a different, more pressing problem that needs attention. As the examples will demonstrate, the reasons for the psychologist's involvement are often critical in determining the outcome of any applied research.

Of course, we are all too aware that often the psychologist is *not* asked to intervene at the time the problem arises; and that their input comes after the fact. Sometimes, the client actively ignores the psychologist's findings! We include examples such as these because they are important in illustrating how problems might have been avoided had a psychologist been approached.

The third question, *what are the important theoretical concepts?*, identifies the theoretical concepts that might be relevant to the psychologist. As we have argued already, good applied research is characterized by allowing theoretical concepts to direct it. As such, the question of theoretical concepts is essential in clarifying the working hypotheses that the psychologist used. The fourth question, *what did the psychologist do?*, clearly specifies the manner in which the psychologist approached the problem, the nature of the interventions that were introduced, and the type of the behavioural evidence that was provided, if any. For example, psychologists may conduct preliminary experiments and summarize their results in a formal written report.

The fifth question, *how was the psychologist's input assessed?*, addresses a fundamental issue. Generally, it is important to demonstrate that the psychological input to the problem has done something. This question of assessment is perhaps the least clear-cut of all. Assessment is likely to be influenced by a host of factors, including the political and economical as well as psychological. One could argue that an obvious assessment is to see whether the problem stayed at the same level, went up, or went down. However, as we shall see, many situations are not quantifiable in that manner.

At the end of each chapter, we provide a list of references, including websites, where the interested reader might go to get further information. We deliberately include traditional academic references alongside less traditional ones; for example television programmes and magazine articles. In this way, the reader is provided with a range of reference sources, some more accessible to the general lay public, others more appropriate for individuals with some background in psychology or related fields. A general bibliography at the end of the book lists the works referred to in each chapter, and also includes materials that were not specifically referenced, but will be of interest to those who may wish to expand their knowledge of Applied Psychology.

■ ADDITIONAL READING

Readers who wish to pursue, in more detail, the topics raised throughout this book will find the following journals useful.

Journal of Applied Psychology (founded in 1917)
Journal of Applied Behavioural Science
Journal of Applied Developmental Psychology
Journal of Occupational Psychology
Journal of Experimental Psychology: Applied

2

The origins and scope of applied psychology

In this chapter we explore general issues in the field of applied psychology. We begin with a brief history of psychology itself before we look at the origins of applied psychology. We look at early interest in the measurement of intelligence, which was one of the first applications of psychological methods to a real-life problem. In the current climate of our more permissive society it seems odd that the measurement of intelligence was initially aimed at identifying and weeding out the unfit. In the century since then we have come to more humanitarian goals; for example, the work of Seligman and of Kahneman in measuring quality of life and the sources of happiness. What does it mean, then, to apply psychology and what is it exactly that is applied? The answers to these two questions involve us in an examination of the major concepts underlying applied psychology. We then look at the diversity of roles that the contemporary world offers to applied psychology. We use the modern hospital as an example of this diversity in which no two institutions are exactly alike. We provide two case studies, or mini-scenarios, to illustrate the discussion.

The role of philosophy

Human beings need an explanation of the world they live in and of themselves and their place in it. If scientific explanations are not available they will adopt some other belief system. In the ancient world, especially in classical Greece, these belief systems found expression in the birth of philosophy. Thoughtful men and women began to ask the questions that we still ponder today: what is the Good Life? why are we here?

Every culture has a set of ideas and beliefs about human nature. This is equally true of religious systems, including the great religions, where they are used to guide believers to some form of ideal behaviour. Whether we choose to call these belief systems psychology is not important. What *is* important is that the cultures of the developed world now use the term 'psychology' to refer to an approach to the understanding of human nature, based on scientific principles of observation and measurement, which has led to a wide variety of applications in the real world. Before looking at these applications it will help our understanding to consider briefly the origins and history of modern psychology.

In the beginning

Most authorities agree that for the Western world psychology began with the Greek philosopher Aristotle (384–322 BC). In his essay *De Anima*, 'Of the Soul', he outlined a system of thought dealing with reason, will, imagination, emotion, and memory; in short, the subject matter of what we now call psychology. In this system the soul, and its properties, was the agent of mental life and determined the individual's interactions with the environment. It is actually not easy to say exactly what Aristotle meant by this term, but we can conveniently think of it as comparable to the entity we now call mind.

One of the properties of the soul was its excitability, the speed with which it responded to events. Another was its stability, the capacity of the response to endure. The reactions of the soul were in turn mediated by the action of the bodily humours or fluids, such as blood, bile, and phlegm, which were regarded throughout the ancient world as the sources of sickness and health. Aristotle used these properties to define a system

---

BOX 2.1 WHY BOTHER WITH HISTORY?

To some, history is merely a list of meaningless dates and the names of people who are dead. How can it help our understanding of anything? There are several answers! We have all been told that history repeats itself. This implies that by knowing what has changed in the past we may know what will change in the present and in the future. This also implies that change itself can be predicted from a reading of history. The textbooks of yesterday are not the textbooks of today and the textbooks of today are not the textbooks of tomorrow. No matter how seriously we regard our concepts and theories we know that they will change. Application follows theory—but always at a distance. This means that when we look at any applied field we are probably looking at the theoretical concepts that have been well established in the immediate past rather than those that are being formulated in the present. Imagine that you have decided to see a film that you think will interest you. You arrive at the cinema only to find that the time you have been given is wrong and the film has been running for twenty minutes or more. You decide to go in anyway. As you watch the remainder of the film you formulate explanations for what is happening, based only on your own perceptions, because you do not know what has preceded it. John is angry with Heather but you don't know why, so you invent. The villain seems to be the man with the moustache but you don't know what he has done. You build an illusion of understanding, but you will not really understand the film, even at the end, unless you have seen the beginning. This seems a good analogy of the way in which history helps us to understand the present. Ebbinghaus, the father of laboratory studies of remembering and forgetting said of psychology that it has 'a long past but only a short history'.

of temperaments, which described what we would now call individual differences or personality. Thus the Sanguine temperament (ruled by healthy blood), the quick and stable soul, reacts to events immediately and sustains that reaction. A person of this sort might make a reliable soldier. This was distinguished from the Choleric temperament (ruled by bile), reacting quickly to events and then changing quickly—quick to anger and careless of its consequences. Today we might say that people with this tempera-ment have a short fuse. The Melancholic (literally, 'black bile') temperament was slow to respond but quick to recover, a creature of changing moods, while the Phlegmatic temperament was not only slow to respond but also slow to recover. This term is still used to describe people who are not easily perturbed.

In modern times, this notion of excitability, of the disposition to react, was used by the Swiss psychiatrist Carl Jung in his influential system of analytic psychology. In his case he came to the idea while watching a family of kittens playing in an orchard (de-scribed in his memoirs; Jung 1963). One of the kittens usually held back, while the oth-ers were eager to explore. This gave rise to Jung's labels of introvert and extravert that formed the basis of his theory of personality. For the hesitant, introverted kitten, the motto might be to look before you leap, whereas the more adventurous extravert kitten would favour the motto to attack first and then ask questions.

The British psychologist Hans Eysenck also borrowed Aristotle's properties of the Soul, but acknowledged their source. The property of stability in his system of individual dif-ferences became the dimension of neurotic behaviour, while the property of excitability became the basis of his dimension of introversion–extraversion. Both of these dimen-sions were first established by the **factor analysis** of large bodies of experimental data. Eysenck and Jung both advocated the practical application of their temperament sys-tems to real-world problems; for example in personnel selection and in the treatment of mental illness. For Aristotle, this was primarily a philosophical system, a way of under-standing the world, not a way of changing it. Applied psychology was not yet ready to take the stage!

Modern origins

Just as most authorities agree on the importance of Aristotle they also tend to agree that the modern view of what we define as psychology began to take shape with the French philosopher and mathematician René Descartes (1596–1654). As well as a philosopher this remarkable man was a soldier who applied his mathematical skills to warfare and an anatomist who learned from dissection rather than from treatises. As a soldier he was offered the rank of General, which he refused. As an anatomist he pioneered the use of dissection as a means of understanding structure. This led him to believe that an-imal bodies could be regarded as machines, obeying the same principles as the clockwork figures that were popular in his day.

The attempt to explain all the behaviours of humans and animals by referring them to observable natural causes was new in a world that was preoccupied largely with faith and authority, and the new empiricism invited the hostility of the religious authorit-ies. This sceptical empiricism was new in European thought but it rapidly gained the support of independent thinkers and become the basis for the developing sciences. These

---

BOX 2.2 CLOCKWORK MICE AND OTHER DELIGHTS

The seventeenth century saw a fascination throughout Europe with clockwork animals and figurines. Elaborate dioramas were built in which mechanical animals and dolls performed simple repetitive gestures. The first edition of Descartes' book, *The Treatise of Man* (1972) contained, as its frontispiece, an illustration of one such garden in the palace of an aristocrat. The figure of the clockwork doll so captured the public imagination that it entered into ballet and opera, where a favourite plot saw the hero falling in love with the prima ballerina only to find that she is merely a clockwork doll. Thus Descartes was responding to a strong cultural influence when he attempted to describe the behaviour of animals and humans as mechanisms. His conclusions were often wrong but they pointed in the direction of what was to become a scientific account of nature.

---

did not then include psychology, as we shall see, but Descartes' thinking led to attitudes and methods that would eventually define our field. We are not meaning to suggest that Descartes was the only pioneer of the empirical approach. The names of Francis Bacon, Thomas Hobbes, William Harvey, David Hume, and many others come to mind. However, it is generally agreed that Descartes ranks as a major contributor to the development of psychology as a science. He was often wrong in his conclusions, but he helped to kick-start a whole new way of looking at the world, the method of empirical observation.

Descartes' contributions took two quite different forms. First, his mechanistic view of human and animal behaviour, including his study of reflexes (coughing, sneezing, swallowing, etc.) were peculiarly modern in their approach. His views in this area were not widely influential during his lifetime. But to view the body as a machine opens the way to understanding behaviour in terms of natural forces, rather than in terms of unobserved properties of the mind. This is very much in accord with modern thinking.

His second major contribution was to bequeath to subsequent generations the mind–body problem, known to philosophers as the Cartesian dualism (see Box 2.4). The importance, historically, of this problem to philosophy and psychology was enormous.

BOX 2.3 DESCARTES' MISTAKES

Some of Descartes' errors were quaint. From his dissections he knew the essential anatomy of the cardiovascular system and he inferred, as others had done, that blood leaves the heart to travel around the body. William Harvey used this information to guess the circulation of the blood and he was right. Descartes, knowing that the blood is warm, concluded that the heart is the furnace that keeps it at this temperature, and that the flow of blood is comparable to the movement of tides. This implied that the circulation of the blood was simply an ebb and flow governed by the nature of the fluid. He was also familiar with the principles of distillation and his dissection of lungs convinced him, correctly, that the blood returns to the heart by way of the lungs. However, he gives an elaborate description of the blood dripping through the lungs as a distillate would in the condensation chamber of a still. Given his importance in the history of thought, he can perhaps be excused these minor errors.

BOX 2.4 THE MIND–BODY PROBLEM

The terms 'mental' and 'physical' are easily understood in everyday language but understanding the relation between them is a difficult puzzle. Can the mind bring about events in the body? Does the body
determine the activities of the mind? Philosophers have long disagreed. For Descartes the two were
independent, hence the dualism. He came to this conclusion through the analysis of his own experience of doubt. In a series of essays, the *Mediationes*, he explored the possibilities of doubt. 'If I doubt
that I doubt then I am still in doubt', he reasoned, and these explorations led him to an awareness of
the self as an independently existing object. The broader concept of mind and body as separate entities followed. The self, aware only of its own thoughts and capable of a disembodied, independent
existence, is capable of doubt and the capacity to doubt defines the self. This notion of an independent self, which is central to our contemporary psychology, was new to his peers. Many solutions to the
mind–body problem have been offered that take the problem to a different level without solving it. In
the twentieth century the Behaviourists tried to deal with it by simply ignoring it (Watson 1913). Others have suggested that mind and body act in parallel, sharing every activity (psychophysical parallelism
and psychic determinism). Another notion is that the mind passively tracks the activities of the body,
with no causal status. More recently the notion of the mind as the software on which the body operates has been popular. It can easily be seen that these notions all have difficulties of their own. None
of them is satisfying and it is safe to conclude that the problems raised by Descartes have yet to find
a solution!

In addition he defined a notion of the self, the novelty of which he himself did not
realize. We take it for granted now, but in the seventeenth century there was no such
concept. Curiously, these were not regarded by him as major part of his work, which
was more concerned with the study of nature.

The eighteenth century: the Age of Enlightenment

Descartes lived at the end of an era in which intellectual activity was dominated by
authority and by theological concerns having to do with salvation and the inner world.
By the beginning of the next century the intellectual climate had changed and we refer
to the eighteenth century as the Age of Reason or the Age of Enlightenment. It was
during this period that most of the philosophers whose names we revere, the great
thinkers of the European world, were active. Many of their concerns fall in the area
that we might now regard as psychology. These included sensation and perception,
the nature of external reality, the nature of truth, and so on. For example, one of the
questions that preoccupied thinkers was the attempt to determine how information
about the outside world reaches the mind. Endless arguments and armchair discussions
dissected the nature of sense data on a purely speculative basis. Today, the answers to at
least some of these questions are emerging in the laboratory.

Part of the philosophical activity of the time concerned what was called Moral
Philosophy. This dealt with the more human concerns of reason, will, conscience,

etc., and was aimed at understanding human nature in its relation to God. The moral philosophers were not interested in practical applications. Questions about the nature of the universe were soon to give rise to the discipline of Natural Philosophy which would come to include physics, chemistry, biology and the other natural sciences. Inevitably, this would give rise, in time, to the enterprise of controlling nature.

The conquest of nature

The nineteenth century can be regarded as the Age of Industrialization. Drawing on the physical sciences, rapid progress was made in the mastery of the natural environment. The invention of the steam engine and its application to factories and to transport systems was one of the most spectacular. These achievements were highly visible to the general public. Between 1850 and the end of the century the Hudson River Tunnel and the Brooklyn Bridge were built in the USA, and the whole of Europe was networked with railway lines. In 1885, British engineers completed the rail tracks that would cross the wilderness of Canada, a distance of some 5000 miles, and breach the towering Rocky Mountains to join the Pacific and Atlantic Oceans. These were extraordinary achievements.

In addition to these achievements the governments of the day bolstered scientific progress in the eyes of the public by sponsoring dramatic exhibitions. In 1851, the Great Exhibition at Crystal Palace brought exhibits to London from all over the world, demonstrating the achievements of science. The Eiffel Tower was built in Paris in 1889 as part of the International Exhibition which similarly displayed the achievements of science and exploration. In the USA the Chicago Exposition attracted huge crowds every four years and in 1893 was even visited by a delegation from far-off Korea!

These events kindled massive public interest and this was paralleled by scientific achievements in the field of medicine. The tyranny of infectious diseases prior to the eighteenth century can hardly be imagined today. Tuberculosis and smallpox claimed millions of lives, as did the common infections of childhood. Widespread prevalence of the venereal diseases brought misery to many. However, the germ theory of disease advocated by Louis Pasteur in France and Robert Koch in Germany during this period (the second half of the nineteenth century) eventually won the day.

In England, in 1796, Edward Jenner successfully vaccinated against smallpox, without benefit of the germ theory, but the success of his technique led in part to the development of adequate theories of infection. Pasteur discovered that by weakening the strength of microbes they could be injected directly to provoke an immune response, and his treatment of rabies using this method became a model for other diseases. Paul Erlich, after many attempts, produced Salvarsan 606, the so-called 'magic-bullet' cure for syphilis, in 1909. This technique was based on the use of selective dyes in the laboratory in order to stain tissues for examination under the microscope. It was the first successful use of chemotherapy, which relies on the property of some chemical agents to attack only specific tissues. These and many other accomplishments bore dramatic testimony to the efficacy of the new and rapidly developing sciences!

BOX 2.5 THE STORY OF VACCINATION

In 1774, two decades before Edward Jenner, Benjamin Jesty, an ordinary farmer, used matter from the udders of a cow infected with cowpox to 'vaccinate' his wife and children. He simply scratched their arms and rubbed in a little of the infected matter. They escaped the ensuing smallpox epidemic and he was soon persuaded to vaccinate other villagers. His action was based on a widely held folk view that dairy maids who were exposed to cowpox rarely contracted smallpox. This was not an application of scientific theory to a practical problem and the germ theory of disease was not accepted until much later. However, Benjamin Jesty's story can be seen as an example of the new spirit of independent enquiry that gave rise to the Age of Enlightenment.

The role of physiology

The success of the physical sciences encouraged scientific interest in life processes and the disciplines of zoology and botany attracted enthusiastic attention. This was influenced by the new concept of evolution, at a theoretical rather than a practical level. However, among the new life sciences, physiology was soon among the most successful. Physiology is the study of the bodily functions of living organisms and includes the study of respiration, digestion, excretion, and other life functions in both plants and animals. These studies are peculiarly suited to the laboratory since they depend upon precise measurement and accurate observation in controlled experiments. The importance of physiology was also partly due to its relevance to medicine and the fact that the discipline lends itself to practical applications. Throughout Europe, physiological laboratories flourished. In Spain, Ramon Y Cajal and in France, Claude Bernard were laying the foundations of a new scientific discipline. These are merely the names of people who are dead and we do not need to look in detail at their work. What is important is that they laid the foundations for a new laboratory science.

In Russia however, Ivan Pavlov, whose motto was 'observe, observe and then observe', was working on the physiology of digestion using dogs as subjects. He was studying the salivary reflex, and had devised an ingenious method of inserting a small tube into the salivary gland in order to measure accurately, to the last drop, the saliva produced. One methodological problem to be overcome was the fact that the dogs began to salivate as soon as they saw preparations for the experiment. Pavlov realized the significance of this. His dogs were *learning* to salivate in anticipation of the change in their environment. Pavlov realized that this mechanism could provide a means of adaptive response to the environment that would increase the animal's chances of survival. This led him to formulate the concept of the 'conditioned' reflex or conditioned response, which became household words for several decades. We still hear it said that children are 'conditioned' to prefer junk food and that soldiers are conditioned to obey. The concept of the conditioned reflex also became the basis for one of the most influential learning theories of the twentieth century, classical conditioning.

Psychology becomes a science

Before this, in 1874, Willhelm Wundt, a German psychologist, had published the first textbook of psychology. He called it *Foundations of Physiological Psychology*, not because he was studying physiology but to make it clear that he meant *scientific* psychology based on observation and experiment. In 1879, in Leipzig, he opened the first psychological laboratory, where he could apply the techniques of careful observation, measurement, and experimental method to the study of psychology. Students from all over the world were attracted to this laboratory and came to study the new methodologies with Wundt. He is thus generally regarded as the founding father of experimental psychology.

The German philosopher Immanuel Kant had declared earlier in the century that the progress of the natural sciences—that is of natural philosophy—or the physical sciences, could not be imitated in the relevant branches of moral philosophy for two reasons. One was that science requires mathematics and he argued that events in consciousness cannot be subjected to mathematical treatment. The other was that science requires experimentation and he argued that experiments with the mind would not be possible. It is sometimes suggested that this was a further motivation among European scientists to develop and pursue the new scientific psychology in order to disprove Kant. For the reasons we have already discussed the general public became interested in the scientific approach to psychology. The bandwagon had started to roll.

Divided opinions

In the USA William James, brother of the novelist Henry James, who was professor of psychology at Columbia University, gave his support to the new psychology, but with some reservations. In 1894 the *Psychological Review*, which was to become the major theoretical organ of psychology for many years, was launched with an editorial by Professor G.T. Ladd entitled 'Is psychology a science?' (Ladd 1894). To this William James famously replied 'Not yet a science but the hope of a science.' From the beginning there was a division of opinion on the issue of how science should be applied. Wundt focused his attention on observable behaviours. 'While experiments can find application in the purely psychological domain,' he wrote 'it must nevertheless be admitted that it is primarily the sensory side of psychic life which accords the widest prospect for experimental investigation.' Thus many of his experiments were concerned with simple sensory experience, reaction time, sensory judgement, reflex movement, and space perception.

For William James these were trivial pursuits and he argued that psychology would not become truly a science until more could be known about the brain. 'When the brain acts a thought occurs,' he wrote. In 1890 he published his own *Principles of Psychology* in which he defined psychology as 'the science of mental life, looking into our own minds and reporting what we discover.'

Others also argued that there could be a psychology, based on scientific principles, but concerned not with observable behaviour but with the workings of the mind. Professor

Ladd, in the article already mentioned (Ladd 1894), enthusiastically described his view of science. 'I regard psychology as the science which describes and explains the facts of consciousness. Unravelling the fibres of consciousness, tracing its genesis and growth, generalising the laws that relate its states together, expounding the conditions of every sort on which the mental life unfolds itself—this *is* for me the science of psychology.'

These two positions, and the controversy they imply, have remained with us throughout the recent history of psychology. The pendulum swings slowly between them. In the early part of the twentieth century experimental psychology consisted largely of a format in which the experimenter (E) interacted with the observer (O), the latter being required to introspect their own feelings, imagery, thoughts, and so on, in response to some form of stimulation. O observed these reactions and reported them to E. In the middle years, when behaviour was the focus of interest, and the behaviourist movement flourished, the typical experiment involved the experimenter (E) but now the subject (S). S was exposed to stimulus situations and E was now the one who observed. With the emphasis on cognitive processes and the reintroduction of the mind, or mind–brain, we now have subjects in both roles and the interest has switched back to mental processes. This movement has been greatly facilitated by the rapid developments of techniques such as **magnetic resonance imaging** (MRI), which allows a much clearer picture of what goes on

---

BOX 2.6 THE EVOLUTION OF THE WORD 'PSYCHOLOGY'

The term *psychology*, from the Greek, meaning 'study of the soul', has had an interesting history. We have seen that Descartes was interested in the study of the Soul and his contemporary William Harvey, in his anatomical exercises, defined *Anthropologie*, the study of man, as having three divisions: *Somatologie*, the study of the body; *Haematologie*, the study of the blood; and *Psychologie*, the 'doctrine of the soul'. This preoccupation with the Soul continued throughout the seventeenth and eighteenth centuries. In 1836 Hamilton referred to psychology as the study of 'states of mind, consciousness and the soul.' This preoccupation ran in parallel with the formal disciplines of moral philosophy. The first use of the term psychology, in something close to our modern meaning, occurred in a curious book by James Prichard, published in 1845 and entitled *The Natural History of Man*. This title was a reflection of a type of book that was very popular at the time, known as natural histories. These consisted of detailed descriptions, accompanied by engraved illustrations, of every known animal together with its habits and characteristics. By this time, most parts of the world had been visited by explorers and Europeans were aware that there was an enormous variety of human 'species' scattered throughout the globe. Pritchard's *Natural History* gave lavish illustrations of primitive folk and descriptions of their way of life. He was motivated by a curious concern. If God had fashioned man in his own image, how could there be so many different shapes, sizes, and colours of people? Prichard wanted to show that they had all diversified from a single species. As part of his scholarly effort he refers to psychology as 'the history of mental faculties' and he suggests that all humans share these in common. In 1892 William James, in one of his collective essays (published in 1920), used the term in its modern sense. 'I wished,' he wrote 'by treating psychology like a natural science, to help her to become one.' And in 1897 Willhelm Wundt in his *Outlines of Psychology* similarly described his work as 'making psychology an empirical science coordinated with natural science' (translated by W. Judd).

in the brain. It is difficult to estimate the extent to which this controversy, or division of interest, is reflected in applied psychology. It seems probable that the influence of the controversy as such is relatively slight. It might even be suggested that new emphases in cognitive behaviour therapy (CBT) represent a rapprochement between the two points of view.

The story so far

In summary, we have seen that the recent era of modern psychology—the 'short history' of Ebbinghaus—grew out of the philosophical preoccupations of Western Europe and that these in turn were inherited—'the long story'—from the ancient Greeks. Our modern era began with the division between natural philosophy, concerned with the nature of the physical world, and moral philosophy, concerned only with will and reason, conscience, and the soul. In the nineteenth century the success of the physical sciences in taming nature and of the biological sciences in promoting advances in medicine attracted the interest of the public and led to a near-religious faith in the possibilities of science. The success of the scientific method, generally, then led from the tenets of moral philosophy to a modern scientific psychology. Public interest in the achievements of science was at least partly responsible for the earliest applications of psychology to mental testing and to industrial efficiency.

The other face of industrialization

While we can admire the scientific and technical achievements of the nineteenth century, there is a downside to the era of industrialization. Families moved from secure rural environments to work in urban factories, resulting in widespread social disruption as extended family ties were lost. There was no system of social welfare and the poor were dependant on charity, which often was administered by agencies that had repressive moralistic concerns. In 1859 Charles Darwin published his theory of evolution in the *The Origin of Species*, which aroused widespread interest and controversy. It also engendered misunderstandings that had serious social consequences. One of the notions in the theory of evolution is that of survival of the fittest, which attributes part of the processes of evolution to the success of species in adapting to their particular environment. This came to be used as a justification for class inequalities and the cultivation of a social elite who felt little responsibility for the so-called lower orders. A mistaken corollary of the theory of evolution was the notion that everything can evolve to perfection. Just as the engineering achievements of the early part of the century had led to the taming and perfection of nature, the doctrine of the perfectibility of man held that the human species could be perfected as well. This led, among other things, to the movement of eugenics, advocating the compulsory sterilization of the unfit.

The literature of the period shows an astonishing preoccupation with notions of decadence and debility. This is evident in the novels of such writers as Dostoevsky and

Émile Zola. The Norwegian playwright Hendrick Ibsen dedicated a whole evening in the theatre to the fate of a boy who has inherited syphilis from a disreputable father. Tuberculosis was widely regarded as a symptom of decadence and we have the spectacle of Bohemian heroes and heroines ravaged by this disease. In this social climate it is hardly surprising that the first major attempt to apply scientific psychology to real-world problems was aimed at identifying the unfit and removing them from society.

The intelligence quotient (IQ)

In 1904 the Commissioner for Public Education in Paris formed a committee to advise on how to identify those children unfit for the classroom and remove them. This was the murky origin of intelligence testing. Some writers have attempted to sanitize this and claim that the goal was remedial education, but the brief to the committee was to identify the intellectually inferior and remove them. One member of the committee was Alfred Binet, a self-taught psychologist who developed the concept of IQ that would dominate educational and clinical psychology for decades. Binet was familiar with the work of Wundt on reaction times in simple tasks and he used this approach to devise a number of short tasks that could be administered easily to children. Examples would be obeying simple instructions, repeating sentences, arranging blocks in patterns, and so on. In 1908 he went a step further and arranged these tasks in ascending order of difficulty. The test now consisted of administering them in this order until the child failed a specified number of items.

By testing a large number of children, Binet was able to determine the age at which each test item could be expected to be passed, and he then proposed an ingenious idea. The age at which a child passed all of the tests would be referred to as the mental age. This might be higher or lower than the child's chronological age. Binet proposed that the simple fraction mental age divided by chronological age, MA/CA, would provide an index of intellectual level. The idea was ingenious, and it was intuitively easy to grasp, though it had no real statistical or empirical foundation. In ordinary language we find it easy to describe a person as twice as bright as his brother or only half as bright as his sister.

The IQ carried this meaning. A child of 10 years of age who passed tests appropriate for the 12-year-old child would receive an IQ of 120 and could be regarded simplistically as 20 per cent brighter than his age peers. Similarly, a child of 10 who failed tests above the 8-year-old level would be given an IQ of eighty, which could be interpreted as meaning that the child was 20 per cent less intelligent than his age peers. The notion of the IQ became immediately popular and the term quickly appeared in daily language. In 1916, in the USA, a revision of the Binet tests was undertaken by Lewis Terman at Stanford University and this test was widely used in schools and clinics for several decades.

How stupid is stupid?

Previously, in 1910, the American Association for the Study of the Feeble Minded had established official guidelines for the definition of stupidity. They proposed three categories, based on IQ scores. Idiots were those with an IQ less than twenty, while those with an IQ between twenty and forty-nine were labelled imbeciles. They needed one more term, so they chose the word moron, from the scholarly Greek word for 'stupid'. Thus a new concept entered into the language and has been a popular colloquialism ever since! A moron is a person who has an IQ between fifty and seventy. The artificiality of these categories is obvious, and they are no longer used in practice.

The following quotation from a paper by Leta Hollingworth, a psychologist at Columbia University, gives a chilling picture of the obsession with mental deficiency or intellectual inferiority that had inspired the development of the Binet tests. Writing in 1922 she says that 'In 1913, one thousand consecutive cases of suspected mental deficiency were transcribed from the clearing house for mental defectives at the post graduate hospital in New York city. This was a public clinic from which children or adults, if found to be feeble minded, might be officially committed to appropriate institutions. Individuals of any age, from any borough of Greater New York, if *suspected* to be of inadequate intelligence [our italics] were admissible to this clinic for mental examination' (Hollingworth 1922).

Another quotation from the same paper reflects the social preoccupations of the time. 'From the standpoint of society it is of interest to know that feeble minded girls feed into the existing social and economic order more conveniently than do boys of the same mental quality. Extremely stupid girls survive and presumably reproduce their kind more easily than do extremely stupid boys. The social order is such that survival for the former depends less on intelligence than it does for the latter' (Hollingworth 1922). This was an era, in both America and Europe, of social confidence in the existing order. The First World War would soon disrupt that confidence but we hear in these quotations an attitude that defined the social order of the day. The notion of identifying the less able was also found in military selection (see 'The war room', Chapter 7) and in industrial psychology, where the emphasis came to be on improving the work level of the individual workers (see 'The work room' Chapter 6).

By 1939, flaws in the statistical concept of IQ led David Wechsler, an American psychologist working at the Bellevue Hospital in New York, to develop a new series of tests whose scoring was based on the normal distribution. One of the difficulties with the Binet test was that the individual items had no coherent relation to each other. Wechsler devised a series of sub-tests, for example vocabulary, general information, verbal comprehension, and so on, that made comparison between levels more meaningful, and yielded qualitative sub-test scores that had diagnostic significance in their own right.

The decline of the IQ

The subsequent history of the concept of intelligence is fascinating but lies well beyond the scope of this book. Intelligence testing and the concept of intelligence became mired in controversy in the following decades, for several reasons. Arguments over the nature of intelligence, whether it is a single ability level or a constellation of several specific abilities, for example, generated more heat than light. Extremely sophisticated statistical analysis of psychological tests were undertaken to attempt to define the components of intelligence: speed, accuracy, strength, and so on. Eventually it was realized that there is in fact no satisfactory definition of intelligence. Is there such a thing as intelligence and if there is what is it? In the 1960s the death knell of the old school of intelligence testing was sounded during controversies over claims concerning race and intelligence. Thus a psychological concept that began in rather murky origins eventually foundered on equally murky political considerations.

The foregoing is not intended to suggest that intelligence testing has no place in applied psychology today. Measures of IQ are good predictors of academic achievement but are less successful in predicting success in the wider world. As we have seen, the notion that society can benefit from the identification of the unfit is no longer popular, but the measurement of intellectual ability still has a role to play. For those who are interested in the details of this story an interesting book by P.D. Chapman with the unusual title *Schools as Sorters* (Chapman 1988) is worth reading.

It should be remembered that there were other positive outcomes from the intelligence-test movement. The fact that it became a movement rather than a disciplined phalanx of professional psychology is reflected in the missionary zeal of some of its supporters in the face of the social and political factors we have noted. On the positive side, the methods of test construction and standardization gave rise to the psychometric school and were of considerable importance. Using these statistical methods it is possible to make measurements of attitudes, preferences, and skills that are reliable and valid and have wide application. The Mental Measurements Yearbook (MMYB), which is published regularly, lists and describes literally thousands of well-standardized tests for use in a wide variety of situations. The current edition (available at www.unl.edu/buros) lists 4000 commercially available tests and provides critical reviews of half of them.

An interesting footnote refers back to Alfred Binet. In his earliest presentation of the IQ test he insisted that the examiner must establish *rapport* with the subject before beginning the test. This is a French word that is difficult to translate and has been retained in our language. Roughly, the dictionary definition equates it with affinity, harmony, and agreement, among many other definitions. In today's terminology it probably means that subject and examiner must be on the same wavelength before a valid test can be undertaken. Alfred Binet thus tapped into an important principle, independent of the issues surrounding mental ability, one that is central to the application of psychological principles in clinical and counselling situations.

The scope of applied psychology

We turn now to the present and examine the diversity of roles and activities that make up applied psychology. First we ask what it means to 'apply' psychology. To answer this we must ask what it is that is applied. We then examine the diversity of roles filled by psychologists, using the modern hospital as an example. We will illustrate this diversity through brief case studies looking at some of the roles psychologists have been called upon to perform in a typical hospital setting.

Pure and applied science

What does it mean to apply psychology? In the informal sense we apply a kind of psychology whenever we persuade a friend to do something that we want them to do. Parents are urged to use psychology in dealing with their offspring and the offspring then apply their own devious versions of psychology to the manipulation of their parents. But, of course, we are interested here in something more formal. It is customary to make a distinction between pure and applied (or sometimes theoretical and applied) in most branches of science: theoretical physics, pure biology, and so on. The students who study biology with a career in mind may end up as teachers or professors of their chosen subject, passing on to future generations the knowledge they have acquired. They are more likely, however, to find employment in some branch of conservation, fisheries, or forestry, where they will *apply* the knowledge they have acquired.

This knowledge base has three complementary components: facts, established by observation and research in the laboratory or in the field; concepts, the theoretical formulations that make sense of the facts in a wider framework; and techniques, the various special skills required in their discipline to establish the facts and concepts in an orderly and repeatable way. In the next chapter we look at some of the major concepts that turn up repeatedly in applied contexts. Here we will examine some of the techniques that trained psychologists bring to problems in the real world.

BOX 2.7 THE KNOWLEDGE BASE: AN ILLUSTRATION

The knowledge base, generated by pure science, is shared by the corresponding applied science. To look at a simple illustration: it is well known that girls acquire language skills more rapidly than boys. This is a simple fact. What concepts help us to understand it? The concept of individual differences is useful here. Individuals differ in language ability. Individual differences have many potential sources; in this case one of them is gender. Others include book and magazine readership in the home, teaching methods in the school, and motivation or interest. A part of the concept of individual differences is the assumption that their origins can be identified. The techniques required to do this include those of measurement or scaling. In order to know that one individual is better at language than another we need to make accurate estimates of language ability. We also need the statistical expertise that will enable us to make reliable comparisons. Confronted with a practical problem, say, of how to improve reading skills of young offenders in a prison population, the psychologist would call on all these elements in attempting to arrive at a solution. Obviously the story is more complicated than this simple illustration would suggest. But the principle is clear. Applied psychology draws on the disciplines of pure psychology and shares them. In this process it often happens that the practical applications give rise to new facts, requiring new concepts and techniques, thereby extending the scope of both the pure and applied branches of the same discipline.

The modern hospital

During the Second World War, psychology proved its usefulness in military hospitals with the result that after the war the Veterans Administration (VA) in the USA, the Department of Veterans' Affairs (DVA) in Canada and the National Health Service (NHS) in the UK began to employ psychologists regularly in their hospitals. The job specifications tended to be vague, other than that they would work with psychiatrists and social workers to administer psychological tests. The psychologists themselves often felt that there were more roles that they could fulfil. They also felt that their employers had hired them without having a very clear idea of what they were expected to do. Rudolph Ekstein, a psychologist who had studied with Freud before the war in Vienna, was appointed as the principal training officer for psychology at the then famous Menninger Clinic in Kansas. His advice to psychologists in training was simple: 'make yourself indispensable'. This is exactly what many psychologists did, defining and fulfilling roles that would make them not only useful but indispensable.

We will use the modern hospital as an example of the wide diversity of roles that come within the range of applied psychology. Box 2.8 lists the departments, services, and clinics offered in the directory of a modern, urban, teaching hospital. Virtually every one of these can use the skills of a psychologist and jobs are advertised on the Internet that refer specifically to individual services. It is not surprising therefore that the modern hospital offers such a diversity of roles.

In this context it is important to differentiate the work of the health psychologist from that of the clinical psychologist. The latter deal with problems of mental illness, maladjustment, personality disorder, and so on (see 'The treatment room', Chapter 8, and 'The sport room', Chapter 9). Health psychologists are concerned with more general health issues, good practice, effective diagnoses, etc., mainly in the context of physical illness. This new discipline already supports its own professional journal, *Health Psychology Update*.

Another recent development is the expansion of specialist hospitals, including the hospice, a special kind of hospital dedicated to the care of patients with terminal illness (contrast this with the Hospital for Incurables in the nineteenth century: Abandon hope all ye who enter here). The hospice movement began in England in the 1960s and has now spread to many countries. The hospice seems to offer unique opportunities for the development of new psychological concepts and techniques. Changing practice in life-support techniques that aim to orchestrate death include the employment of hospital ethicists, who are trained initially in law, philosophy, or psychology.

The theme throughout this book is that the action taken in an applied psychology problem should be determined by the nature of the situation and not primarily by the expertise or professional orientation of the individual psychologist. In this section we will look at some of the skills that can reasonably be expected of a person trained in psychology. It should be remembered however that not every psychologist will have all the skills to be listed.

BOX 2.8 SERVICES, CLINICS, AND DEPARTMENTS OF THE MODERN HOSPITAL

The following list is taken from the directory of a large, urban, teaching hospital. Given the vast array of functions in the modern hospital it is hardly surprising that psychologists find many diverse roles. Try to guess which of these services are likely to employ psychologists, and why.

Accident and Emergency

Administration

Anaesthesia

Breast-Screening Unit

Cardiology (diseases of the heart and blood vessels)

Diabetes Clinic (supervision of diabetic treatment, e.g. insulin intake)

Enterology (diseases of the intestines)

Falls Clinic (treatment of falls, usually in the elderly)

Fracture Clinic

Gastrology and Hepatology (diseases of the stomach and liver)

Genitourinary Clinic (diseases of the urinary and genital systems)

Geriatrics (treatment of the elderly)

Gynaecology (diseases of women)

Immunology (diagnosis and treatment of immune deficiencies)

Intensive Care (Adults)

Intensive Care (Children)

Medical Genetics (management of inherited illness)

Neonatal Unit (care of the newborn)

Neurology (diseases of the nervous system)

Neurovascular Unit (problems of blood supply to the brain, e.g. strokes)

Obstetrics (management of childbirth)

Oncology (cancer diagnosis and treatment)

Orthopaedic Clinic (treatment of bone and joint injuries)

Paediatrics (illnesses of children)

Pain Clinic (management of chronic pain)

Personnel (staff administration)

Psychiatry (medical assessment and treatment of mental disorders)

Psychological Services

Rehabilitation (follow-up treatment, e.g. after a stroke)

Rheumatology (management of inflammatory joint disease)

Spinal Injury Clinic

Urology (diseases of the urinary system)

BOX 2.9 A VOLUNTARY PROJECT

Imagine that you have completed your training as a psychologist and are ready to offer yourself for employment. You find the idea of work in a hospital appealing but you are not certain what sorts of work will be available. Go to the Internet and use your ingenuity to find some of the answers. Hint: as a start, log on to your favourite search engine and click the advanced-search button. In the window offering (exact phrase) enter the term 'job application'. In the window offering (all these words) enter the words 'hospital' and 'psychologist'. You will be surprised at the number of different job situations that are open. Use your own experience of the Internet to explore these further.

Technical skills in applied psychology

The list of specific skills will include counselling. Reading through the list of services in Box 2.8 it is easy to imagine how patients in each service could benefit from expert counselling. As yet, no standard constellation of roles has been established and every hospital has its own pattern. Counselling services may be confined to patients or may include relatives who face such problems as unexpected death and bereavement. Staff encounter difficult decisions, including the decision to treat or not to treat, and the problems of life support in terminal illness. Counselling, in some hospitals, includes these issues.

Hypnosis also has an important place in hospital settings, especially in the management of pain. Although relatively few psychologists are trained in the technique, it nevertheless tends to be more or less the preserve of applied psychologists. In addition, psychologists are expected to have skills in social analysis; that is, in the observation and interpretation of social situations.

Importantly, in a medical setting, psychologists are very often regarded as experts on experimental design. It is frequently the experience of a psychologist working in a hospital setting that medical personnel approach them who want to do research but who need help with designing their study. The important consideration here is that the psychologist must be seen as accessible. This will include both the willingness to listen and the avoidance of technical jargon. Ideally, medical staff must be trained to come for help *before* beginning the study, rather than after. This is more likely to happen if the psychologist is seen as approachable and helpful. In addition to the design of experiments, psychologists in the hospital setting are expected to have considerable expertise in statistics and the analysis of data. Many psychologists have had training in the basic techniques of psychophysiology as well. In the medical setting they are asked to contribute their knowledge and expertise to the solution of measurement problems involving bodily functions. An example will be found in case study one below.

Communication skills

Another interesting area in which psychologists have recently begun to make contributions is the area of communication. A number of studies over recent years have shown that patients often do not understand the information given to them by medical staff.

There are many reasons for this. Medical staff tend to take the setting for granted and to forget that the patient is present on a once-only basis and that everything is unfamiliar. The dialogue between patient and doctor or patient and nurse may encounter problems of specialized vocabulary and medical staff are not usually trained in this aspect of communication. Some research has looked at the quality and nature of dialogue (Gill 1995) with a view to improving the quality of information transferred. A typical example occurs in the description of pain. The doctor, ever since student days, has learned to discriminate various constellations of pain, and to recognize their diagnostic significance. Examples are sharp and stabbing, or dull and boring, intermittent or acute, and so on. Note that the term boring refers here to a quality of the pain, seeming to bore into the tissue, not to boredom as such. When the doctor asks the patient about the quality of pain experienced—is it sharp or dull?—the two are not using a shared vocabulary. In particular patients for whom English is a second language complain of this problem. However it is not confined to language problems as such. Patients are simply not familiar with the appropriate vocabulary.

Questionnaire design

Doctors are trained to look carefully for signs, the things that they can observe, and symptoms, the things that the patient tells them. It is with the latter that the problem of vocabulary obviously arises. Apart from sophisticated methodologies for improving dialogue, the other solution to this problem of communication lies with the psychologist's expertise in test construction. A number of questionnaires have been devised to assist patients with the description of their symptoms. The oldest and best known of these is the General Health Questionnaire (GHQ), which includes items referring both to physical and to mental problems. (Zigmond and Snaith 1983). Questionnaires dealing specifically with pain include the Oswestry Back Pain Scale (Fairbanks et al. 1980), the Quebec Back Pain Scale (Koper et al. 1996), and more recently the Roland–Morris Pain Scale (Fairbanks and Roland 2001). Each of these has been standardized on appropriate populations.

A good way of using questionnaires is to have the patient fill in the items and then go through their answers with a competent nurse or psychologist who can check whether the meaning is precisely what the patient intended (is this what you really mean? can you think of a better word to describe what you feel?). The importance of these scales is that they have been properly constructed and have the necessary validity and reliability for widespread use.

Scaling

The use of questionnaires raises the important question of scaling methods. Psychologists are expected to have particular expertise in devising and using a variety of scales. A scale is simply a device for measuring some quantity in a reliable way. Because psychologists are required to measure properties that are not straightforward, a number of scaling concepts have emerged. We may be required to measure the severity of anxiety or tension, the depth of depression, or simply a person's ability or aptitude in some skill. The issues involved in scale construction are complex and lie beyond the scope of this chapter. There are many good textbooks dealing specifically with scaling methods e.g. Van der Ver (1980). For our present purposes we will look merely at the essentials of scaling.

If you want to measure the length of something, a curtain or a cupboard door, you will probably use a metre stick. This is the ideal scaling tool because the scale in centimetres has several desirable properties. Each of the centimetres is the same length throughout the whole of the scale. Compare this with scores on a maths test where the difference between two scale points will depend on the difficulty of the items, and will therefore never be exactly the same. Another advantage of the metre stick is that the scales are proportional. Half the length of the metre stick yields two equal segments. Suppose you are asked to say on a scale from one to ten how much you enjoyed a new brand of cola. If your friend rates the drink as four, but you rate it as eight, does this *necessarily* indicate that your rating is twice as favourable as that of your friend? The simple answer is that it does not. Finally, though it is not obvious, your metre stick offers a value of zero. Suppose that you are asked to measure the height of a fence post standing in the ground. If all that is required is the height above ground there is no problem. Your metre stick begins at zero ground level. However, if you want to replace the fence post and you need to know its overall length you need to know the length that is buried under the ground. In this case your metre stick cannot be used and you therefore have no notion of where zero may lie.

It is not usual for the accomplishments of applied psychology to be recognized outside the field. However, in 2002 the Nobel Prize was awarded to a psychologist, Daniel Kahneman, for scaling complex preferences relating to the choice of stocks and bonds by investors under different sorts of favourable and unfavourable conditions. In the words

---

BOX 2.10 SCALE PROPERTIES: BASIC CONCEPTS

Scales that have all of the properties described above are known as *ratio* scales, reflecting the fact that they can measure proportions accurately. Below the ratio scale in level of precision is the scale for which the units have equal lengths but there is no way of measuring the distance from zero. You use your metre stick as an interval scale and determine that the length of a fence post above ground is fifty-four centimetres. You cannot say whether this is one-third or two-thirds or any proportion of the overall length because your scale has no zero point. These are called *interval* scales. Often, in psychological scaling, it is only possible to assign some sort of rank order; more than or less than. This is often true for example in measures of preference. You wish to find out which of five brands of coffee is most preferred. There is no accurate numerical scale, so what you must do is ask your subjects to arrange the five brands in the order from least preferred to most preferred. By simply assigning the numbers one to five to each of the brands you produce a simple scale. These are called *ordinal* scales because they reflect only the order of preference. The simplest level of scaling is a mere category. Examples are male/female, old/young, and definitely infected/possibly infected/not infected'. For scaling purposes these are known as *nominal* scales because they merely name the categories. The importance of scaling to applied psychology cannot be over-emphasized.

of the citation: the award was given 'for having integrated insights from psychology research into economic science, especially concerning human judgement and decision-making under uncertainty.' Interestingly, Kahneman's work has included careful and ingenious scaling of hedonic preferences; that is, of the elusive quality of pleasure (see Kahneman and Tversky 2000).

Selected case studies

The following two case studies illustrate, briefly, some of the points we have discussed. They are each based on actual cases and they are chosen to represent the situation in which the psychologist is approached for help with a problem that lies outside their formal job description.

Case study one: consciousness under anaesthesia

Modern anaesthetic agents may not induce full coma; that is, loss of consciousness. Some patients complain of having felt pain or having heard conversations during surgery. Some patients may sue. The surgeons are entitled to believe, as they make the first incision, that the patient will feel no pain: no surgeon wants to torture their patients. Yet the American Society of Anesthesiologists reported in its 1996 newsletter that the incidence of awareness under anaesthesia can range from 11 to 40 per cent in some circumstances. Depth of coma is very hard to measure. The early anaesthetics, chloroform and ether, produced easily recognizable stages as they took effect: (1) euphoria and disinhibition; (2) diminished consciousness with tendency to struggle; (3) quiet breathing, loss of reflexes; and (4) coma, unresponsive to stimuli (followed by profound coma and death, if prolonged). Thus they reliably produced loss of consciousness and freedom from pain. The classical ether stages no longer apply. A wide range of newer anaesthetics produce potentially a wide range of activity, some of which may not include loss of consciousness. The anaesthetic triludin used in childbirth, the so-called twilight sleep, is an example.

One solution would be to monitor reactivity to external stimuli unconnected with the operation. One of the most important concepts in psychophysiology, the branch of psychology dealing with bodily reactions, is that of the orienting response. In humans and animals any significant or unexpected stimulus produces this response automatically. It is not under conscious voluntary control and can be used to detect awareness of events. In humans, one component of the orienting response is sweat-gland activity on the palmar surfaces of the hands, which can be measured fairly easily.

The anaesthesia department in a large, urban hospital approached two psychologists who worked in the research department of the hospital asking them to investigate the feasibility of measuring awareness under anaesthesia (Levey and Goldmann 1986). Normally, non-medical staff are not welcome in the operating theatre. However, the anaesthetists were able to arrange for them to attend regular sessions where the operation of arthroscopy on the knee joint was being carried out in a standard routine procedure. It was essential that every patient had the same surgical treatment. With the agreement of the surgeons and anaesthetists, changes in sweat-gland activity were recorded from the palms with the patients' consent. Notes were made on the recording of specific surgical events (e.g. first incision), of comments by operating-theatre personnel, and of responses, if any, to a tape cassette played to each patient through earphones during the operation. The content of the tape included the chimes of Big Ben, a barking dog, and comments on current events. In addition, the patient's name was spoken from time to time.

The results of this investigation showed that some, but not all, of the patients were processing stimuli while under anaesthesia. Responses tended to be made to stimuli that would be unexpected in an operating theatre. These included the barking dog and Big Ben. Studies in hypnosis have raised the notion of a hidden observer, who remains aware throughout the hypnotic session although the subject is not. It is as if the patients were opening their minds to stimuli that took them by surprise. None of the surgical events provoked responses, probably because they were expected by the patient. Research in this important area continues (for a review, see Andrade 1995).

Case study two: day-case anaesthesia

In the 1980s the pressure to reduce numbers of hospital beds led to day-case treatment for minor surgery. Patients were lightly anaesthetized during the surgical procedure and then discharged the same day. Many patients, however, were apprehensive, making them more difficult to anaesthetize at the shallow levels required. A proportion of all patients could not be anaesthetized as this level and had to be admitted a second time for conventional in-patient surgery. Two psychologists who had worked previously with anaesthesia were invited to join a team of surgeons, anaesthetists, and nurses to explore this problem (Goldmann et al. 1988).

Exploration of the problem with the medical team suggested that an appropriate model would be to regard patients' apprehensions concerning anaesthesia and surgery as a type of phobia. Trials were run using a de-sensitization programme that would normally deal with phobic anxiety. In this case it was applied to patients awaiting surgery in the day-care unit. To this was added a simple method of training in self-hypnosis, used by psychologists in pain clinics, which combines imagery with relaxation. A nurse, at the bedside, instructed patients in this technique for twenty minutes prior to the surgery. They were then left to practise while they waited for the surgery. A matched control group of patients, who did not receive this treatment, were asked to take part in discussion sessions of comparable length.

Questionnaire assessment of anxiety levels showed a significant reduction in anxiety for the treated group but not for the control group. The quantities of anaesthetic agent required to maintain anaesthesia in these patients, during the surgical procedures, was significantly reduced. In addition, the proportion of patients tolerating the day-case procedure increased. The hospital in which the study was carried out now uses these methods routinely in the management of day-case surgery.

■ ADDITIONAL READING

Agnew, N.M. and Pyke, S.W. (2004) *Science Game: an Introduction to Research Methods in the Behavioural Sciences*, 7th edn. Oxford University Press, Toronto. A good, readable overview of research methods and concepts that has been popular for years.

Herrnstein, R.J. and Boring, E.G. (eds) (1966) *A Source Book in the History of Psychology*. Harvard University Press, Cambridge, MA. This is a collection of excerpts from original sources in the history of psychology. The items are arranged by subject and supported by brief commentaries. York University in Canada maintains another collection of original sources on the Internet. The website is www.psychclassis.yorku.ca

3

Applying theory to practice

We now introduce the organizational structure for the book, the concept of a room. A room represents a general class of real-world contexts where there is a common goal. For example, 'The crime room' (Chapter 4) involves contexts that arise in the course of investigating crime, while 'The court room' (Chapter 5) represents situations that occur in the process of judging whether a crime has been committed. 'The work room' (Chapter 6) looks at the way problems emerging from our working environment impact on how we feel, act, and think, while 'The war room' (Chapter 7) summarizes problems that arise regarding national security and during war. 'The treatment room' (Chapter 8) provides the general label for a group of situations that focus on the treatment of emotional and mental difficulties, in either clinical or non-clinical populations. 'The sport room' (Chapter 9) is the general context for situations where we engage in physical activities, and shows how psychological concepts derived from mainstream, empirical research are applied to issues about performance and skill learning.

Content of rooms

We organize this book on the basis of real-world settings, which we call rooms. Each room should be viewed as a label for a general class of naturalistic contexts. For example, we have the crime room where, as the name suggests, crimes are investigated. This general context of crime investigation includes the more specific activities of analysing psychological evidence at a crime scene, and interviewing an eyewitness in a police station. In each room we consider the different ways in which psychologists can make an impact, and the scenarios that we provide illustrate how specific questions and problems are addressed through the application of psychological theories and findings.

We believe that our focus on the naturalistic contexts, or rooms, allows us to consider a broader range of topics than if we were to base our discussions exclusively on the skills of the psychologist. For example, most texts organize applied psychology around the discipline and training of psychologists. So, there will be a chapter on forensic psychology, a chapter on occupational or organizational psychology, a chapter on clinical psychology, and so on. Without question, this is a perfectly acceptable way of dividing up applied psychology; and, it has the advantage of mapping directly onto the different professional divisions that are represented in governing bodies (e.g. see professional divisions of the British Psychological Society at www.bps.org.uk).

However, the disadvantage is that such classifications obscure the richness and diversity of issues in the applied problem. So, sometimes, real-world problems will arise out of a forensic context that do *not* require the expertise of a forensic psychologist, but rather require the expertise of a cognitive psychologist. For these reasons, we choose to focus on the general class of naturalistic contexts, or rooms, and contend that it is the nature of the applied problem that determines what kind of psychological skills and expertise are most important.

We start with 'The crime room' (Chapter 4), which, as we have stated, illustrates problems arising in the course of investigations of crime, like how to interview a witness or obtain confessions from suspects. There is so much media coverage of crime investigations—either factual or fictional—that the crime room, and the activities of psychologists working therein, is familiar to most lay-people. The next chapter, 'The court room' (Chapter 5), follows the theme of jurisprudence and discusses the important roles psychologists play in courts of law, both civil and criminal. For example, we question how juries come to understand evidence, and show how psychologists have aided in better understanding this process. Chapter 6 focuses on problems associated with 'The work room'. Here the problems concern the working environment, such as stress management, team building and personnel selection. Theoretical explanations that dominate the work room are also found to be important to 'The war room' (Chapter 7), which represents one of the earliest applied contexts in which psychologists made a significant impact. The war room is particularly interesting, focusing as it does on issues regarding national security, where psychologists have played major advisory roles. 'The treatment room' (Chapter 8) includes issues that arise in the treatment of emotional and mental problems. We include problems that are associated with clinical populations, like obsessive-compulsive disorders, as well as those that affect non-clinical populations, such as sleeplessness. 'The sport room' (Chapter 9) focuses on physical activities and sport, including the roles that psychologists can play in enhancing athletic performance. This chapter is interesting in that it combines the classic theories of motor skills—historically linked to **behavioural psychology**—with techniques more traditionally associated with the treatment room, such as counselling and mood enhancement.

We note that our choice is by no means comprehensive, and we may have omitted rooms that the reader feels are more relevant, or intriguing. To this end, we invite the reader to think of their own list of rooms, and to consider the applied problems that a psychologist might be asked to help resolve.

Major theoretical themes

In the following section we identify the major themes, or theoretical questions, that pervade all of the rooms we discuss. One theme focuses on how we learn and remember. The second theme asks about individual differences, like why some of us make good leaders and others do not. The third major theme asks what motivates or drives our behaviour. Motivation is a complex topic and we use different definitions, from why we do things to how we maintain a level of physical vigour. The fourth major theme is the impact of emotion on behaviour, and reminds us of the need to develop multi-level explanations of human behaviour.

While the rooms and their related activities may be diverse, there are common themes that link them all. These themes can be formulated into different questions about human behaviour. First, we have the general question of knowledge acquisition and knowledge retention, or how we learn and remember. In the laboratory, learning and memory have been somewhat arbitrarily divided into two separate theoretical and empirical enterprises. For example, learning studies might measure the number of times (or learning trials) a person needs to see a list of twenty words, before he can recall all twenty words correctly. In contrast, memory studies would look at how many of the twenty words the person could recall after a single exposure, and after some delay of minutes, days, or years. While we acknowledge that the distinction is a traditional one in psychology, for the present purposes we combine questions of learning with questions of memory.

The question of how we acquire knowledge, and show evidence of retaining it, is one that is relevant to every room. This is not surprising, as explaining how we learn and remember is essential to all levels of our being, from the most molecular to the most global. We can question how learning occurs at the pre-synaptic site of a neuron, as when we discuss the process of **habituation**, which is a very basic form of learning. We can as easily discuss how we learn what is and what is not socially acceptable in our peer groups. In fact, some psychologists, like Steven Kosslyn in his 1980 book *Image and Mind*, believe that learning and memory should not be independent fields of study *because* they represent the basic mental processes that underlie most of our cognitive abilities. Instead, Kosslyn suggests that we should study learning and memory in the context of perception, problem solving, and personality. While we find Kosslyn's arguments stimulating, we merely use them here to illustrate that learning and memory are central issues in most, if not all, areas of psychological study.

The importance of understanding learning and memory appears somewhere in each of the rooms. For example, the crime room introduces naturalistic problems that are clarified by the theoretical distinctions between *incidental* and *intentional learning*, as when an eyewitness to (or victim of) a crime is asked to identify a possible perpetrator from a line-up. Similarly, *investigative profiling* raises questions about how criminals learn, and remember, to execute serial crimes, such as murder or arson. The court room, and its related problems, may not immediately seem to involve learning or memory. Nonetheless, we show that explanations regarding attention, learning, and memory are used to introduce improvements to the jury process. Problems arising in the work room require descriptions of how people learn and later remember skills as well as information. A good example is the usefulness of **task analyses** when a worker is asked to learn a new skill. Basic theoretical hypotheses regarding how we learn and remember have been highly useful for problems that arise in the treatment room. For example, some psychologists maintain that mental health problems, like *affective disorders*, are the result of improper **learning schedules**. Psychological descriptions regarding how we remember traumatic events are central to the treatment room as well as the war room, as in the treatment of post-traumatic stress disorders and battle fatigue. The sport room also introduces problems that are helped by the application of learning theory, such as the effects of extended practice on behavioural and physical skills.

The second major theme can be called **individual differences**. This concept has a long history in psychology. Alfred Binet, whom we met in the last chapter as the founder of the IQ, wrote in 1895 that 'Studies of individual differences are one of psychology's most important practical applications' (Binet and Henry 1966). No one can dispute the fact that, in the same situation, some people will behave one way, while other people behave another way. We act differently from each other, see the world differently, have different attitudes, and have different reactions. For example, some people will respond to a traumatic event, like a near-miss car accident, by being shocked and highly distressed, and engage in a series of worrisome thoughts, like 'what if we had been going a little bit faster?' In contrast, other people will show little reaction and appear well adjusted and calm, claiming that 'a miss is as good as a mile'. The idea that there are such things as individual differences—factors in our personal make-up—is one way of explaining the diversity in human behaviour.

The question of individual differences is one that arises time and time again in all of the rooms we discuss. In fact, in many applied problems, it is more essential to know how the *particular* individual in front of you will respond, rather than how some *average* person might behave. A classic example is the concept of leadership: are leaders born or are they made? Such questions are at the core of many problems that arise in both the work room and the war room, where selecting the incorrect person to be responsible can have serious consequences. Explanations of individual differences emerge in the crime room, and underlie many of the assumptions behind investigative profiling; for example, the assumption that the criminal leaves his unique psychological fingerprints at the scene of the crime. Problems associated with athletic training, as discussed in the sport room, must also consider individual differences and how they mediate the success of different training regimes. Why is it that some people prefer to join in activities that involve team efforts, while others are happier engaging in physical activities that involve no one else? These questions, and others like them, fall under the general heading of individual differences.

The third major theme that keeps appearing across the different rooms is motivation. Motivation is a particularly complex topic. It can be used to describe physical, tangible states such as vigour and physical exertion, as well as hypothetical constructs like will or intention. Motivation can be used to explain why we do things, such as the intentions behind our actions. Motivation can also refer to how willing we are to engage in some behaviour, such as our motivation to adhere to an exercise programme. We can question a person's motivation to commit a crime, and try to link this to the person's underlying needs. Equally, we can consider what motivates some people to be a pilot as compared with a soldier, and show how this can be related to general intelligence. Many applied problems, in many different contexts, benefit from the application of psychological explanations of motivation.

Our fourth theme highlights how central our ability to feel, or to emote, is to our existence; and looks at the effects that our emotions have on our behaviour. Our ability to emote undoubtedly affects our social interactions, and our emotions can convey important social signals to those around us. More importantly, our emotional state impacts on our mental and physical behaviour. Examples from the crime room are easy to find, such as the impact that emotions can have on a victim's ability to report on a traumatic event. The problem of false confessions also requires some discussion of the effects that anxiety and panic can have on a person's ability to resist the pressure to confess. Problems in the court room similarly focus on the impact that emotions have on behaviour, as in the impact of emotive evidence on the emotions of the jury or the way the anxiety of a witness will affect the way in which he remembers a crime. Explanations about the effects of emotions on behaviour are relevant to problems arising in the work room, such as the impact that worker satisfaction can have on productivity. We also consider the impact that fear can have on the behaviour of the soldier, when we enter the war room. Similarly, problems that arise in the sport room, such as the effects of performance anxiety, require a description of the impact that our emotional states have on our mental and physical behaviour.

These major themes—learning and memory, individual differences, motivation, and emotions—are by no means exhaustive. However, they are themes that have been prevalent throughout the history of psychology; and still continue to be so today. Importantly, these themes are major mainstream topics within experimental psychology. This means that they continue to have a well-established empirical and theoretical base from which applications to the real world can be made.

General approaches to applied problems

Just as there are many different types of psychologist who can operate in the different rooms, there is a choice in the range of approaches that a psychologist can adopt when addressing an applied problem. Very simply, an approach is a way of describing human behaviour, and is very much defined by the theoretical assumptions and terms that are used, and the methods through which its proponents amass evidence to support their theoretical explanations.

One general approach is biological, and assumes that all behaviour can be reduced to explanations that focus on biological processes, such as the neural changes that accompany habituation to a noxious stimulus. Generally, observable responses, as in changes in biochemical levels, are used to support theoretical ideas; and quantitative measures, like the mathematical mean of a treatment population, are relied upon. Experimental methods that are particularly suitable for parametric statistics, such as linear regression and the t test, are the most commonly used ways of obtaining evidence. The biological approach had very prestigious early proponents, such as Sigmund Freud, and is currently one of the most dominant approaches. The advent of new technologies that enable precise brain mapping is likely to mean that this approach may soon make obsolete the other approaches that follow.

The second general approach is the behavioural approach, which seeks to explain how the *person*, rather than some physiological portion of the person, behaves. Behaviourists are interested only in observable responses, so share with their biological colleagues a preference for quantitative measures and analyses; and experimental designs that enable factorial variables to be considered, such as frequency and amount of a reinforcement schedule. Classic and operant learning theories are most notable of this approach. Indeed, early **verbal learning** theorists like Ben Underwood and Leo Postman used terms borrowed directly from the animal literature on conditioning, such as stimulus–response associations, spontaneous recovery, and even extinction. Importantly, the behavioural approach has been very successfully adapted to explain developmental questions regarding the aetiology of social behaviour, and social learning theories are among the most accessible and adaptable to the applied context. It has also served as the basis for highly successful treatment interventions for very debilitating health problems, such as phobias and depression.

The cognitive approach is the third approach, and also relies on experimental methodologies, with a long-term bias towards factorial combinations of different variables such as word frequency and word length. Ulric Neisser first coined the term cognitive psychology in his seminal 1967 book of the same name (Neisser 1967). Cognitive psychology frames questions in terms of information processing. Cognitive psychologists describe the world in terms of units of information, and ask about basic processes, such as *attention* and *perception*. David Marr's theory of perception (Marr 1982) is one of the most exciting examples of a cognitive approach to perception, with its emphasis on the gradual building up of information based on progressively more complex analyses of our retinal images. Psychologists adopting a cognitive approach discuss how information is organized, as in schemas or schematic processes. Schemas are representational devices that abstract the invariant properties across the general class of events, as in the schema for eating at restaurants. Mainstream theories developed from this cognitive approach have proven to be very useful in helping solve applied problems.

We note that explanations of cognitive operations have recently dominated theories of learning and memory, for example the Working Memory model. However, other approaches can, and have, been used to address questions of learning and memory. Therefore, we remind the reader that the cognitive approach is bound clearly by descriptions of information processing.

The other major approach that is consistent throughout the rooms has as one of its core principles the assumption of psychic determinism, and is traditionally associated with the term *psychodynamic*. As the term implies, the psychodynamic approach assumes that all behaviour is the expression of some underlying need; and that some of our needs are outside our conscious understanding. Our needs, be they conscious or not, serve as the basis to motivate us to behave the way we do. Note that this is the only approach that explicitly considers motivation to be a central explanatory concept. Terms like drives and needs provide the basis for explaining all aspects of our behaviour, from our ability to perceive a situation as dangerous, to our inability to remember a particularly nasty, traumatic event.

We need to be clear that there are other approaches that, while not dominant in all rooms, are certainly important in some. The humanist approach is a good example of what we mean. The roles of the observer and the observed, typical of the other approaches discussed above, are discarded. Instead, the humanist approach focuses on the person's unique experience and its explanations are directed at understanding the conditions that enable the person to reach some inner potential or achievement. Terms like phenomenal experience, or subjective understanding, are used to show the importance of the person's views and attitudes. This major theoretical shift is associated with a shift in the type of methodology and analysis that is used. With this approach, the quality of the person's experience is of interest. So, gross methods of testing large numbers of participants are uninformative. Instead, single individuals are selected, and more in-depth techniques are used, such as quasi-structured interviews. Analyses look at the type, rather than amount, of detail. For example, this approach would want to identify the different themes that occur in a person's life. This approach is very popular in some applied problems found in the treatment room, such as in the treatment of depression.

Whereas this approach has not been as dominant in some areas of psychological study, it has influenced the development of the social constructivism, of which Kuhn (1970) represents one of the best-known advocates. Social constructivism challenges the very basis upon which most of experimental psychology rests, through its rejection of logical empiricism (see Chapter 1). Logical empiricism states that theories are evaluated on the basis of the observable evidence that can be amassed to support or refute them. In contrast, social constructivism suggests that the basis for accepting, or rejecting, any theory has more to do with the social preferences operating at the time within the discipline, rather than anything else. Reality is constructed through social concepts that are mutually agreed by the group. In the case of psychology, these social concepts are represented through the use of paradigms—or ways of seeing the world in terms of subject and experimenter, and so on. In this way, theories come and go, not because they are demonstrated to be true, but because of the arbitrary fashion of the science at the time. While social constructivism has not been accepted wholeheartedly by many psychologists, it is an important approach to consider.

■ ADDITIONAL READING

Anderson, J.R. (1983) *The Architecture of Cognition*. Harvard University Press, Cambridge, MA.

Fodor, J. (1983) *The Modularity of Mind: an Essay on Faculty Psychology*. MIT Press, Cambridge, MA. These are two classics in the field of cognitive psychology, influential books that have provided the descriptive framework for the study of mental functions.

Gruneberg, M., Morris, P., and Sykes, R. (eds.) (1978) *Practical Aspects of Memory*. Academic Press, London. A useful early collection of applied memory research.

PART TWO

The Rooms

PART TWO

The Rooms

4

The crime room

This chapter discusses the different issues that arise when crimes are investigated, and refers to the general context under which these issues occur as the crime room. The crime room represents the first stage of our criminal justice system: the stage of investigation, which is the domain of the police. We show how extensively psychologists are used to help resolve difficulties that arise during the investigation of crime. We first consider the traditional topics associated with the crime room generally regarded under the heading of forensic psychology. We then go on to discuss the different phases that an investigator might go through in the course of conducting an investigation. We include a discussion of how psychologists have introduced improvements in procedures for eyewitness line-ups or identification parades, in procedures for interviewing witnesses, and in the manner in which suspects are questioned. We also consider the important development that has occurred in the context of motiveless crimes, in particular the work of those psychologists involved in investigative or offender profiling. In general, the crime room is an ideal, real-world context in which the psychologist can successfully apply many mainstream theoretical concepts. We provide two scenarios that illustrate how important psychological explanations are regarding memory, and the effects of emotion on our behaviour, when witnesses and victims of violent assaults are interviewed. We also show how developmental issues, such as the age of the witness or victim, are crucial in determining the nature of the interview techniques that might be used.

Crime

We start out this chapter by asserting that crime is an inevitable consequence of living in a civilized society. We suggest that, when enough people live together for a long-enoughbreak time, someone will engage in a social taboo, or behave unlawfully. It may be that criminbreak ality is a *natural* behaviour, that crime is linked to normal development, out of which most of us mature; or it may be that crime is restricted to a deviant minority, and is largely the consequence of the debauchery of the society in which it occurs. This debate is still raging, and we offer no further insight into the matter here. Regardless of the aetiology, we can be assured that crime, ultimately, exists in every society and every culture.

Crime is, by definition, behaviour that violates social laws or taboos; so, we can only consider what crime *is* in the context of the culture or society in which the crime occurs. However, regardless of how we define crime, we find that most cultures share a common feature when it comes to law enforcement. In most countries, the police investigate crime. In some countries, the police are public servants; in others, they are little more than extensions of the military arm of a government. Sometimes police tactics are questionable and highly unethical; other times the police follow fair and transparent procedures. While we deplore the use of violence and brutality, the exact police tactics are irrelevant for our purposes here. Our point is that, in most countries, when someone commits a crime, the society delegates the responsibility of enforcing the law to a specific group of people, generally the police, who respond by investigating the crime. The police want to find out who committed the crime, and wish to apprehend this person so as to prevent them from continuing to engage in the criminal acts. We group the issues and problems that arise during the course of an investigation into the general world context, the crime room.

It is the primary job of the police to amass and investigate the facts in order to determine whether an unlawful act has been committed. To do this, the investigator collects and reviews evidence, so that when a crime has been committed a charge and arrest can follow. However, solving crime and apprehending the person(s) responsible are difficult tasks, in that most criminals do not wish to be caught. In some cases, as with motiveless crimes, the task becomes even more difficult, as there is little in the way of clues to help the investigator narrow down his field of search.

Because crime is defined in terms of a person's behavioural responses, it is not surprising that psychologists have become an indispensable source of help to investigators. Importantly, psychologists from virtually all disciplines are now able to provide support to the different facets of crime investigation. For example, experts on abnormal personality characteristics have long been essential in understanding the reasons behind why people commit crime; their impact is still operating in the most modern of techniques, like offender profiling. Equally, though, the recent advances in **neuropsychology**, particularly in the development of techniques used to monitor brain activity and biochemistry, are also very useful in helping the police understand the effects of closed head injuries on a victim's ability to report on an assault. The crime room is one group of applied settings where psychologists are likely to remain useful for many years to come.

The complexity of crime investigation

We have already stated that crime can only be considered within the particular culture in which the act takes place. Different cultures have different beliefs, and hence they have different laws, and social taboos, regarding what is and what is not acceptable social behaviour. For example, two young people arguing in public may be socially condoned in one culture, whereas it may be associated with serious and severe punishment in another. Because of the obvious impact that culture has on crime and law enforcement, societal values must be considered in parallel with any discussion of crime and its investigation, rather than considered in some *post hoc* fashion. This is true for virtually every type of crime we might want to consider.

This means that some elements of the crime room will vary from one culture to another, in the way that the execution of some crimes clearly varies from one culture to another. For example, when we consider investigative profiling (see pp. 52–6) we see that the geographical distances and diversity afforded to a serial rapist in the United States—with its extensive freeway systems and overuse of motor cars—is very different from the possibilities that exist for a serial rapist in England.

At the same time, though, some elements of the crime room are common regardless of the culture. For example, it is likely that the developmental age of the child needs to be considered when deciding on an interview strategy, regardless of whether the child lives in Damascus or Toronto. Equally, if a person sees an event under poor conditions—such as when visibility is reduced to half a metre—this will impact on the ability to identify an unknown perpetrator who was eight metres away, regardless if the crime was committed in Canada or in Mexico.

We focus much more on the common elements of the crime room, rather than emphasizing the cultural differences. This is in part due to the fact that we wish to demonstrate the great success that psychologists have had in applying general psychological principles to investigations. Nonetheless, we wish to stress that a comprehensive discussion of crime must include a clear description of the impact of cultural standards, and social taboos.

Traditional topics in the crime room

In this section, we discuss those topics that are traditionally associated with the crime room. In particular, we spend some time discussing how psychology impacts on the jurisprudence system generally, although we restrict our attention to only those aspects that are relevant to crime investigation. We then go on to identify the different steps of an investigation, and show how concepts from cognitive psychology can be used to describe mental processing like hypothesis formation. We also discuss the different roles that psychologists can take in the crime room, which are clinical, experimental, actuarial, or advisory. Importantly, these roles are not restricted to the crime room, and will apply to all other rooms.

Issues discussed in the crime room fall under the more general heading of law and psychology. Traditionally, psychologists working within the context of law and psychology would be considered as criminological, or forensic, psychologists. Most authors agree that the development of what traditionally is known as *criminological* or *forensic psychology* began in the early twentieth century, with Munsterberg's book, *On the Witness Stand*,

---

BOX 4.1 THE SATIRICAL TRIAL OF MUNSTERBERG

Most modern scholars acknowledge that Otto Munsterberg was one of the first psychologists to ap-ply psychological principles to the understanding of eyewitness testimony. His essay, *On the Witness Stand* (Munsterberg 1908), was the subject of a rather tongue-in-cheek article by a well-known lawyer of the day, J.H. Wigmore (1909). Wigmore describes the trial of Munsterberg, who was allegedly being sued by a group of lawyers. The lawyers claimed that the psychology professor's book was endorsing views that were not only unsubstantiated, but libellous. For example, Munsterberg had allegedly ac-cused the legal profession of professional neglect, as they failed to use psychological data that would help to promote more accurate eyewitness accounts. In his defence, Munsterberg's counsel said that his client had only wished to draw attention to the fact that psychology, as a science, could be very helpful, primarily through its explanation of memory, as well as through psychologists' understanding of motivation and intention of witnesses and suspects. What is so delightful about Wigmore's review is that the trial was, in fact, a complete hoax. Munsterberg had never been sued for his views. However, Wigmore's article seemed to reflect the views of the legal profession regarding the use of psychological concepts in legal proceedings.

---

in 1908 (see Box 4.1). However, it was not until the latter half of the twentieth century, and particularly since the 1970s, that psychologists have become famous and sometimes notorious players in the justice system.

Haward, in his book *Forensic Psychology* (Haward 1981), provides a good description of a traditional forensic psychologist. For him, a forensic psychologist is a professional who lends psychological expertise to the different stages of the criminal justice system. In order to understand Haward's definition, we will take a moment to review the stages of our criminal justice system.

Our criminal justice system has three stages. The pre-trial is what concerns us here in the crime room, and involves all aspects of crime investigation. The second stage is the trial. This stage is dominated by the prosecution system, which, in our system, involves a prosecuting and defending counsel, a judge, and a set of individuals or jury. The roles of each are clearly defined, so that it is the job of counsel to present and argue evidence, while it is the job of the jury to assess the evidence in terms of whether the defendant is guilty, or not guilty, of the charges. The third stage, sentencing, is when the defendant receives the formal consequences of being found guilty, through sentencing by a judge. Haward suggests that forensic psychologists can operate at all of these three stages, al-though it is only the pre-trial phase that interests us here.

Another very useful taxonomy for considering the more general area of law and psychology comes from Haney (1980), who suggested a threefold classification: psychology *in* law, psychology *and* law, and psychology *of* law. Psychology *in* law refers to psychologists providing expertise during what can be regarded as the normal procedures of the law. One good example is when counsel or defendant(s) enters pleas of insanity or another mental disorder, such as a **post-traumatic stress disorder** (see 'The treatment room', Chapter 8). In these cases, the psychologist (or psychiatrist) may be asked to provide expert testimony to facilitate the court's decision on the defendant's psychological or mental state (see 'The court room', Chapter 5, pp. 89–9). Another example is the selection of jurors. Psychologists may be asked to provide expert opinion on who might be inappropriate (or appropriate) to serve as a juror in a case, identifying whether the potential juror would be biased against or in favour of the prosecution (or defence). When considering psychology *in* law, it is 'the legal system that dominates and . . . dictates the form and application of psychology . . .' (Haney 1980, p. 170). Psychology simply serves the law. Psychological findings are used to clarify legal points, rather than change them.

In contrast, psychology *and* law, Haney's second classification, is more controversial in that psychology, its theories and its empirical literature, are used to argue for or against the 'correctness' of legal procedures, such as is the case with poor identification parades or improper interview techniques. Not surprisingly, these situations are potentially controversial because the psychologist's expertise is used to identify or illustrate where miscarriages of justice might be occurring in normal legal procedures. When considering psychology *and* law, it is the psychologist who attempts to 'assert power and compel legal change' (Haney 1980, p. 170). A good example of this is the application of cognitive theories of memory to conditions of false testimony, or misleading *post-event information*. We illustrate this in scenario one (see pp. 61–8), where we discuss how cognitive theories of **episodic memory** can be used to help identify appropriate interview strategies for victims of crime.

Finally, there is psychology *of* law, a more esoteric subject and one that has received less attention in the psychological literature. In these circumstances, the focus is on the development of the law as a social institution, and examines the underlying psychological principles that contribute to its development, e.g. 'why, how and under what circumstances people obey the law' (Haney 1980, p. 156). For example, a psychologist may consider the circumstances under which members of a society decide that a law is unjust, and display mass civil disobedience. The first two, psychology *and* law, and psychology *in* the law, will be the focus of this and the following chapter, 'The court room'.

The stages of crime investigation

Psychologists and crime investigators have been associates for a long time and, this collaboration has been immortalized in fiction, from novels to film thrillers (e.g. Conan Doyle's arch detective, Sherlock Holmes, and Clarice Starling in *Silence of the Lambs*). At the present time, the police are probably more comfortable in using a psychologist's skills and expertise than ever before. It is certainly true that relative to the 1950s, psychologists are now not only important but also used habitually in many aspects of police investigation. To better understand the roles that a psychologist might take, it is useful to consider first what investigators normally do in the course of their work in the crime room.

Most investigators agree that good crime detection involves a series of stages. The stages are not necessarily described or labelled in the same way across different countries. Nonetheless, there is a general pattern that emerges in spite of the country in which the investigation is taking place. Janet Jackson and her colleagues, van de Eshof and de Kluever, provide a clear and useful description of this pattern (Jackson et al. 1998). First, the police must collect evidence (sometimes referred to as data capture). This includes evidence from the crime scene, any statements from witnesses or victims, and additional information, for example medical evidence or details about other similar crimes being committed. In the next stage, the investigator analyses the evidence. This would involve all forensic data, for example genetic testing, as well as careful consideration and review of non-forensic evidence. Third, the police must derive hypotheses regarding the crime. This will require the use of inferential reasoning to establish a motive and possible suspect. On the basis of this, the police then set out to apprehend suspects that conform to the hypotheses formed regarding the crime.

Jackson et al. (1998) point out that investigators proceed through these stages in different orders. They use two distinctions that have become important in discussions of cognitive processing, **bottom-up processing** and **top-down processing**. Some investigators operate in a bottom-up fashion, relying on the details of the case to help form hypotheses about the crime. In contrast, others take a more top-down approach. The investigator first considers higher-level features of the crime, for example links between how the crime was committed and the characteristics of the victim. Jackson et al. (1998) suggest that some investigators even adopt a 'hybrid' approach, using top-down processes at some points, and bottom-up analyses at others.

Roles in the investigation of crime

Psychologists can take at least one of four roles during the investigative phase—*clinical, experimental, actuarial,* or *advisory*. These roles are defined in terms of the nature of the psychologist's input more than any other defining feature. When a psychologist takes a

---

BOX 4.2 BOTTOM-UP OR TOP-DOWN?

Bottom-up and top-down processing were first introduced as concepts in theories of perception. Bottom-up processing involves the perceptual system abstracting details from the sensory environment that then serve to support more sophisticated perceptual processing, like object recognition. For example, our bottom-up processing identifies that there are three, perpendicular lines, which then allows us to recognize the object and see a triangle. In contrast, top-down processing is when perception is directed by higher-order hypotheses, which guide the identification of perceptual details. Steven Palmer (1975) provided an empirical demonstration of this when he showed the effects of context on the perception of ambiguous objects. Palmer presented participants with pictures of ambiguous objects. For example, one object could be either a post box or a bread box, depending upon the context. Palmer showed that when the visual context was a kitchen, more people 'identified' the object as a bread box. However, when the visual context depicted an outdoor scene, more participants identified the object as a post box. This elegant example shows how easily object recognition is influenced by higher-level information such as context. We expect to see a bread box in a kitchen, so we 'see' a bread-box when the object is presented within the context of a kitchen. This clearly illustrates that top-down processing, which is guided by our expectations and general world knowledge, can distort what we see.

BOX 4.3 THE CLINICAL APPROACH

We define the clinical role as one where the psychologist focuses on psychological and behavioural disorders in terms of abnormalities. This role is most often associated with clinical populations, which we discuss more fully in 'The treatment room' (Chapter 8, pp. 169–203). Clinical populations are often considered in terms of deviancy, against some normative population. Hence when a psychologist operates in a clinical role, she may be required to use standardized tests to measure some personality characteristic, in order to assess whether the person has some 'abnormality' relative to the statistical norm. The conceptual basis for understanding these abnormalities will vary according to the particular therapeutic framework that is adopted. For example, *psychoanalytic theories* argue for different levels of awareness and raise questions about the nature of consciousness. The psychological battle between different levels of the personality, the *id, ego,* and *super-ego* are believed to be play havoc with our mental state. In contrast, *cognitive behavioural theories* stress the importance of beliefs and cognition on emotion and behaviour. Regardless of the particular theoretical background, psychologist adopting a clinical role are likely to have some understanding, or expertise, in clinical syndromes, personality disorders, general medical conditions (e.g. *epilepsy, dyslexia*), or social and intellectual impairments (*learning disorders*).

---

clinical role, he or she is likely to adopt a *single case-study* approach and rely on theories of personality, both normal and abnormal, as the basis for discussing the psychological or mental state of an individual (the witness, victim, or defendant) (see Box 4.3). The clinical role can include the psychologist having one-to-one, in-depth interviews with relevant people (e.g. key witnesses, defendants) and conducting **standardized tests** that are designed to assess some aspect of the person's psychological state. The psychologist is likely to rely on both **quantitative data** (e.g. the numerical score on a psychometric test for depression) and on **qualitative data** (e.g. general themes observed when answering certain questions in an interview), when operating in a clinical role. A psychologist might also be asked to describe possible motives of a perpetrator, as in investigative profiling (pp. 52–6).

An experimental role is when the psychologist gives expert opinion regarding an issue, based on the empirical or experimental literature. The psychologist may summarize the current experimental literature and offer an opinion or conclusion; or the psychologist might be asked to conduct psychology experiments in order to ascertain the extent of a problem. For example, in cases of trademark infringement, a psychologist might be asked to determine whether a competing brand has borrowed too extensively from a more popular brand's packaging. The psychologist would use theories of perception to identify and address important issues, for example perceptual similarity in colour, shape, objects displayed, and logos. This could be accomplished by running an experiment to determine whether people suffer any perceptual confusion over the packaging of the two brands. Depending upon the outcome of the study, the psychologist would offer empirical evidence and provide an expert opinion on the psychological processes that may underlie perceptual similarities, so as to warrant a trademark infringement.

Actuarial roles can be seen somewhat in almost direct contrast to the single case study, in that they often involve the psychologist interpreting and analysing large data sets, for example official government statistics. For example, suppose a government agency tries out a procedure designed to reduce the amount of time that an investigator has to do paperwork. The agency finds that 5500 out of 10,000 investigators report less paperwork, 4000 report no improvement, and 500 claim that their paperwork actually got worse with the new procedures. Is 5500 a big enough improvement for the agency to announce that is has developed a wonder procedure? Here is where a psychologist, acting in an actuarial capacity, can be very useful. The psychologist's expertise is in being able to identify trends in the data, analyse data with appropriate statistical methods, and provide summary conclusions based on statistical analyses that might otherwise bewilder the intelligent, but untrained, professional. Most recent examples have included investigative profiling and, in particular, *geographical profiling* which advantageously uses large data sets to determine *cognitive maps* of offenders. Finally, an advisory role is one where the psychologist directly counsels the professional on the course of action that might be taken. For example, the psychologist might be asked to advise on how best to interview a suspect who committed the crime while under the influence of alcohol or drugs. Alternatively, the psychologist might be asked to give advice on the manner in which questions might be posed to victims or witnesses who have experienced extensive trauma.

Collaborations between psychologists and the police

In this section we consider some of the most important collaborations between psychologists and the police. We begin by using Gary Wells's definitions of estimator and system variables (Wells 1978). Estimator variables are those features of the investigation over which the investigator has no control, such as the age of the victim. System variables are features over which the investigator does have some control, such as where a victim is interviewed. We then go on to discuss the problem of identification parades, or line-ups, as it is one area where psychologists have introduced dramatic changes in procedures. We then go on to discuss the work of Elizabeth Loftus, who has been the most influential, modern psychologist in the crime room, contributing extensively to questions regarding interview techniques, and the fallibility of memory. Another important collaboration has been through the application of personality theories, although we treat this topic only briefly here, as it forms the basis of other chapters. We also consider the recent impact that investigative and offender profiling has had on criminal investigations, and distinguish between two general approaches, the clinical approach and the experimental approach.

The psychologist Gary Wells, in 1978, distinguished applied psychological research that focuses on what he calls estimator variables from research that focuses on system variables. He suggests that research on system variables has more direct application to the crime setting than research on estimator variables. However, this is likely to be due

---

BOX 4.4 CLASSES OF VARIABLES

The distinction between *estimator* and *system variables* is useful, as it helps to unify the areas of forensic interest. Estimator variables refer to features over which the investigator has little or no control. Examples include viewing conditions for an eyewitness (e.g. the amount of time looking at a perpetrator), the complexity and seriousness of the crime (e.g. whether the crime was a robbery or a hit-and-run), individual characteristics of the alleged perpetrator, and the victims and witnesses (e.g. race, age, and sex). In contrast, system variables are features over which the investigator (and psychologist) has some control. These include the length of delay between the crime and statements being taken from witnesses or victims, the structure of questions that are used by interviewers (e.g. open-ended versus closed), and the suggestiveness of the interview style (e.g. coercive or misleading). Not surprisingly, investigators have been very interested in developing system variables, as these variables provide them with at least some control over the conditions under which witnesses and victims are interviewed. Theories of memory have been particularly influential in helping investigators develop techniques that improve the accuracy and amount of recall, but that do not influence the reporting of errors, such as the cognitive interview technique (CIT) of Ed Geiselman and Ron Fisher (see main text, pp. 62–5).

---

to the fact that variables over which the investigator has some control are simply easier to implement changes for than those over which there is no control. Even so, it is likely that research into estimator variables, such as the sex of an eyewitness, will have a dramatic impact on criminal investigation procedures. Most recently, studies combining behavioural and neurological methods have suggested that women process emotional information differently from men, and similarly show better retention of certain kinds of emotional information. If such data are replicated and verified, these findings will have important implications for the reliability of eyewitnesses on the basis of the type of crime and the sex of the eyewitness.

One of the prime examples of system-variable research is that done by Wells and his associates, focusing on the identification line-up or identification parade. The consequences of mistaken (or false) identification are replete in both real cases of crime and popular literature and film (e.g. the film, *The Fugitive*). Regardless of the admonishments about the fallibility of witnesses, if a witness has positively identified a suspect, the suspect's chances of being arrested and questioned by the police increases.

The problem of identification

The applied psychological work in this area has maintained an outstanding level of theoretical integrity and quality; it represents psychology *and* law at its finest. One feature that has been examined in empirical studies is the instruction given to eyewitnesses prior to the line-up. Suppose a witness is called in to help in an identification parade. Rightly or wrongly, she may assume two conditions have been satisfied. One is that the police have enough evidence to organize a line-up; the second is that the police will include a

BOX 4.5 INDIVIDUAL DIFFERENCES AND CRIME

One of the most enduring examples of how psychologist work in the crime room comes from the work on individual differences. The notion that different people behave in different ways is one that has fascinated psychologists for many years. There is no other place that their interest has been more piqued than in the context of the crime room. Essentially, the questions we want answers to include why some people commit crime and others do not; and why some people commit some types of crimes while others do not. We deal extensively with this topic later, when we consider 'The treatment room' (Chapter 8, pp. 169–203), as it is there that the notions of social deviancy can be best understood. So, for the moment, we merely note that psychologists are vital in helping society to understand why some people commit crimes. Virtually all approaches in psychology have contributed to this understanding. For example, work done with men in Sweden examined the effects of both genetic and environmental factors on criminality (Cloninger et al. 1982). Cloninger et al. concluded that men who had backgrounds of criminality in both genetic and environmental factors were far more likely to show criminal behaviour than those who had no history of criminal backgrounds. Equally, criminality can be explained in terms of social learning theory, whereby the argument is that children learn to be anti-social and engage in criminality through observing such behaviour in their daily lives. Support for this position comes from the work done on the effects of violence on young children (e.g. Osofsky 1995).

person in the line-up who *they believe* might be the offender. Given these assumptions, the witness is likely to believe that one member of the line-up is the true offender. As Wells points out in his 1988 article, if the witness detects *which* member of the line-up is the suspect, the witness will be inclined to select this person. Evidence has shown that any suggestions to witnesses, either verbal or non-verbal, that the suspect is present in the line-up will significantly increase the chances of a false identification.

Another factor that influences suspect identification is the structure, or characteristics, of the line-up itself. Elizabeth Loftus, in her seminal 1979 book, *Eyewitness Testimony*, in addition to Wells, points out that the prior knowledge a witness has will interact with poor identification parades, especially when one member fits the 'description of the suspect' more than the others (Loftus 1979). Wells (1988) refers to this as the functional size of the line-up; and distinguishes between the nominal size of the line-up and its functional size. The nominal size of the line-up is based on the absolute number of people in the line-up. So, in a line-up of six people, the likelihood of one particular person being selected is one in six. In contrast, the functional size of the line-up is based on the number of individuals who could be wrongly selected by chance. This functional size is estimated by a 'mock' group of witnesses who are given a basic description of the 'offender' and asked to pick one member from a line-up. For example, the witness may know the offender's physical features, for example blonde, male, roughly six feet tall, and slight of build. So, if only one member of our line-up with six people matches this description, it is likely that there is a 100% chance that he will be picked, regardless of his innocence or guilt.

A disturbing example

Wagenaar, in his book 1988 book, *Identifying Ivan*, provides one of the most dramatic examples of poor identification procedures. The Nazi war criminal Ivan the Terrible, or John Demjanjuk, was alleged to be responsible for the deaths of 850,000 people at Treblinka, Poland, during the Second World War. The entire basis for the case against Demjanjuk was, exclusively, identification evidence given by some of the survivors of Treblinka, about thirty-five years after the atrocities were committed.

Wagenaar was asked to act as a defence witness—a task that others had declined due to the highly sensitive nature of the accusations and the crime. He took as his theme the identification of Ivan by surviving witnesses, after thirty-five years; his focus was on the procedures that were adopted by the prosecutors. As Wagenaar points out in great detail, the procedures of identification violated 'rules' that psychological research stipulates are critical for accurate eyewitness identification. For example, neither of the prosecutors was trained in the proper procedures for identification, as defined by Israeli law (Wagenaar 1988, pp. 127–31). As a consequence, Israeli laws were violated; for example prosecutors directed witnesses' attention to specific pictures of mug-shots, and photospreads containing insufficient numbers of foils. Similarly, the photospread itself, used to identify Ivan, contained pictures that were not matched to the suspect's description. Details that might have indicated the identity of people in the spread were not removed. Wagenaar rightly argued that the interviewers had introduced biases, thereby casting doubt on the veracity of the victims' identification. Wagenaar bravely demonstrated that, at times, being an applied psychologist has graver consequences than being theoretical and detached. The morality and ethics of the applied problem are often an issue for the psychologist.

Developing interview techniques

Another major area of collaboration between psychologists and the police has been in the context of interview techniques. The more general psychological issues that arise when we consider interview techniques are explored in more detail below in the two scenarios. However, we feel that it is important to highlight the contribution that psychologists have made in the context of misleading, or leading, post-event information. Most psychology undergraduate textbooks contain numerous references to the work of Elizabeth Loftus. In her book, *Eyewitness Testimony*, Loftus (1979) outlines the critical importance of what she termed 'post-event information'. Post-event information, or PEI, is any information that a witness receives, or is exposed to, after an event has occurred. Examples of PEI include a witness rehearsing the event with other witnesses, the witness being exposed to media coverage of an event, and, importantly, leading questions posed by interviewers, such as the police. Experimental evidence on PEI has led to major improvements in the manner in which the police interview witnesses, as we shall see below.

While much of the research on eyewitness testimony has been focused on the unreliability of memory, some researchers have been more interested in determining whether eyewitness reports could be made more accurate with the introduction of new techniques. One technique that has received a considerable amount of attention is hypnosis. The exact psychological processes behind hypnosis are controversial. Some early practitioners believed that hypnosis produced an altered state of consciousness, or *dissociation*. This notion of dissociation, where one part of the mind gets 'cut off' from the other, is popular with many athletes, who attempt to ignore aches and pains in order to continue their performance, as in long-distance running (see 'The sport room', Chapter 9, Scenario Two). In contrast, other practitioners viewed hypnosis as a normal state of consciousness, where the person's suggestibility is merely heightened.

The modern view is that promoted by Ernest Hilgard, called the neodissociation theory, which favours the assumption that hypnosis is an altered state of consciousness. Hilgard referred to the hidden observer, which is that part of the mind still available for processing information while another part is in a trance-like state. Hilgard gave credibility to the concept of hypnosis when he established his laboratory for hypnosis research at Stanford University in California in the late 1950s. Most psychologists believe that the process depends more on the characteristics of the person being hypnotized than the skill of the person who is doing the hypnotizing! While there is evidence that hypnosis can aid in eyewitness recall (e.g. Geiselman et al. 1985), there is also evidence to suggest that hypnosis carries with it some dangers. For example, hypnotized witnesses seem very confident in the information they recall while hypnotized, regardless of the accuracy of the information (e.g. Weekes et al. 1992). Since it is well established that juries place more credence on testimony from confident witnesses and victims (see Wagstaff et al. 1992), this means that hypnotically induced accounts can carry more weight, even though they might not be more accurate. For a more recent review of the literature on hypnosis, the reader is advised to refer to the article by Theodore Barber (2000).

Serial crime and profiling

Most crimes are understood in terms of motive and intent. The motive reflects the reason for the crime; *why* someone does something. The motive is that which *drives* the person, energizes the person to commit the act. In contrast, the intent is *what* the person wants to do, or what consequences the person wants his actions to take. For example, suppose a long-suffering wife hears of her husband's most recent affair; distraught over her husband's continued fecklessness, she loses her temper while they are arguing and strikes him with a pan that she has in her hand. The wife's intent was not to kill her husband; she hit out at him simply to silence his lies. But, as it happens, her blow is delivered in such a way that her husband breaks his neck and is killed instantly. The wife goes on the run.

Now, one of the first questions that a crime investigator will ask is about motive: is there anyone who would want this man dead, or would want to harm this man? By focusing first on a possible motive, the police immediately narrow down the possible suspects for the crime. By asking the question, who would have the motive to kill this man?, the police would eventually be led to the wife, particularly after they discovered the details of the husband and wife's private lives. Generally, the police assume that most perpetrators somehow know their victims, or know of their victims; and, that, when there is a link between the perpetrator and the victim, the motive is easier to establish.

In fact, it is the case that in the overwhelming majority of violent crimes that are committed, although the exact percentages vary, the victim and the perpetrator *either* know each other *or* have some relationship.

However, in a small percentage of cases, there is no obvious link between the perpetrator and the victim. The victim does not know the perpetrator; the victim seemed to be picked at random, or haplessly was in the wrong place at the wrong time. The motive for the crime is not clear. Why, if the victim were *unknown* to the perpetrator, would the perpetrator commit the crime on *that* victim? Criminal investigators refer to these types of cases are motiveless crimes. These motiveless crimes are immensely difficult for most investigators. Without a motive, the proverbial 'anyone' could be the perpetrator; and anyone is a lot of people. Forensic evidence is undoubtedly helpful, but often not useful until the police have a suspect in custody. For example, suppose that we have a motiveless crime, and we have a strand of the perpetrator's hair. We do forensic analyses and we discover that the hair is from a woman with dark hair, possibly Mediterranean descent; we even conduct a DNA analysis. However, we have over 15,000 women who fit this description. Obviously, interviewing each and every one, and doing DNA matching, would be costly and ineffective. We must have some way of narrowing the size of the net, some way of restricting the number of women who might be our suspect.

It is exactly in these types of cases that psychological concepts are very useful; and, consequently, the motiveless crime represents an ideal place where psychologists can apply basic principles about behaviour. However, it is these very cases that have served to

---

BOX 4.6 INVESTIGATIVE VERSUS OFFENDER PROFILING

Investigative and offender profiles are very useful when it is suspected that a serial criminal is at work. Serial criminals are those who repeatedly commit the offence, as in the case of serial rape and serial arson. It is important that we distinguish between *investigative profiling* and *offender profiling*, as the two are very different. We use the term investigative profiling when we refer to a psychologist operating at investigative stages. There are no suspects apprehended and there may be few leads as to where to look for suspects. The profiler is asked to develop a structured description of the perpetrator, particularly in terms of socio-demographic variables, such as age, marital status, history of employment, and so on. Depending upon the profiler's approach, the profile might include personality characteristics such as types of leisure activity or other interests. Most profiles would probably include some idea as to the general geographical area of operation of the perpetrator. In contrast, offender profiling is when the offender has been captured and, usually, is incarcerated. The offender has already been sentenced, so there is the assumption that the perpetrator is known to the investigator. Under these circumstances, the investigator conducts an in-depth analysis of the offender, including uncovering family background and upbringing, exploring any childhood traumas that may have contributed to the offender's behaviour. Performance on standardized tests and quasi-structured interviews are used to provide some understanding as to why and how the offender committed the crimes. Investigative and offender profiles offer very different insights into crime and are useful for different reasons. Consequently, they are not to be confused.

become a source of controversy, as there is serious disagreement between professional psychologists as to how to best proceed. We begin by discussing the area of investigative profiling.

Before discussing the different approaches to investigative profiling, we first want to identify what all investigative profiling techniques, and profiles, have in common. One assumption is that of **psychic determinism**. While we discuss this concept extensively in a later chapter (see Chapter 8, pp. 174–79), we need to introduce the concept here, as it serves as the basic assumption behind all profiling. In its most simplistic form, psychic determinism assumes that all behaviour is determined, or motivated, by internal drives, states, or needs. There are any number of different theoretical approaches to discussing the exact nature of these internal drives or needs, but they do not concern us here. What is important is that investigative profiling is predicated on the belief that the internal states or needs of the individual directly determine why and how that person commits a crime.

The concept of psychic determinism is particularly useful when we consider serial crimes. It is assumed that when people repeatedly commit the same offence, or similar offences, they develop a pattern in their behaviour, a signature to their crime, which directly reflects their needs, internal states, or motives. Their pattern reflects the unique elements of their motive to behave in the way that they do. So, the way that you would commit crime will be slightly different from the way that we would commit the same crime. While different psychologists will proffer different types of evidence as psychological fingerprints, all investigative profilers must assume psychic determinism.

The second pervasive feature of investigative profiling is the assumption that there is a ceiling, or some *asymptote*, to a criminal's learning curve, so that, when the person has committed enough crimes, they will have reached some stable point, where their behaviour no longer changes. We must make this assumption if we want to believe that there is a stable behavioural pattern to the criminal's behaviour to which we can subject our profiling techniques. This is an interesting assumption for a number of reasons, as it flies in the face of some empirical literature. First, the literature on motor skills suggests that even after 80,000 trials a person is still improving in their performance of quite simple tasks like rolling a cigarette. So, it is quite likely that even after a good number of crimes, the criminal will still be learning her 'trade'! Second, the literature on how we learn complex tasks strongly suggests that we will learn different components of a complex task at different rates. For example, a multi-skilled task like driving a car is learned at different levels, in different stages. Some elements of the skills, such as clutch control, become automatic long before other elements of the skill, such as reversing around a corner. So, we would expect that a complex task like committing a burglary would similarly show different learning rates. Investigative profiling does not take such things into account, however.

Two approaches to investigative profiling

There are two generally acknowledged approaches to investigative profiling. One approach is best described as a case-study approach. The individual perpetrator is considered at great length, identifying personal, social, mental, emotional, and environmental factors that might be influencing this person's behavioural patterns. All aspects of the evidence are considered in detail, and viewed in terms of their potential relations to each other. From this detailed examination, some hypotheses about why and what led to the behaviour are formed. The intent of the profile is to provide the motives behind the crimes, the personal themes that dictate the person's behaviour. From their detailed analyses, the profiler identifies themes that are important for the person, for example maintaining control of the victim. Psychologists who adopt this approach generally rely on *psychoanalytic frameworks* to explain deviant behaviour, or use theories that are developed from clinical or specialized populations. For example, this latter approach is reflected in the work of the US Federal Bureau of Investigation, wherein the profiler attempts to understand the underlying motives behind the crime.

The second approach is different in terms of the methodology through which it derives its profile. We will label this second approach as the experimental approach. The experimental approach relies on as large a database as possible in order to draw conclusions about the *relationship* between different elements of a crime, such as the type of victim, type of force used, and other features at the crime scene. It uses government and crime statistics as its sources, and then applies statistical analyses to discover whether any particular features of crimes group together. So, for example, if someone uses a gun in a robbery, how often is that associated with other features, such as verbally abusing or battering the victim. In the main, statistical analyses relying on correlations, and family and factor analyses serve as the ways in which psychologists interpret these huge amounts of data. Through careful analyses of the relationship between different features of the crime, psychologists hope to identify the salient characteristics of the criminal, including where he lives, what he does for employment, what hobbies he might have, and so on. In the main, these profilers are less concerned about the underlying personality motives than they are about identifying real or tangible variables.

The experimental approach borrows extensively from theoretical concepts derived mainly through experimental methodologies. In particular, concepts from cognitive psychology—such as the importance of **schemas**—have been appropriated to discuss how elements of the crime reflect the criminal's internal world. For example, David Canter (2000), a well-known profiler in the United Kingdom, makes good use of the notion that criminals develop a schema for the crime, including sequences and habitual responses to various elements of the crime. Canter suggests that, with practice, the criminal's behaviour becomes more and more schematic, driven by their habitual patterns. According to Canter, the criminal leaves behind, through his behaviour, the remnants of his internal schemas.

It is important for us to mention that investigative profiling is suitable only for crimes wherein the criminal can execute a unique pattern of behaviours. For example, arson is a good candidate for investigative profiling, in that there are many ways in which to execute the act, including different types of building, types of incendiary device, and so on. Murder is another serial crime that lends itself to investigative profiling. There are many ways in which to unlawfully kill someone, and it is because of the inherent variability in the way this crime can be committed that makes the crime a suitable candidate for profiling. In contrast, other types of repeated crime are very poor candidates. For example, car theft is quite often a serial offence; and, while the *type* of car may be important to

---

BOX 4.7 PROFILING SERIAL CRIMES

Investigative profiling has received a good deal of public attention, particularly through its association with serial killings. Serial killings are the cause of much public concern and fear, and, understandably, those cases where profiling has been used have received considerable media coverage. Serial killings capture our imagination and offer powerful, cultural images to us. Thus we have the idea of a hero, in the form of a behavioural profiler, Clarice Starling (from *The Silence of the Lambs*), who combats evil, as delightfully personified by Hannibal Lecter. In fact, serial killings are often very low-frequency events, in that most police officers will never investigate a case of serial killing in their career. However, because they are so rare, and police officers have so little experience, serial killings can actually go undetected, with the investigator suffering linkage blindness, a term coined by an English investigator, Rupert Heritage. The investigator does not know the signs of behavioural patterns, due to a lack of experience with serial crimes. As a consequence, the investigator fails to detect the pattern. So, while rare, serial assaults can pose a real threat, and obviously provoke extreme reactions from society when they go undetected!

---

note, there are only so many ways that people can steal a car; for example, disarming the security systems, breaking a window, and 'hot-wiring'.

There are many factors that influence whether a psychologist is called in to help with an investigation. One is whether the investigator believes that profiling has much to offer. Some police investigators feel that profiling essentially involves good detective work, and that an investigator's role is not that dissimilar to that of a profiler. Other people argue that profiling is *not* the same as investigation; that a good profiler must have an understanding of the psychological processes behind criminal behaviour. Regardless of the profiler's orientation, the profiler has expertise in psychological concepts and the psychological literature that can uniquely inform a criminal investigation. We do not feel that there is a clear-cut answer, for criminal behaviour, like so much of the real world, is largely difficult to predict, and many factors will influence decisions as to how to best investigate a specific incident of crime.

Summary of the crime room

We have discussed the traditional topics associated with the crime room, and also outlined the various roles that psychologists can play. We have noted that certain collaborations between psychologists and law enforcement have resulted in vastly improved techniques for suspect identification and the interviewing of witnesses or victims. We have also considered briefly the use of psychological principles in investigative and offender profiling. There is no doubt that in our modern world new kinds of crime are evolving, such as those crimes involving the Internet. With the advent of information technology, the nature of crime and the way that it must be investigated had changed so dramatically that the laws are struggling to keep up with the issues. Similarly, the nature of global conflict, as it exists today, means that new ground is being broken with

---

BOX 4.8 CONFESSIONS OF GUILT

There are many important applied issues that need further attention. One notable example is the understanding of confessions. This area is one in which psychologists and investigators have been known to have confrontational interactions, as it raises questions regarding police interrogations and the probative value of confessions. The act of confessing to a crime is one that has grave consequences for the accused. As Marquita Inman (1981) notes, a confession, once made, is difficult to retract, and any further protestations of innocence are regarded with disdain and the accused is often under great pressure to enter a plea of guilty. Inman points out that the act of confessing is a highly complex one, combining social and psychological elements. For example, it has long been known that innocent people can be made to confess to crimes, and in some cases may even come to believe in the confession themselves. There are many ways in which psychologists might explain this. Conditions of the interview procedure, such as whether the suspect is deprived of sleep, can lead to temporary states of hysteria and abnormality. Psychoanalytic theory can be used to argue that guilt anxiety can affect even emotionally stable people, for example subjective feelings of guilt or sinfulness can merge with intense external accusation during a guilt-oriented interview. Psychologists using clinical or experimental approaches will be invaluable in helping law enforcement ensure that the techniques used for investigating crime are fair, just, and based on sound, psychological evidence.

---

international laws, such as the internment and incarceration of insurgents on foreign lands. How crimes are investigated, and how criminals are treated, is very different than it was only twenty years ago.

Scenarios one and two

The two scenarios that follow consider examples of system variables, since both look at factors or variables over which the investigator and the psychologist have some control. While both scenarios emphasize the problems that arise when interviewing witnesses or victims, the two scenarios are very different in nature and in the extent of their application. The first scenario illustrates how psychologists used their expertise to help in the specific case of a victim who had been seriously assaulted. This scenario relies heavily on the experimental literature relating to adult memory, and extends cognitive hypotheses about episodic memory, and the effects that emotion has on memory. This scenario is particularly useful as it shows how psychologists may need to consider the *interaction* between estimator variables—like the emotional state of the victim—and system variables—like the interview technique used.

The second scenario represents another real-world situation where interview techniques were the focus. However, in the second scenario, the psychologists were asked to review and assess governmental guidelines proposed for the interviewing of a vulnerable group of victims and witnesses; children. This second scenario demanded that the psychologists take on a variety of roles, and required them to use a variety of diverse, empirical methods, including *qualitative analyses* and *descriptive statistics*. Child development—mental, physical, emotional, and social—and the effects that trauma can have on a child were particularly important, as were issues regarding the development of personal memory, and the suggestibility of young children.

SCENARIO ONE

THE CASE OF THE WOMAN JOGGER

In this first scenario we discuss how serious violent assaults are investigated. Violent assaults introduce a variable over which the investigator has no control: the level of trauma and emotional distress of the victim. The emotional state of the victim, which is an estimator variable, is relevant not only at the time of the interview, but also at the time the crime was being committed. For example, victims who dissociate during the commission of a crime may be less likely to report on details than those people who stay focused and 'present'. Without question, our emotional reactions greatly impact on our ability to remember traumatic events.

One of the problems with interviewing victims of violent crime is that these victims often have gaps in their memory about what happened. There are a number of reasons why this might occur. For example, extreme states of stress are likely to reduce cognitive resources that are available at the time of the event, and this affects what a person attends to and how much they store and later remember. We know that the emotional salience of an object, like its threat value, will influence whether a victim does or does not attend to it. The phenomenon of weapon focus, introduced in 1978 by Brian Clifford and Ray Bull, is the result of an emotionally salient object, namely the weapon, virtually hijacking the victim's attention. Given that the weapon is a threatening element of the environment, the victim is likely to attend differentially to the weapon and as a consequence will better remember what the weapon looked like, simply because of its importance. A gun pointed directly in one's face will capture the victim's attention at the expense of other important details, even perhaps the physical description of the offender!

Stress has a tendency to make the person focus on things related to the threat, and so incidental but important details might go unnoticed. Information may go unreported regarding things that happened prior to the attack; for example, was there another person who might have been walking by at the time? Details that are not related to the attack, for example the address on a pack of matches, may also go unreported. However, we must note that individual differences, and pre-morbid traits, like cognitive style, will also interact with other variables, so that not all people will react to the same traumatic event in the same way.

Cognitive psychologists have been very influential in applying principles derived from laboratory studies to real-world investigations. There is no more successful application of cognitive theory than the cognitive interview technique (CIT) (Geisleman et al. 1985). CIT has always had the advantage of using very sound, empirically reliable principles. As we shall see below, the original version was unique from all other attempts at improving interview techniques, by virtue of the fact that it relied on certain empirical findings about events, or episodic memory that were true across many, if not most, situations.

An American woman, aged 33, was in a rural part of England, visiting her aunt for a holiday. She had gone for a run along a path, near a park, where a group of allotments are, where people grow vegetables and flowers. It was about 9.30 a.m. The woman had run about fifteen minutes, passing a few people. She stopped for a moment to tie the laces on her trainers. As she knelt down to tie her shoes, someone grabbed her from behind and threw her to the ground. Everything else was a blur. All she remembers is that someone attacked her and tried to tear her clothes off her body. She cannot remember seeing her attacker, although she has some vague recollection of a man asking her directions just before she was attacked. She does remember fighting with her attacker, or being forced to the ground. There were bruises over the victim's limbs and upper body. She thought her attacker hit her with something, although there was no evidence of any head wounds or other facial injuries. She was not able to say how long the attack went on, apart from the fact that it 'seemed like hours'.

According to the victim, the assault was interrupted when a dog and its owner approached. The victim remembers hearing the dog barking loudly and also remembers hearing someone call a name. The victim believes that her attacker became scared and ran off, leaving her face down on the path. The victim was too scared to turn around immediately. When she did, the dog owner and the dog were standing next to her asking if there was something wrong. The victim asked the dog owner to take her home, where she got a change of clothes before going to report the assault to the police. As a witness, the dog owner gave their details to the victim.

Once at the police station, the victim agreed to be examined by the police surgeon and also agreed to a preliminary interview with the lead investigator. The clinical examination suggested that the colour of the victim's bruises were more consistent with an assault that might have occurred within the last ten days, but certainly not within the last twenty-four hours. The investigator interviewed the dog owner, who claimed that no one was there when she approached the victim. The dog owner said that some of the victim's clothes had been removed, and that she clearly was distressed and traumatized by the attack.

A male police officer was assigned to lead the investigation. When he first interviewed the victim, she could not remember very much, and she was clearly more interested in returning to the United States. The investigator was aware that the victim's memory for the event was patchy and often unclear: she had only a vague impression of the man who asked for directions; and she had no memory of her assailant. The victim was also very vague about the exact details of the assault: she could remember tying her shoes, and was clear about details that occurred before the attack. However, her memory of the attack itself left much to be desired. All she could remember was fighting with her attacker and feeling scared that she was going to die. Her time estimates were also questionable. While the victim felt that the attack had 'lasted for hours', it was clear that the attack only lasted a few minutes, as the dog owner had found the victim around 10.00 a.m. The investigator had interviewed the victim for a second time and she failed to report any new information. He was concerned whether he should proceed any further.

The investigator was aware that the victim's inability to report on much of the attack might be a normal reaction to traumatic assault. The investigator had been trained in basic rape trauma syndrome so he knew that the victim would be going through different emotions as she came to terms with her assault. Consequently, the investigator knew that he needed to be sensitive in how he was going to interview the victim. For example, he knew that were he to accidentally express any doubts regarding anything the victim said about the attack, the victim might interpret this as him disbelieving her. This in turn would significantly reduce the victim's motivation and ability to report on details.

Importantly, the investigator had attended a workshop where psychologists had discussed the use of memory-enhancing techniques to improve victim's reports. He was keen to discover whether his victim would benefit from the use of any of these kinds of technique. His police training had already included experience with the CIT. He did not regard himself as an expert in the CIT, however, and was not convinced that he could rely on his judgement alone.

What was the situation?

Unfortunately, violent crime is not uncommon. The investigator had experience with interviewing victims, and also had a good appreciation of the potential psychological factors that might be important. As a consequence, the situation was one in which other professionals in the crime room *welcomed* the input from a psychologist.

Obviously, the situation required a relatively quick assessment of the major psychological variables that might be operating. Importantly, this was an ongoing case and it was clear that the victim was eager to leave the country and return home to her family within the next day or two. Some action had to be taken. The investigator knew the contact details of the psychologists who specialized in applied memory problems and contacted them directly. After an initial meeting, the investigator asked that the psychologists be formally involved as consultant memory experts in the case.

Why were the psychologists used?

The investigator had two clear objectives that he wanted the psychologists to fulfil. First, he wanted the psychologists to tell him whether memory-enhancing techniques should be used with his victim, and, if so, what kinds should be used. Clearly, any suggestions were obviously restricted by statutory law. For example, hypnosis could not be used, even if there was unequivocal evidence that proved it was a highly effective technique, as it is not an acknowledged technique in English courts. Also, the investigator was highly concerned that the memory-enhancing techniques did not promote a fanciful account from the victim that contained incorrect information.

The second objective was more problematic. While the investigator did not doubt that the victim had been attacked, he also had to acknowledge that there was virtually no conclusive forensic evidence that supported anything the victim remembered. Unfortunately, the victim's account was very sketchy and incomplete at times. Even more problematic, his immediate superior officer was not convinced that the victim was telling the truth, and this put additional pressure on the investigator.

Given these difficult circumstances, the investigator hoped that the psychologists could help him prove that the victim's account was truthful. Based on what they knew about memory, he wanted the psychologists to comment on whether or not the victim's account had truthful characteristics to it.

What psychological concepts were relevant?

The psychologists realized that they could draw on the huge literature that has been amassed on how people remember events that are highly personal and unpleasant. There were a number of factors that were obviously important to consider. First, the psychologists had to understand the more general question of how people remember events. The psychologists would obviously be guided by the literature on explicit, auto-biographical memory, as asking the victim to remember her attack is asking the victim to engage in explicit, autobiographical memory retrieval. In fact, there is a fairly straightforward match between theory and the real world, which meant that translating theory into practice should be somewhat easier.

The psychologists knew that the investigator specifically wanted to know whether any memory-enhancing techniques might be useful, and particularly wanted to know

---

BOX 4.9 AWARENESS AND MEMORY

One of the most exciting developments in memory theory came when psychologists started to consider the *act* of remembering, particularly in terms of the person's awareness and intention. Very simply, there are different ways in which we remember. The distinctions are in terms of (1) how aware we are of engaging in the act of remembering, (2) why we are remembering, and (3) what is the task of re-membering. So, for example, suppose a student is taking an exam, and has a series of test questions that must be answered. The test is designed to assess how well the student has learned the course materials. The student is fully aware of the fact that he is remembering: he knows that he is retrieving information that he has read in the past, or heard presented in lectures. The student is also knowingly remembering this course material in the service of answering the test question. This type of remember-ing has been called **explicit memory** or *intentional memory*; the task would be described as a *direct memory task* (Jacoby 1984; Johnson and Hasher 1987). The memory is explicit because the student is fully aware that he is engaged in retrieving past learned information. The memory is intentional, as the student is deliberating attempting to engage in the act of remembering. The task is direct, in that the student knows that the question is directly assessing his memory for the course materials. In con-trast, take the case of someone stopping you for directions to a famous local landmark. You begin to tell the person directions, when suddenly you have an image of last Sunday, when you were standing and looking at the very landmark. In this circumstance, you unintentionally remembered last Sunday, as you were actually in the process of telling someone directions; no one directly asked you to remem-ber your personal experience, so the task would be an *indirect memory task*. The concept of **implicit memory** has been highly useful in explaining behavioural dissociations in some clinical populations, such as *amnesic* syndromes (e.g. Cermak et al. 1995; see also Roediger and McDermott (1993) for a discussion of implicit memory in 'normal human subjects').

about the appropriateness of the CIT. Critically, CIT is based on well-founded principles regarding how people remember specific events. We briefly outline the four basic cognitive components of CIT, as these are most relevant. These four represent the major techniques of CIT and distinguish it from all other types of interview technique that have been devised.

Ed Geiselman, Ron Fisher, and their colleagues were the original proponents of CIT (Geisleman et al. 1985). The original CIT, as it has come to be known, relied on techniques that had been shown to be effective in producing accounts that were more accurate, but without increasing the number of errors. Four basic techniques formed the basis of CIT, and serve to distinguish it from any other approaches.

The first technique can be called context reinstatement. We experience things that happen in our lives, like going to the cinema, in a specific spatio-temporal context: we go to the cinema at a particular time, on a particular day, to see a particular movie, with particular people, and so on. When we are asked to remember our trip, we remember a specific experience, filled with details surrounding the specific place and time. With the technique of context reinstatement, we are encouraged first to remember details of the context, before we attempt to report on the event itself. The assumption is that if we remember details of the context, this will subsequently enable us to better remember details of the event itself. The logic of this assumption is based on the psychological theories that postulate memory retrieval, especially free recall, to be one of recreating event-specific information. There are many routes to which event-specific information might be accessed; reinstating some of the contextual cues are assumed to facilitate this process dramatically.

As there is no way of knowing which contextual cues might be the best, CIT suggests that the person reinstate as much of the original context as they can. So, we would be asked to go back to the time when we were waiting to get tickets, then imagine that we are going into the cinema. We would be encouraged to focus on the details, including any sights or sounds, like other people talking. We would also be asked to recreate our internal mental environment, such as any thoughts we may have had, as well as any emotions or feelings we might have been having at the time. Any details that reinstate the original context are considered to be important.

The technique of context reinstatement, where the person builds a picture of the context, was actually appropriated by CIT from an earlier technique, which was developed by Malpass and Devine in 1981, called the guided memory technique. The guided memory technique directs the person through the event, starting at some point before the incident up to the critical moments, in a systematic fashion. So, with our cinema example, we might be encouraged first to imagine ourselves at the ticket booth, then going into the cinema, then going to get some refreshments, and so on. This systematic retracing would occur up to the critical point that someone wanted us to recall.

A second component to CIT is the instruction to say everything, regardless of how important it is. This instruction is in direct response to the fact that when people talk to the police they often have some pre-conceived notions about which details are important to an investigation. Because of these pre-conceived notions, people will omit or edit out details about an event if they believe that these details are unimportant. The only problem with lay-people's pre-conceptions is that they are often wrong! In fact, a good

---

BOX 4.10 THE IMPORTANCE OF CONTEXT

One of the best-documented findings in the cognitive literature on memory is known as *encoding spe-cificity*. Endel Tulving and Don Thomson (1973) described the principle of encoding specificity, when they showed that recall was far superior when recall conditions reinstated the original learning condi-tions. The general principle is that the more similar the learning and recall contexts are, the better recall will be. This is similarly referred to as context-dependent memory. A simple example is provided by the work of Duncan Godden and Alan Baddeley (1975), who looked at the effects of encoding specificity on divers' recall of words. Divers were first asked to learn a list of words, either on land or while they were underwater. The divers were then asked to recall the words. Half recalled the words in the same context under which they were learned; the other half were switched contexts. So, for those divers who learned the words while under water, half of them would be asked to recall while under water, while the other half would be asked to recall the list on dry land. Godden and Baddeley (1975) found that when the learning and recall contexts were the same recall was better, with the divers recalling roughly 30 per cent more than when the contexts had been switched. The practical implications of such demonstrations are dramatic. This suggests that when we want an eyewitness to remember an event, if we take the eyewitness back to the scene of the crime, she should recall more information due to the effects of encoding specificity. This technique of taking people back to the scene of the crime has been used in many cases of serious crime. Investigators also conduct a reconstruction of events in the hope that the reinstatement of the contextual features will prompt someone to remember more about a crime.

---

investigator is interested in *all* details. Good crime investigation involves examining all the facts and then making inferences. What seems to be an unimportant detail may have great significance later in an investigation. For these reasons, the person is asked to report everything, regardless of whether he thinks the detail is evidentially valuable or not.

The third technique in CIT asks the person to alter the perspective from which they recall. In the original CIT this meant, for example, asking the person to imagine that they were standing in a different part of the room, and then recall the event from that perspective. This shift in perspective is assumed to introduce new cues that in turn may result in the person remembering more information. However, there is an obvious problem with this technique. It introduces a perspective that person *did not experience*. As a consequence, if the person is basing recall from a totally *imagined perspective* they are just as likely to introduce information into the account that is incorrect.

Because of these obvious potential problems, the modified CIT dropped this tech-nique. Instead, the person was asked to change the order of their report. Here, the per-son would be asked to report the event from beginning, middle, end, and then reverse the order, recalling from the end through to the beginning. The person might then be asked to report the event from the middle, and so on. The assumption behind this technique is again based on the belief that recall involves accessing event-specific in-formation through cues. When we ask someone to reverse their order of recall, different cues become available, and so too does new, correct information. Thus, the technique can improve and promote new information because the person is forced to consider the event from a different, although experienced, perspective.

The fourth technique of CIT addresses the complex issue of confidence and memory. In the context of crime investigation, sometimes people—witness or victims—want to be completely sure that they are correct in what they are saying. In this way, the person only wants to report information that they are absolutely confident is correct. What this means, though, is that often the person fails to report otherwise correct information simply because they do not feel confident enough in the accuracy of what is being remembered. However, the memory literature tells us that there is a highly complex relationship between confidence and memory. While the empirical research is equivocal, the fact still remains that confidence is not an infallible indicator of whether some piece of information is correct. To this end, under the original CIT, the person is encouraged to adopt a more lenient confidence level when reporting details, and to report details even they are unsure about their correctness.

Understandably, psychologists have been more concerned about the issue of witnesses and victims being confident about otherwise *false* information. Indeed, as we will see in The treatment room, (Chapter 8 Scenario One), the idea that someone can be highly confident about events that have never happened has served as the focus of debate for topics like **recovered memories**. However, it is equally important to remember that in the crime room the consequence of a person *failing* to report otherwise correct information can be devastating to the investigation. Consequently, while there is no question that confidence is not the best indicator of accuracy, CIT notes that in the real world any information has the potential to be useful from an investigator's viewpoint.

It transpires, though, that this fourth technique has had its practical problems, particularly in the context of the court room (see Chapter 5), where cross-examination occurs. If a defence counsel knows that the victim had been encouraged to *report even if unsure*, then counsel can easily discredit the details. Counsel can suggest to the jury that the victim had been prompted by the investigator to report the information in spite of feeling unsure of its accuracy. Because juries believe, erroneously, that confidence is a good indicator of accuracy, they are likely to discredit any information in which the victim lacks confidence. Due to these practical problems, the modified CIT encourages people to give multiple reports. With each new report, the victim is told to forget what she said before, and, using context reinstatement, remember the event as if it were happening in the present. The assumption is that repeated recalls give the victim additional opportunities to access new information.

The psychologists in this case were also aware of empirical evidence to suggest that there were some potentially problematic consequences of using CIT. First, CIT has been known to increase the number of errors in an account as well as increasing the amount of correct information. The problem for a real-world investigator is that it is rather difficult to know what is an error and what is correct information. Further, if an error is introduced into an account while using such powerful techniques as context reinstatement, the victim may become highly confident in an otherwise erroneous piece of information. Additionally, empirical evidence has suggested that CIT should not be used with people who suffer problems of *reality monitoring*. Reality monitoring reflects our ability to distinguish between things that we have actually experienced and things

---

BOX 4.11 THE REVISED CIT

In addition to the revised CIT including new cognitive instructions, it also advised interviewers to be careful of interrupting the victim or witness. Allowing the person to talk uninterrupted is considered to be important for a number of reasons. For example, if the interviewer consistently interrupts a victim, the victim's memory processes will be consistently interrupted, making the report disjointed. The victim will find it more difficult to provide an initial account of what happened. Further, it is known that oral reporting is more difficult than written reporting, in that the person has to remember what she has said with an oral report, whereas a written report can be reviewed much more easily (see Bekerian and Dennett 1990). As a consequence, the modified CIT suggests that the person be given the opportunity to produce an account that is free from any cues or interruptions. This free narrative phase—where the victim or witness is invited to tell the interviewer everything that she can remember—has been incorporated in most guidelines for interviewing witnesses and victims. The revised CIT also argues that the interviewer should take time with the questions, and proceed very slowly. This slow process, although tiresome, allows the victim or witness time to imagine the situation as they are reporting it. Importantly, these techniques are indirect and do not intervene extensively while the victim or witness is reporting. The interviewer is also encouraged to use the terms and phrases that are reported by the victim or witness so as to be confluent with how they are remembering.

---

that we imagine we have experienced. Marcia Johnson and her colleagues have been largely responsible for investigating processes involved in reality monitoring. Her research suggests that the mental state of the person will strongly influence their ability to distinguish fact from fantasy.

So, while CIT is supported by an impressive amount of experimental and empirical evidence, there are also some potential problems that can be associated with its use. These would have to be carefully considered by the psychologists.

The psychologists also knew that the emotional nature of the event, and its personal significance to the victim, would be critical variables to understand. Arguably, the victim's emotional reaction might be the deciding factor in whether the psychologists recommended the use of an interview strategy like CIT. The psychologists would need to consider whether the victim was suffering any traumatic reactions, and would need to consider how any stress or anxiety would affect the victim's ability to report on her attack.

Unfortunately, the experimental literature on emotional memories is not consistent. Generally, the method of study has been to compare people's memory for emotionally neutral events to events that have some emotional relevance. Some studies have shown that relative to neutral events, people are less able to recall negative events, and may suffer highly specific memory problems. An example is the experimental simulation of *retrograde amnesia*, for example as reported by Loftus and Burns (1982). This refers to poorer memory for details that occur immediately before the emotional or unpleasant event. For example, suppose that your friend is driving you to your doctor's appointment. You are looking out the window, and you notice that there is an elderly gentleman walking his dog. You turn to tell your friend something and suddenly you see that a bicyclist has crossed in front of the car and your friend unavoidably hits the cyclist. If we were to then ask you, 'what was the elderly gentleman wearing?', you might find that your memory for the gentleman's clothes, or even his dog, was not clear. Under similar circumstances, a certain percentage of us would have poorer memory for details that occurred immediately before we witnessed the emotional event of hitting the cyclist.

However, other researchers have shown that emotional events are better retained than neutral events. For example, Christianson and Loftus have argued this point, illustrating in their 1987 article that central details of emotional events are better retained than central details of non-emotional, or neutral, events. To make matters even more confusing, some researchers have shown no difference!

The psychologists were also aware that there is an equally impressive body of literature based on clinical observations suggesting that emotional events may be very difficult to remember, particularly in the short-term. Here, clinical experience—based on single case studies and extensive qualitative analyses of interviews—suggests that details of emotional events may be inaccessible for some time after the event occurred. One explanation is provided by psychoanalytic theories of trauma, which would argue that some people might use the **defence mechanism** of repression. Repression is a mechanism by which the unpleasant memory stays blocked from the person's conscious awareness. This enables the person to continue with everyday life, and protects them from the possibility that the painful memory will ever enter their *focal awareness*. This view would suggest that the victim in this case might be motivated to repress her memory for the attack. Certainly, clinical experts argue that there is substantial evidence to suggest that a victim may not be able to remember the details of an attack until some time afterwards (see, for example, the work of Karon and Widener 1998).

The psychologists were also aware that other factors, such as guilt, might lead the victim to repress her memory for the assault. There is a substantial literature on the emotional aftermath of attacks, particularly those of a sexual nature. Judith Herman has written many excellent books on the topic of trauma and provides comprehensive discussions on the variety of negative thoughts and feelings that a victim of trauma can experience. One of Herman's biggest contributions to the understanding of trauma is her distinction between type one and type two trauma. Type one trauma is where the person experiences a unique, highly unpleasant and potentially life-threatening event. Type two trauma is where the person has experienced extensive, chronic abuse or trauma, such as in cases of incest or political torture (Herman 1994).

It appeared that the victim in this case was experiencing type one trauma. Victims of this type of trauma can feel a sense of guilt or responsibility for their attack, in spite of the fact that this is obviously an irrational belief. The victim may harbour irrational feelings that they somehow invited or caused the attack, as the thought of being so helpless and out of control is too terrifying to contemplate. Rather than being able to direct anger against the attacker, the victim assumes responsibility. The mechanism of repression would be very successful in helping the victim avoid further feelings of guilt.

Much of the literature on serious assaults suggests that victims of type one trauma can go through a series of stages. The first stage is one of disbelief and shock, where the victim is particularly sensitive to any external suggestions. This initial phase can vary and is characterized by fairly poor memory recall. The second phase can be called the acute reaction phase. Here, the victim may go through a variety of different reactions at different times. They may experience heightened arousal and be overly vigilant, scanning the environment for any signs of threat or danger. Alternatively, the victim may experience intrusions, in the form of either intrusive thoughts or intrusive images. A third common reaction is constriction, where the victim adamantly avoids thinking about the event, experiences feelings of dissociation (e.g. trance-like states), or denies that anything is wrong. The victim can feel any number of emotions, such as anxiety, guilt, or fear, and may begin to feel anger towards the attacker. The victim can experience any or all of these reactions at different times. Generally, the acute phase will last for up to twelve weeks after the event. Importantly, Janoff-Bullman (1992) suggests that many of a victim's firmly held beliefs about the world are seriously challenged when an attack occurs. For example, the beliefs that the world is safe, that the world is just, and that the world is under the person's control are all seriously challenged when one becomes the victim of a serious attack. During the acute phase, the victim becomes acutely aware that their long-held beliefs about the world are violated, and this naturally affects the victim's emotional state.

The third phase can be thought of as an adjustment phase. Here the victim may be 'getting on with her life', and will have introduced major changes, such as a new job, new partner, or new hair style. Again, the victim may experience many feelings, such as anger or guilt, and may also engage in reparative thinking, such as *counterfactual thinking*; for example, 'if I had not screamed, then he would have killed me'. These new cognitions are in aid of helping the victim to better comprehend the event. Some psychologists hold the view that these new cognitions are also the victim's way of preventing any similar events from happening in the future. Importantly, the victim may actively not wish to return to anything that is a reminder of the negative event. This means that the victim may be very reluctant to talk to anyone, including the police, about the attack.

The final phase is referred to as assimilation, or failure to assimilate. Here, the victim has integrated the negative event into their life narrative and is able to return to normal life. Failure to assimilate can result in the person being haunted by the event, and generally leaves the victim feeling depressed and hopeless over the future.

Of course, the psychologists in this case also knew that the reactions of the victim at the time of the event, as well as at the time of the interview with the investigator, would determine how well she was able to report on details. For example, if the victim were highly anxious during her attack—a completely reasonable reaction—she may avoid threat-related details, so that her memory for these details would later be poor. Equally, if the victim responded to the attack by dissociating—such as having feelings that it was happening to someone else—she would be less likely to have attended to features. At the time of recall, were the victim to be depressed, then her memory would be poor, as it is a well-established fact that depression reduces a person's ability to report on lower-level details. Thus the psychologists knew that they would have to consider the victim's emotional reactions very carefully before making any recommendations regarding memory-enhancing techniques.

Finally, the psychologists had to consider the question of truthfulness. The investigator had expressed an interest in finding out whether the victim's accounts had the characteristics of a true account. This was tricky, as the psychologists knew that while there was an extensive literature on the topic, it was impossible for *anyone* to say whether someone was giving a truthful account or not. Even with extensive corroborative evidence to suggest one way or the other, how could the psychologists ethically consider such a request? The psychologists decided that they would still review the literature on reality assessments. Given the extensive literature, they decided that they would focus on the methods of the German psychologists Udo Undeutsch, Max Steller, and Gunther Koenken (e.g. Umdevtsch 1982). This decision was based more on the fact that the psychologists had some familiarity with these researchers, and also had been involved in workshops with all of these psychologists, so could rely on them for professional advice if necessary.

The issue that was important here was whether the victim was motivated or willing to produce a truthful account. The assumption behind the research into this area is that a truthful account contains characteristics that can distinguish it from an account where the person is deliberately giving false information. These characteristics form the criteria upon which the psychologist assesses the account; hence, the approach is often referred to as criteria-based content analysis. For example, one of the characteristics of truthfulness is that the person will provide contextual information surrounding the incident, and so will embed the story: 'I had to go to the dentist early in the afternoon, so I decided to take a shorter run than I normally would have liked.' This statement places the event, namely the run, in a greater context of what the person had to do later in the day. The proponents of content-based criteria assessment argue that if an account has such detail, the account is more likely to be a truthful one. Depending on which approach is taken, there are between nineteen and twenty-three different criteria that need to be fulfilled in order for the psychologist to come to the conclusion that the account is true.

What did the psychologists do?

The psychologists reviewed all of the evidence including all witness and victim statements. They also asked the investigator to share his feelings about the case and, in particular, asked the investigator to state what he felt were the weaknesses and strengths in the evidence. This was done so that the psychologists had some idea of where the investigator might need support. Of course, the psychologists had to be careful that the investigator's opinions did not influence their own, as the psychologists were called in to be objective consultants rather merely to confirm what the investigator thought.

Most critically, the psychologists analysed the victim's statements. They paid particular attention to the structure of her accounts—for example, how she told the story—and the content of her accounts—namely what details she could remember about the attack. The psychologists also noted other more subjective features, such as the victim's comments about how she was feeling at the time of the attack, as well as her motivation to continue with the investigation. In particular, the psychologists wanted to highlight the ways in which the victim's accounts were compatible, or incompatible, with what memory theory might expect.

BOX 4.12 THE PROBLEM OF MEMORY AS A LAKE

There are some major difficulties with any approach that attempts to analyse the *contents* of a report (see Bekerian and Dennett 1993). One is the general metaphor of memory as a repository, or something that things are put into and taken out of, like a lake. This metaphor assumes that the interviewer 'fishes' information out from this repository. Continuing with our rather simplistic fishing model of memory, the interview process is viewed as something quite passive. All the interviewer does is 'hook' the information. Once retrieved, the reality-assessment procedures can then examine the information in an effort to determine whether the account has the requisite characteristics associated with truthful accounts. While we do not concern ourselves here with the arguments against such a metaphor, we do suggest that this view leads to an overly simplistic assumption about how an account is produced. Instead, we suggest that memory, particularly memory for a traumatic event and memory under police interviewing, is likely to be the result of a combination of factors, only one of which is the information that the person might be able to retain. These other factors include the interviewer and how he approaches the person; for example whether he is friendly, aggressive, or suggestive in his questioning. Similarly, the nature of the interview technique will also largely restrict what the person produces in her account; for example whether the technique is structured as questions and answers.

The psychologists also considered briefly the applicability of any reality-assessment criteria. However, all of the approaches require that the statement be relatively lengthy and one that contains considerable details. Given that the account was rather short, and also given the psychologists' general misgivings about assessment approaches, they were reluctant to engage in any procedures that might suggest the victim was or was not telling the truth.

Next, the psychologists commented directly on whether CIT would be appropriate. They pointed out that while it was likely that the victim could report more information, the victim consistently stated that she could not remember any more than she had already said to the investigator. The psychologists suggested that the CIT is probably better used with someone who is actually interested in remembering more information and that it might be a good idea to find out whether the victim wanted to pursue the case further, or not. The psychologists suggested that the investigator inform the victim that the evidence she had provided might be too sparse to pursue the case further, particularly as they did not currently have a suspect in custody. This gave the victim the option of continuing or not, and would at least serve to empower her.

The psychologists made all recommendations formally in a written report that was given to the investigator. The psychologists suggested that the victim be informed that they had been asked to act as consultants and were willing to discuss any details of their report with the victim.

How was the psychologists' input assessed?

Upon receiving the report, the investigator asked to see the psychologists to discuss their recommendations further. In general, the investigator felt that the psychologists had confirmed what he suspected were difficulties with the case. The investigator informed the psychologists that he had approached the victim, and suggested that she should try using the CIT. However, the victim refused and left the country within the following week. Importantly, the investigator shared some new information with the psychologists: the victim had been suffering from depression for a number of years, and was on medication. The victim had failed to inform the investigator of this, as she had been afraid that such a disclosure would lead people to disbelieve her allegations. This would have been important information to know from the outset. The case was never solved.

SCENARIO TWO

INTERVIEWING CHILDREN IN CASES OF ALLEGED CHILD ABUSE

One of the most disturbing problems that faces all societies today is child abuse. Statistical assessments of exactly how many children suffer abuse, and what type of abuse they suffer, are difficult, for obvious reasons. For example, not all cases of child abuse are substantiated, in that the victim's allegations may never be proven, and hence the allegation will not be considered *bona fide*. Equally, many cases of child abuse are simply not disclosed. Another difficulty is that we may have clear ideas about what constitutes certain kinds of abuse, such as sexual abuse, whereas we may find it more difficult to identify when emotional abuse occurs, in spite of the fact that this form of abuse is arguably the most damaging. While the statistics vary from city to city, from country to country, and from year to year, what is not in dispute is that child abuse is an international problem. Children are abused regardless of the culture, society, or socio-demographics of the individual child; and pursuing allegations of abuse pose highly specific problems for the investigators. The following scenario is based on the work of Bekerian and Dennett (1996), who used psychological principles to help inform investigations of child abuse.

In England, many law enforcers were finding investigations of child abuse to be fraught with difficulties, particularly in the early 1980s. Importantly, there were a number of public agencies that shared statutory responsibilities for child protection; for example the social services and the police. Both had independent power to investigate suspected cases of child abuse and neither was required to operate in conjunction with the other.

Unfortunately, this independence resulted in the proverbial situation where the left hand did not know what the right hand was doing. In a relatively short space of time there were a number of notorious cases where dozens of children were taken from their homes on either the basis of improper interview techniques or the basis of unsubstantiated forensic evidence. Significantly, these actions were unilateral decisions made by one of the statutory agencies responsible for investigating child abuse. The newspapers and media referred to the act as one of 'abduction', since the children's homes were raided in the early morning hours, much in the way that police would raid criminals' houses! It was later discovered that there was insufficient evidence to support the majority of allegations of abuse, and that some of the children had *never* made allegations in the first instance. Because of the reaction of the public—as well as those parents who were not guilty of abuse—the government was forced to consider how changes might be introduced (*Criminal Justice Act 1989/1991*). These changes were formally documented in the *Memorandum of Good Practice* (MoGP; *Criminal Justice Act 1989/1991*), which provided investigators with clear guidelines regarding procedures for interviewing children who allege abuse.

The guidelines were very specific regarding how interviews should be conducted, what types of questions should be asked, what details must be included in the interview, and so on. For example, open-ended questions, such as 'what happened?', were preferred to direct questions, such as 'did X do this to you, or did Y do this to you?'. These changes were introduced so as to protect children from the possible effects of misleading questions and to maximize the child's ability to report accurately on any alleged abuse. Critically, the guidelines stipulated that children alleging sexual abuse should be given the opportunity to be interviewed on videotape, if that served in the best interests of the child. The function of the videotape was two-fold. First, a tape would allow the investigator to obtain a coherent account and importantly preserve the evidence. Second, the videotape could spare the child the difficult task of providing evidence in chief. The child would be spared the further trauma of testifying in court, with the defendant being present.

The guidelines also strongly urged the two statutory agencies to cooperate with each other. In particular, any video interviews with children should be conducted co-jointly, with a representative of each statutory agency being present. This working together was seen to be a way of preventing the pitfalls of unilateral investigations by either agency. The interviewing of children was no longer the exclusive domain of either statutory agency.

One particular county in England was concerned that their practitioners and police officers were making the transition smoothly. Feedback from the local Crown Prosecution Service (CPS)—responsible for prosecuting cases—had been rather uncomplimentary. The CPS complained about the quality of video interviews, and in particular the quality of children's accounts. According to the CPS, the poor prosecution rates of the county were the direct result of the poor video-interviewing skills of the police and social services. Interviewers were either not following the guidelines or were not able to work with each other sufficiently so as to successfully interview the child. Either way, it was either impossible to sustain the charges or secure prosecution on the basis of what was said in video interviews.

What was the situation?

The situation was a serious, real-world problem, in that there are serious consequences to any investigation of an allegation of child abuse. At the time, co-joint interviewing had just begun and there were no precedents for the police and social services to work so closely together. Not surprisingly, there were apparent differences in the approaches of the two agencies. For example, the two agencies often had different goals and statutory responsibilities. The police were responsible for protecting the child, by virtue of establishing evidence for or against the commission of a crime. In contrast, social services would be primarily concerned with establishing what interventions would be in the best interests of the child. A social worker would be less concerned about establishing whether a crime had been committed, and more concerned about the child's overall well-being.

The situation also revealed another problem, and this had to do with experience in conducting formal, evidential interviews. The police were trained in interviewing in accordance with the rules of evidence and felt confident about interviewing, although admittedly apprehensive about the video procedures and about talking to children. In contrast, social workers felt better equipped and skilled at talking to children, and not comfortable with conducting an evidential interview, particularly when their police counterparts were present. Given the differences in statutory responsibilities, skills and training, the relationship between professionals from different agencies was not always warm and friendly.

Adding to these tensions was the fact that CPS firmly placed the responsibility for failures in prosecution on poor joint investigations. The agencies, however, felt that they had provided sufficient evidence and were consequently surprised that these cases were not prosecuted successfully. Given the serious consequences of failing to protect children who needed help, the problem was of grave concern to all professionals involved.

Why were the psychologists involved?

Trainers and managers from both statutory agencies approached two psychologists who had experience in working on investigations of child abuse. In particular, the psychologists had expertise in applied memory issues, including the effects of trauma on child development, and had been involved in early pilot schemes on co-joint training. After a preliminary meeting, the psychologists agreed on an empirical project that focused on three specific, applied questions. The first concerned how well interviewers were adhering to guidelines. This was an essential point to address, as CPS had complained that interviewers disregarded many of the guidelines.

The second question concerned whether interviewers were applying techniques that were based on sound, psychological evidence. In particular, the psychologists agreed to assess the interview techniques in relation to the known academic literature on memory and child development. This was an essential point to consider, since children have different abilities to report on events as they develop. The interviewers needed to demonstrate that they were sensitive to the different developmental changes that occur across childhood.

The third question focused on recurrent problems that emerged with either special populations or specific age groups. Anecdotal evidence suggested strongly that interviewers were finding certain children difficult to interview in accordance with the guidelines, particularly those with learning difficulties. The main reasons for these difficulties seemed to be that the guidelines were designed to operate with children who have a certain level of linguistic competency and skill. Interviewers felt that the guidelines were biased against children with special needs. Unfortunately, these children are particularly vulnerable to abuse.

The psychologists felt that it was essential to consider their results in relation to the co-joint training programmes that were currently being offered by the county. For example, the weaknesses and strengths observed in the video interviews might correspond to gaps in the content and emphasis of training programmes. Once problem areas were identified, more in-depth training could be provided.

The project proposal was agreed by all agencies. In addition, the psychologists were asked to comment on specific interviews, for example, on how a particular interview might have been improved, or how a given interviewer might improve. This required the psychologists to consider different methodologies, such as qualitative methods like *content* or *thematic analyses* of interviewer–interviewer–child triads.

What psychological concepts are relevant to the problem?

The psychologists knew that the task of interviewing a child, particularly a child who may have experienced negative or traumatic events, was highly complex. Any number of different approaches, and different conceptual frameworks, would be relevant. For example, the interview can be construed as a social situation, one where the dynamics between interviewers and child directly affect the nature of any account the child might produce. This *constructivist approach* would have us consider all social dynamics between dyads and triads, such as how the interviewers define their roles in the interviews, how interviewers delegate responsibilities, and so on. However, other conceptual frameworks would be equally useful. For example, the concepts regarding a child's moral and emotional development, such as the psycho-social developmental stages described by Jean Piaget, or Erik Erikson, would also be undoubtedly essential to consider. Theoretical explanations regarding the ways in which adults and children interact, such as the different kinds of parenting that children might have experienced, would also be highly informative. Finally, the psychologists could look at the cognitive approach, and have at their disposal an impressive amount of empirical literature.

Given the applied questions, the psychologists decided to restrict their review to the literature on child development, and focus extensively on memory development. Concepts related to or impacting on memory development, such as the development of different emotions, was included to the extent that they were relevant.

The restrictions of the investigative procedures meant that only children above a certain age would be considered as suitable for further investigation; for example children over the age of three-and-a-half years. So, the applied situation dictated that the ages of interest would be between 3 and 16 years. What particular concepts would be important?

It was clear that the task of interviewing involved explicit remembering. Sometimes the child would be acting in the capacity of a witness, while at other times the child would be the victim. Significantly, the guidelines required the child to provide an account that demonstrated that the child could report on major actors (who) and major actions (what), and could isolate the event in space and time (where and when). Described in these terms, it was clear that the literature on the development of event-specific and autobiographical memory needed to be reviewed carefully.

Researchers in child development have provided clear demonstrations of children as young as thirty months having autobiographical memory recall (see Fivush et al.

BOX 4.13 THE DEVELOPMENT OF HUMAN BEINGS

Developmental psychology is concerned with the physical, mental, emotional, and social changes that occur over our lifetimes. Mental changes include those associated with our ability to perceive objects, our ability to use language, our ability to solve problems, and our ability to acquire and retain knowledge. There is still debate over whether certain developmental milestones, like learning how to talk, are constrained by critical periods or are better understood in terms of sensitive periods. Critical periods imply that the child must accomplish the milestone within the developmental period, or be impaired, or subnormal, in their skills or abilities. The notion of a sensitive period is more flexible, and implies that certain abilities are easier to acquire during periods where the child is more receptive, but that the child might still be able to reach the normal milestone at a later date. The most recent evidence suggests that some abilities once thought of as tied to a specific time period can be acquired later. For example, post-natal depression was once thought to have irreversible negative effects on *attachment behaviour*. This does not seem to be the case (see Barnes 1998). While most of the dramatic changes occur during our formative years, from birth to early adulthood, it is certainly true that we change continuously throughout our lifetimes. Most of the early work on human development started in the later nineteenth century, and was restricted to the changes occurring in childhood. G. Stanley Hall, at Clark University in Worcester, Massachusetts, USA, is credited with establishing the first research centre specifically aimed at understanding child development and is largely acknowledged as the founder of child psychology. Since the 1950s psychologists have expanded their interests to include developmental changes that occur across the lifespan, including changes occurring across advanced old age.

BOX 4.14 THE DEVELOPMENT OF MEMORY SKILLS

Just as adults show a distinction between different types of memory, so too does child development. One of the most interesting findings is the relatively early development of recognition memory as opposed to recall. Recognition memory is characterized by our ability to identify something, or someone, as 'old' or familiar to us, or 'new' or unfamiliar to us. It is clear from the developmental literature that recognition memory is easily intact by the time the child has developed primary attachments, for example once the child reaches 8 months old. In fact, some researchers argue that as early as 4 months old the infant develops *object permanence*, meaning that the child is able to recognize and anticipate the constancy of material objects. For example, suppose you play peek-a-boo with an infant—you pretend to hide behind a piece of paper, and then emerge from behind. The child is only able to appreciate this social game because she has object permanence. While recognition memory is one that develops early in infancy, the same is not true for recall, or verbally reproductive memory.

1996 in their chapter on memory development). For example, a child of 30 months can give correct and highly vivid details about a sequence of actions, and interactions between characters in a favourite film. However, children as young as this would be highly reliant on prompts and external cues in order to provide the extensive amount of information that is required to prove points of law. Thus, while very young children may be able to report on autobiographical events, they fail to achieve the standards set by law.

The literature suggested a certain consensus regarding the development of explicit, autobiographical memory. It seemed that most researchers agreed the importance of language development as a signal for the impending development of autobiographical memory. For example, Howe and Courage, in their 1997 review article, provide an excellent summary of the empirical evidence, suggesting that the child cannot have autobiographical memory until she has a firm concept of I and me. Their argument is that autobiographical memory requires the development of self-awareness, both as an objective and subjective agent; and that this development occurs roughly around the time that the child develops language competency, for example after 24 months. Thus, it seems that while a very young child can have vivid memories for personal events, these do not take the form of autobiographical memories, where the child is aware that *she* is reflecting on her *own* past. This type of autobiographical memory—where we knowingly report on our past—is reliable only after the acquisition and development of language skills.

The literature was also consistent in suggesting that once the child develops good language and *pragmatic skills*—for some children as young as 3 years old—he or she is easily able to report on autobiographical events in a manner that can include who, what, and where. Although the type of details and the amount of information increases with age, the basic structure of the child's account is not dramatically different from an adult's. Provided the child is interested in the event, and is motivated to recall the event, the manner in which the account is constructed will show a familiar pattern to that demonstrated by adults.

Nonetheless, there are still very important developmental changes that occur in childhood. Most of the evidence shows that accounts from a younger child will lack enriched details, such as contextual embedding. A younger child will also be unable to reproduce complex sequences and fail to show any sophisticated understanding of the causal relationship between two events. Again, much of the research has suggested that the young child is highly reliant on the adult, or interviewer, to produce structured, narrative accounts of what happened.

The psychologists in this case were particularly interested in the review provided by Ceci and Bruc in 1993, who showed unequivocally that young children, say 4 years old, are highly susceptible to misleading information and suggestions from adults. Furthermore, Ceci and Bruc (1993) argued that, once young children had been misled, there was very little that could be done. For example, suppose a child sees an event and we make a misleading suggestion about a detail, such as a woman's hair colour. Before we ask the child to recall what she saw, we give them a warning, saying, 'some of the information about the woman's hair colour might not be correct. Forget what I said and just remember what you saw.' While adults and older children are able to use this warning, and avoid the misleading detail, younger children do not seem to be able to use such a warning. It seems very apparent that young children, those 6 years and under, would be particularly susceptible to misleading suggestions about events that did not happen.

BOX 4.15 DOING DEVELOPMENTAL RESEARCH

There are a number of different methods that are used by developmental psychologists. Some advocate an observational approach, where the child is placed in a simulated (or real) situation and her behaviour is observed. A good example of an observational approach is Mary Ainsworth's Stranger Situation (see Bretherton and Main 2000 for a good review). The Stranger Situation involves a mother and infant in a room. The mother leaves and a stranger enters (modern tests assess the child's behaviour at this point). The stranger then leaves and the mother returns. The child's reaction to the mother, for example seeking physical contact, is assessed. The other method is an experimental method where the child is placed in a simulated situation and their behaviour is assessed. A good example of this is the experiments on the theory of mind. For example, a child is shown a box of crayons and is asked 'what do you think is in the box?' Most children respond with 'crayons'. The child is then shown what actually is in the box, a chocolate bunny. When later asked 'what did you think was in the box when I first showed it to you?', some children will respond 'the chocolate bunny'. These children do not show that they have grasped the concept of self as being distinct from the other. Developmental studies also rely on two general types of design: longitudinal and cross-sectional. A longitudinal design is one where children are followed throughout their development, for some time span. So, if we want to know how children develop physical skills between the ages of two and six, we follow the same child, or children, through their development and repeatedly test their skills. The cross-sectional design uses cohort ages, and compares children at different developmental ages. Each has their advantages and disadvantages. The longitudinal approach better identifies the development of specific children, the cross-sectional approach takes into account cultural differences that might occur during longitudinal studies.

What did the psychologists do?

The psychologists were given access to forty-four evidential videotapes that were conducted across a six-month time frame. This number was consistent with the number of interviews that had been used in an earlier government audit at the same time (see Davies et al. 1995). All interviews were with children who were alleging abuse. The interviews were conducted by a single agency (police officers or social workers) or were conducted co-jointly. All interviewers were considered to be mature, in that they had experience in videotaping and more generally in child-abuse investigations. General demographic features of the children and the interviewers were noted, including age of child, length of interview, sex of interviewer(s), dominant interviewer, multiple or single accusations, and type of abuse. These data were important in order to compare the findings with the other empirical studies.

The psychologists did not want to know whether the case had resulted in any arrests, or whether any subsequent prosecution had been successful. The psychologists felt that this information would have only biased their conclusions.

They decided that a good interview technique was one where the child was given the best conditions under which to disclose a crime, in the event that a crime has been committed. A good interview technique would promote a clear, unprompted account, and, at the same time would not bias the child to produce false accounts. A good interview technique would balance the need to obtain comprehensive information with the certain knowledge that children can be misled into saying things that did not happen.

They then conducted content analyses on the videotapes. Each tape was first transcribed and, using a time code, broken into scenes, as defined by general topics that were discussed. This division of tapes into scenes was first done independently by each of the psychologists, and then in discussion.

A number of factors were documented. One was how well the interviewer adhered to all guidelines; for example did the interviewer stress the importance of telling the truth to the child? Did the interviewer tell the child what time it was? Interviewer's questions were also documented, in terms of both content and type. For example, content analyses revealed what topics the interviewer had discussed in an effort to develop rapport.

The behaviour of the child was noted in terms of how responsive the child was regarding different types of questioning. The child's willingness to engage at different times during the interview and with different interviewers was also carefully monitored. In particular, the psychologists observed how effective the interviewer's style was in engaging the child. This did not mean that the child needed to make a disclosure. Rather, the psychologists were concerned about how well the interviewers could interact with the child. The psychologists also paid attention to any glaring problems or if good practice was outstanding, as well as any recurring patterns. For example, practical problems sometimes prevented the child from being heard, such as microphone not being in a position to pick up any of the audio. On average, a twenty-minute videotape took ten or twelve hours to analyse satisfactorily.

The psychologists provided individual reports for each tape, and also provided a general report that outlined more general patterns that emerged across all interviews, children, and interviewers. In addition to specifically addressing the three research questions, the general report also provided descriptive statistics regarding features of the interviews, like the average age of the child, as well as statistics regarding lead interviewers. After highlighting general problem areas, the report also made specific recommendations regarding the improvements that could be made in training and in the supervision of investigators of child abuse.

The report also compared the findings with respect to the government study that had been conducted. In fact, the two studies were slightly different in their remit. The government audit had a much larger, but less detailed, remit: to look at the investigation, prosecution, and effects on children. In contrast, the psychologists were asked to look exclusively at the evidential video, without concern for any other evidence, information, or details about the case. Therefore, the only true comparisons that could be made were with respect to the characteristics of the population, for example the ages; and characteristics of the interview, for example how many social workers conducted the interviews compared with police officers.

How was the psychologists' input assessed?

The project and its recommendations were assessed in two very different ways. One was based on the reactions of the interviewers. All practitioners and investigators who had participated in the project were given the opportunity to meet with the psychologists in order to give their opinions on any aspect of the project. Uniformly, the practitioners and investigators involved felt that the research provided them with some objective assessment of their strengths and weaknesses. This was significant to them, as all expressed the great need to get more direct input, and receive comments on their interview techniques. The practitioners and investigators also commented that the research project had given them the opportunity to air their views, and this too was sorely needed.

A second, more formal, assessment came, indirectly, through an independent government audit of different counties' training programmes for co-joint investigations. The audit was designed to assess the extent to which competency criteria in training had been introduced, and also wanted to document any research that had been commissioned by the county agencies. The main aim of the audit was to inform future government curricula regarding training for child-abuse investigations. A very well-known professor, who was an expert in the area of applied memory problems, was responsible for leading the audit team. As part of their larger remit, the audit team reviewed the project, including the recommendations for changes in training, and confirmed that they were compatible with the intended government curricula.

Importantly, the major recommendations that the psychologists made about training were implemented by the statutory agencies. All co-joint training came to include a review of important issues in child development and a review of cognitive theories of memory and the experimental evidence on event memory. This meant that any investigation of child abuse would be informed by the best current psychological literature. In this way, the project could be considered a success, as it helped to encourage professionals to integrate psychological principles in investigations of child abuse.

■ ADDITIONAL READING

Arrigo, B.A. (2000) *Introduction to Forensic Psychology: Issues and Consequences in Crime and Justice*. Academic Press, London. An authoritative recent review of major issues involved in forensic psychology.

Gudjonsson, G. and Haward, L. (1981) *Forensic Psychology: a Guide to Practice*. Routledge, London. A comprehensive introduction to forensic psychology and its practices.

Jackson, S. and Bekerian, D.A. (eds) (1997) *Offender Profiling: Theory, Research and Practice*. John Wiley, Chichester. This book is recommended for readers who are particularly interested in offender profiling.

Wells, G.L. and Loftus, E.F. (eds) (1984) *Eyewitness Testimony: Psychological Perspectives*. Cambridge University Press, New York. An essential tool for those interested in the problems of eyewitness testimony.

■ **QUESTIONS**

Scenario one

1   How might this case help the police officer to improve his general questioning techniques with victims and witnesses?

2   What other factors might the psychologists have considered?

Scenario two

1   What were the benefits of using more than one methodological approach?

2   Were there any serious theoretical omissions in the work?

5

The court room

In this chapter we consider psychology's contribution to the criminal justice system. We first give some background about the functions and processes of the court. We then look at a way of categorizing the interface between psychology and the law, before proceeding to examine a number of examples of the way in which psychologists have influenced criminal procedures. As before, the psychologist can adopt a clinical, experimental, actuarial, or consultant approach, or some combination of these. The chapter highlights the many and diverse applied roles that psychologists can adopt within the general context of the court, and the extensive range of empirical and theoretical psychology that underpins them.

Functions of the court

The functions that the court fulfils, and the processes that it uses to execute its functions, will shape the nature of the roles that psychologists can play in the court room. Two very different systems operate, as we will now illustrate.

Regardless of the country in which it is located, the court room gives the state the opportunity to accuse an individual of a criminal act (or acts). The state presents evidence that supports the charges, and the accused or their representative provides evidence to counter the claims made. Jurisprudence ensures that certain procedures are followed in order that the due process of law is maintained. However, there are vital differences in jurisprudence across countries and these differences will influence the characteristics of the court room. Scotland, for example, allows for the distinction of three verdicts in contrast to England's guilty and innocent verdicts: innocent of the charges, guilty of the charges, and not proven.

The adversarial system

There are two general types of justice system that are used in countries of the western world, the *adversarial system*, and the *inquisitorial system* (see the next section). Adversarial systems are adopted, for example, in the USA, the UK, Canada, and Australia. The adversarial system pits one adversary against the other (i.e. prosecution versus defence). Each side is required to present evidence to a judge and jury, which is generally comprised of representative members of the society, or a 'jury of one's peers'. The jury are responsible for evaluating the evidence and returning a verdict. The presumption of innocence (i.e. that the defendant is innocent until proven guilty) is a consistent feature across all countries that adopt an adversarial system.

The adversarial system involves a judge who, in the case of a jury trial, serves to assist the jury with information regarding legal procedures, instructions regarding verdicts, the status of evidence, and so on. The judge also represents the final decision-maker, as it is they who determine the sentence of the defendant. The judge can also act as an interpreter of the law when pronouncing a sentence. While the law provides the rules for society's conduct, the courts can execute a degree of discretion when sentencing an individual and thereby help to shape these rules. The psychologist's expertise may be invaluable in helping to inform a judge's decision-making, particularly when questions of recidivism arise (see Jackson and Bekerian 1997 for more detailed discussions of this point).

The inquisitorial system

An inquisitorial system, as adopted in most European countries, shares some of the features of the adversarial system. Evidence regarding the charges is presented to the court (e.g. by prosecution and defence counsel) as in the adversarial system. However, the court operates on the assumption of guilt, with the defence responsible for proving the defendant's innocence. In many cases the defendant is tried without a jury. Instead, a judge (or panel of judges) evaluates the evidence, determines the verdict, and

---

BOX 5.1 THE JURY CONCEPT

The jury concept arguably has its origins in the *Magna Carta*, 1215. One article of this charter forbade the punishment of any free man without the consent of his equals. The intention was to judge the justice of the punishment, not the guilt or innocence of the accused. This was meant to curtail the power of the Sovereign. The notion of selecting at random a panel of peers and equals, from among citizens judged to be a comparable group to the accused, was first enshrined in the American Constitution and became the basis of jury selection in all English-speaking countries. The right of defence and prosecution to reject unsuitable jurors (i.e. biased jurors) is in effect a judgement of the issue of comparability. In some cases defendants may opt to be tried by a judge in the absence of a jury, if they feel that a jury would be swayed by spurious arguments. This is also a right embodied in the court procedures.

BOX 5.2 HISTORICAL BACKGROUND OF THE JUDICIAL SYSTEMS

Both the adversarial and the inquisitorial systems have very ancient roots. The inquisitorial system is founded on civil law; that is, on a system of laws established by the state and written for all to read. The civil code in force throughout most of Europe was first put in place by the Emperor Justinian, known to historians as the Law Giver, in the fourth century AD. His laws derived originally from Roman law and remained in force throughout the Holy Roman Empire. Later they became the basis for legal reforms in France under the Emperor Napoleon. As most of Europe eventually fell under his rule, the Napoleonic Code became the basis of law. In a system based on the concept of civil law the primary function of the courts is not to ensure that the law is interpreted correctly, but that it is strictly upheld. The arguments of both defence and prosecution are directed at this outcome. The adversarial approach derives from common law; that is, from a body of loosely defined ideas of natural justice and fairness generally accepted by the community. It became the basis of legal process in England, during the thirteenth century, when Henry II established the first circuit courts, presided over by itinerant judges whose aim was to clarify and standardize local court practices to conform to the common law. The ideas invoked in common law are written *about*, but not usually written down. Hence, the main function of the courts is to decide how justice has been achieved in the past in similar cases, and the arguments of both counsels are directed at interpretation of earlier findings or *precedents*. Thus the terms inquisitorial and adversarial, and the approaches they represent, can be seen to originate in profoundly different concepts of law, not merely in differences of procedure.

---

sentences the defendant. It should be noted that in certain jurisdictions within the UK the government departs from its normal system of justice and, unusually, adopts an inquisitorial system. An example of this was seen in the trials involving terrorism in Northern Ireland.

The type of justice system will help determine the nature of the psychologist's involvement. For example, in an adversarial system, the psychologist may be asked to provide expert opinion to either the defence or the prosecution. This raises the possibility that the psychologist will become a partisan advocate and be inadvertently biased to form conclusions that support the contentions of the counsel requesting their assistance. This is not surprising as the psychologist will be aware that counsel wishes to have the psychologist's support or endorsement. This can result in an overstatement, or an over-generalization, of the psychological findings. Psychological knowledge is rarely as absolute as legal counsel (or the law) might ideally desire. In contrast, an inquisitorial system affords the psychologist the opportunity to be appointed as a friend of the court, or *amicus curiae*. Freed from any allegiance to either adversary, the psychologist may thereby be able to provide a more balanced view of the evidence.

In recognition of these concerns the British government recently commissioned the Woolf Report (1996), the recommendations of which have led to new rules of court known as the Civil Procedure Rules, 1998. Lord Woolf's objective was 'to enable the courts to deal with cases justly' (Statutory Instruments 1998, no. 3132 (L.17)) by reducing the adversarial nature of civil proceedings, thereby making litigation fairer, faster, cheaper, and more accessible. In pursuit of this end, Lord Woolf recommended limiting the scope of expert witnesses in various ways. One of the provisions of the new rules is that wherever possible expert witnesses in civil cases (including psychologists) are to be appointed jointly by both parties. Where the parties are unable to agree on a witness, the Court can appoint one. The function of the expert witness is to assist the Court and their duty is therefore clearly to the Court rather than to the instructing solicitors. Opinions expressed by the expert witness need to be impartial and objective. Civil cases most frequently employing psychologists at present are those concerned with compensation for personal injury. For example, a defendant may claim that they have suffered post-traumatic stress disorder (PTSD) as the result of an accident and the psychologist is called upon to make a clinical assessment of the validity of this claim, based on interviews and appropriate tests.

Psychological issues involved in the court room

Regardless of the justice system, there is extensive overlap in the issues that emerge from the court room, and we will now consider some of these. We first outline the different stages of the judicial process that psychologists might be involved with. We then go on to examine the different approaches that characterize the psychologist's roles within the court room.

The issues that arise, both theoretical and practical, are traditionally viewed as belonging to the domain of forensic or criminological psychology. For the student who is particularly interested, Gisli Gudjonsson and Lionel Haward, both of whom are widely experienced in the area, have provided a practical review of this branch of psychology (Gudjonsson and Haward 1981).

Forensic psychology encompasses the pre-trial, trial, and post-trial phases of the judicial process. The issues involved in pre-trial phase include those concerned with plea-bargaining, false confessions, and fitness to stand trial. Issues during the actual trial include the nature of questions used during cross-examination, reliability of witnesses, and jury decision-making. Finally, the post-trial phase introduces issues of sentencing and mitigation, as well as those concerned with rates of recidivism. As can be seen, these issues arise from a variety of concerns.

Within the general context of the court room, the psychologist can adopt one or more of a number of approaches.

1 The *clinical approach* is when the psychologist gives an expert opinion regarding normative psychological states (e.g. psychological testing for clinical depression). The emphasis is on assessment of normality, relative to some standardized measures or set of theoretical concepts. Abnormal psychology and personality theory will inform the psychologist acting from a clinical approach.

2 The *experimental approach* may similarly have the psychologist acting as an expert witness. However, the issues here will concern the empirical psychological research, or psychological literature, that pertains to a particular legal procedure. For example, the psychologist may report empirical data on *false memories* in order to help inform

the court whether the defendant is falsely confessing to charges as a result of police procedure, or prosecution coercion.

3 The *actuarial approach* is valuable in the context of interpreting large data sets and deriving predictions about behaviour (e.g. the risk of re-offending). Generally, an actuarial approach requires the psychologist to have expertise in statistical analyses, particularly those that are relevant to larger data sets (e.g. **multiple regression, factor analyses, analysis of covariance**).

4 Finally, psychologists can adopt the *consultant approach*, where they offer assistance with decisions regarding evidence, interviews, or selection techniques.

Two of the categories defined by Craig Haney, and discussed in the previous chapter (psychology *in* law versus psychology *and* law; Haney 1980), offer a convenient framework within which to examine the issues arising from the interface between psychology and the law.

Psychology *in* law

In this section we examine a number of examples of the way in which psychologists contribute to the judicial process. In doing so, we include a consideration of such topics as plea-bargaining, false confessions, and risk assessment.

Psychology *in* law represents those situations where psychologists provide their expertise as an intrinsic part of the normal procedures of the law itself. For example, the court may need to be convinced that a defendant is mentally competent to stand trial. The psychologist may provide the court with an expert opinion, either in the form of formal assessments and reports (see scenario two, pp. 96–102) or by presenting their opinion in court as a witness.

Plea-bargaining

One of the most popular topics within the court room that illustrates psychology in law concerns the study of plea-bargaining. Plea-bargaining represents a significant component of the criminal justice system. The defendant is given the opportunity to enter a plea of guilty in exchange for some compromise from the prosecution, either in the form of reduced charges, reduction in the number of counts, or a recommendation for lenient or alternative sentencing. While it is difficult to estimate accurately the percentage of cases that involve some form of plea-bargaining, one authoritative study places the figure as high as 90 per cent. On first inspection, plea-bargaining appears to offer advantages to both defendant and prosecution. The act of pleading guilty to a crime essentially results in the defendant waiving all rights to a trial. The defendant is thus allowed to forego the potentially disastrous consequences of a trial. The prosecution avoids the possibility of defeat, always a potential outcome in any trial, and, importantly, saves the state the responsibility of paying for costly trial proceedings.

However, legal experts and forensic psychologists have long been concerned about the dangers involved in plea-bargaining. The major concern centres on the essential requirement that the defendant is *competent* to enter a guilty plea. The question is whether the defendant rationally enters a plea, or whether the plea is the result of the defendant's fear, played upon by the prosecution. Most authors stress the importance of examining the circumstances under which a plea bargain is made. For example, Arrigo (2000) points out that a guilty plea may be the result of the defendant wishing to avoid a less-favourable outcome, rather than a logical, positive decision. Practices of overcharging (i.e. charging the defendant with the maximum number of crimes associated with the defendant's actions) and over-recommending (i.e. the suggestion by the prosecution that a more severe sentence will result) are prevalent in criminal investigations. Such coercive tactics may be sufficient to frighten the defendant into pleading guilty to the charges.

False confessions

The focus of psychology in law also covers the study of false confessions. The issues here are conceptually similar to those discussed for plea-bargaining. As before, due process of law requires that the defendant's confession is one based on the fact of guilt, rather than coercion. Gudjonsson (1992) suggests that false confessions must be viewed as an interaction between individual and situational factors, the latter of which includes the social and cultural contexts. Empirical research has focused on identifying individual differences, using both prison populations and undergraduate populations. Some of the psychological factors that have been identified include intelligence, anxiety, antisocial personality characteristics, and a previous history of substance abuse. More recent research by forensic psychologists suggests that the extent and severity of an individual's offending will be a further discriminating factor for people who falsely confess.

BOX 5.3 VARIETIES OF FALSE CONFESSION

The literature on false confessions suggests that there are three categories of false confession, and each has different psychological implications. The first represents situations where the defendant makes a false confession without any obvious external pressure. For example, the person makes self-incriminating statements in order to protect a loved one. The second classification is a coerced confession where the person believes in their innocence. The person complies with the pressure to confess in the hope that a confession will reduce negative, or enhance positive, outcomes (e.g. a reduced sentence or reduced charges). Under these circumstances, there is a real possibility that the confession is based on fear rather than a rational decision. The third classification is what some authorities identify as coerced internalized confession. This is a disturbing state where the individual, although innocent, comes to believe that they have committed the offence. Individuals with mental health problems or psychiatric disorders may be particularly sensitive to coerced internalized confessions. In part, the justice system has recognized this in England through the passing, by Parliament, of the Bill *Achieving Best Evidence with Vulnerable Witnesses and Victims 2001*.

False memories

One area of memory research that is particularly relevant to discussions of false confessions pertains to the study of falsely created memories. Experimental psychologists have examined the extent to which people can be convinced that something happened to them when in fact it did not. This research typically involves asking participants to report on a number of personal or autobiographical events. The experimenter then introduces a false event and asks the person about it (e.g. 'tell me about the time that you got lost at the zoo'). Importantly, the event must be one that fits into the person's life narrative; that is, is consistent with general world knowledge and personal schemas. The event must generally be endorsed by some authority figure, thereby confirming to the person that the event did indeed happen. Another aspect of this research methodology is that the person is questioned repeatedly about the event over a number of recall sessions.

On the whole, the research has consistent results. People start reporting on the event that never occurred, and provide a range of details in their accounts of it. Thus, a person can be misled into believing that they experienced, or did something, that did not happen. Experimental psychologists argue that if, under these relatively innocuous circumstances, people can be misled into reporting on false events, the chances of this occurring under conditions of distress (e.g. police interrogation), or other emotionally charged situations (e.g. counselling, see 'The treatment room', Chapter 8), are uncomfortably high.

BOX 5.4 HOW RELIABLE IS YOUR MEMORY?

One of the most important distinctions that psychologists make when they discuss **episodic** or **event memory** is the distinction between *reproduction* and *reconstruction*. The difference reflects the extent to which the person's memory report is distorted by their prior knowledge, or schematic knowledge. When someone is engaged in the act of reproductive remembering, their memory report is generally restricted to details that actually occurred in the event, and their intent is to provide an accurate description of what they can remember of the event. While such remembering can be incorrect, the nature of the errors is not linked to the person's schematic knowledge of the event. The classic empirical examples of reproductive remembering are verbal learning studies, in which nonsense syllables were used (e.g. Postman and Underwood 1973). Part of the reason that psychologists used nonsense syllables was to prevent any real-world knowledge, or schematic information, from contaminating the person's memory. In contrast, when someone is engaged in the act of reconstructive memory their memory report is biased by their schematic knowledge. While the person may want to provide an accurate account, what they know *should happen* rather than what *actually happened* will influence their report. For example, reproductive recall processes are probably dominating when we attempt to remember exactly what we wrote down on our shopping list that we accidentally left at home! On the other hand, if we decide to buy something on the basis of our memory of what we *usually need*, we are relying on schematic knowledge and are using more reconstructive recall. Ulrich Neisser (1981, 1984) uses the terms 'literal recall' and 'constructive recall', respectively, and concludes that most of our remembering in everyday life is governed by processes of constructive recall, rather than literal recall.

There are serious caveats that must be placed on any conclusions drawn from experimental research, particularly if one wishes to generalize to real-life conditions of false confessions. First, not everyone gets misled. Some people are highly resistant to any false suggestions, regardless of the conditions. This clearly indicates that an examination of individual differences is absolutely essential. Research on individual differences had a considerable impact on psychological theorizing in the late 1960s and early 1970s and these studies included measurements of suggestibility, a dimension that is heavily involved in false-memory phenomena.

Second, not all situations are equally believable, or plausible, as false suggestions. One factor that may be important is the extent to which the person is confident regarding the false event, or false information. A good example of this is a study on Bugs Bunny and Disneyland. The experiment demonstrated that many people could be misled into believing that they had interacted with Bugs on a visit to Disneyland, in spite of the fact that Bugs Bunny is a Warner Brothers cartoon character, and hence could not possibly be anywhere near Disneyland. However, it could be argued that not many people accurately remember Bug's affinity with Warner Brothers prior to the suggestion. Thus, the false suggestion that Bugs belongs to the world of Disney would not conflict with any strong factual memory. Similarly, provided the person had been to Disneyland, the false information does not contradict their known history. Further, the results suggest that a person's report on a false event may contain some correct personal information. This means that the report, while based on a false event, can nonetheless reflect accurately on a person's own history.

Assessment of risk

Another prominent example of psychology *in* law is risk assessment, and how it can be used to help inform the courts regarding sentencing. It is of obvious importance that sentencing takes into account the likelihood of an individual repeating the crime, or being a threat to themselves or society at large. Ideally the court would like to know whether the defendant is likely to commit the same offence again, or another offence, and when they might be likely to do so. It is here that a psychologist's expert opinion can have a huge impact on the severity of the sentence imposed.

Risk assessment can be based on the clinical approach (i.e. the psychologist's clinical experience), the experimental approach (i.e. use of empirical research and literature), or on the psychologist's expertise in interpreting data sets that pertain to the crime. For example, the defendant's score on a standardized test that is known to be correlated with recidivism (the actuarial approach) can be used in this way. As is often the case, different experts do not agree whether one approach is more or less problematic than the other. For example, the clinical approach is partly based on the psychologist's professional training and experience with particular clients. As professional experience is so variable, the psychologist's opinion might not be one that is shared by most colleagues.

The actuarial approach is based on interpreting large data sets, and consequently might appear to have more scientific credibility. However, a number of serious criticisms can be made. First, the non-psychologist (i.e. the court) does not necessarily find statistical concepts easy to assimilate into the legal framework. For example, Roesch and his colleagues argue that one of the quintessential differences between law and psychology is in terms of the concept of certainty versus that of probability (Roesch et al. 1999). Second, the data are usually based on psychological tests, which in turn may be criticized. As some of the most common tests rely on the skill of the examiner (see scenario two, projective tests, pp. 96–102), they cannot be regarded as infallible implements. Third, the psychologist bases their opinion on an interpretation of the data which, by definition, is limited to *central tendency*, or *normative values*. This means that the psychologist is basing their opinion of the defendant on what *most* people might or might not do. This is not a problem found with clinical approaches. Quite the contrary, the clinical approach, like the law, considers only those facts relevant to the specific case in question.

Regardless of their approach, the psychologist can never predict any individual's behaviour with complete certainty. Melton and his colleagues suggest, in their influential textbook (Melton et al. 1997), that the most important issues concern how to make the expert's opinion more accurate. There are a number of factors that are likely to be important. The accuracy of risk assessment will be a function of dynamic, interactive factors, which pertain to the individual, the justice system, and the individuals operating on behalf of the justice system, as well as more general social factors, like religion, culture, and political climate.

Psychology *and* law

In this section we principally look at psychology's contribution to helping the court understand that the way in which questions are phrased contributes to the way they are answered. We have used this example to illustrate the second category of interface between law and psychology.

The category of psychology *and* law refers to the psychologist's role in monitoring legal processes from outside the system. For example, there are circumstances where their expertise is used to identify potential miscarriages of justice that are occurring as a consequence of legal procedures. The psychologist still acts as an expert witness; however, the expert opinion concerns the interaction between psychological processes and legal procedures. In particular, legal procedures are challenged in terms of whether they have or have not resulted in any potential biases that could lead to miscarriages of justice. Essentially, issues emerging under the heading of psychology *and* law are those designed to challenge legal rules and procedures, and induce change.

Asking the right question

One of the most interesting areas to develop from psychology *and* law concerns the experimental work on questioning techniques. Much of the earlier work focused on the techniques adopted by the police while interviewing defendants in custody. More recent evidence has considered the manner in which witnesses, plaintiffs, and victims are questioned in the court room during both direct examination (i.e. *evidence in chief*) and cross-examination. A recent study examined the structure of questions used during rape trials. It was found that question styles tended to restrict the range of possible responses and hence did not promote the most complete, or accurate, accounts from the witness. For example, 'did you have a lot to drink or was this just a normal night out?' cannot be answered accurately without adding other alternatives. Too often, in a sensitive interview situation, the person being questioned is unable to offer the more meaningful alternatives out of fear, shyness, or embarrassment. This restrictive style of questioning was used with both complainants and defendants. The authors suggest that more open-ended styles of questioning should be utilized, particularly by the prosecution. Open-ended styles of questioning, such as 'how much did you have to drink?', afford the opportunity to report evidence without an external bias. With more open-ended questions, the possibility of evidence remaining relatively uncontaminated is greater. Judgement based on an open-ended questioning style is obviously better for the legal system, members of society, and the individuals involved in the case.

Inevitably, Haney's classifications of psychology in relation to the law are difficult to distinguish in practice. Nonetheless, the classifications are useful as they serve to unify what has become a rapidly growing discipline. Research, and the resultant literature on law and psychology, are growing at astonishing rates, so that some integration and organization of topics is essential. Similarly, psychologists now play an increasingly significant part in the court room and this has given rise to an increasing number of roles as they become major players. It is essential to maintain some way of understanding and integrating what these diverse roles have in common.

The 'expert' witness

In this section we highlight some of the issues that can arise with the psychologist's role as an expert witness. In particular, we note the difficulties in defining and accrediting expert-witness credibility.

Whether a psychologist is regarded as an expert witness depends in part on the justice system, and in part on the individual judge. For example, courts in the USA admit expert evidence from cognitive psychologists on memory issues, while English courts are much less likely to rule that memory issues require expert evidence. In circumstances where a psychologist does provide an expert opinion, it is essential that the psychologist is, indeed, an expert. This begs the question of who is an expert, and what are the criteria necessary to regard oneself as an expert. Standardizing the criteria is a problem that continues to concern legal professionals, professional organizations, psychologists, and the general public.

Most professional bodies and organizations agree that an expert must have completed appropriate, formal training in some psychological domain. Various professional bodies, such as the American Psychological Association (APA) and the British Psychological Society (BPS), are designated as accrediting bodies for formal training programmes in different divisions of psychology, such as research, clinical, and forensic. To become a chartered psychologist with the BPS an applicant must demonstrate that the necessary academic qualifications have been fulfilled. For those readers who are interested in a career in psychology the appropriate organization's website will give full information (www.bps.org.uk, www.apa.org).

The importance of experience

It is widely acknowledged that qualifications alone are not sufficient for a psychologist to regard themselves as an expert. **Formal knowledge** alone cannot replace the practical, or **tacit, knowledge** that comes with direct experience. The psychologist should also have experience. Clearly the experience gained must be relevant to the opinion being proffered. This is clearly advantageous in situations where the expert psychologist adopts a clinical approach (see Scenario Two, below). One would want the psychologist to have experience in working with the particular client group, before proffering an expert opinion. Similarly, one would expect that a psychologist acting as an expert within an experimental approach could demonstrate adequate research experience and an ability to review the empirical literature, as demonstrated by the publication of peer-reviewed papers. In the same way, a psychologist providing expert opinion from an actuarial approach would need to have experience in conducting, interpreting, and discussing complicated statistical analyses involving large data sets. In most circumstances where a psychologist is claiming to be an expert, formal training must be accompanied by relevant practical experience in order for the claim to be justified.

BOX 5.5 THE REAL PROBLEMS OF EXPERT WITNESSES

Expert opinion is an issue that raises heated debate amongst professionals in psychology and in law. Jurors place far too much emphasis on eyewitness statements, in spite of the fact that the psychological literature is replete with examples of how poor eyewitness accuracy can be (see Kassin et al. 1989). Similarly, juries assume that witnesses who are highly confident are also likely to be the most accurate, again in spite of the evidence from psychological studies. In part, it is precisely because common sense is not necessarily accurate that expert opinion has become so important. For example, it is essential that both the judge and jury understand how people can come to believe they know something, when in fact their so-called knowledge is simply the result of some misleading post-event suggestions by an interrogator (see Loftus 1979). However, there is an inherent problem when using expert opinion, particularly within the domain of psychology, and this is that no two experts will necessarily agree! This is the direct result of the nature of the evidence upon which each bases their expert opinion. Where there is controversy, it is likely that the evidence is equivocal. So, some literature suggests that eyewitnesses can be highly reliable under stress, whereas other literature suggests the opposite (again, see Kassin et al. 1989). The outcome is often a battle between the experts, where one expert argues against the other's opinion. This divergence in expert opinion can have the effect of confusing, rather than aiding, the jury's understanding of important issues, and inevitably leads to more complex, lengthy, and expensive trials.

Both training and experience can be assessed and quantified, so some of the criteria regarding experts could be reliably specified. However, there is still the problem of deciding who should hold the accrediting power. There are many professional bodies within psychology, each adopting a slightly different set of criteria for professional accreditation. The question of whether one accrediting body is better than another is difficult to answer. Some employers may prefer a particular accrediting body because of historical links. Importantly, the salaries offered by employers will depend on the nature of the accreditation held by the psychologist. Eventually, the issue of accreditation is likely to require government regulation, given the rate at which psychologists from all disciplines now operate as experts in the courts.

SCENARIO ONE

THE USE OF JURIES IN COMPLEX LITIGATION

The literature on juries is a fascinating mixture of topics. Much of the research has used simulations, based on the use of mock juries, due in part to the restrictions that are placed on jury research. In England, for example, jurors are prohibited from discussing any aspects of a trial. Some studies have looked at issues of comprehension and understanding; for example, the effects of judicial instructions on jury comprehension. Other studies have focused on the make-up of a jury, identifying factors that might contribute to a juror's decision-making; for example, the effects of social conformity or the attractiveness of the defendant. Being tried by a jury of one's peers is assumed to be one of the most steadfast characteristics of the adversarial system. This scenario challenges this by examining the effectiveness of peer juries in complicated litigation. The scenario is interesting in that not only does it directly address the effectiveness of a peer jury, it also involves a group of psychologists rather than a single psychologist. The issues raised in this scenario represent most of the mainstream areas in cognitive psychology.

What was the situation?

The 1980s in England reflected a time in which people, particularly those who had been educated, were interested in making money fast, in big city deals and share trading (reflected in films such as *Wall Street*). Not surprisingly, the occurrence of so-called white-collar crimes increased in parallel (e.g. corporate fraud, stocks and shares embezzlement). Significantly, changes in trading and developments in technology meant that white-collar crimes became highly technical, where money would not only change hands but also change shape (e.g. stocks, then liquid assets, then overseas bonds, then dot.com businesses, etc.). Because of the increasing complexity of these types of crimes, investigations and prosecutions were better led by people who had similar training, or expertise in the area; for example, elite investigative teams specializing in complicated fraud cases (the Flying Fraud Squad).

While the number of such investigations, and subsequent arrests, continued to increase, there had been an overwhelming failure to convict successfully in these complicated fraud cases. Not surprisingly, prosecutors were called upon to justify the poor conviction rates. They argued that the police were providing adequate evidence to convict, and that they, the prosecutors, had presented the evidence clearly. The problem was with the jury.

Much of the evidence in complicated fraud cases required the juror to follow extensive and complicated 'money trails'. The evidence was numerical, with graphs, tables, pie charts, and other types of diagram (e.g. flow diagrams) illustrating the trail of money. Having a good working knowledge of business and money transactions, and being comfortable with numbers, could almost be regarded as a necessity. Prosecutors argued that, while most jurors were undoubtedly numerate, few had the background and expertise to comprehend the evidence. Because the jury failed to understand the evidence, they naturally returned verdicts of 'not guilty'.

Why were psychologists involved?

In 1983, Lord Roskill was asked by the UK Lord Chancellor's Office to form a committee (the Lord Roskill Fraud Trial Committee), which would address the possibility of replacing peer juries in cases of complex and complicated fraud, such as corporate fraud. Professionals from law, psychology, and sociology were asked to participate in a forum to discuss the various issues raised. The psychologists who were present raised their concerns that the *extent* of the jurors' problem had not been established. The assumption had been that, because jurors could not comprehend the evidence, they were returning verdicts of not guilty. However, the psychologists pointed out that this had not actually been established. The basis for not-guilty verdicts *might or might not* have been related to the jury's understanding of the evidence. The Committee agreed that this was a basic question that needed addressing and asked the psychologists to present a research proposal outlining how it might be examined.

This situation represents a stunning example of psychology *and* law: a normal feature of the legal system, jury trials, was being examined. The importance of this situation cannot be overstated. Juries represent an integral component of the adversarial system. Any suggestion of removing them immediately divides opinion. For example, some legal professionals identify proposals to replace peer juries with panels of experts (or judges) as a risk to justice (e.g. Rozenberg 2003). It was clear that any recommendations made by the Roskill Committee could impact dramatically on the future of the legal system.

What psychological concepts were involved?

As the psychologists were focusing on the jurors' comprehension and understanding of the evidence, their general questions concerned the **information-processing** abilities of jurors, and whether these might be improved. While the views of some members of the legal profession may dismiss the jury as old-fashioned or naive, there is ample evidence to suggest that jurors are competent at, and committed to, making informed and balanced decisions. In fact, some psychologists argue that the average jury, once appropriately informed, has exactly the same strengths and weaknesses, and is prone to exactly the same biases, as any panel of so-called experts, or judges. The entire project

---

BOX 5.6 JURIES SEEN THROUGH THE EYES OF THE LAW

The issues raised in this situation go to the heart of the jury concept. While laymen and philosophers view the jury as the embodiment of democratic process, the legal profession sometimes sees them in a different light. Neitzel and colleagues (1999), having reviewed the available literature, offer the frank suggestion that the law actively mistrusts jurors. They are not alone in this observation. Many authors, including those within the legal world, have raised doubts about the adequacy of juries in arriving at the truth. Witness one anonymous American critic, a trial judge, who described juries in the following unflattering terms: 'We commonly strive to assemble twelve persons colossally ignorant of all practical matters, fill their vacuous heads with law which they cannot comprehend, obfuscate their seldom intellect with testimony which they are incompetent to analyse or unable to remember, permit partisan lawyers to bewilder them with their meaningless sophistry, then lock them up until the most obstinate of their number coerce the others into submission or drive them into open revolt.' While this may somewhat overstate the case, others have found more serious grounds for doubt. Diamond and Casper (1992), writing in the official journal of the Law Society, criticized the ability of jurors to understand the testimony of experts. Johnson and Wiggins (1994), also addressing the legal profession, note that the law seems to dismiss juries, assuming that the average juror is incapable of understanding the more complicated aspects of litigation.

---

involved issues that are in the mainstream in cognitive psychology, and included attention, learning, and memory. Arguably, when an individual is confronted with a complex situation they are required to selectively attend to some aspect of the environment and ignore everything else. This concept of *selective attention* is central to information processing. Concepts that would be immediately relevant include hypotheses regarding **short-term memory** and **limited processing capacity**. It has been argued that individuals can become overloaded with information, particularly when the information is not familiar.

One possibility was that the jurors were finding it difficult to maintain their **focused attention** on evidence, particularly if the evidence required the processing of complicated arguments, or extensive amounts of statistical or numerical information. Another issue involved examining how the evidence was being *presented* to jurors with a view to improving the jury's comprehension and understanding, including

---

BOX 5.7 THE ROLE OF ATTENTION

Attention has been one of the most frequently studied areas in cognitive psychology. As a topic, attention was very dominant in theories emerging during the 1960s and early 1970s with theoretical arguments surrounding the issue of where the bottleneck in attentional processes occurred. Methodologies that have been developed from research on attention have been particularly prominent in empirical work on various clinical disorders, such as anxiety disorders. Because of the precision of experimental work on attention, it has become a favoured area in which to apply new developments in the careful study of brain functions, using **functional magnetic resonance imaging (fMRI)** techniques.

knowledge acquisition and retention (i.e. the ability and opportunity to absorb and retain new information).

What did the psychologists do?

There were two stages involved. The first required the psychologists to provide a research document. The research document would outline a number of things: the questions being addressed; why these questions were important to the main remit regarding jury trials; how these questions might inform any recommendations regarding jury trials; and how any research might proceed. This document required the psychologists to review all empirical and related psychological literature, and provide details regarding how any empirical investigations might proceed, including the length of time required to complete the project, costings, and 'deliverables'.

The research document was prepared by members of the UK Medical Research Council (MRC) Applied Psychology Unit who had attended the original forum. It was comprised of a number of independent research proposals, each taking an experimental approach. All projects focused on whether a juror's understanding and knowledge of complex evidence could be improved. The separate proposals looked at different aspects of the general issues surrounding how juries attend, understand, and remember evidence. Robert Logie, John Duncan and Alan Baddeley proposed looking at issues of focal attention (Logie et al. 1986). The argument was that it was important to establish how long a juror stayed attentive to the evidence. If a juror lost interest and stopped attending within ten minutes of the trial proceedings, they would not be expected to return a verdict of guilty, at least not on the basis of the evidence.

Debra Bekerian and her co-workers (1986) investigated the effect that summaries could have on a jury's ability to remember evidence. They were also interested in examining whether a juror's retention of evidence was in any way related to the verdict they returned. As it is impossible for researchers to investigate real juries, all projects involved mock jurors. The work focused on the ability of individuals to remember different types of evidence that might appear in a fraud trial. The researchers speculated that jurors find some evidence easier to understand than others (e.g. evidence regarding the defendant's personality versus evidence regarding tax-rebate forms). Because of this, they will find the more familiar evidence easier to remember, and rely differentially on this information when making judgements of guilt. This implies that some of the evidence, namely that which the jurors found too difficult to remember, was not being used to informs the jurors' decision-making.

Such questions focus on concepts regarding the facilitative effects of knowledge structures on memory and the dangers that may result from utilizing existing knowledge structures. The investigators also questioned how memory for 'difficult' evidence might be supported. They suggested that summaries which repeat key aspects of the prosecution and defence's arguments may enable the juror to remember evidence that otherwise might be too difficult. The use of summaries relies on the notion that memory will be improved through repetition, or **rehearsal**. Repeating information should facilitate the jurors' ability to remember evidence over the longer term and this would enable the jurors to utilize more of the relevant evidence when making their decision of guilt.

Another proposal by Logie and his colleagues focused on *selective attention*. In particular, they were concerned with identifying lapses of attention. Lapses of attention occur when the individual cannot focus on the environment and becomes mentally distracted. The investigators were most concerned with first identifying when these lapses occurred, and second with whether concentration lapses might be remedied by providing jurors with breaks. Issues regarding concentration and the mental effort required to process unfamiliar information were also highly relevant.

The work of Alison Black (1986) focused on the *presentation* of information and particularly on the effects that prior knowledge can have on the comprehension of information. One question posed by her looked directly at the effects of providing jurors with a glossary of terms that would be used during the course of the trial (Black 1985). One of the major problems with complicated fraud is the terminology used to describe various actions, or assets (e.g. portfolio development). Failing to understand complicated terms obviously would impair a juror's ability to assess the evidence. A glossary would provide the juror with prior knowledge of terms, and serve as a mnemonic for aiding their comprehension. This manipulation was derived from theories that suggest that prior knowledge can promote new learning by providing a structure or basis for the integration of the new knowledge.

More generally, issues of how existing knowledge structures can aid the comprehension of new information were at the heart of these investigators' concerns. For example, they were interested in the differential ease in understanding growth in financial assets, when this growth was displayed as a numerical table versus a pie chart. They suggested that most people would find a pie chart, which graphically demonstrates changes in size, easier to comprehend and remember than a comparison of two numbers. Part of the reason for this is that perceptual size is perceived and understood at a much earlier developmental age than numerical size. For example, even young children (e.g. aged four or five) will demonstrate differences in size in their perceptual depictions. In contrast, a child's ability to use and understand numbers when depicting quantity develops later (e.g. at ages 7 or 8). The manipulations considered by Black (1986) rely on assumptions that the ease with which people assimilate new information will depend largely on their pre-existing knowledge structures and the extent to which the new information is compatible with them.

How was the input of the psychologists assessed?

The Roskill Committee produced a report in 1986, which recommended that two further bodies be established. One was the Serious Fraud Office, which has now supervised several complex fraud trials. Its functions include investigation as well as presentation of new cases and its staff includes experts in a variety of fields. Interestingly, they include experts in information technology, as the psychologists had recommended. The other body is a standing Advisory Panel that issues recommendations in the form of Working Papers. These recommendations have no force in law but serve to advise the courts.

One of their recommendations is that the Rules of Court should expand and formalize procedures to assess the competence of juries. This would take the form of questionnaires designed to determine literacy and numeracy. This is not unique. In France,

---

BOX 5.8 CAN COMPREHENSION BE MEASURED?

Comprehension is defined as the person's ability to understand information. The manner in which comprehension is assessed generally involves presenting a person with information, and then, some short time later, asking the person to make judgements or inferences that are based on the information they received. Accurate inferences, or judgements, indicate that the person has successfully comprehended the information. For example, suppose the person is given the information that Tom is ten-year old and has a younger brother. The person may then be asked to select from the following: (a) Tom is an only child; (b) Tom has no sisters; (c) Tom has at least one brother. Given the information, option (c) would indicate accurate comprehension. Notice that the other options, (a) and (b), differ importantly in the quality of information they offer. The first flatly contradicts the original statement and hence relies only on memory. The second (no sisters) may be *either* true *or* false, as it is neither confirmed nor denied in the original. Its correct rejection therefore relies on both memory and inference.

---

for example, all the jurors in jury trials must be able to read and write. What is new, however, is the use of a questionnaire designed specifically for the purpose. Again, this follows from the findings of the psychologists. Another recommendation has been that judges should have the authority to set time limits on speeches by both prosecution and defence. This recognizes the important role of attention, and the hazards of compromising understanding when too much material is presented at once. They further recommend the use of information technology in the presentation of evidence in a clear fashion by means of flow charts and diagrams presented on computer screens.

Most importantly, from our standpoint, the panel explicitly referred to the contribution of the psychologists from the MRC Applied Psychology Unit in recommending that juries be provided *before the trial* with coherent summaries of both the prosecution and the defence cases in order to provide a framework within which their ability to understand and remember the evidence would be 'significantly improved'. Finally, and most importantly in terms of the judiciary process, the panel has advised that further research should be commissioned on the ability of juries to understand these cases before sanctioning the removal of juries in complex fraud trials.

SCENARIO TWO

A CLINICAL PSYCHOLOGIST IN COURT PROCEEDINGS

Our next scenario is concerned with the role of the clinical psychologist in a personal injury court case. Occasions arise that call for the input of a clinician, for example when fitness to stand trial is questioned, where there is a suspicion of mental illness. In the example to be dealt with here the problem was more specific. It was not a typical case but it raises some interesting points.

What was the situation?

Mr G, a 24-year-old warehouse worker, claimed that he was the victim of an accident at work. He reported that a heavy block and tackle came loose and swung towards him, striking him in the small of his back. He was knocked to the floor but not otherwise hurt and he resumed work for the rest of the day. Unfortunately, no one had seen the accident and this was to become a difficulty. In the course of the following week he gradually developed severe back pain. The pain eventually led him to leave his job and seek the state benefits to which he was entitled.

Two years passed and Mr G remained unable to work. His friends suggested that he take his case to one of the legal firms advertising help with accident claims, on a no-win, no-fee basis. He was reluctant to do this initially, believing that if he approached his old firm they would find him a lighter job within the company. In fact, the personnel office refused to consider him. In the end therefore, he accepted his friends' advice and decided to seek compensation.

The legal team notified his former employers of their intention to sue. This brought a response, which resulted in a meeting between the two teams. At this meeting it was agreed that it might be advantageous to both parties if they were to settle out of court. As a condition of this settlement Mr G's employers asked that the case be referred for a medical opinion. If the case went to court the expert opinion would be available. The medical specialist chosen was a neurosurgeon with wide experience of back injuries and their associated neurological deficits.

The request to the neurosurgeon was that he assess the extent, severity, and probable cause of the damage claimed. Routine investigations in such a case include the use of X-ray and **magnetic resonance imaging (MRI)**, as well as a thorough physical examination. As the neurosurgeon worked in a large teaching hospital he was also able to call on the expertise of neuropsychologists. Neuropsychological assessment is increasingly called for in personal-injury litigation. Indeed, a recent survey showed that legal referrals to neuropsychological services rank third in frequency after neurological and psychiatric referrals (Sweet et al. 1996). The rapidly developing discipline of neuropsychology offers a number of specialized tests. These are mainly aimed at investigating brain function, however, and in this case were all negative. They did not include a routine psychological assessment; that is, an exploration of personal and emotional factors.

The routine surgical investigations showed that Mr G had a small nodule on one of his lumbar vertebrae. This could cause pressure on the afferents to the sciatic nerve and might account for the pain and limitation of function. However, it was impossible to judge from the X-ray or MRI scan when the small lesion had occurred. It might have been caused by the accident or by some earlier injury. Furthermore, because there had been no witness to the accident, Mr G could not prove that he had been hurt in the way he claimed. As Mr G was seeking damages, the *real* problem was to determine whether his claim was genuine.

Back pain is very common, particularly among males, and is one of the most frequent reasons for losing time from work. However, as the perception of pain is purely subjective and is not necessarily related to tissue damage, diagnosis is often difficult.

This is particularly problematic with back pain, and more than two-thirds of patients with lower back pain have no observable pathology. Back pain is therefore one of the conditions that are referred to frequently as contested illnesses. They include chronic fatigue syndrome, myalgic encephalomyelitis, Gulf War syndrome, and others. In these conditions there is a strong belief on the part of the patient that they are ill, even though health-care professionals are unable to substantiate the illness. In Mr G's case, as is all too common, his general practitioner had made no serious attempt at diagnosis and therefore had not referred him for investigations. Too often, complaints of back pain as the major symptom are simply referred to pain-management clinics whose function is to help the patient to develop a range of strategies to manage the perceived pain (see Chapter 8).

Where personal injury is involved, there is always a strong possibility of *malingering*; that is, the patient pretending to be ill in order to gain compensation. In this case, the lawyers for the employers would almost certainly try to argue that Mr G was malingering in order to receive a larger sum of money. The fact that the medical evidence was inconclusive would be likely to strengthen their argument. The neurosurgeon felt troubled by this, as he had become interested in this patient. He believed Mr G to be honest and sincere in his claims.

Why was the psychologist involved?

The neurosurgeon was aware that his report might be disadvantageous to Mr G. As an expert witness the neurosurgeon was entitled to offer his *opinion* that Mr G's claim was genuine, but he felt uncomfortable about giving this opinion without firm evidence to back it up. His strong hunch was that the story was true, but he could not support it on the basis of any evidence. In his exasperation, the neurosurgeon had even considered using a so-called judgement of Solomon and offering to operate on the young man's vertebrae. If Mr G accepted the offer it would mean that he was mainly interested in returning to a normal life. However, if Mr G refused the operation, it would suggest that his overriding interest was in the compensation money! Instead, he decided to discuss the case with one of his colleagues, a clinical psychologist of several years experience.

Although he respected his colleague, the surgeon was frankly sceptical of the value of psychological tests. However, as they talked they both decided that it would be helpful to see whether a psychological assessment would clarify the issue of possible malingering.

If the psychologist's assessment suggested that Mr G was not malingering, it would strengthen the neurosurgeon's case. The psychologist agreed to undertake the assessment. Note that the psychologist has not been appointed as an expert witness in his own right, but was acting as a consultant to the expert witness.

The problem for the psychologist now became one of trying to assess whether the patient's account could be believed. Unfortunately, there is no psychological test that will examine this directly (see 'The war room', Chapter 7, for a discussion of the lie detector). In any event, whatever the results of the psychological assessment they would not clarify the real problem, viz. whether the alleged accident had actually caused the lesion in the spine.

What psychological concepts are involved?

The first concept that is relevant here is the role of patients' subjective beliefs about illness and disability. Ecclestone et al. (1997) studied the explanations of chronic pain offered by patients and by their health-care professionals. Typically, patients regard the cause of their condition as originating in the body. Often there is a history of injury that originally resulted in an episode of acute pain, and the patient sees this as the cause of their chronic pain. However, the professionals tend to view the development of pain from acute to chronic as a form of dysfunctional reaction. That is, they believe that, in many of these cases, psychological or psychosomatic factors maintain the pain.

Worry may also serve to exacerbate and perpetuate the pain, though the patient sees it as entirely organic in origin. Modem research methods include **discourse analysis** in which the patient's detailed description of the condition is examined systematically for clues that there is some hidden awareness of the role of stress, childhood experience of illness, or unusual sensitivity to stressful activities. These analytic methods have evolved from *post-modern* theories and methods, and examine the subtext of patient's accounts. A full description of these methods can be found in Rogers (2001). In the case of Mr G the psychological assessment would look for these factors underlying the complaint.

Another psychological concept of relevance here is that of malingering. The term 'malingering' normally refers to fairly uncomplicated attempts to feign illness in order to achieve some gain. It is said to be common in military situations where personnel hope to be excused duty (in Army parlance it is called 'swinging the lead'). It is common among children who want to avoid school and in undergraduates who want to avoid exams. However, there are more serious forms, two of which, Ganser syndrome and Munchausen syndrome, will be described here. In the case of Mr G, the psychological assessment would need to be aware of them.

The defining characteristic of Ganser syndrome, at interview or in psychological tests, is a tendency to give seemingly absurd or silly answers to straightforward questions. An example, often quoted in the textbooks, is the question, 'how many legs has a horse?'; answer, 'three'. This type of response has been called talking past the point because the answer shows clearly that the patient understands the question; it is not a cognitive disability as such. The answer makes sense if it is appreciated that it is a near miss. The question is understood and the answer is in the correct domain but is incorrect in a silly way. Symptoms may also include inattention and drowsiness, or **conversion symptoms**; for example, paralysis or loss of function and rarely, hallucinations. Ganser syndrome is sometimes called prison psychosis because it occurs more frequently in prison populations where there is a vested interest in getting special treatment.

Munchausen syndrome is a class of disorders in which the person deliberately causes illness or self-injury, but denies that they are doing so. They may genuinely be unaware of their own actions, even of such bizarre ones as eating rotten matter, inhaling noxious substances, and so on. There is no clear understanding of this condition and it probably ranges from fully aware manipulations through to deeply unconscious acts. Recently there have been accusations of Munchausen syndrome by proxy (MSBP) in which parents are accused of causing illness in their children. This has disturbing similarities to allegations of child abuse though they need not concern us here. In the present context the psychologist would need to consider some milder form of the same underlying psychopathology; the possibility that the injury in question was self-inflicted. Both of these syndromes are often thought to reflect a need to avoid responsibility.

Finally, the psychologist would need to consider the possibility of a **hysterical disorder**. While not regarded as a form of malingering, hysterical symptoms usually stem from an unconscious desire for gain, demonstrated in the form of physical symptoms.

What did the psychologist do?

First he decided what psychological tests to use, if any. A recent five-year survey of clinical practice in the USA (Holub 1992) found that two-thirds of the settings used the same set of tests: the Minnesota Multiphasic Personality Inventory (MMPI), Wechsler Adult Intelligence Scale (WAIS), Rorschach Inkblot Test, Thematic Apperception Test (TAT), and Bender Visual Motor Gestalt Test. There has been no comparable study in the UK but it seems probable that there would be some overlap in those settings using standard psychological tests. These five tests are all very well known and together they constitute a test battery.

The MMPI is designed to measure important aspects of personality. It yields a profile of subtest scales based on established norms. Such tests, based on statistical concepts of normality, are called psychometric tests. The MMPI consists of a large number (660) of simple statements printed on cards (e.g. I enjoy a good party). The subject is asked to sort these cards into one of three piles: agree, disagree, or don't know. The subtest scales are formed by adding up the relevant items. For example the item 'I am a special agent of God', would be unlikely to go into the agree category of a normal person. Several items of this sort would fall into a scale intended to identify psychotic thinking. The test differs from the WAIS (see below) in that new subscales can be formed from subsets of the existing items. They should then be standardized on a sample of normal individuals before being widely used.

The WAIS is another psychometric test. It is a standardized intelligence test containing a number of subtests that yield an estimate of the examinee's various cognitive abilities, compared to those measured on a very large normative sample.

In contrast to the psychometric tests are the projective tests. In these tests a series of ambiguous stimuli is presented to the subject who is asked to interpret them, having been told that there are no right or wrong answers. These tests rely on the so-called projective hypothesis, which states that faced with an ambiguous stimulus an individual's response to it will be determined by their own needs, tendencies, and 'psychological organization'. This intuitive concept was gradually developed in the first part of the twentieth century. It was given formal status by Lawrence Frank who attempted to examine and clarify its implications systematically (Frank 1948). Whereas various scores can be derived from tests of this type, they differ from the psychometric tests in that they aim to produce an overall dynamic picture of the person's current functioning rather than a numerical comparison with a normal sample.

The two best-known projective tests are the Rorschach Inkblot Test and the TAT. In the former, the subject is presented with a series of ten symmetrical inkblots and asked to say what they resemble. A wide variety of responses is possible, ranging from human or animal shapes to clouds, maps, and so on. The significance of the responses is assessed through complex procedures derived from personality theory. An advantage of the Rorschach test is that deceptive responses are easily recognized as such by a trained and experienced examiner. Although the Rorschach test has generated controversies in the past, a recent review has justified its use (Donnelly 2003). A full discussion of projective tests lies beyond the scope of this book but a good overview is offered by Semeneoff (1976).

The other well-known projective test, the TAT, uses pictures of undefined persons or groups of people in deliberately ambiguous situations. The subject is asked to invent a story about the picture. There are thirty of these pictures and the usual practice is to select, on the basis of the subject's age, gender, and problem areas, a subset of relevant pictures. Rather than yield an overall picture of the personality, this test is used to identify significant themes in the subject's experience, such as anxiety or guilt, and to suggest the areas towards which they are directed.

Finally, the Bender Visual Motor Gestalt Test presents the subject with a series of eight very simple geometric forms that they are asked to copy. This test is sensitive to certain types of brain damage, revealed by errors in copying, and is used as a screening test where there is reason to suspect cognitive deficit. It is peculiarly sensitive to malingering, since the subject is tempted to produce abnormal designs that are easily recognized as deceptive.

The MMPI, the principal personality measure in the list above, is self-administered and it has been claimed that this deprives the examiner of the opportunity to assess the truth of the answers. This is an obvious disadvantage where the truthfulness of the subject is itself in doubt. For this reason some examiners use the MMPI as the basis for a searching interview based on the answers given. However, many of the MMPI items are transparent in the sense that the subject can easily guess their meaning and intent and thus will provide the answers that they want the examiner to believe. For example, a statement such as 'I am often in pain', that is intended to get at neurotic or hypochondriachal concerns, would not be answered truthfully by an individual seeking compensation for injury! It has been suggested by Gacono and Meloy (1994) that tests having high **face validity** in this way should always be avoided where the possibility of malingering is an issue.

The psychologist was trained in the use of the Rorschach test and had considerable breadth of experience in using it. Indeed, he was widely regarded as an expert. In view of the considerations outlined above, he therefore selected the Rorschach test as the principal tool in his examination of Mr G, supplemented by careful interview and discourse analysis. If the interview suggested specific worries or concerns he would use the TAT to explore them. Since the young man's intelligence was not at issue the WAIS was not used. The psychologist decided that he would only add the Bender gestalt test if the Rorschach test suggested that Mr G's responses were deceptive, as it would function as an invitation to deceive.

In summary, the clinical psychologist was applying his experience and skill in psychological assessment to the specific question asked by the neurosurgeon: 'In your opinion is this person likely to be lying?' He was invoking the hypothesis that if the subject were motivated to deceive, his responses to the inkblots would be deceptive.

The young man readily agreed to a psychological assessment and it could be argued that his very agreement might support the view that he was honest. He cooperated fully in both the interview and the inkblot test. The latter showed no evidence of deliberate deception in the sense of identifying misleading percepts and he was judged to be frank and forthcoming during the interview. The psychologist concluded that there was very little likelihood that his case for compensation was based on deception. He reported his findings verbally to the neurosurgeon.

How was the psychologist's input assessed?

The assessment of results in any psychological investigation is usually rather complex. In this case it was simple. The surgeon, feeling supported by the psychologist's findings, was able to give his expert opinion that Mr G was making a genuine claim. Furthermore, he offered to operate on the young man's back. His offer was accepted without hesitation. After a brief period on the waiting list, the operation was carried out and the young man was successfully treated and returned to a normal life. The case was settled out of court and a costly litigation was avoided. The case described, though not typical, shows how the approach of applied psychology was useful in the court room, although the case never came to court.

■ **ADDITIONAL READING**

Fox, D. and Prilleltensky, I. (1997) *Critical Psychology: an Introduction*. Sage Publications, London. This book argues that both the theoretical and applied branches of psychology serve to support the interests of the status quo. It is controversial but very interesting!

Melton, G., Petrila, J., Poythress, N., and Slobgin, C. (1997) *Psychological Evaluations for the Court: a Handbook for Mental Health Professionals and Lawyers*. Guilford Press, New York. A useful source for those interested in issues of mental health as they affect the law.

Roesch, R. Hart, S., and Ogloff, J. (eds) (1999) *Psychology and Law: State of the Discipline*. Kluwer Academic, New York. A good review of recent issues.

■ QUESTIONS

Scenario one

1 What ethical issues arise from the different research findings?

2 What changes in court-room proceedings would *you* introduce on the basis of the findings?

Scenario two

1 What limitations might there be in the psychologist's use of projective tests?

2 What physiological measures would have complemented the psychologist's approach?

6

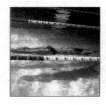  

The work room

In this chapter we examine the changing trends in the way that psychologists apply their knowledge and skills to our working environments. We first give some background into the early studies of the working environment that focused on the working environment in terms of productivity and efficiency. Two early approaches are depicted; one, scientific management, which dissected tasks into components, and two, the human-relations movement, which was more concerned with the attitudes and feelings of workers. We then see how the progression from the Industrial Revolution led psychologists to more modern concerns that highlight individual differences and group behaviour. In particular, we consider how psychology has been influential in promoting better selection, performance assessment, and training of workers. We also consider the importance of psychological investigations on groups and how groups are formed, operate, and maintained within the work environment. The chapter illustrates the many areas of psychology that have infiltrated our working environments. The scenarios show the great diversity in the way that psychologists can inform and improve our working environments.

The concept of work

For those of us living in Western societies, the concept of work forms a significant part of everyday life. There are many ways in which we define the notion of work. For example, we can argue that work involves some amount of sacrifice in order to achieve some desired outcome, for example exchanging our time and effort for money. Using this definition, we can contrast work with pleasure. Pleasure is not usually associated with any sacrifice, and we often seek it for its own sake. Similarly, we can distinguish between work and labour, work and occupation, or work and profession. However, no single definition can encompass all aspects of work for all people. As Porteus has pointed out (Porteus 1997), the distinction between work and pleasure, for some individuals, is an anathema, as work *is* the major source of pleasure and fulfilment in life.

Regardless of how we define the concept, work and the workplace impact crucially on our lives. Work influences our attitudes, beliefs, perceptions, feelings, the clothes we wear, and our physical actions: things that fascinate psychologists. Not surprisingly, therefore, the workplace has been favoured by psychologists as a venue for exploring some of the most important aspects of human behaviour.

The psychologist's role

It is essential to remember that psychologists respond and react to the current socio-economic and political environment; and this is clearly demonstrated in the way psychologists have been involved in the workplace. For example, during the early twentieth century psychologists were encouraged by factory owners to identify physical conditions that increased production efficiency on the factory floor's production line. In contrast, the domination of modern societies by information and information technology has meant that psychologists consider other factors, such as the mental strain placed on an individual and their psychological well-being (see Arnold et al. 1995 for further discussion).

Similarly, the political environment in which the psychologist operates will promote different lines of study, simply because different environments afford different opportunities. For example, war and its atrocities offer the psychologist situations, and chances for observation, that are unlikely to be available unless serious ethical violations are committed. Perversely, much of our psychological knowledge has been gained through observing the effects of war on individuals, e.g. post-traumatic stress disorders and battle fatigue (see 'The war room', Chapter 7; see also 'The treatment

---

BOX 6.1 THE ROLE OF CULTURE

Different national cultures emphasize different aspects or dimensions of work; and national cultural attitudes are good predictors of work performance. For example, the acceptance of a psychologist in the workplace was established with greater ease in the USA than in the UK. This difference was in part due to the increasingly dominant roles that trade unions held in the UK at the beginning of the twentieth century (Hollway 1991). It is probably fair to say, without involving unnecessary value judgements, that the British trade unions at this time were more combative and isolationist than their American brothers. They tended to see any change introduced by management as an infringement of workers' rights. A few researchers have examined directly the international differences in the concept of work. The work of Hofstede (1980) provides highly useful and informative analyses of the different dimensions or factors that emerge as important indicators of national cultural attitudes towards work (see also Buchholz 1978). As a consequence, it is essential to remember that much of the theorizing that has emerged from the psychological study of work reflects Western cultural values; for example the need for achievement (McClelland et al. 1953).

room', Chapter 8). This just serves to remind us that, whenever psychologists operate in the real world, the real world directs, dictates, and determines the ways in which the professional psychologist can explore and explain human behaviour.

In the following we consider how psychologists first examined work and the workplace. We will then consider the different issues that arise when psychologists focus on the individual person as the unit of their study (e.g. **occupational psychology**), as opposed to when they focus on larger units of analysis, such as groups or organizations (e.g. **organizational psychology**).

Early investigations in the work room

Early investigations of the workplace focused on how to improve the worker's productivity and efficiency. Many psychological concepts that emerged from this early work continue to be dominant today. They include scientific management and the human-relations movement. Scientific management focused on improving worker's efficiency through analyses of task components, consideration of individual differences, development of training, and provision of incentives. The human-relations movement was more concerned with workers' attitudes and feelings, and focused on the social aspects of the workplace.

The work room represents one of the earliest, formally documented applications of psychology to real-world problems, with Munsterberg becoming the first recognized applied psychologist in the USA. As indicated by the title of his book, *Psychology and Industrial Efficiency* (Munsterberg 1913), his interest directly reflected the dominant socio-economic concerns of the newly industrialized Western world. Industrialization offered a chance to produce goods on a mass scale as never before. The employer wanted the psychologist to improve work productivity and efficiency within the context of an industrial environment. Munsterberg was particularly interested in the interaction between the worker and the job; and accordingly he emphasized the importance of selecting the correct individual to do the job.

The first time-and-motion studies

This interest in achieving the most efficient and productive work force is well illustrated in the work of Taylor (1911) and Gilbreth (1911), who undertook what are known as *time-and-motion studies*. Taylor's interest was to determine the most efficient way of performing tasks, and, to do this, he systematically broke down each task into small, discrete units. These units were measured in terms of the time it took to complete them. For example, suppose a worker was required to affix a badge onto the bonnet of a car. Taylor's idea was to break down that task into a series of sub-tasks, each of which contributed to the final goal of affixing the badge securely onto the car. The worker would first have to pick up the badge, make sure it was free from defects, apply adhesive to the badge, and then place the badge onto the car so that it was secure, while making sure that no damage occurred to the body or paintwork. Each of these actions would be timed, and an overall quality rating applied. On the basis of this type of breakdown of components, Taylor would then be in a position to instruct the worker how to avoid unnecessary movements that were reducing efficiency and productivity. Because Taylor's approach involved the identification and objective measurement of component behavioural units, his general approach came to be called *scientific management*.

Importantly, Taylor did not consider the performance of *any worker*; rather, he analysed performance on only those individuals he regarded as good workers. Thus, Taylor identified the importance of individual differences as factors that affect productivity. He also demonstrated an understanding that individual differences would require modifications not only in the work apparatus, but also in the working environment, in order to enhance maximally the individual's productivity. Taylor also considered the importance of *incentives*: if the workers were motivated by some incentive, then overall productivity would be higher. The argument rests on the assumption that people will work harder, more efficiently, or achieve some desired goal, if you provide them with the right incentive.

The role of incentive

For example, if each time a worker surpassed a particular, achievable goal they were given a bonus to their wage packet, the worker would be likely to want to surpass that goal. This is the reason why sales-driven business organizations are often commission-based. It is easy to see how the notion of incentives can be viewed under the more general heading of motivation. As human beings and mammals, when we are more motivated, we are generally more inclined and more willing to comply with the demands of the work environment.

When incentives are provided by management, the incentives are regarded as *exogenous*, in that they are introduced external to the worker and therefore can be manipulated directly. An example is the extra bonus given to our worker who surpasses a specified goal. These are to be contrasted with *endogenous* incentives, which are considered to be internal to the worker and therefore cannot be manipulated directly. Endogenous factors are best considered in the context of theories of psychological needs and goals (see McClelland et al. 1953; Herzberg 1966; Locke 1990 for extended discussions of these concepts). Workers may feel, for example, that when they surpass a particular goal, they are achieving their potential. As a consequence they experience feelings of greater *self-esteem*. Studies on human behaviour suggest that endogenous incentives can be more powerful incentives than exogenous; for example, greater self-esteem can be a more powerful incentive than more money (see Katzell and Thompson 1990).

Two basic approaches

Two distinct approaches to the study of work emerged from Taylor's seminal studies. The first attempts to change the person so that they are better able to do the task, or *fitting the worker to the job*. This approach focuses on training the worker to perform the task in the most efficient manner. A modern example would be training an operator to use pop-ups

---

BOX 6.2 THEORIES OF MOTIVATION

The notion of motivation received more attention in the past than today. The topic of motivation was particularly important in discussions of animal learning (e.g. Hull 1943). Theoretical models depicted motivation as an energy that can be depleted or stored, with the force behind the energy being the organism's need, such as the need to eat, the need to be safe, etc. As a consequence of its need, the organism is driven—motivated—to achieve and satisfy this need. Increased motivation resulted in more energy to perform the behaviour. The impact of incentives on behaviour, particularly in the form of **reinforcements**, was a core concept in *learning theories*. Incentives are meant to tap into the organism's needs, thereby inducing motivation. For example, in **operant conditioning**, the organism's behaviour is 'shaped' using positive outcomes or rewards. Behaviour that approximates the desired one is reinforced with a reward of food (based on some schedule). Eventually the organism produces the behaviour that conforms to that which is required. In the 1950s to the late 1960s most psychology students conditioned laboratory animals to perform some tasks as a function of different reinforcement schedules. For example, the animal (mainly the proverbial white rat) would be placed in a **Skinner box**, which contained a bar. The animal was required to push the bar down, and in return a food treat would be dispensed. The animal was reinforced on successively closer approximations to the desired behaviour, thus **shaping** the new response. **Reinforcement theories**, and learning theories in general, continue to be major theoretical frameworks for discussing problems in the work room.

---

in performing computer operations. The second approach changes aspects of the job to map better onto the person, or *fitting the job to the worker*. Here, differences in performing the tasks are identified and features of the work environment are changed accordingly.

An early example of fitting the job to the worker is that of Taylor redesigning work tools in accordance with the height and size of the worker. There are at least two factors that will contribute to the worker's ability to operate a piece of equipment, the worker's height and the worker's size. Height will determine the person's reach, while size in part determines the person's overall strength. A shelf that is too high (or too low) for the worker to reach without making additional, unnecessary movements reduces efficiency. Lowering (or raising) the shelf, in accordance with what is the optimal height for the worker, therefore improves performance. This would in turn lead to re-designing equipment, as in having flexible shelf height.

The political context under which psychologists first became interested in the workplace was the First World War. Government departments, concerned about workers' health and productivity in ammunition factories, first introduced questions about personnel selection—getting the right person for the job—and personnel training—training the person to do the job successfully. After the war the direct involvement of psychologists like Sir Frederic Bartlett, and the foundation of the National Institute of Industrial Psychology (NIIP), led to the *human-relations movement*. Its members held that the workers' feelings and attitudes were important, as these feelings and attitudes would directly affect productivity and efficiency.

The Hawthorne studies, conducted between 1924 and 1939, at the Hawthorne Electrical Plant, are justly famous. Their findings helped to shape the human-relations movement (see Riggio 2000 for a review). The general goal of theses studies was

> **BOX 6.3** THE HAWTHORNE EFFECT
>
> It is important to note that an unexpected finding from the Hawthorne studies was that the workers' behaviours seemed to be influenced by the fact that they were being observed. As Schein (1988) points out, changes to the working environment may have resulted in the workers believing that they had more freedom, which, in turn, influenced their attitudes towards their work. This effect, whereby the mere act of observation changes the individual's behaviour, has come to be known as the *Hawthorne effect*. The Hawthorne effect is particularly important, as it is not the result of any manipulation of the psychologist, and can bias results of observations and experiments in ways that are unexpected.

to establish the relationship between conditions of the working environment and productivity. However, the studies reported surprising findings. Although the physical environment, for example the level of ambient lighting, somewhat affected productivity, the effects were not consistent, and nor were they necessarily in the anticipated direction. Instead, the more important features of the environment seemed to be social in nature, for example group cohesiveness and **group norms**. The Hawthorne studies are important in that they represent a significant change of emphasis away from the physical environment, towards the social environment present in the work room (see Mayo 1933 for a more detailed description).

These traditional approaches to the work room led to two rather distinctive ways in which work was viewed. On the one hand, there was the scientific-management approach as typified by Taylor and by Gilbreth. This approach was concerned with dissecting the task into small, discrete components, training the individual to execute these components in the most efficient manner, identifying individual factors that contribute to increased productivity and efficiency, and offering incentives to increase motivation. In contrast, the approach of the human-relations movement focused on the social aspects of the work environment, stressing such things as group cohesiveness and group norms. While neither approach in itself could adequately account for workers' performance, in combination the views provide a coherent, and comprehensive understanding of many of the most important issues that arise in the work room.

The suggestion that people can be trained to be more efficient, and that different people have different requirements, may be obvious in a modern, post-industrial society. However, at the time of their inception, these ideas were revolutionary. As we will discuss later in this chapter (see pp. 112–14), training and personnel selection are still major problems that psychologists help to solve. As such, we must not underestimate the profound influence that people like Munsterberg, Taylor, Gilbreth, and Mayo have had on how psychologists function in the work room.

Recent topics considered in the work room

Attitudes towards work and workers have evolved considerably. However, psychologists still vary in their unit of study. Some psychologists analyse the behaviour of the individual, whereas others analyse the behaviour of groups or organizations. Recently, popular topics include personnel selection, training, and development; group behaviour and group norms; and human factors including ergonomics or human engineering. Because of the importance of computers and information technology in the modern workplace, human-computer interactions and user-friendly technology have become important areas of investigation.

Unlike the early twentieth century, it is taken for granted today that workers have attitudes, feelings, and beliefs. Progressively, more and more employers are being held responsible for maintaining workers' well-being and satisfaction. In parallel, our modern societies have come to include more jobs that involve mental skills, like operating a computer. The theoretical approaches used by early investigators have not been completely overshadowed. For example, scientific management is still considered as an essential tool of the occupational psychologist (e.g. Coolican et al. 1996). Learning theory and reinforcement schedules are still highly valuable in developing training programmes. However, newer psychological frameworks, particularly those from cognitive psychology and mainstream psychology, are more frequently used to understand behaviour in the workplace.

Personnel psychology

Personnel psychology is concerned that the individual doing the job is well suited to perform the requirements of the job. This worker–job matching can be achieved in a number of ways. Common issues include personnel selection, performance, and assessment, and personnel training. More recent developments are coaching and mentoring.

Personnel psychology focuses on the individual as the unit of analysis. The assumption is that work performance will improve when there is a good match between the tasks that are required to perform the job and the individual performing those tasks. It is a fact that different jobs require different skills and abilities, and that individuals differ in their abilities, skills, and aptitudes. The key to successful worker–job mapping, then, is first to measure what skills are needed by different jobs and which people have those skills, and then to match the two. The worker–job matching can be achieved either by *fitting the worker to the job* or by *fitting the job to the worker*. In practice, both approaches are essential, as neither in isolation can accommodate all of the factors that influence the goodness of fit of the worker–job match. In practice, fitting the worker to the job includes such things as training people how to operate machinery or software. In contrast, fitting the job to the worker is more related to the domain of human factors. For example, we identify what it is in the work environment that is unhelpful for the individual (e.g. shelf height) and modify that factor to produce an overall more comfortable fit with the worker (e.g. lowering or raising the shelf).

There are certain prerequisites for having a good worker–job match. These include a good description of the job and what it entails (task analysis), and a good description of the person who is likely to be best suited to the job (individual qualities and characteristics). Task analysis requires a comprehensive and accurate analysis of the requirements of the job—the physical, mental, and emotional requirements. This in turn leads to a job specification, which tells the person what they will be expected to do.

Task analysis

A good task analysis is not easy, and requires the job to be broken down into essential component parts, tasks and activities (see Eldridge et al. 1994 for a detailed discussion). Two different methods can be used to provide essential task analyses. The distinction between these two methods involves the level of description, and also the ease with which desirable, individual characteristics can be identified. The goal-oriented method provides general descriptions of the tasks involved in the job, with the focus being on the task outcomes, or goals. For example, the general descriptions might be to meet with the public, or to liaise with multi-agency representatives. The alternative, the action-oriented approach, provides more specific descriptions of the activities involved in achieving the tasks; for example answering telephone queries or ensuring that post is delivered by 3.00 p.m. The decision to use one method over another is in part due to the nature of the tasks. Tasks where the goals can be accomplished in a variety of ways may be better discussed in terms of general features, since a specification of the way tasks might be achieved is restrictive. For example, there are many ways in which a job candidate might be expected to liaise with representatives from other agencies, whereas there are a limited number of ways in which post would be delivered.

Let us distinguish between these two methods by discussing the job of a university lecturer or professor who is required to teach a course. The job of the professor can be described in two different ways. One focuses on the tasks involved in terms of successful results or goals; for example, to provide students with scholarly review of the area and to provide students with comprehensive understanding of current literature. The other is focused on the specific actions involved; for example, giving oral lectures on selected topics, providing written handouts and overheads, being available for students during office hours, and so on. This latter description arguably can be more easily translated into individual requirements, or person specification. The job specification, to give oral lectures, can be translated into the person specification, such as the need to have good communication skills.

As the label implies, personnel psychology is concerned with assessing individuals and selecting the right person for the job. Research into psychological characteristics, such as intelligence and personality traits, has had a huge impact on individual recruitment and selection (see 'The court room', Chapter 5, p. 100 for a discussion of personality tests, and p. 101 for a discussion of projective tests). In particular, **standardized psychological tests**, which aim to measure stable, individual characteristics, are regular tools in personnel selection. Many standardized tests rest on the assumption that people have core characteristics in their personality that stay constant across different situations and contexts (see also 'The crime room', Chapter 4, pp. 52–6, on criminal profiling). The standardized test is designed to measure these stable traits, and, as a consequence, help employers to select people who have the necessary requirements to do the job.

To be useful, standardized tests should demonstrate satisfactory levels of **validity** and **reliability**. Validity can be loosely defined as a demonstration that the test is actually

---

BOX 6.4 AN ALTERNATIVE VIEW OF INDIVIDUAL DIFFERENCES

Some psychologists argue that there is little convincing evidence for stable personality characteristics, and point out how unpredictable the same person can be in different situations (Mischel 1968). Instead of stable internal characteristics they argue that it is the similarities in the situational demands in which people find themselves that create apparent stability in behaviour. For example, Lambie and Marcel (2002) challenge the notion of a unified self, and consider multiple selves. Each different self is appropriate for and responds to different aspects of the individual's emotional life; for example, professional self, mother self, daughter self, etc. (Lambie and Marcel 2002). According to this view, there are critical features in all everyday situations that dictate the behaviour of the person. Any consistency in the person's behaviour is due to the overlap in the features of situations, not to any stable personality traits. This view has more in common with the **existential approach** to personality (see Chapter 8, pp. 183–4), where the person's psyche is said to be in a constant state of choice, development, and change.

---

measuring what it claims to be measuring. For example, if a test claims to measure a person's ability to fixate rapidly on visual objects, the researcher must be sure that it is not measuring some other factor, like colour blindness, that might affect performance. Reliability can be loosely defined as the stability of the measurement, across time and different testing sessions. A reliable test is one that is not affected by changes in testing situations or contexts. For example, if a test claims to measure a stable psychological characteristic, like **trait anxiety**, the test should demonstrate consistency, so that the same person scores roughly the same across different testing sessions. A person who scores high on trait anxiety at time 1 should also score high on trait anxiety at time 2. Note that it is this characteristic of trait anxiety that distinguishes it from **state anxiety**, which is expected to vary form situation to situation.

Training and assessment

Another important aspect of personnel psychology involves training and assessment. In training, the psychologist is concerned with developing ways in which the individual can be supported to learn new skills or improve old skills. In assessment, the psychologist focuses on ways in which the individual can learn to self-assess and monitor their own performance. Often the two are related: generally, those skills that are the focus of training and are those that employers want to assess.

There are two approaches to training and assessment. One addresses the needs of the hypothetical average worker whereas the other addresses the specific needs of the individual. Many formal training programmes in organizations and institutions take the average-worker approach to training and assessment. With this approach, the minimum essential skills, information, and knowledge needed to perform the task(s) are identified and then presented to all individuals in the same manner. No provision is made for the fact that different people learn in different ways and at different speeds; or that people come to training with different attitudes, experiences, and abilities. As a consequence, people can leave the same training with vastly different levels of accomplishment. Because the training has adopted the average approach, assessment of competency, too, must rely on the principle of the least-common denominator; competency is thus based on the *minimum* acceptable level of competence, as defined by the organization or institution.

In recent years, institutions and organizations have been concerned with making assessment procedures more transparent. This has given rise to the notion of training aims, goals, or outcomes. Aims and goals identify for the person what the intention of the training is and what the person will be learning; for example, 'to improve your ability to deal with the public, we will be teaching you how to engage the audience'. Outcomes typically tell the person what they will be able to *do* after the training; for example, 'you will be able to make more eye contact with the audience more often'.

The second approach focuses on the specific requirements of the individual. In recent years, the concepts of *coaching* and *mentoring* have emerged as popular models in this tradition. Coaching and mentoring support the individual by assessing their own individual strengths and weaknesses, and providing a training that suits that person's specific requirements. Attention is given to the individual's unique abilities, aptitudes, and skills. Areas of improvement (goals), and how to assess change (outcomes), are identified in a concrete fashion. For example, a coach or mentor may be asked to help a person improve communication skills when delivering formal talks to prospective clients. The person is asked to give a short talk and a videotape is made. The coach then views the tape with the speaker, noting the different positive or negative non-verbal signals they were giving; for example, the number of times the person made eye contact with the audience. Improvement is then monitored in terms of concrete behaviour; for example, the number of times the person looks at the camera across successive talks.

Learning and individual differences

There are very good reasons why training *should* be concerned with individual differences. It is possible that average-worker training courses can create learning environments that are not only foreign, but also hostile to the individual. For example, Satinder Gill (1995) has found that the learning methods preferred by nurses on professional development courses allowed group discussion, where participants were allowed to exchange personal experiences. However, these teaching methods were completely unacceptable to doctors and consultants, who consistently preferred formal, didactic methods of training with little personal self-disclosure. The problem for large institutions or organizations is that the sheer number of people who require training and assessment make individual coaching and mentoring inefficient. At the same time, it is impossible to develop a programme of training that can accommodate the needs of all individuals and all organizations. Such questions are difficult to resolve and decisions about training and assessment must ultimately consider convenience and financial restrictions.

Nevertheless, mainstream psychological theory has been very influential in helping organizations come to terms with the problems of training and assessment. For example, Bandura's **social learning theory** (Bandura 1969) has been one of the single most important influences in the development of training programmes. This learning theory argues that through the act of observation, a person learns how to behave and how to act. This passive viewing of the other is called **vicarious observation**. Vicarious observation in part forms the basis of traditional, on-the-job apprenticeships, whereby novice workers are given the opportunity to observe and work alongside other experienced, skilled workers. Social learning theory argues that such vicarious observation can be as powerful as formal training in which the individual is being taught skills for the job directly.

The place of cognitive psychology

In recent years, developments in cognitive psychology have become progressively influential in devising training programmes. For example, many cognitive theories assume that the learner is an active participant in acquiring skills and knowledge (e.g. Gibson 1966). The person actively searches the environment and selects and responds to its conditions, rather than being passive, like a sponge, soaking up the available information. This notion of active learning has been appropriated into training programmes, with the individual actively engaging with the materials to be learned, as in practical exercises or role plays.

Other imports from cognitive psychology are the distinctions between **formal, declarative**, or **explicit knowledge** and **tacit, procedural**, or **implicit knowledge** (see Box 6.5). With formal knowledge, the emphasis is placed on the worker being trained to know *what is required of them*; with tacit knowledge, the emphasis is placed on the worker being trained to know *how to perform their skills*. A good example is a nurse taking blood from a patient. The nurse must have formal knowledge regarding the procedures, or must know *what* to do; for example, knowing what procedures must be followed before the needle is inserted in the arm and knowing what to do after the needle is inserted. The nurse similarly must have procedural knowledge, or know *how* to do; for example,

---

BOX 6.5 WAYS OF KNOWING

One of the most important theoretical arguments in cognitive psychology involves the debate over the nature of knowledge. Knowledge can take different forms, and each form has different characteristics associated with it. For example, some theorists have distinguished between formal and tacit knowledge, while others make the distinction between **declarative** and **procedural knowledge** (e.g. Anderson 1983). While the terms differ, as do the specific characteristics, the overall distinction is between knowing *that* or knowing *what* versus knowing *how*. Formal, or declarative, knowledge refers to information that can be verbalized, or imparted through formal communication, such as lectures, papers, etc. In contrast, knowing *how* is usually associated with tacit or procedural knowledge. Such knowledge is generally assumed to be difficult to impart through verbal means, and reflects the person's ability to know how to do something.

knowing how to put the needle into the vein, knowing how much pressure to put on the arm, etc. Arguably, the nurse cannot satisfactorily do her job unless she is competent in both. Failure in knowing what to do could endanger the patient. However, failure in knowing how to do the task will result in pain and discomfort for the patient. Training courses now appreciate the importance of workers developing sufficient competencies in both formal and tacit knowledge.

It is not surprising that training is an important area for the psychologist's input. Of course, as technology has developed, so too have the ways in which we work. Without question, the computer has become a dominant feature of many working environments. Because of this, psychologists have been forced to consider quite specifically how best to train people to use computers, and how to make computers easier to use. In response to this, the area of human–computer interaction (HCI) has developed into one of the major topics of interest for psychologists acting within the work environment.

Human–computer interaction (HCI)

Cognitive psychology and theories of information processing have been highly influential in dictating the manner in which such investigations occur. A great deal of attention has been placed on discovering ways in which human–computer interactions could be improved. The early work, when computers were still in their relative infancy, focused on a variety of factors, such as text display and **means-steps analyses**. In the main these early studies were interested in mapping computer operations onto normal cognitive operations, so computers could become friendlier to the user. For example, early work provided clear evidence that people need to be able to see a certain amount of text in order to understand what they are reading. When the screen displayed too little text, the person was unable to remember sufficiently what had come before. This resulted in considerably poorer comprehension, and meant that they were forced to return to the earlier text, an unnecessary and cost-ineffective action. This early work had a significant impact on computer design; for example, the modification of text sizes (e.g. the zoom function).

The work of Barnard and Grudin (1988) provided essential evidence regarding the ease with which names and icons depicting software functions can be understood by the user. For example, the term 'edit', as a mnemonic to describe a function, is only useful if there is a clear semantic relationship between the term and what the user believes the act of editing to mean. If the user would not describe the act of changing text as editing, then the mnemonic will prove difficult to learn.

Early computers were often plagued by using terms that bore little resemblance to those that would be used by the average, non-computer user of language. For example the term 'stack', used to identify currently active memory, bears no convincing relation to the ordinary uses of the term. The layperson has no way of knowing that it refers to the sequential organization of the memory store and hence has no reason to use it.

Other research examined the functions of pictorial instructions, and the use of icons to specify actions. For example, Barnard and Marcel (1979) were asked by the Post Office to provide a pictorial way in which postal workers could be trained to use new equipment. They found that pictorial instructions were only effective to the extent that they provided a clear indication of the *sequence* of actions, the necessary pre-conditions for an action to occur, and a clear depiction of what the action should produce. Similar attention has been given to what might be considered the ergonomics of human–computer interactions—the size of visual display units, workstation layouts, and so on.

The problem of stress

As our views towards work change and what we do evolves, so do the topics that preoccupy psychologists operating in the work environment. One of the fastest-growing topics is work-related stress. Regardless of the organization—from governments to the local bank—employers are progressively more concerned about the cost in terms of time and money of work-related stress and resultant employee absenteeism, litigation, and premature retirement. Psychologists are becoming more actively involved in assessing the healthy, and unhealthy, dynamics of the work environment. Work-related stress is likely to be the result of a combination of two sets of factors. One of these comes from individual differences in resiliency; for example, how much outside social support the person has. The other arises from organizational sources of stress, such as those that are associated with being the professional and doing the job. Factors that influence an individual's resilience to stress will be discussed in more detail when we consider the treatment of stress disorders (see Chapter 9, pp. 221–43).

Cooper and Marshall (1988) have identified factors that contribute to organizational stress. These include factors that are intrinsic to the job, as well as roles with the organization. For example, factors intrinsic to the job for a police officer include dealing with crime and the immediate effects of crime on its victims. On the other hand, part of the role of a police officer is to *protect* the general public against crime. Arguably, both of these intrinsic and role factors directly influence the amount of stress experienced by the average police officer. Cooper and Marshall also classify factors in terms of the organizational culture—work relationships—and career prospects and development.

For example, the organizational culture of the police is not one that promotes discussion of anxiety and stress. The police officer is meant to be able to deal with the job and the emotions that go along with the job. As such, the anxiety or stress that a police officer may experience is in the context of an organization that does not formally recognize the need to deal with anxiety or stress. All these organizational factors are assumed to interact with external, non-work-related factors, like domestic problems, social support, and physical robustness. Together, they determine how well the person responds to the stresses and strains of everyday working life.

Organizational psychology

Organizational psychology is concerned with understanding all aspects of groups, from how individuals form groups and develop group norms, to how groups make decisions. Groups require people to interact socially. Some social interactions are formal, such as those designated by job roles, and others are informal, such as those that develop because of common personal interests. Groups go through stages of development, commonly referred to as forming, storming, norming, and performing. Many things affect how a group develops, like leadership and perceived cohesiveness between group members.

Groups are one of the most important aspects of our working environment, and they are the major focus of interest for what is traditionally called organizational psychology. Regardless of what we do for our living, our working environment requires us to interact with people at two different but related levels. One level is the social interaction that comes from us *working in* the organization, and represents our *formal social interactions*. The other level is the social interaction that results from *working with* other people in the organization who have similar interests or opinions, and these represent our *informal social interaction*.

What we do, and how our job role fits within the formal structure of the organization, largely determines formal social interactions. Obviously, formal social interactions will be different depending on the more global structure of the organization or institution. For example, the Fire Service has a very well-defined structure based on levels within a rigid hierarchy. Because of the nature of the organization, formal social interactions generally acquire an autocratic style, where people in the lower hierarchy are told *exactly* what to do by people higher up in the hierarchy. So, in the Fire Service, fire-fighters are told to do specific job, and are assigned specific roles, such as operating machinery, entering buildings, and so on. People who outrank them, such as junior officers, give them orders.

In contrast, other hierarchical organizations have formal social interactions that are less autocratic. For example, university departments are hierarchical, in that they have different levels of seniority, and different roles, tasks, and responsibilities within the department. Still, the characteristics of the formal social interactions are very different from the Fire Service. A lecturer will, of course, have some explicit, non-negotiable formal social interactions. There are yearly assessment exercises, where the line-manager, usually someone senior in title or experience, will consider how the lecturer might develop professionally, such as to publish more peer-reviewed papers. However, it is highly unlikely that the line-manager would tell the lecturer *exactly* what paper to write.

Informal social interactions reveal the sub-groups that form within the larger organization or institution. Sub-groups are formed through common interests, and can develop into friendships outside the work environment. Informal social interactions can have a massive impact on an individual's performance. A good example of the power of an informal social interaction is the office romance, which is notorious for changing the working environment, not only for the lovers but also for the innocent co-workers who happen to be bystanders!

The evolving group

Most psychologists agree that groups go through different phases, or stages of development. Early on, Tuckman (1965) identified four distinct levels in small groups. These include forming, storming, norming, and performing (Tuckman 1965). The first stage, forming, establishes the group initially. Forming requires the individual members of the group to identify their common goals or attitudes and embark on negotiations with each other. Potential group members must compromise, so that the group can actually be established. For example, during the forming stage individual members may feel that one of the main goals of the group should be to promote better general health awareness at work. However, one member may not be concerned with general health awareness, but only with the effects of stress at work. However, rather than demand that stress at work be the focus, this person will concede, be confluent, in order to ensure that the group can form.

Storming, as the name implies, is less about compromise and more about the emergence of conflict between members. Once the group is sufficiently formed—so that the group is actually established—conflict erupts. Group members can argue over the specific procedures that are to be adopted, or the specific roles that each group member is assigned. For example, one person in the group may feel that they are particularly well suited to the role of leader, as they have more experience than the other group members have. However, one or two group members may dispute this, and a leadership battle will ensue between sub-groups. While uneasy, storming is an essential stage of group formation, as this is when group members get some idea about one another's personalities and behaviours. Conflict is a vital element in any healthy group; without it, the potential strengths and weaknesses of the group will not be realized.

Norming involves the group becoming more ordered, with conflicts beginning to get resolved. During this stage, individual members begin to agree on formal and informal rules of the group—such as what is acceptable group behaviour and what is not. For example, suppose most of the group agrees that it will, as a whole, informally support all health claims made by workers, in the first instance. However, suppose one individual member disagrees and believes that each specific worker's claim should be viewed separately to see if it merits support. The group may take explicit sanctions, and the renegade member may be asked to resign or withdraw from the group. There may also be implicit sanctions. The wayward individual may fail to receive e-mails regarding dates of important future meetings.

The final stage is performing. The group becomes a stable unit, and has well-defined characteristics. Individual members operate in conjunction with each other to fulfil the goals of the group. Individual members do not indulge in inter-personal conflicts, although some disagreements or differences may never be resolved. The group develops a collective identity, with individual members knowing what and how to perform their roles within the group.

Cohesion and leadership

Obviously, many factors affect whether a group is successful. One of the more important factors is *group cohesiveness*. Some definitions of group cohesiveness put emphasis on the levels of interaction and compliance among group members (e.g. Coolican et al. 1996,

p. 230). More frequent and significant interaction between members promotes better cohesiveness. For example, a group will obviously be more cohesive if it conducts regular weekly, three-hour meetings rather than have two, semi-annual, one-hour meetings a year. Groups that are more cohesive also have group members who are compliant, and go along with the rules.

However, we must remember that group cohesiveness is just a general term for *how group members are like each other*. For example, members can be like each other in the way that they behave. They can act the same, wear similar clothes, or have similar haircuts. Members can also hold the same beliefs, or attitudes. For example, members of an advertising group are likely to hold similar beliefs and attitudes regarding the importance of their own occupation to the world's economic growth. Finally, individual members feel the same about some things. All members of the advertising team feel confident in their abilities, and are highly motivated to acquire large, lucrative accounts.

Significantly, outside threat is potent in increasing group cohesiveness, as is illustrated in trade-union disputes. The improper intervention of management can promote more group cohesiveness than often was present prior to the intervention, and lead to the us-versus-them attitudes sometimes verbalized by both sides of a trade-union dispute. Intriguingly, once us/them develop into intransigent positions, only a mediator, an independent person who facilitates discussion, can resolve the impasse.

Leadership is another factor that influences group cohesiveness and it has captivated psychologists' attention, for good reasons. The leader can determine the success or failure of a group, and can unite or divide the group. Psychologists have been interested in understanding different characteristics of leadership and linking these to outcome measures, such as how group productivity or group satisfaction is affected. For example, the group can select or choose its own leader, like some political leaders. In contrast, employees are not given any power in the appointment of their line-manager, and an external factor, the organization, makes such decisions. It is assumed that when groups select their leaders, group members are more satisfied and happier to comply with the demands of the leader. There are certainly different styles of leadership. Some leaders listen to subordinates' views, while others offer little in the way of guidance and allow people to get on with their jobs. Regardless of a person's leadership style, a leader can only be assessed in terms of the group members, and the task of the group. Certain circumstances, like war, may require leadership that is less democratic and more autocratic, in order to ensure the survival of the group itself (see Chapter 7, pp. 143–4).

A long-standing debate is whether leaders are born, or made. This is essentially the age-old debate regarding nature versus nurture. Here, the question is whether a leader is someone who has a genetic predisposition to lead, or whether a leader is someone whose experiences and environment have promoted and facilitated the development of leadership qualities. Psychologists have similarly debated whether it is the character of the person that makes a leader, or the actions of the person that make a leader. As with most debates, the answer seems to be that a leader does have certain qualities—some inherent, others learned through experience—as well as possessing the ability to execute the tasks required of a leader.

SUMMARY

We have shown that the early interests of psychologists over a century ago are still as important in today's working environments. While the nature of the way we work has changed, the problems we encounter are the same: how to train people to do the job, how to select the right person for the job, the importance of good leadership on group morale, and so on. The work room is somewhat unique in that it offers more possibilities to apply psychology than any other real-world setting. We have shown that cognitive psychology, animal psychology, social psychology, personality theories and standardized testing, and motor and movement psychology have all contributed towards our understanding of our working environment. Given the amount of time we spend in it and the importance we place upon it, the work room must continue to explored by psychologists. The work room, more than any other, allows us to explore and understand human behaviour, both of the individual and of the group.

SCENARIO ONE

TRAINING INTERVIEW STAFF

This first scenario looks at the problem of training (see above, pp. 112–13). As we have already shown, training can be made to fit the average worker, or, as happens in coaching, can be made to apply to a specific worker. Regardless of the particular type of training, generic or individual, there are two general aspects that training must provide. One is that training must enable the person to do the job: the training must provide sufficient information so that the person can actually execute the job in hand. The other is that training must enable the person to believe that they can do the job. This aspect of training involves more the psychological component of readiness and preparedness for the skills required of the job. In order to establish that both these aspects are covered in training, there must be some evaluation of the relevance and appropriateness of the training programme. Evaluation requires two things: an assessment of the objective performance of the worker, and a subjective assessment of how well the worker feels prepared to do the job. Importantly, the two are not necessarily correlated. One deals with the person's actual performance; the other deals with the person's feelings regarding their performance, or how well prepared they feel that they are for the job.

For example, suppose a training programme instructs a worker on how to use a new piece of software. An objective evaluation of how well the worker performs may be the number of errors the user makes with the new software. The subjective evaluation will include how well the worker felt the training programme addressed issues that concerned them, how well the trainer put across the information, how clear were the instructions for use, and so on. This distinction between objective and subjective is reminiscent of the Hawthorne studies, which stress the importance of the psychological robustness of the worker within their environment, rather than just the performance of the tasks.

It is interesting to consider which aspect of evaluation is more important to an organization. While it is important that workers feel they have improved, it is likely that an organization will want some objective way to measure this improvement. Should no objective improvement be noted, the company or organization may decide that the training programme is unsuccessful, as is the case in the following scenario.

The following scenario also illustrates the importance of considering the cognitive components of a task confronting the worker. Names of the firms involved have been changed in the interest of confidentiality. The working environment is often filled with conflicting and competing bits of information, as is the case, for example, with air-traffic controllers. Given the huge amount of changing information that they must process, it becomes essential to train them to attend to the appropriate pieces of information, and integrate them appropriately, ignoring some aspects in favour of others. Attending, or not attending, to the wrong piece of information at the wrong time can result in serious consequences. In the scenario that follows, workers are confronted with a similar problem regarding how to attend to and retain different bits of information while doing their job.

What was the situation?

A market-research company, Atlas Market Research, had recently won a very large contract from a very large multi-national car company, Nukar, to evaluate the car company's recent training programme. Nukar's training programme not only focused on customer relations, but also was designed to promote the newest model of an economy car that needed to sell well in order for the company to reach projected targets. The training programme instructed people in a variety of topics known to influence customer attitudes and relations. For example, conversation is more effective when the customer feels welcome, and this can be accomplished by using the customer's name regularly, and by making regular eye contact. Nukar wanted to be sure that the sales people were not only using effective communication devices, but were also promoting the new model sufficiently.

BOX 6.6 THE IMPORTANCE OF BODY LANGUAGE

A substantial part of effective communication involves the role of body language. Here the emphasis is on the unconscious signals that a person shows through their body movements or facial expressions. It has long been assumed in psychotherapy that the body has a direct link with both cognitions and emotions; and that the body movements and facial expressions betray how the person is really feeling. For example Willhelm Reich, an early disciple of Freud, argued that early psychological and physical traumas are kept in different parts of the body, such that certain movements result in deep emotions being felt. The work of Satinder Gill and her associate (Gill and Borchers 2003) on social gestures within the work context also illustrates how gestures can encourage or discourage help from co-workers. For example, they have shown that large, vertical movements are used to get a co-worker's attention and draw them into the 'problem space'. These elements of non-verbal communication are important determinants of human interaction.

In response to Nukar's request for an evaluation, Atlas came up with the novel idea of the pseudo-shopper (PS). The PS would pose as a real customer, pretending to have real requirements, but would, in fact, be a stooge for the company. They would report back on various aspects of their interactions with the sales people. Critically, the PS could be directed to look out for any specific techniques that had been promoted during training. Nukar embraced the idea of pseudo-shoppers, and Atlas secured the contract.

Atlas did not have much experience with the concept of a PS, so had not carefully considered whether the PS would need much training. After some discussion, Atlas decided that each PS should be given an information booklet that specified showrooms, times of visits, and a personal background; for example, whether the PS was single, had children, used the car for business, and so on. Given that Nukar was concerned about promoting its new economy model, each PS was given specific dialogue to learn, with questions that they had to ask about the new model. In addition, the PS was asked to pay attention to a variety of other factors, such as the general physical condition of the showroom, the type of background music that was playing, and other details.

Each PS was asked to visit three different showrooms over the course of three days. In order to reduce costs, the PS was only allowed to make one visit to each showroom. After each visit, the PS filled in a 100-item questionnaire that asked about various aspects of their visit: overall friendliness, number of staff visible, number of staff wearing name tags, number of times staff made eye-contact, and so on. The PS was required to return the information packets, with all questionnaires completed, at the end of the three days.

Why was the psychologist involved?

Within days it was apparent that something had gone badly wrong. Few of the PSs had visited the requisite number of showrooms, and even fewer were able to complete the questionnaires. The situation was urgent. Atlas had only a few weeks before the scheduled meeting with Nukar, at which time they were meant to demonstrate whether or not Nukar's training programme was succeeding. Atlas had charged Nukar a very substantial sum of money and it was apparent that if they failed to 'deliver the goods', not only would their contract with Nukar be in serious jeopardy, but their reputation would also suffer. Atlas could afford neither outcome. With these serious consequences in mind, they felt that they had little choice but to import some psychological expertise. Atlas contacted a national accrediting body for psychologists, who gave them the telephone number of a specialist in applied psychology. At the initial meeting with the psychologist, Atlas outlined the problem. They were clear that they wanted to continue to use PSs, although they acknowledged that there were real difficulties. The psychologist asked to see completed questionnaires, the information packet given to the PS, and a copy of the original contract with Nukar. The psychologist also asked for any comments that the PS had made, in order to understand any difficulties that might have arisen for them.

What concepts might be relevant?

The psychologist realized that a task analysis would provide the best indicators of the problems confronting the PS and hence the concepts that might be important to consider. Having broken down the tasks of the PS into their components, the psychologist began to identify the problem areas. The PS had to perform multiple, complicated tasks. For one, they had to remember to ask certain questions about the new model, and so had to remember verbatim details of what to say. Importantly, they also had to remember how the sales persons responded. In addition they had to attend to a variety of perceptual features, like the condition of the showroom, how many cars were on display, the number of staff wearing name badges, the number of times the sales person used their first name, and much, much more! Thus the psychologist began to develop a picture of the problems confronting the PS. Most had to do with problems about attending to the correct information, and retaining the information long enough to fill in the questionnaire.

One concept that is obviously relevant is that of *selective attention*. This type of attention can be described in a number of different ways. Gestalt theories of perception discuss the selection of **figure** versus **ground**, while **signal-detection theory** discusses the identification of *target* or *signal* above noise. The basic ideas are the same. Figures or signals have recognizable properties: they have shape, contours, or regularity in patterns that distinguish them from the background, and they seem more important to the person, or have more meaning attached to them. An example is a person sitting in a room, having a conversation with their friend, when someone suddenly shouts 'Fire! Get out!' and a fire alarm goes off. The person will probably stop talking, regardless of where they are in the conversation, re-direct their physical orientation, and regard the pending danger from the fire alarm as being more important than continuing the conversation with their friend. Under circumstances where the environment is particularly rich, and teeming with differing modalities of sound, smell, vision, and touch, the level of distraction is greatest and it becomes more difficult to attend selectively to a single signal or figure. It requires more effort to discriminate between figure and ground when much is going on. For example, suppose your task is to notice whenever a particular person's name is announced over a public address system in a hotel lobby. In one situation, the hotel lobby is heaving with people coming in and out, there are delegates for two or three conventions that are checking in, and messages are being regularly broadcast over the system. In the other situation the hotel lobby is quiet, with only a few staff behind their desks, and no messages are being announced. It is obvious that one situation is more enriched and distracting than the other and that the task of hearing the name is more difficult as a consequence. As far as the psychologist was concerned, the task of the PS was like that of the person in a busy hotel lobby. It was apparent to the psychologist that the PS needed some form of help in learning how to make use of selective attention.

The problem would certainly be improved were the PS allowed to have some sort of reminder of the details to which they were meant to attend. However, notes or memory aids were not allowed as such aids could make staff suspicious and undermine the PS's disguise. As such, the PS had to remember to attend to certain bits of information and

---

BOX 6.7 IMPROVING YOUR PROSPECTIVE MEMORY

Current literature on prospective memory suggests that prospective tasks can be made easier or more difficult, depending upon the extent to which the person utilizes already existing schematic structures. For example, assume that you want to remember to pick up your dry cleaning. Research suggests that if you link this into some existing structure for the day, like picking up the children from school, it will be easier for you to remember to pick up the dry cleaning. Problems of prospective memory are frequently experienced by people who suffer frontal-lobe damage and have been the basis for important work done on memory aids.

---

ignore others, regardless of their personal significance, saliency, and so on. This type of memory, where the person is required to remember to do something in the future, is referred to as *prospective memory*. While not yet studied extensively, prospective memory problems are extremely common in everyday situations. For example, remembering to take one's pills, or remembering to pick up the dry cleaning, both reflect prospective memory.

Importantly, the PSs had no prior experience in the type of selective attention required of them. Evidence from studies on learning illustrates that tasks for which the learner has little prior experience benefit from practice trials. Practising a musical instrument, for example, allows the person to develop physical skills and competence in the techniques of playing the instrument through sheer repetition. Thus, part of playing the piano involves being able to move the ten digits independently of each other and practice enables the person to become more proficient at this. With more practice, the task requires less conscious awareness and can be performed implicitly. The pianist has to 'think less' about moving the fingers and the ability becomes more automatic, freeing the player to divert attention and effort to other tasks. The pianist attends more to the quality of the finger movements, rather than whether they can produce them in the first instance. The effects of such practice, whereby the learner engages in learning how to do the task(s), have long been referred to as **warm-up** effects, and **learning-to-learn** effects.

The psychologist felt that the concept of warm-up effects and learning to learn would be important to consider in addressing the problems met by the PSs, since they had no previous experience of the task and no prior knowledge. In essence, they needed to learn first how to do the task required of them before going into the showroom. The psychologist felt that this could be achieved through some form of role play, where each PS could take on a different role, and get feedback on difficulties they were experiencing.

Another important concept is the nature of the memory task confronting the PS, in that the learning is *intentional*, in contrast to *incidental*. Intentional learning means that the individual deliberately wishes, or means, to learn and later remember the information. A good example of this is a consumer who hears an advertisement for a car loan and decides that the repayment conditions sound reasonable. The person will deliberately want to remember the details, including the telephone number, and so will repeat the number to themselves while they find a piece of paper on which to write it down. The consumer is deliberately interacting with the materials with the express purpose of wanting to reproduce the information later.

In contrast, incidental learning and memory occur when the individual interacts with some stimulus, or aspect of the situation, but does not have the deliberate intention of learning or remembering anything. Advertising campaigns often rely on incidental learning and memory, although they are unlikely to know this. An example of this is seen in promotional advertising in motion pictures. When a particular character is seen drinking a brand of soft drink, the consumer is given subtle information regarding the product, including what type of people use the product, what the consequences of using the product are, and so on. Later, the consumer will select that brand of soft drink when having a party, in part because of their exposure to the brand name during the movie. Exposure through incidental learning can work regardless of whether the person remembers being exposed to the target or not. Subliminal advertising works on the assumption that people do not need to know that they have been exposed to a target in order for them to learn about and remember that target later.

Other concepts focus on factors that relate to improving retention; that is, the ability to reproduce the information after the event. In the case of the PS, the method of retention required **recognition memory**, as well as **cued recall**. While recognition memory is generally considered an easier task than recall, both types of memory reporting are facilitated by **rehearsal**. This involves the individual repeating the information, and there are different kinds of rehearsal. Our consumer who wants to remember the telephone number for a car loan can do so by simply repeating the information. The rehearsal is regarded as superficial in that the person is not doing anything actively to change the information, or to relate the information to knowledge they already have. They are simply repeating it so that they can remember until it is written down. In contrast, if the person remembered the loan number by relating it to something they already knew, this type of rehearsal would involve organizing the information and would be considered to be deeper. For example, the number might be 1019513. The person could remember 10 as the month they were born, 19 as the day they were born, 51 as the year they were born, and 3 as the number of children they have. While much more complicated than merely repeating the number, this deeper, organized rehearsal enables the person to remember the information better and longer. The PS would be better off if they could use some form of strategy to remember, as sheer repetitive rehearsals would not work, given the huge amount of information that they needed to remember.

The psychologist also realized that the PSs had to remember different types of information, some very specific and some more general. Very specific information included the number of times a sales person used the PS's first name; more general information regarded how the PS rated the overall tidiness of the showroom. Some information is easier to remember than others. For example, imagine that you are asked to repeat verbatim the words used in an advertisement. It is likely that you will be able to give a reasonably good idea about the gist of what was said immediately after you see the advert and for some while after that. In contrast, it is much less likely that you

BOX 6.8 MODELS OF MEMORY

In early information-processing theory, where memory was described in terms of a *spatio-temporal metaphor*, rehearsal was thought to result in information being transferred from some short-term store to a more permanent, longer-term store. However, this view was challenged by theorists who were concerned with how information was processed rather than merely transferred. One particularly dominant hypothesis, put forward by Craik and Lockhart (1972), considered the quality of processing, in terms of *levels of processing*. For example, information processed in a shallow way would result in the person retaining superficial, sensory details; for example, the number of syllables in a word. In contrast, information that was processed on deeper levels would result in the person retaining semantic, conceptual or thematic details; for example, whether something was important or unimportant. A different approach was adopted by Baddeley and Hitch (1974), who were interested in defining the *functions* of the short-term memory store. They suggested that this store serves as a working memory, having limited capacity, that is used to bring together and hold in temporary storage the information needed to accomplish a particular ongoing task. Such a store would be a functional unit, independent of the nature of the current task, which might involve problem solving, learning, comprehension or other cognitive activities. The working memory model proved capable of predicting and explaining a wide range of experimental results.

BOX 6.9 STRATEGIC OR AUTOMATIC MEMORY?

The psychological literature has distinguished between attributes of an event that are automatically encoded and learned, from those that require more strategic efforts to be learned (e.g. Schneider and Shiffrin 1977; Shiffrin and Schneider 1977). For example, familiarity judgements, namely the ability to distinguish 'old' from 'new', seem to be the result of the automatic encoding of frequency information and do not require strategic efforts. This is certainly consistent with most recent evidence from neuropsychology, which highlights the role that the more primitive systems play in detecting old from new; for example, hippocampal activity. Equally, the developmental literature points to the finding that recognition memory develops very early in infancy, in some cases within hours of birth. Such diverse, converging evidence argues strongly that certain attributes of an event are easy to learn, and appear to be automatically perceived or hard-wired.

will be able to remember the exact words within a few seconds after you see the advert; and it is extremely unlikely that you will retain the exact words for weeks afterward.

What did the psychologist do?

The psychologist felt that one reason the project was failing so badly was that the PSs had not been trained to do their job properly. The psychologist believed that Atlas had failed to do an adequate task analysis of the multiple goals confronting the PSs and as a consequence had not prepared them adequately in training. For example, given that they had to fill in a questionnaire, it would be useful to have each PS familiarize themselves with the details to be remembered. In short, part of training someone to be a PS should be to make them familiar with the job they would be doing. If filling in a questionnaire were part of the job, then becoming familiar with the questionnaire would obviously help the PS to do the job more successfully. Unfortunately, Atlas's training programme had largely ignored such task-relevant details, and this resulted in the PS being poorly equipped to do the job at hand.

To this end, the psychologist considered what cognitive requirements were demanded from the PSs. On the basis of an initial task analysis, the psychologist developed a modified handbook. The new training handbook explained clearly the different things that the PSs would be expected to remember, and gave a series of tips that were intended to help them with their tasks. Suggestions included reviewing the questionnaire three or four times immediately before going into a showroom, as this would help the PS to remember details later. The handbook also discussed potential mnemonics that the PSs might use to help their memory. For example, the PSs were encouraged to make each visit to a showroom unique, say by going to showroom one in the morning, and showroom three in the early afternoon. This would make it easier to remember each visit, as there would be distinctive features that would distinguish one visit from another. The handbook also warned how memory could become less accurate with delay, and encouraged the PS to complete the questionnaire as soon after the visit as they could.

The psychologist was especially critical of the format and structure of the questionnaire. In particular, some of the questions were impossibly difficult to answer. For example, the PS was asked to specify the exact number of times the staff had used their first name: the options given were 0, 1, 2, 3, and 10 times or more. The psychologist pointed out that it would be very difficult for anyone to remember such precise details, and instead provided some suggestions for more general, easier ratings, like 'never used my name', 'used my name sometimes', or 'used my name extensively'. This more general information would be as informative and considerably easier to report.

The psychologist also told Atlas that the questionnaire asked for too much information, and that it would be difficult for anyone to remember so much information correctly. The easiest and most sensible remedy was to reduce the number of questions on the questionnaire. However, in order to do so, it would be essential to identify what Nukar wanted to know *most* about. For example, if Nukar wanted to know whether their staff were friendly, and that was very important, then a question should be included that asked the PS to rate how friendly the staff were, rather than how many times they used the PS's first name. Atlas claimed that it would be impossible to go back to Nukar now, as the company was expecting a final report within the next fiscal term. If they were to go back to Nukar at this late date, with such essential questions, it might not look good. The psychologist could therefore not proceed further, but did make some suggestions about how the questionnaire might be streamlined. For example, some questions were redundant, like Were the staff personable? and Were the staff friendly? These might be subtly different, but not sufficiently so as to warrant both of them being on the questionnaire.

How was the psychologist's input received?

The psychologist presented a modified handbook and a completed report to Atlas, reviewing the PS project, and noting the serious problems inherent in the design of the questionnaire. In the report, the psychologist concluded that the PS project was largely a disaster, and that Nukar was still not in a position to know about the behaviour of their staff, the conditions of their showrooms, and so on. Atlas was very disturbed that the psychologist had suggested so many major modifications to their project. The company was in a difficult position, as Nukar had already contracted out large sums of money for the PS scheme and were expecting a detailed report outlining the positive results of the project. Atlas regarded the psychologist's input as problematic and refused to take any further action regarding the PS project.

Nukar discovered, through insider information, that a psychologist had been involved and contacted the psychologist directly, asking for a copy of the report to Atlas. However, as the report was formally the property of Atlas, the psychologist could not ethically provide anything to Nukar. Out of courtesy, the psychologist informed Atlas of Nukar's request. Atlas provided Nukar with a report of their own, which, rather than criticising the PS project, argued how effective it had been. The psychologist was informed that their services were no longer required, and given a reminder that the contents of their report were the property of Atlas and could never be distributed without the company's permission.

SCENARIO TWO

EVALUATING AN ADVERTISING CAMPAIGN

In this scenario, we look at the problem of producing a good advertising campaign. Advertising represents a major way in which companies, organizations, and product providers communicate with potential consumers. Not surprisingly, psychology has played a large role in developing ways in which advertising can be most effective. Much of the energy for this work has come from *social psychology*; in particular, the study of attitudes. Attitudes would of course be important in consumer psychology, as it is assumed that our attitudes towards objects, products, and images will determine the way in which we act, including what we buy, what we chose to eat, what we choose to wear, and so on.

Because advertising relies on successful communication, the classic issues raised in the **information-processing** approach have also received a lot of attention. How much information is presented in an advert, how the information is presented, the number of repetitions or exposures to the advert, when the information is presented: all these will have a major impact on the quality of the communication to the consumer. Advertising campaigns must consider other factors as well, such as the affective or emotional component. The emotional component must be considered carefully; if the advert is too negative, people will not attend to it as they will find exposure to the advert too uncomfortable.

The following scenario highlights how difficult it is to develop a good advertising campaign, without considering details like the nature of the information that is being given, the manner in which people use the information, and the motivation people might have for changing their behaviour. As we shall see, advertising campaigns can be helped through a psychologist's input, and when no input is given they can often result in a waste of considerable sums of money, time, and energy.

The British Broadcasting Corporation (BBC) is a national media organization that provides the general public (both nationally and internationally) with radio and television programmes through its sponsorship from government funds and public licenses. In the late 1970s, the BBC announced that it planned to make major changes to the wavelengths assigned to its four radio channels, BBC Radio 1, 2, 3, and 4. Each channel provides very different types of programmes and each appeals to vastly different audiences. For example, BBC Radio 1 broadcasts what might be considered as popular music—for example the Top Twenty—whereas BBC Radio 4's programmes are concerned with news, current affairs, productions of radio plays, etc. The BBC had decided that two of the channels (BBC Radio 1 and 3) would occupy frequency positions on the medium-wave reception band (MW). In order to achieve this, some confusing changes were to be introduced. BBC Radio 4 would move from MW to a frequency on long-wave reception (LW) that was occupied by BBC Radio 2. In turn, BBC Radio 2 would move to the MW position held by BBC Radio 4.

Not surprisingly, the BBC was concerned that the public knew when the changes were to occur, and what the changes were. Any losses in the listening audience would have serious financial implications, as listening figures could be used to reduce government subsidies. Consequently, the BBC decided to introduce a campaign, extending roughly eight to ten weeks before it intended to introduce the changes. The campaign adopted a so-called saturation approach: there were repetitive jingles and formal announcements on all of the four radio channels; flyers were sent to all householders; and newspaper and television advertisements were taken out. On average, jingles and formal announcements were presented about ten times during the day's radio coverage.

Importantly, all of the jingles, announcements, or advertisements referred to the changes in terms of the new numerical position of the channels; for example that Radio 1 would be moving to 98.5 MW. These numerical frequency values were the only format in which information about the changes were presented, with one single exception; adhesive labels that were sent along with flyers. These labels were designed to adhere to radio dials so as to identify where the new location of each channel would be (radios in the 1970s, including car radios, were analogue, not digital, and all took the form of spatial dials).

Two psychologists at the then Applied Psychology Unit in Cambridge, UK, were curious as to the extent to which the campaign was being effective. After a few days they felt, as listeners, that the campaign had little impact on their memory. Despite being repeatedly bombarded with advertisements on the radio, neither psychologist could accurately report what the new numerical frequencies were. Both also experienced a certain amount of annoyance every time one of the catchy jingles was featured. Informal interviews with their colleagues confirmed that others were similarly ignoring the campaign, and that a majority had also found the campaign annoying. The two psychologists therefore decided that they would examine how effective the campaign actually was to the general public.

What was the situation?

The situation had to be viewed as a 'one-off': the BBC had decided to change wavelength frequencies and was unlikely to do so again. Importantly, the campaign was to continue for only eight to ten weeks, so there was a strict time constraint on any empirical investigation. As the campaign had only just begun and was still in its first week, the psychologists had to act promptly if they were to examine the effectiveness of the campaign across the time it continued.

Why were the psychologists involved?

The scenario represents an intriguing situation, where the client *did not* request any input; rather, the psychologists' involvement was self-motivated. However, it is essential to point out that, had the BBC requested advice, it is likely that the psychologists were not in any position to offer any *a priori* advice. There was little prior research on how people remembered radio channels. Although the psychologists doubted that the listening audience remembered their favourite radio channel by numerical frequency, they had no evidence to support their case. Consequently, the psychologists probably could not have advised the BBC on how to develop the best advertising campaign.

What concepts might be useful?

In order to consider what concepts were important, the psychologists paid close attention to the details of the advertising campaign. The campaign involved saturation advertising, to the extent that advertisements were repeated across weekday and

---

BOX 6.10 ORDINARY MEMORY FOR ORDINARY EVENTS

There are a number of important lines of research that examine how people remember everyday information. One example is the work of Ley and his associates. This investigator was concerned with how well people remember medical information imparted during doctor–patient visits, and found that many communication problems arose so that patients often did not have good memories for their visits (Ley 1978). This work highlighted the importance of well-known psychological principles such as the *serial position effect*; that information presented first is well remembered while information presented later is likely to be forgotten. Other work by Wagenaar (1978) investigated retention for publicly broadcast weather reports. Wagenaar reported that people's memory for weather reports was very low, in spite of the fact that the information was of high personal significance. He suggested that this poor retention was due to the fact that there was no higher-order structure, or **schema**, to the presentation of the information. These early investigations into learning and retention of everyday information offer excellent examples of research with **ecological validity**; that is, research with practical implications for the real-life environment (see Neisser 1976).

weekend programmes. The psychologists hypothesized that frequency of exposure over the period of weeks would be an important factor. A **total-time hypothesis** would suggest that eventually people would learn the new frequencies simply on the basis of this repetition alone. Given that advertising was repeated at regular intervals across the day's programmes, the campaign operated on a **distributed-practice** schedule. This approach separates different repetitions, so that the repetitions occur after some break. Theoretically, distributed practice should be more effective than **massed practice**, where repetitions are given in sequence, without any breaks. Traditionally, for best learning results, people should be given distributed rather than massed practice.

The psychologists also felt it was important to consider the attitude that people might have towards the changes. For example, it was important to determine whether listeners would care about any other channel than their favourite one. As such, they might only be concerned about where the new Radio 1 would be, rather than where any of the other channels would be. This attitude would ultimately effect people's attention as well.

How people attended to the campaign was also a serious problem. It would be obviously difficult for people to learn any new information regarding the changes if they could not sustain their attention to the advertisements. The psychologists assumed that many listeners would be performing more than one task while listening to the radio, such as driving a car or doing household chores. Therefore, it was possible that the competition in the environment restricted the listener's attention to the advertising campaign.

The psychologists were also were concerned with how the information was being presented. New information is easier to learn if it fits into an already existing structure. For example, consumers associate the colour green with nature. If an advertiser makes the product cover of an environmentally friendly soap green in colour, this is relying on an already existing structure, that green is associated with nature. The problem with radio frequencies is that no one knew how people were most likely to store and remember the information in the first instance. This, ultimately, would make learning more difficult, as was demonstrated in Wagenaar's work on memory for weather forecasts (Wagenaar 1978).

The psychologists strongly suspected that people do not normally remember radio channels in terms of their radio frequencies. However, the BBC's entire campaign

---

BOX 6.11 THE COCKTAIL PARTY PHENOMENON

The power of personal significance to grab attention is well illustrated in what is known as the cocktail party effect first described by Colin Cherry in 1953. This effect is based on a mundane observation. A person can be in a very crowded room, such as in a cocktail party, and be totally absorbed in conversation with someone. Suddenly, one's attention is re-directed by someone mentioning their name at the other end of the room. Cherry argued that the personal significance of one's name captures attention at the expense of all other information. Much of the early work on attention was concerned with establishing how this selective, filtered attentional system worked (e.g. Broadbent 1958).

BOX 6.12 UNDERLYING STRUCTURE IN MEMORY

The notion that there are organizational tendencies, or structures, has had a long traditional in discussions of learning and memory. Barlett (1932) considered the notion of **schemas**, which he borrowed from Sherrington's (1933) description of neural patterns in the brain. Barlett argued that schemas are means through which information is organized habitually. Schemas exert such effective influence that over time, or in the absence of detailed information, people will report information in accordance with what is dictated by prior schematic knowledge alone.

---

largely rested on the assumption that people remembered numerical frequencies, rather than the positions of the channels on the radio dial. In fact, it could be argued that any knowledge people did have regarding the position of radio channels was likely to be highly idiosyncratic and contextually dependent on the listener's own radio device.

The psychologists were also concerned about the difficulties people would have in re-learning information. In its most simple form, listeners had learned to associate radio channels and wavelength frequencies, for example that Radio 2 went with wavelength B, which is known as **paired associate learning**. One possible difficulty in learning the changes would result from **proactive interference**, where prior learning interferes with learning something subsequently. A good example of proactive interference is forgetting where you parked your car in a regularly used car park. Your memory for where you parked your car this particular time is overshadowed by all the other times that you've parked your car in the car park. However, the changes the BBC were introducing were even more problematic. The changes required people to re-pair old associations, so that Radio 2 now went with the wavelength associated with Radio 4, and vice versa. This re-pairing of **associations** is known classically in the **verbal learning** literature as an **A–B, A–Br paradigm**. Suppose you are asked to learn the pairs train–black and dog–queen, but are then asked to relearn train–queen and dog–black instead. This paradigm is generally associated with great difficulties in re-learning information, much more so than would be expected from other forms of interference.

What did the psychologists do?

The psychologists assessed the effectiveness of the radio campaign through two questionnaires presented to volunteer subjects from the existing subject panel of the Applied Psychology Unit. The first questionnaire provided some baseline measure of the extent to which people knew the current radio positions, and was completed eight weeks after the campaign had started, and one week before the intended changes were to be made. This was important if any assessment of the campaign's effectiveness was to be made. The questionnaire contained three sets of items. The first asked about people's listening habits for each channel. People were also asked to provide a brief description of the nature of the programmes that they would expect to hear on each of the channels. The last item in this set asked people to position each of the channels by placing a mark on a drawing that represented three radio receiver bands (VHF, MW, and LW). Each band provided a middle position, and two end positions, so as to give the person some scale. People were asked to write the frequencies under each placement for each of the channels, using the band to which they normally tuned. For all items they were allowed to respond with 'don't know' whenever appropriate.

The second set of items asked people about the proposed programme changes. Questions asked for general and specific descriptions of the intended changes, when the changes were to occur, and the source of their knowledge about the changes. This latter question provided alternatives such as formal or informal radio announcements, postal leaflets, television commercials, newspaper advertisements, or magazine advertisements. The last question in this set asked people to indicate the *new* position for each of the channels. The format for this was exactly the same as described for the old placements. Again, people were asked to write the new frequencies beneath their marks. A final set of questions asked people about any self-imposed memory strategies that they were using to learn the new positions, and whether they had made any conscious attempt to learn the exact frequencies of either the old or new channels.

Some two to three weeks after the changes were introduced a second questionnaire was distributed. People were asked if they had experienced any difficulties in learning the new positions; whether they had made any strategic attempt to learn the information; and, importantly, to specify any advertisements, etc. that were particularly useful in helping them learn the new channel positions.

The results of the first questionnaire showed that most people listened to the radio an average of two-and-a-half hours daily. Given that they had been tested roughly eight weeks after the start of the campaign, the average listener answering the questionnaire had been exposed to more than 1000 radio presentations regarding the changes. All people were aware of the nature of the changes, and nearly 85% could give the exact date for the changes. Postal information and radio announcements were cited as the most common sources for the changes. On the basis of this, the psychologists concluded that the campaign seemed effective in alerting the public to the changes, and when they would occur.

However, the data from the rest of the questionnaire were not as positive. First, there was the problem of people's lack of awareness of the numerical frequencies. Few of the people could accurately cite the numerical frequencies for the old channels and even fewer could accurately cite the new numerical frequencies. Given that the psychologists had suspected that numerical frequencies were not the mode in which people remembered radio positions, they decided to observe how well people placed their marks on the radio dials. The accuracy of the marks would correspond to visuo-spatial knowledge the listener had regarding the different channels.

The data were no better. For old channel positions, over half the listeners were unable to make an estimate, and less than a third were able to give an accurate placement for the best-known channel. For one of the band frequencies, more than 90 per cent of the people responded with 'don't know'. The same pattern emerged for knowledge of the new positions. Over 70 per cent could not provide any estimate of the new positions, with less then a quarter being accurate about even the most well-subscribed channel. On the basis of these data, the psychologists concluded that the campaign had largely been ineffective. People had very poor memory for old radio frequencies and positions, and, by and large, did not show much evidence of having learnt much from the saturation campaign.

The data from the second questionnaire confirmed these conclusions. Over 70 per cent of the people reported having great difficulties in remembering the new positions. Critically, the most helpful aid in remembering the new positions was the adhesive label, with nearly 50 per cent of people claiming that they were using the adhesive solely to remind them of the new positions. Thus, the campaign, which had been pursued vigorously over weeks and which had cost a considerable amount of money, was shown to have spectacularly little effect.

The psychologists delivered their findings to an international conference, and also submitted their data for publication. They also provided a preliminary report to the BBC.

How was the input assessed?

The psychologists' findings were peer-reviewed and considered acceptable for publication in a scientific journal (Bekerian and Baddeley 1980). The work was considered to illustrate the importance of integrating experimental psychology with real-world problems. The BBC chose not to respond to any correspondence and in some sense this was understandable. The psychologists had undoubtedly provided an interesting example of applied psychology. Equally, however, they had demonstrated that, in spite of considerable effort and money, the BBC, as an organization, had failed to produce an effective campaign.

■ **ADDITIONAL READING**

Hollway, W. (1991) *Work Psychology and Organisational Behaviour*. Sage Publications, London.

Porteus, M. (1997) *Occupational Psychology*. Prentice-Hall, London.

Riggio, E.R. (2000) *Introduction to Industrial/Organisational Psychology*. Prentice-Hall, London. These three books are among those most frequently cited as references in the field of occupational and work psychology.

■ **QUESTIONS**

Scenario one

1   Was it ethical for the psychologist to withhold his report from the companies who had commissioned the original project?

2   Given the psychologist's conclusion, how would you devise an organizational training scheme for employees to know whether they were complying with the requirements of organization?

Scenario two

1 Why should government agencies automatically consult psychologists before they introduce major changes that require the general public to learn new information?

2 Rather than take a cognitive approach, what other approaches may have been equally fruitful to consider?

7

The war room

In this chapter we consider the war room, which includes all topics traditional to the study of military psychology. Over the centuries tacticians and leaders have consistently used psychological concepts. While the execution of war changes with technology, many elements of the psychology of war do not. We consider the more general area of military psychology and discuss how psychology has been applied to practical problems such as assessment, selection, leadership, motivation, and morale. We show that the impact of the group is important not only for military precision, but also to ensure the emotional well-being of the soldier. We provide two scenarios that highlight very different applications of psychology. One of the scenarios illustrates how psychologists have been useful in improving the design of military machines, and reflects how psychology has influenced man–machine interactions. The other scenario shows how a psychologist's scholarly skills were put to use in a situation involving espionage.

The nature of conflict

In this section we first look briefly at the nature of conflict and conclude that we are an innately aggressive species. We then look at the distinction between the psychology of war and military psychology, our own area of interest, before proceeding to a recognition that the importance of psychological principles to warfare has a very long history.

We start out by concluding that we are a species that engages in violent behaviours against each other. We assault each other as individuals, and we assault each other as groups, whether as gangs, tribes, clans, religious groups, or nations. Some scholars argue that the absence of any other species of hominids is evidence that we, *Homo sapiens*

sapiens, are an aggressive, combative, social animal—so much so that we wiped out our more docile 'cousin' species.

Wars start when we, side A, cannot agree with you, side B, over some issue, and are unable, or unwilling, to use non-aggressive communication to resolve our differences. Once having decided that aggressive conflict is the way forward, we form strategies, and execute a plan, or plans, that will, we hope, result in us winning the dispute. Necessary to our success is, of course, an assessment of risk and loss. We must decide how much we are willing to sacrifice, how many lives we are willing to lose in order to secure our victory. However, regardless of the victor, we want to ensure that we have the necessary means to win another conflict—should the need arise—or, at least, protect and defend what we may have left. We will call the general context in which the planning and development of strategies for conflict and for peace occur the war room.

The war room exists in the real world whenever there is a conflict, or a truce, between two or more identifiable groups of people. For example, a conflict between the armed forces of different nations and a conflict between two local gangs would both yield some strategy of aggressive tactics, goals, etc. We shall see that most of the input that psychologists have had in the war room has been motivated by large, military organizations. Not surprisingly then, many of the topics we discuss are more clearly relevant to formal military organizations, like combat psychology and personnel selection. However, some of the topics are relevant to conflicts and truces, regardless of the sizes of the group, such as the importance of good morale and the effects of propaganda.

The psychology of war versus military psychology

Before beginning our discussion of some of the more traditional topics found in the war room, we first need to distinguish between the psychology of war and military psychology. The psychology of war is concerned with all elements of combat; for example, tactics, performance fatigue, duty rotation, and weapon use. Psychological principles are applied within the context of a combative environment where casualties are anticipated. Given that casualties are anticipated, the psychology of war must by necessity include discussions of highly specific topics. For example, leaders and commanders expect their soldiers in combat to become desensitized to seeing dead bodies and hearing the cries of the wounded. In some sense, being among casualties is part of the job and the soldier must somehow become immune to the emotional effects that this might have. However, seeing one's best friend die is likely to have an entirely different effect on the soldier, and may require specialized psychological treatment.

In contrast, military psychology is much more general, and covers aspects of war *and* peace. The *Corsini Encyclopedia of Psychology and the Behavioral Sciences* (2001) defines it as 'the application of psychological principles and methods to military needs . . . military psychology is not so much a separate field of psychology, but rather is defined by its area of application: military personnel and organizations . . .' (p. 957). For example, military psychology would include the examination of the effects of the combat environment on the soldier, as well as research regarding the effects of environmental factors that are present in everyday, non-combat life, such as the effects of having families on base, or the effects of reassignments.

In this chapter, we discuss issues that are traditionally considered under the general heading of military psychology, which by definition can include factors pertaining to combative environments.

The historical context of psychology and war

All scholars agree that modern military psychology is lodged firmly in the twentieth century, as we discuss below. However, we feel that it is essential to remember that, when we examine the war room, we are looking at a very old, surprisingly unchanged, real-world context. While the discipline of psychology may not have emerged until the late nineteenth century, the application of psychology to war has been common since the time of the ancients, and testimonials to this fact abound. There is Sun Tzu (*c*.500 BC), who considered open confrontation to be destructive ultimately, and instead advocated strategic manoeuvring so that you 'bend others without coming to conflict' (*The Art of Strategy*, p. 12, translated by R.L. Wing 1997). Sun Tzu argued that central tactical leadership and psychological manipulation were the elements of success: '[good leaders] lure through advantages, and take control through confusion' (ibid., p. 25). The importance of healthy morale among soldiers was noted by the Greek mercenary Xenophon two millennia ago: 'whichever army goes into battle stronger in soul, their enemies generally cannot withstand them' (quoted in Richardson 1978). This point was not lost, centuries later, on Napoleon, who claimed that 'Morale makes up three quarters of the game—relative balance of manpower accounts only for the remaining quarter' (Heidl 1967).

These quotes demonstrate that concepts of tactical leadership, strategic manoeuvres, and psychological manipulation were as relevant to past generals and leaders as they are to those operating in the twenty-first century. In this way, many topics pertinent to the war room remain as important today as they did 2000 years ago, in spite of the obvious changes in technology, weaponry, and combat practices. We admit that it is beyond the scope of this chapter to do justice to this fact. Nonetheless, we can still acknowledge that the leaders of ancient times knew the importance of psychological principles, and used them to secure victory and maintain peace, just as their modern, military counterparts continue to do.

Assessment, selection, and training

In this section, we consider the related topics of selection, assessment, and training. We look at the situations in which psychologists have been called upon to devise task analyses in order to ensure that the right soldier is selected for the right military task. We then look at how psychologists helped to discover the differences between good fighters and poor fighters, as well as identify the characteristics that make good leaders. Finally, we discuss the role psychologists have played in increasing the effectiveness of training. Modifications have included better opportunities to learn necessary skills and more realistic training programmes, such as those offered by simulations.

The First World War

The First World War was the starting point for modern military psychology as the Allied military forces needed fast answers to important questions. For example, there were the related problems of assessment and selection. Not everybody is equally well suited to join an army; and once in the army, not everyone is equally well suited to the same job. While these observations are obvious and probably universally accepted, the military still had the practical problem of discovering, in an efficient and speedy manner, the recruits who were unfit for military service. An obvious example was the problem of low intelligence. The military needed to know which recruits were of such low mental ability that they could not successfully engage in training. Another goal was to screen recruits so that the most appropriate recruits were allocated to each assignment. Yet another challenge was to devise the most efficient methods for training recruits, which would have to include not only training recruits to use weapons, but also preparing them for the realities of combat.

Psychologists were asked to help in these matters, to devise reliable and cost-efficient ways of assessing a recruit's abilities, to map these abilities to the most appropriate military job, and to develop effective training programmes. In this way, the First World War provided psychologists with their first formal opportunity to fit the worker to the job. In fact, many of the topics that we have already considered in 'The work room' (Chapter 6) first flourished in the context of the war effort, such as the application of **task analyses.** For example, the roles of a foot soldier require different physical and mental abilities from the roles of a vehicle driver. A psychologist's expertise in task analyses was invaluable. The psychologist could provide a way of identifying the actions that the task required and could identify the abilities that were needed to perform those actions. In this way, the psychologist was essential in helping to devise tests that could discriminate those who were unsuitable. In fact, during the First World War psychologists dominated the business of assessing ability and aptitude.

Psychological expertise in research design and analysis also proved vital. Psychologists could devise a series of standard questions to discriminate between those recruits who

---

BOX 7.1 THE BEGINNINGS OF PERSONNEL SELECTION

The earliest psychological studies on job–worker match, personnel selection, and leadership, and the effects of the physical environment, were in direct response to military questions that arose from conflicts during the First World War. Robert M. Yerkes, who was then president of the American Psychological Association, assembled leading psychologists to help in the war effort, in particular to help with the enormous task of assessing and selecting recruits. Under Yerkes's guidance, these psychologists developed a selection programme that assessed the mental suitability of recruits for different military jobs. The resultant standardized tests, the Army Examinations Alpha, for those recruits who could read, and the Army Examinations Beta, for those recruits who could not read, were used to screen about one million recruits. This early work with the military served as the starting point for many popular areas of psychological enquiry, especially those that are now considered under the traditional headings of organizational and occupational psychology.

would make good fighters and those who would make good pilots. However, without having expertise in research design and data analysis, we could not guarantee that our standardized test had any **reliability** and **validity**. Further, there was a limit to the extent to which the psychologist could *guarantee* an accurate prediction of a recruit's ability from performance on a standardized test.

Sir Frederic Bartlett, in *Psychology and the Soldier* (1927), addressed this issue directly when he cautioned against over-interpreting a recruit's fitness to perform a military task on the basis of his performance on examination tests alone. He concluded that it was relatively easy to devise tests that identified the unfit; however, it was much more difficult to be confident in decisions about the 'fit' candidate. Bartlett pointed out that examination tests, whether they measure mental abilities or practical skills, do not reliably take into account other factors that may have an effect on a recruit's ability to perform a military task. Bartlett cited an example where a recruit's condescending attitude towards his fellow recruits, and his lack of social cohesion with his *primary group*, resulted in '[his] high intellectual capacity...[being] prevented...from finding expression' (Bartlett 1927, p. 35).

Barlett felt that there were many factors that must be considered if selection and training are to be effective; among them is the person's **temperament**. Temperament does not reflect a single trait and is determined by a variety of personality factors, like a person's ability to tolerate change and ambiguity, their amicability and popularity, their ease in new situations, and so on. As Bartlett stated 'when a man presents himself for entry to any important social group in his country, the records of his intelligence rating and of his temperamental make-up ought to be as readily available as his ordinary health records. If these were made seriously at the proper time, the problems of building and training an efficient army would be considerably simplified' (Bartlett 1927, p. 37).

The Second World War

By the time of the Second World War, psychologists were major players in the recruitment, assessment, selection, and training of military personnel. Not surprisingly, as technological advances changed the manner in which war was conducted, selection tests had to change, becoming progressively more sophisticated. This meant that problems of allocation, namely how to match the recruit to the job, took priority. For example, as artillery equipment became more complex, the aptitudes and abilities of those who would be controlling them changed accordingly. Unlike rifles, some of these new weapons, such as anti-aircraft batters and aircraft guns, required collaborative efforts between groups of individuals. As a consequence, much of the selection and assessment procedures during the Second World War classified recruits not only on the basis of their ability to learn new tasks, but also in terms of their ability to work with others, and under stressful situations.

The Second World War also marked a change in the training of recruits. For example, during the First World War, the major model for training a soldier was through an apprenticeship, or **vicarious learning**. The novice soldier watched the experienced

---

BOX 7.2 ACTIVE COMBAT

One of the most important psychological studies that emerged from the Second World War is that of S.L.A. Marshall, who systematically examined the behaviour of combat troops, in his 1950 book *Men Against Fire*. Significantly, Marshall reported that only a small, consistent percentage of fighting soldiers actually ever fired at the enemy. Depending upon his sample, this varied from 15 to 30 per cent, with the latter only occurring in exceptional companies. These estimates stayed surprisingly constant, regardless of the type or length of combat action in question. Generally, if a man were to pull the trigger, he would do so from the start of his combat experience and continue to do so until the end. Importantly, the difference between fighters and non-fighters was not their courage, as the non-fighters were as likely to expose themselves to danger as their counterparts who pulled the trigger. Marshall's work highlighted how essential it is to consider the individual soldier's psychological make-up.

---

soldier and received tuition when necessary. In this way the novice learned what things needed doing, the sequence of actions required, and so on. This type of learning is compatible with the notion of *on-the-job training*, and is effective in that we all learn much of our everyday skills through social, vicarious learning. However, this type of learning is more likely to be successful when the person has repeated opportunities to learn, and is not under stress. Obviously, the conditions of war do not afford either to the newly enlisted recruit.

The psychologist was in an ideal position to provide some advice on how to improve training. At the forefront of any military training are two goals. One is to equip the recruit with some mastery of the skills necessary to perform his military duties, and the second is to prepare the recruit for the conditions of war. Fortunately, many psychological concepts could be directly translated into military training. For example, the importance of feedback on performance was introduced in the so-called quick-kill training method. A quick-kill training method has targets of silhouettes pop up unexpectedly and the soldier has to make quick decisions as to whether to fire or not. One of the basic principles of learning theory is that feedback (i.e. knowing how well you perform) improves performance. Applying this helped to promote target accuracy. When training programmes were reworked to include sound psychological principles, the recruit had a better opportunity to improve his military skills, and to be prepared for some of the conditions of combat.

The Korean War

By the time of the Korean War, there was sufficient evidence to suggest that careful selection, followed by adequate training, could dramatically improve the effective use of military resources. In particular, the earlier work of Marshall (1950), who showed that only a proportion of men actually fire against the enemy (see Box 7.2), indicated clearly

---

BOX 7.3 TASK MAINTENANCE

A related topic, which still poses one of the most important problems in today's military operations, regards skills maintenance. That is, how often does a person need to have a refresher course in order to maintain his level of skill? This is by no means a straightforward question as the answer requires at least three things. One, some task analyses must be performed in order to determine the necessary component skills to complete the task (e.g. to fire a rifle). Two, there would have to be some break-down of the differential rates at which these components are learned to a stable level. For example, aiming accurately to hit your target may be more difficult to learn than pulling the trigger once you have aimed. Three, there would need to be a similar breakdown of the differential rates at which these components are forgotten. For example, the skills necessary to aim accurately may require more prac-tice to maintain than the skills necessary to pull the trigger. Given the increasing complexity of the skills required to operate technologically advanced weaponry, it is not surprising that psychologists continue to be vital in the context of military training.

---

that the killing effectiveness of military units could be enhanced dramatically if the appropriate people were recruited and selected. To this end, much attention was given to identifying those individuals who had an aptitude, or ability, to be good fighters. While there were a few studies undertaken, the research conducted by the Human Resource Research Office (HRRO; an organization that was funded by the Army) is considered the more reliable.

Who makes a good fighter?

Researchers at the HRRO first focused on identifying the two groups of soldiers that they would be comparing: a *good* fighter group and a *poor* fighter group. (Note that this is different to Marshall's earlier comparison of *fighters* versus *non-fighters*.) The initial as-sessment of whether someone was a good or poor fighter was based on verbal reports, commendations, and first-hand reports from other men. Researchers found that good fighters exposed themselves more to enemy fire than poor fighters. However, even when being exposed to the same amount of fire, a good fighter systematically behaved differ-ently to a poor fighter. They assumed leadership when necessary (e.g. when the desig-nated leader is not operative), they engaged in aggressive acts outside the normal role of a leader (e.g. attacking another unit offensively), or they performed a supporting role (e.g. protecting another injured soldier while medical help is called). In contrast, poor fighters physically withdrew from engagement (e.g. when under fire they refused to re-turn fire), psychologically withdrew from engagement (e.g. obeyed orders only at gun-point), showed signs of mental dissociation (e.g. saw or heard things that were not there), and became emotionally labile (e.g. trembled and cried).

Soldiers in the two groups were asked to complete roughly eighty-six psychological tests, and consistent differences were found. Good fighters scored higher in terms of leadership, as assessed in terms of poise, spontaneity, extroversion, independence, and freedom from anxiety. Good fighters were also more likely to engage in adventurous

---

BOX 7.4 PROBLEMS WITH RELIABILITY AND VALIDITY

Such was the success of these standardized tests that many of them have been applied to other contexts, such as education and aptitude testing. Nonetheless, we need to be cautious about what we conclude from this early research. For one, the sheer number of psychological tests employed, and the possibility of extensive **covariability** among them, requires us to take a conservative view. For example, whenever there is a large number of tests, researchers must be concerned with increases in **experiment-wise error rates**. Simply put, the more tests we conduct the more likely it is by chance alone that we will accept a finding as significant when it is not. This problem certainly exists with the HRRO research, given that more than eighty tests were used. Second, there is the real question of co-variability among the different tests used. For example, the tests used to assess leadership may have examined factors that were highly correlated with other measures used to assess emotional stability. Therefore, we may simply be measuring different components of the same factor. Furthermore, while the data are reliable and consistent, there is no unifying psychological explanation for the findings. We need to stress this, as the presence or absence of a coherent psychological explanation is essential to good applied psychological research. Without a unifying theory, we run the risk of accepting and acting on findings for which we have no real understanding.

---

activities or sports and body-contact games. The researchers noted that *differences in masculinity* were among the most significant ones that they found between good and poor fighters.

Good fighters were also more intelligent, although there is a caveat to this. There was ample documentation that, as a group, combat soldiers were significantly *less* intelligent than men in other military branches, a problem that still confronts the Army today. Perhaps smarter people do their best not to get assigned to the front line! Nonetheless, the researchers concluded that the intelligent combat soldier made a better fighter than his non-intelligent counterpart. Perhaps related to this, good fighters preferred humour that was witty and sarcastic rather than simply telling jokes. Finally, good fighters were more emotionally stable, and less prone to anxiety or depression.

We cannot overestimate the importance of the early HRRO findings. Most crucially, many of the psychological tests identified could be administered *before* an individual engaged in combat, and this was highly advantageous to the military. The HRRO data were also important in helping to refine how soldiers got allocated to assignments. For example, the proportion of good fighters in a unit, relative to average or poor fighters, could now be manipulated. This in turn would have an impact on the effectiveness of different military operations. For these reasons, the research by the HRRO is one of the most important examples of applying psychology to the war room.

Who makes a good leader?

A related problem to the selection of a good fighter is the problem of selecting a good military commander and leader. This problem was particularly acute during the Second World War, and especially in the UK, where the normal methods of obtaining officer candidates (i.e. recruiting officers exclusively from public schools) became impractical.

BOX 7.5 ARE LEADERS BORN OR MADE?

The debate between nature and nurture is particularly relevant to a discussion of the selection of leaders. Are leaders born with the ability to lead, or can we make someone a leader by training them properly and putting them in the right situations? The question centres around the issue of whether the characteristics of an individual, be they personality traits, mental abilities, or emotional intelligence, are determined by genetic influences (i.e. nature), or by environmental and situational factors (i.e. nurture). As is often the case with psychological debates, there is evidence for both sides of the debate. Studies with twins are particularly popular in this context as they provide built-in controls for heredity and environmental factors. **Monozygotic twins** (i.e. identical twins) who are reared together show greater similarities on certain traits, like achievement, than **dyzygotic twins** (i.e. non-identical or fraternal twins), who are reared together. Such data support the view that nature determines who they will be and how they will act. On the other hand, identical twins who are reared together show greater similarities in achievement levels than identical twins who are reared apart. This provides evidence that environmental factors influence the person's development. The correct answer is undoubtedly a combination of both.

Some highly creative procedures were adopted to determine a candidate's leadership and command qualities, such as problem-solving situations rather than standardized question-answering sessions. These novel procedures included giving candidates real-life scenarios in which no solutions were obvious and where group cooperation was essential.

One of the most famous examples of a problem scenario is cited by Shelford Bidwell (1973, p. 112 ff.). The candidates were told that they had to make their way across a shark-infested river using only an oil drum, a plank, a piece of rope, and a few other tools. Candidates were observed in terms of how they performed, whether they emerged as leaders, and whether they showed flexibility in their problem solving and united the group's efforts. This method of selection proved successful and is still used today.

After the Second World War, psychologists were more directly involved in identifying the psychological characteristics that made for a good leader and commander. Psychologists discovered that a good leader is aggressive and good at problem-solving. They communicate clearly and explain reasons for commands. They demand a high level of performance from subordinates, explicitly reward good performance, and deal with failure constructively and without threat. A good leader is also able to mediate and dissipate tension between members of the group. Finally, a good leader identifies the outstanding qualities of his subordinates and uses them to best effect (i.e. assigns the most appropriate person to each task).

However, one of the most startling findings to emerge was that non-combat leadership and combat leadership required different characteristics and abilities. For example, a good non-combat leader was rigid with respect to rules, athletic, physically imposing, and tactful. This was not the case with a good combat leader. Highlighting these differences enabled the military to distinguish between the leaders needed during combat and those who were more useful during times of peace.

SUMMARY

By the end of the Korean War, assessment, selection, and training were major factors in determining the combat behaviour of both individual soldiers and their units. In this section we have reviewed research on soldiers' experience in combat zones and shown how these findings provided the basis for developing more sophisticated selection and training procedures. We have illustrated how better selection, through the development of standardized tests, allowed the right soldier to be assigned to the right military job. We have also shown that through better training, the soldier is better equipped to perform his tasks, thereby ensuring that he is more efficient and effective at his job. Improvements in training included better identification of the requisite skills that need to be mastered, and more realistic opportunities to engage in practice, such as in simulations.

This leads us directly to our next topic—the soldier's morale. Giving more opportunities to practice skills, and more realistic situations under which to practise, understandably improves the morale of the fighting soldier and his unit. Training prepares the soldier; and being prepared reduces the soldier's apprehension and unease about going into combat. However, the best selection and training in the world is useless if the soldier is unwilling to fight—has little 'heart'. The soldier must be willing to sacrifice and endanger himself, and must be willing to engage in hostile activities when directed to do so or when the situation demands it. To be truly effective, the soldier must be motivated to fight.

Morale and the fighting spirit

The morale of a soldier is a topic that has long captured the attention of students of military psychology. Morale is a complex concept and it is not easy to provide a clear-cut definition, as it is best seen as a combination of related factors. There are both situational and psychological factors that influence morale and these interact with each other. One of the most important psychological components is the soldier's motivation to fight.

While ancient leaders may have appreciated the vital importance of good morale, it has taken some time for modern military leaders to realize this. For example, leaders of the nineteenth century considered rigid discipline and routine to be more effective in producing effective soldiers than positive incentives like the promise of getting a few days leave. In fact, despite the extensive breakdown in morale after the First World War (notably in Russian and Austro-Hungarian armies), the formal study of morale did not emerge until well into the Second World War.

Components of morale

Morale is not an easy concept to define. Part of the difficulty is that it is a psychological term that covers many levels of explanation. There are physical and situational factors that will affect a soldier's morale. For example, if we are fighting in terrain that is highly unfamiliar and treacherous, and we are outnumbered, we may suffer from low morale simply because we are at a clear disadvantage relative to our enemy. Similarly, if we are starved of proper food, or rest, our morale will be lower than the morale of soldiers who are well fed and physically rested. Physical factors can be environmental, such as the climate, and also institutional, such as poor tactics and management of supplies to troops.

At the same time, there are internal or psychological factors that contribute to the soldier's morale. These, too, are complex as they may be emotional, physical, and mental. Although the influence of emotions is not always easy to predict, there is clearly an affective or emotional component to morale. For example, we could argue that extreme fear is unlikely to yield high morale on the battlefield. However, there are many instances where soldiers, out of sheer fear for their lives and a desire to live, fought the enemy ferociously. Their morale, and willingness to fight to the death, was supported by their instinct for self-preservation.

Then there is the person's physical state, or vitality, which will be affected by a number of things such as sleep loss, fatigue, and arousal levels. These obviously interact with situational factors and institutional responses from the military. For example, institutional responses to promote good morale include rest and leave, and appropriate rotations, where limits are imposed on the length of combat duty that a soldier must serve before he receives a change in duties.

A definition of morale would also need to include some description of mental components. We would want to consider cognition generally, such as the soldier's ability to be vigilant during a watch, to identify a target correctly, or to remember the correct sequence of actions when under stress. We would also need to consider what are called the **hot cognitions**, or beliefs the person holds, since morale is influenced by beliefs. For example, wars are conducted for reasons, although the ones that are given explicitly are not necessarily the real reasons for the conflict. Still, if a soldier believes in the reasons, the justness of the cause for the fight, his motivation will be greater than if he *does*

BOX 7.6 PEER-GROUP INFLUENCE

The work of Asch (1956) is one of the most cited empirical demonstrations of the power of groups on an individual's behaviour. Asch's experiment involved the use of *confederates* who pretended to be students in a psychology class, and a naive participant (i.e. a student who was unaware of the purpose of the experiment). Asch presented two lines, one that was clearly longer than the other, and asked each student to say if the two lines were equivalent. Each of the six or seven confederate 'students' agreed that the lines were of equal length. The last person to be asked was the naive participant. Asch documented that naive participants were often persuaded to agree with the group's decision, and conclude that the two lines were equivalent, in spite of the evidence of their eyes. Although there are criticisms of this experiment, Asch's findings nonetheless provide startling evidence for the impact that the group, and its values, can have on the individual. The military applications of this finding are important. People can be led into seeing, believing, and behaving a certain way, in spite of what their senses tell them!

not believe in the cause. These beliefs are 'hot' because they are ones to which the person ascribes great personal significance. Hot beliefs underlie how we feel about ourselves and how we understand the world, and dictate how we relate to others. Psychologists are all too aware that horrible atrocities can be committed in the name of extreme feelings of patriotism and religious fervour, when cognition is at its hottest.

Morale is also influenced by how the individual interacts *with* the world. In this instance, group cohesiveness, and feelings of belonging to his primary fighting group, will be important. A soldier who is highly committed to the group's common goal, and has bonded well with his group, will have higher morale. The power of the relationship between the individual soldier and his group cannot be underestimated as a protection against the conditions of war, as we shall see.

Motivation

In this section we consider how aggressive combat behaviour can be understood in terms of innate drives and personality traits. We also consider explanations that view aggressive behaviour as learned, and explore what incentives or rewards might be useful in motivating the soldier.

One of the most important aspects of morale is the soldier's motivation. While morale and motivation are closely linked, there are important differences. For example, the concept of morale has been largely restricted to discussions of military environments, and to a lesser extent, working environments (see Chapter 6). In contrast, motivation is a psychological concept that has been extensively studied by psychologists and has formed a major part of many theories of animal and human behaviour.

The topic of motivation is so central to the study of psychology as a whole, that we cannot consider it fully here. Essentially, the question of motivation is the question of *why*? Why does the soldier obey commands, why is the soldier willing to fight? The answer depends on which conflict we choose to examine. For example, Genghis Khan told his troops that 'The greatest pleasure in life is to defeat your enemies, to chase them before you, to rob them of their wealth, to see those dear to them bathed in tears, to ride their horses...' (quoted in Bidwell 1973, p. 20). This suggests that the opportunity to be aggressive and to pilfer was sufficient to motivate the ancient soldier. While the modern military may claim to deplore such glorification, they, too, realize that *aggression* is a powerful motivator on the battlefield.

Why are soldiers motivated by aggression?

How can we explain why normally placid individuals are able to commit aggressive acts when commanded to do so during war? As before, there are many different types of possible explanation. Biological explanations were originally developed in the context of animal behaviours. Concepts like **drives** and innate tendencies were

---

BOX 7.7 THE ORIGINS OF AGGRESSION

Konrad Lorenz was renowned for developing the study of **ethology**. Ethologists observe animal behaviour in the animal's natural habitat, under natural conditions with little or no intervention. Ethology
is in direct contrast to an **experimental methodology**, where the psychologist deliberately manipulates or alters various aspects of the environment in order to observe the effects of these components
on behaviour. Lorenz viewed aggressive behaviour in human beings as an innate drive, much like our
need to eat, sleep, and drink. His description is analogous to the idea of a reservoir, where drive builds
up and the animal needs to release this stored up energy periodically. For Lorenz, soldiers are motivated to be aggressive because they have an innate drive to do so. Some soldiers have higher drives than
others, or bigger reservoirs, and so are more likely to fight than other soldiers. This significance of this
view to military psychology is enormous, as it suggests that some people are more aggressive due to
their biological make-up and hence would make better soldiers than other people.

---

common. Examples of drives include feeding, drinking, and some social behaviour, like
hierarchical dominance in social groups and mating. These explanations focused on the
need for the animal to disperse energy associated with the drive.

Although psychologists continue to study the biological basis for emotions, with the
development of sophisticated technology, psychologists can now examine the physiological and neurological factors that underlie emotional behaviours like aggression. For
example, the limbic system (i.e. the thalamus, hypothalamus, amygdala, and hippocam-
pus) has been implicated as important for the expression of many basic drives (e.g. hunger, thirst, and sex) as well as being responsible for the control of emotions like fear and
rage. Similarly, new techniques have helped to describe the function of chemical altera-
tions in neurotransmitter substances (e.g. epinephrine (also known as adrenalin), GABA
(γ-aminobutyric acid), and glutamate) in emotions such as anxiety, fear, and rage. Such
research will go some way towards helping us to understand the biological basis underlying a soldier's motivation to fight. However, there are important ethical issues that need
considering. For example, there is the worrying possibility that we may be in a position,
in the near future, to turn someone into a good fighting machine simply by giving him
the appropriate cocktail of drugs.

Explanations of individual differences in aggression and motivation are also
concerned with inherited components of aggression. For example, the military has long
been known to attract a particular type of personality, one who is more rule-bound,
more conservative, and more inflexible in outlook. That is, the classic *authoritarian
personality*. The authoritarian personality is more likely to conform to institutional
regulations and procedures, more likely to adapt better to group demands and more
likely to be socialized with respect to training. Interestingly, studies have shown that
good commanders are more rigid in terms of routines and regulations and expect high
levels of conformity from their subordinates.

Other explanations propose that aggressive behaviour is a learned characteristic,
subject to the laws of reinforcement, as developed by Skinner and Pavlov. We have
already discussed **social learning theory** (see Chapter. 6), which argues that our social

behaviour is learned. According to such theories, a person will be motivated to fight given the appropriate reinforcement. This leads us to consider what a soldier might regard as *incentives* or rewards for fighting.

Internal and external motivators

There are two classes of motivator, internal and external. Internal motivators serve as incentives because of their inherent value to the person. An example of an internal motivator is the desire for higher *self-esteem*. Our self-esteem is positively associated with our feelings of pride and satisfaction in how we act, or how well we behave in a situation. Some psychologists, like Abraham Maslow, have argued that self-esteem and self-satisfaction are as strong internal motivators of human behaviour as the most basic of needs, such as hunger or safety (see 'The treatment room', Chapter 8, pp. 180–4). A soldier who has pride and self-satisfaction in performing his duties will have higher self-esteem. His higher self-esteem, in turn, would be associated with increased motivation.

Examples of external motivators are awards or promotions that a soldier receives, or group recognition of his performance in combat. The attractiveness of certain external rewards has changed. Five hundred years ago the prospect of plunder may have been a sufficient incentive for the soldier to fight. Even today, the promise of material gain is sufficient for some soldiers, as when mercenary fighters are recruited. However, monetary or materialistic gain is not as powerful an external reward to the modern soldier as is external recognition, be it from the military itself, or from the public. A hero's welcome is a greater incentive to fight than the promise of more money.

Not surprisingly, most studies show that external rewards, such as peer recognition, self-pride, or increased autonomy (as in having more recreational leave) can seldom outweigh internal motivators. Internal rewards have more significance to the individual and are more intrinsically valuable. Most modern military institutions now recognize that a

---

BOX 7.8 MORALE AND PUBLIC SUPPORT

We should note that the public's attitudes towards military action affect morale. If there is little public support, this will have a negative effect on the psychological states of those engaged in military action. A modern example of this is Vietnam and the impact that the peace movement had on combat soldiers and veterans returning to the USA. In recent conflicts unprecedented access to combat manoeuvres has been given to the media. Modern communications and technology now ensure that public dissent is transmitted to combat soldiers more rapidly than ever before. This is a factor that will need to be considered in future conflicts, particularly when public support is lacking. However, even when the public does support a course of military action, soldiers often feel that they do not receive the recognition for their actions that they deserve. Military historians note that soldiers throughout all major conflicts have felt that the public remained largely ignorant of the conditions and consequences of war. Some studies of the Second World War have shown that combat soldiers returned home with a sense of being owed some status in the post-war world. More often than not, these expectations were never realized, leading to feelings of bitterness and betrayal.

soldier who is fighting to achieve some internal reward or goal will endure more hardship than will a soldier who is fighting simply for money, or external recognition.

Identification with the primary group

In this section we discuss how the soldier's identification with the group influences morale. We then examine the different psychological roles that individuals must perform in order to keep combat units effective. Finally, we look at how the individual's emotional relationships within the group can provide some protection against the horrors of war.

Military historians uniformly note that while beliefs and other motivators are important, it is often the more intimate feelings of friendship and comradeship that instil the will to fight. It is the primary group that sets and reinforces standards of behaviour, such as fighting or following military procedure. At the same time, individuals in the group, such as a 'buddy', provide emotional support and companionship during times of stress. Studies from the Second World War, the Korean War, and Vietnam all confirm the critical function that friendship plays in supporting the soldier.

A soldier's feelings of belonging to his group develop as a consequence of many factors. For example, close spatial proximity and the ability to have intimate conversations with at least one other trusted comrade will encourage a soldier's bond to his group. Equally, more intimate relationships between members of the group, as with buddies, increase group cohesion, as individual soldiers come to rely on and trust each other more.

Research conducted after the Korean conflict was concerned with understanding the *inter-personal dynamics* between members of the same primary fighting units. Anecdotal evidence often suggested that different members of the group fulfilled different roles. For example, a soldier might choose to share a night-watch with person A because the person was a good marksman and was highly dependable under stress. However, the same soldier might choose person B with whom to go on leave because person B was more likeable and a closer confidante. Such observations led military psychologists to conclude that different psychological functions must be fulfilled in order for the group to be effective, and for group cohesion.

Psychological roles within the combat group

From these anecdotal findings, psychologists began to understand that a good fighting unit is supported by the quality of the human relationships its individual members have with each other. For example, the American psychologist, Rodney Clark, identified five psychological duties that must be fulfilled in order for a combat group to operate (Clark 1953). One was managing the group; for example, ensuring that the supplies and provisions were distributed equitably. Another was defining and maintaining group norms, which involved making sure that all members of the unit were clearly told what was and what was not acceptable behaviour. This included initiating discussions to resolve conflicts and explicitly stating what was expected from each member of the group. Modelling was another function that had to be fulfilled, where senior members operated as role models for junior group members. Related to this is the fourth function of teaching. As we have already discussed, teaching through demonstration, or vicarious learning, was one way in which a novice soldier could learn. The teacher had to be a person who was perceived by the other group members as having sufficient knowledge to be an expert; the teacher also had to be good at communication, so that he could present the information in a way that other group members could understand. Finally, someone had to take responsibility for containing the emotional conflicts that would inevitably arise between group members. Clark suggested that this function was more than just being able to listen or sympathize. Rather, this function seemed to be more akin to therapy. People who served this function had an ability to sense 'when an individual's desires were in conflict with the welfare of the group...' and helped the individual to '...adjust his conflicting efforts to harmonize with the squad's goals' (Clark 1953).

We can see that some of the functions are likely to be fulfilled by the formal leader of the group. For example, managing the group is likely to be done by higher ranks, or those people who have organizational responsibilities to perform managerial duties. In contrast, men from lower ranks are equally likely to fulfil other functions, such as containing emotional conflict by being someone's buddy, or teaching a junior soldier how to rest during breaks in firing.

The emotional consequences of combat

There is no doubt that all soldiers suffer from demoralized feelings and fear at some time. However, one factor that mediates these negative emotions is the soldier's bond with his group. When a soldier feels that he belongs to the group, he is better protected against intense and prolonged combat reactions. It seems as though being with others in the same boat, even if it is a lousy boat, is some comfort and helps the soldier deal with the emotional consequences of war. In fact, reports of psychiatric breakdowns or **combat trauma** were less likely when the soldier felt strongly attached to his primary fighting group. The group, and the bond it afforded, provided the soldier with some resilience in dealing with the emotional battering that war inflicts.

Of course, there is a negative consequence of being attached to your fighting comrades. The prospect of your best friend dying or being injured from enemy fire is an entirely realistic possibility; and, when this happens, the emotional impact is so considerable that some soldiers cannot continue, and suffer symptoms of combat trauma. There are a variety of reasons why soldiers suffer combat trauma, and the symptoms are equally varied. However, we defer discussion of combat trauma here, since the treatments that military psychiatrists developed for combat trauma have had an enormous impact on the treatment of trauma in the general population. For this reason, we consider combat trauma and combat psychiatry in 'The treatment room'.

SUMMARY

We have considered some of the traditional topics that have been central to the application of psychology in the war room. We have shown that psychologists were essential in developing methods of assessment, selection, and allocation and that their involvement directly affected military campaigns. These early efforts, like mapping the worker to the job, served as the basis for much of the later work done in non-military working environments (see Chapter 6). We suggested that the questions posed by these early researchers in the context of war and combat highlighted debates that are still central to psychology today, such as the biological basis of emotions and the effects of nature versus nurture. We illustrated how psychologists used basic principles derived from learning theory, particularly notions like reinforcement and incentives, not only to improve training and performance, but also to sustain the soldier's morale and motivation. We also considered how important the soldier's affiliation to his fighting group is in ensuring well-being and emotional resilience.

SCENARIO ONE

THE ROLE OF PSYCHOACOUSTICS IN THE DEVELOPMENT OF AUDITORY WARNING SIGNALS

This first scenario looks at the problem of designing auditory warning signals on aircraft. This work is derived from a series of studies conducted by Dr Roy Patterson and his research team. It is an excellent example of applied psychology that combines the field of human *ergonomics*, including issues regarding man–machine compatibility, with theories of perception. This scenario illustrates the effectiveness of experimental methodology and design in addressing questions that have great significance in the context of the war room.

Every military action requires resources, including personnel, and combat tactics reflect this fact. To ensure their effective use, risk assessments are conducted to determine whether the benefits of the action outweigh the costs to resources. Human life is simply another resource in combat and military leaders must ultimately decide what are acceptable losses. They acknowledge that a certain number of people on both sides will be injured or killed in order to achieve their objectives. These losses are judged to be acceptable as they are the unavoidable consequence of combat action. The military feels that it can justify them to the public, and to the loved ones of those who are lost.

However, military personnel also die, not through combat, but through failure or error on the part of the military (e.g. through so-called 'friendly fire'). These losses are unacceptable, as they can be avoided or averted. Unacceptable losses pose a serious problem for military leaders. The public is not as easily swayed into believing that the people who lost their lives due to the negligence of the military died for 'a good and just cause'.

The following scenario provides an example of how unacceptable losses were reduced through the input of a group of psychologists. It is a wonderful illustration of how psychologists and psychological theories can directly influence the safety of military personnel through the development of more user-friendly machines.

What was the situation?

After the Korean conflict, war technology became significantly more advanced. The highly sophisticated technology on board the new helicopters required the crew to assimilate a considerable amount of diverse information and to perform many tasks at once. That is, the environment was **multi-modal**, with different sounds, lights, and background noises. The workload was distributed across all members of the crew, so that the safety and success of any mission was reliant on a number of people performing different operations in certain sequences. This meant that it was essential for the crew to communicate information accurately with each other.

Very soon, it became apparent that signals warning of danger (i.e. that required immediate action) needed to override all other perceptual information. In response to these requirements, designers adopted a visual warning system, and this served as a prototype for all warning systems on certain types of military helicopter up to the mid-1980s. For example, flashing yellow lights were used to signal that the craft was descending to a dangerously low height.

Unfortunately, there are various factors that render a visual warning system less than optimal. First consider how we might get people to attend to visual information. We could flood the environment, as occurs with strobe-lighting effects. Under these conditions, the ambient light is flashing so dramatically that our attention cannot help but be alerted. Unfortunately, it would be very difficult to read flight-deck instruments accurately if the ambient light were pulsating! Another way to attract attention is with flashing lights. The rhythmic pulsation of light is salient, particularly under the light conditions of a flight deck. However, in order for the signal to capture our attention we need to be *facing* it. If our back is to the signal, or if we have our heads down looking at something else, we might not see the signal and this could lead to disaster.

Next, let us consider what happens during an emergency on a flight deck. As already mentioned, the members of the flight crew are doing more than one task at any time and this is particularly the case in an emergency. In psychological terms, they will be **parallel processing** or **serial processing** (see Box 7.9), will be engaged in a **multi-task situation**, and are likely to be in a state of heightened alertness and anxiety.

Significantly, the crew will be focusing on other visual information, such as instruments that need to be monitored. Last but not least, the act of flying itself relies primarily on vision, and even during night flights most of the flight panel is visual. Thus the crew would be processing a huge amount of visual information in the course of their normal duties, let alone under emergency conditions. A visual warning signal would be in stiff competition with other visual information for the crew's attention; and this would increase the chances of the crew not attending to the warning signal in sufficient time to avert disaster.

Sadly, this proved true when a helicopter came down, killing all personnel. It appeared that while the pilots were looking for landfalls within fog, they had been able

---

BOX 7.9 SERIAL AND PARALLEL PROCESSING

The distinction between serial and parallel processing is an important one for psychologists. Many of the early theories of attention, such as that of Donald Broadbent (1958), argued that people could do more than one thing at once through rapid serial processing: attention and its processes would be switched from one task to the other. These types of models suggest that attention can become 'bottle-necked', with too much information resulting in only a subset being processed. In contrast, modern theories of perception and cognition, such as those of Hinton and Anderson (1981) and Barnard and Teasdale (1991) argue that information is processed in parallel across different information units. The limitation of the person to do, or attend to, multiple tasks is determined not only by the amount of information, but also the quality of the information processing involved.

---

to ignore the flashing yellow light signalling that the craft had descended dangerously low. Subsequent military investigations concluded that if the warning signals had been auditory, the accident could have been avoided.

Eager to avoid any future disasters, the military decided to produce an auditory warning signal that would not fail to dominate attention. They decided to model their warning system on the ambulance siren, which cuts through all other traffic sounds and noise by sheer volume. Importantly, because it uses the auditory modality, a siren does not require the driver to be oriented to it spatially, so it will not interfere with the act of driving itself, which is dominated by vision. Given the similarity of the conditions between driving and flying, the military decided that this type of auditory signal would ensure that the crew could not ignore the warning. In addition to the visual warning system, new helicopters were therefore fitted with auditory signals that would dominate all other perceptual information. For economic reasons, high-frequency tones were selected for the majority of warning signals, with the major distinctions between the different signals being their absolute frequency (pitch) and their intensity (loudness).

BOX 7.10 THE PRIMITIVE WARNING SYSTEM

Psychologists who study hearing argue that the auditory modality is far superior to the visual modality as a perceptual warning system. Patterson (1990) points out that hearing is a primitive warning sense. For example, the sound of our enemy rustling through the foliage will reach us far faster than the sight of our enemy. Patterson also notes that an auditory warning signal does not require the pilot's attention. The pilot can be engaged in another visual task, or can be quietly taking a rest with their eyes closed; in either case, an auditory warning will be detected. As Patterson clearly argues, the military needed to consider the psychology of hearing and examine how the brain processes auditory information. If they had, they would have seen that the question was not whether helicopters should have auditory warning systems, but rather how they could construct warning sounds that would promote the best and most reliable detection.

Why was the psychologist involved?

The new design, using auditory and visual warnings, solved the problem of the flight crew ignoring the warning signals. Unfortunately, it introduced new and equally disturbing concerns, and the number of incident reports that cited problems with the new warning system increased. After a sufficient number of complaints, and near-miss disasters, the military decided to enlist the help of applied psychologists who were experts in the area of human hearing. Through collaboration with private companies, government departments, and research councils, the psychologists agreed to address the flight crews' complaints. One of these regarded the level of the auditory warning. Pilots had complained that some of the warnings were so loud that it was impossible for them to hear anything else, which made communicating information to each other difficult. Ironically, pilots claimed that often their first action was to *turn off* the warning system, so that the flight crew could talk to each other and find out what the problem was!

A second complaint was that warnings were not always easy to discriminate from other sounds that shared the same **spectral characteristics**, such as when turbines or pumps became worn (see Box 7.11). Members of the crew were uncertain whether the sound they were hearing was a warning signal, or just a normal part of the background noise of the aircraft. A third problem was that the warning signal reached its highest intensity immediately, going from a completely quiet situation to full volume. This had the consistent effect of startling the pilots so that they could not respond to the situation with composure and objectivity. When we are startled, our natural reaction is to experience muscular tension and prepare for an immediate response. The problem is that if a pilot reacts too rapidly, their reaction is likely to be incorrect because they have insufficient information, which is why instantaneous reactions are always *discouraged* in pilot training.

BOX 7.11 THE WAY WE HEAR

We perceive sound as a pattern of changes in the pressure of air. Our hearing system is designed to tell us about three things: wavelength, amplitude, and location. Wavelength, or **frequency**, refers to the time it takes for the sound wave to complete one cycle. This is generally measured in cycles per second, or **Hertz**, also known as **Hz**. Humans are sensitive to frequencies between 30 and 20,000 Hz. High-frequency sounds, such as screams, have very short cycles, whereas low-frequency sounds, such as Buddhist chants, have very long cycles. Any complex sound, such as that produced by a musical instrument, is a combination of many simpler sounds. Each component sound will have a particular frequency, or cycle, and can be thought of as having **spectral characteristics**. Amplitude is the size of the wave, as would be measured as the loudness or intensity of the sound. Sounds of greater amplitude are louder than sounds of smaller amplitude. Generally, intensity or power is referred to in **decibels** or **dB**. Finally, we are sensitive to the location of the sound as those that are closer to our ear are processed quicker and received faster by the brain. The ability to utilize differences in the speed in the processing of auditory information is the basis for the *echo-location* used by some species of mammals.

A fourth criticism was that there were too many warning signals. For example, on some aircraft, there were as many as fifteen different auditory warning signals, from those signalling evacuation procedures to those associated with over-speed problems. Crews therefore had difficulty learning which sound signalled which danger. Furthermore, the majority of warning signals were of high frequency. This was a problem because the human ear is designed to discriminate between changes in sounds rather than absolute sounds. To compound the problem even further, when two or more warning signals came on simultaneously, their combined sound made it difficult for the pilots to recognize the component signals involved.

What psychological concepts are relevant?

Concepts developed from the discipline of **psychoacoustics** were of obvious relevance. The study of psychoacoustics combines experimental methodologies developed from psychology with an understanding of the anatomy and physiology of the ear, to explain how people process and perceive auditory information from the environment. In this case, the psychologists felt that the problems were related to some fairly basic theoretical concepts regarding how people detect patterns of sound, how they learn to associate meaning to patterns of sounds, and how they remember them.

The first problem was to produce a warning sound that would be easily detected above the background noise of the helicopter. Flying an aircraft is a noisy business with multiple sounds coming from outside the aircraft as well as the engines and the flight deck itself. Similar problems have been addressed by psychologists interested in how we single out, and selectively attend to, one perceptual feature when there are many other things going on in the environment that are competing for our attention. Although there are many possible answers, we shall turn to **signal detection theory**, one of the most familiar explanations to arise from the work of *psychophysics*.

BOX 7.12 THE CLASSIC AREA OF PSYCHOPHYSICS

The area of psychoacoustics belongs to the more general area of *psychophysics*. Psychophysics attempts to explain the processes of perception through analyses of molecular sensory processing of the five main sensory systems (i.e. vision, hearing, touch, smell, and taste). In particular, discussions focus on how information from our physical environment is translated, or *transduced*, into information that can be understood and processed by our brain. Psychologists interested in psychophysics would be concerned with descriptions of *sensory receptors*. They examine how sensory receptors detect the presence of physical events in the external world, how they convey the occurrence of physical events to the brain, and how they process this information so that the brain can receive it. Through the use of experimental methodology, psychophysics provides a level of explanation that is based around descriptions of sensory receptors and action potentials. This level of description is different from that provided by more cognitive approaches. For example, a cognitive theory may not only discuss sensory receptors, but also consider non-sensory aspects involved in perception, such as the effects that emotion or memory might have on our perceptual abilities.

Signal detection theory operates on the assumption that people detect a target, in this case the warning sound, from a background of non-target sounds, as a consequence of two independent processes. One process relies on differences between the sensory features of the target and non-targets, such as the spectral characteristics of the sound (see Box 7.11). The overlap between the sensory features of the target and the non-target is assessed by d'. This is a measure of the ratio that reflects the difference between target and background, and ranges from zero to one. The smaller the ratio, the more similar the target and background, and consequently the more difficult it is for us to detect the difference. For example, suppose you are asked to press a button when you hear speaker A (the target), but not when you hear speaker B (the non-target). If both of the speakers are men, you will find it more difficult to distinguish between the two than if speaker A is a woman and speaker B is a man. Part of the reason for this is that the two male voices share more perceptual features.

The second process has to do with how readily we are able to *accept* that the sound we are hearing is the target. This process involves us making a decision and is related to the level of certainty we have to reach in order to decide that this is the target and not some random noise. This is measured by beta (β), and is referred to as our *criterion*. Typically, criteria are discussed in terms of whether they are lax or strict. For example, suppose we are given the task of identifying a song by the first four notes of its music—a task commonly used in television game shows. If we have a lax criterion, we may decide that we only need two notes to identify the song. However, if we have a strict criterion, we may want to wait until all four notes have been played. These decisions have nothing to do with the sensory information but with how willing we are to accept that we have heard a target, given the amount of information we have received.

Regardless of their explanatory framework, the psychologists knew that it was essential for the perceptual features of the warning signals to be distinctive from the background sounds of the flight deck and sounds of flying. The original designers had dealt with this problem by selecting a very high-frequency sound and making it very loud: one hundred decibels. What they had failed to take into account was the fact that sounds over eighty-five decibels are generally quite unpleasant, particularly at high frequency. The psychologists knew that they needed to examine closely the perceptual features of the warning signals in the context of the environment under which the crew was operating. Their main focus was how to increase the perceptual distinctiveness of the warning signal. In order to do this, the psychologists would have to analyse the nature of the competing sensory information on the flight deck, in particular the spectral characteristics of other sounds common to a flight deck (e.g. engine noises and rotor-blade sounds).

Analysing the spectral characteristics of the other sounds would also address another criticism, which was the problem of detecting a meaningful pattern of sound. In psychological terms, the problem is how we assign meaning to sensory information. To put it another way, how do we combine bits of sensory information into whole objects, or patterns? A good example from the visual modality is the three-lines/triangle. This well-known figure consists of three straight lines arranged to form the outline of a triangle, but with the corners not joined. If we ask most people what they see when they look at this figure, they will respond with 'a triangle'. However, what are actually present are three disjointed lines. So, how is it that we are able to *see* a triangle where none exists? According to **Gestalt** theory, we take the sensory information that is present, and then actively impose some organization or structure on it in order to *see* something meaningful. We fill in the spatial gaps, and using our knowledge about objects, and about triangles in particular, impose structure so that the three lines become a set of lines forming a triangle. Of course, our ability to impose this organization on the figure is aided by the fact that the three lines are angled in such a way that is consistent with how they would look as a triangle. According to Gestalt theorists, the organization inherent in the sensory information and our ability to impose our own organization on the environment allows us to *perceive* a meaningful object, where, in fact, there is none.

In the case of auditory information, we associate certain temporal patterns, or rhythms, with whole units or sets. For example, the sound series, da-da-da, da-da-da, is perceived by most people as two sets of triplets. In this way, we would use rhythm to indicate a set, or whole. Unfortunately, the warning signals did not make use of any distinct temporal patterns. Because the sounds comprising the warning signals lacked any inherent structure, the crew failed to recognize them as *a set of sounds that meant something*. The psychologists knew that if the warning signals had contained better structure, such as a recognizable rhythmic temporal pattern, the crew would have been better able to distinguish this systematic pattern from the random patterns of noise and sound around them.

Another issue was that the large number of auditory warnings meant that the pilots were experiencing perceptual confusion. It became difficult for them to tell whether warning A or warning K was occurring. Additionally, the pilots found it difficult to learn and remember so many different warning signals. There are two separate issues that the psychologists felt needed considering, and both were relevant to psychological concepts regarding learning and memory. First, the crew had to recognize a large number of signals. The psychologists realized that the crew had not been allowed to learn each signal to a stable level so that they could recognize them automatically and without hesitation. Furthermore, given that the crew only heard the warning signals occasionally (i.e. during an emergency) the large number of signals was clearly going to stretch the crew's ability to remember them all, particularly during states of high emergency and stress.

The second problem was that the crew was also required to learn and remember what each signal meant. Learning to associate two things together is an area that has been studied extensively by psychologists. One feature that can make learning associations easy or hard is the extent of *class* or *set similarity*. Learning theorists have long argued that, when two or more sets or patterns are to be learned, the more similar the two sets are, the more difficult it is to distinguish one from the other. For example, suppose you are learning two lists of **paired-associate** items and your task is to remember which list contained a particular pair. In one, set A, you are presented with a series of word–word pairs, like train–black. After learning set A, you are asked to learn set B, in which you are presented with a different series of word–word pairs such as plane–white. If you are then asked to identify whether a word pair came from set A or set B, you will experience some difficulty, as the two sets share significant properties. However, if set B has number–word pairs, like 7–blue, your task would be much easier, as the set similarities would be greatly reduced.

The psychologists could immediately see why this principle needed to be taken into account. As the majority of signals shared similar properties (e.g. most were high-frequency), this made it difficult for the crew to learn and remember the specific association between signal and emergency condition. The psychologists knew that they needed to find a set of signals that not only would be easy to learn and remember, but could also be easily distinguished from each other.

What did the psychologists do?

The psychologists decided that they would approach the problem by devising a research programme whereby observational studies would be combined with experiments involving flight crew and pilots. For example, the problem of deciding what was the appropriate level of intensity for warning signals was addressed by first analysing the spectrum of components of a flight deck, and their corresponding intensity levels. This provided an indication of the level of intensity at which background sounds were operating, which would have to be surpassed if the warning signal was to be detectable. Analyses of flight-deck noise also provided critical information about similarities between the sensory characteristics of the warning signals and other flight-deck noises. This could provide an initial way of addressing the problem that pilots had in distinguishing the warning signal pattern from other rhythmic patterns.

Bearing in mind that anything louder than one hundred decibels would be uncomfortable and distracting, the psychologists plotted background noise on the flight deck. From this, they developed a model that predicted the appropriate range of intensity levels that would maintain the distinctiveness of a warning, and still be acceptable to the listener. The psychologists then conducted experiments with pilots in flight. The pilots were given six different warning horns and were asked to select the one they felt was the most appropriate. Interestingly, the pilots selected the warning horns that corresponded to the levels that were predicted by the psychologists' model.

The problem of learning and remembering the different warning signals was addressed by another set of experiments. Naive listeners were asked to learn and remember a set of ten auditory warning signals that were drawn from flight decks in aircraft. Some of the warning signals shared spectral characteristics (i.e. frequencies), some shared similar temporal characteristics (i.e. rhythm or pulse-repetition rate), whereas others shared both spectral and temporal characteristics. By varying the type and extent of similarity, psychologists could advise how to create warning signals that were not only easy to learn, but also easy to remember.

The data from the naive listeners proved fascinating. First, the listeners had relatively little trouble in learning six warning signals. However, once the number of signals exceeded six, the learning rate declined sharply and listeners found the task much more difficult. The psychologists knew that these results could not be translated directly to the flight-deck situation, as they were using naive listeners who were unaccustomed to the task of identifying different sounds. However, they felt that these results certainly reinforced the view that aircraft with more than ten warning signals may be putting undue stress on the flight crew.

Equally informative were the analyses of the types of error that the listeners made. It was very interesting that the most confusion seemed to occur when there were temporal similarities between the signals. That is, signals with vastly different spectral components but sharing the same rhythm were often confused. Again, although the psychologists were aware that they could not apply their results directly to the flight-deck situation, the importance of rhythmic patterns in the recognition of signals was underlined. Their results clearly demonstrated that the potential for confusion could be reduced dramatically by introducing more variation in the temporal patterns of warning signals. On the basis of these data, the psychologists conducted a subsequent study with helicopter pilots. Pilots were given the standard set of ten signals used previously, and a new set of ten signals that introduced variability between the temporal patterns of the signal. The data showed that the learning and retention rates for the newly devised set of signals far exceeded those of the standard set, and that the confusion rate was much lower.

Another problem that the psychologists felt was essential to address related to the time needed for a warning to reach its full intensity. The psychologists knew that the majority of warnings came on at full intensity, producing the highly undesirable effect of startling the crew. The psychologists addressed this problem by developing a model of a prototype warning sound. The prototype served to identify what might be optimal features in terms of the onset and offset of a warning, the intensity or loudness of the warning, and its rhythm or pulse pattern. The prototype was made of a sound pulse with distinct spectral features and a pulse pattern was used to provide a distinctive rhythm. The pattern of pulses was a basic grouping of four clustered pulses followed by two, irregularly spaced pulses, which completed over a few seconds. Each pulse could be manipulated to have different on/off contours; for example, rounded contours meant that the onset and offset of the sound was slow, and sharp contours reflected abrupt onset and offset.

On the basis of this prototype, the psychologists were able to develop a warning that could capture the crew's attention without risking a startle response. They suggested that, in an emergency situation, the first burst of a warning-sound pattern should be at a relatively moderate level, one that was audible but would not interfere with any ne-cessary actions that might be required. The successive bursts of pulses after the initial pulse would quickly increase in intensity and then recede again slowly as the pulse pat-tern concluded. The psychologists believed that this envelope of amplitude differences, with its pattern of sudden up then down, would give the impression of movement, of first moving forward rapidly and then receding slowly, and that this apparent motion would draw the crew's attention. The pattern would then be repeated for a second time, with a gap of a few seconds. In the event that some action had been taken, the pitch, level, and speed of warning bursts would be lowered, so as to indicate less urgency, and should be repeated after four or five seconds. Importantly, gaps in the bursts would al-low the crew to communicate with each other. If, however, no action were taken after the first pattern, successive patterns would be introduced at increasingly higher pitch, intensity, and speed. This would ensure that they would override any ongoing speech and would demand immediate attention.

How was the psychologists' input assessed?

This is one example where applied research was not only well received, but also acted upon. On the basis of both the spectral modelling and the behavioural data, the psychologists devised a set of warning signals that addressed all of the criticisms of the old system. The new, modified set of warning signals were first tested on flight crews. The results indicated that the new set substantially increased the chances of the flight crew responding appropriately to emergency situations. The military was delighted with the results and lives were unquestionably saved as a result of the psychologists' input.

SCENARIO TWO

ASSESSING THE USEFULNESS OF LIE DETECTORS

Our second scenario has espionage as its backdrop. As the nature of war has changed, so too has the nature of peace. The end of what was known as the Cold War helped to lessen the immediate worry of major nuclear conflict between two or more superpowers. However, while there may have been an overt change in the relationship between traditional opponents, there was an increase in what might be called covert operations. Covert operations include such things as special operations, intelligence units, and other techniques of psychological warfare. These covert operations, as their name implies, are conducted largely outside the awareness of the general public. To be most effective, they must also be kept secret from our allies, national partners, and political adversaries.

As we have already discussed, one of the most pressing problems that has consistently confronted the military is how to select the right person for the right job (see above, pp. 138–45). Indeed, we saw that this was a problem for virtually every branch of modern military organizations, from deciding who should be a ground soldier to who should be leading a battalion of men. A similar, perhaps more pressing problem existed when considering special operations. Special operations require special skills and abilities. Modern military leaders realize the seriousness of the problem of selection, and invest considerable amounts of energy and resources into utilizing standardized tests that would highlight candidates' aptitudes, as relevant to the job.

For example, suppose we want to select people to do a special job, such as to infiltrate a counter-insurgency cell. We can assume that there are going to be certain characteristics, or aptitudes, that will make for better, or poorer, agents. These might include the person's general level of anxiety: given the stealthy nature of the task, we would want people who maintain a level of calm and clear thinking under pressure. We might also want to select people who show few outward reactions when they are lying, and select people who are convincing in their false portrayals. It would make sense for us to devise some means of assessing whether our prospective candidates had these qualities, and determine how much these qualities affected how well different people did the job.

This next scenario demonstrates how things can go wrong when this approach is not adopted. It outlines how a government bureau responsible for intelligence and counter-intelligence ignored the hard-learned lessons of the military. As a consequence, the government was put in a highly compromising situation, and national security was put at risk.

What was the situation?

In the late 1980s the British Civil Service, in consultation with the military, established a network of counter-intelligence units. One unit, Unit Z, had the task of listening to chatter, or eavesdropping, on radio communication between members of a known guerrilla organization, the Freedom Fighters. The Freedom Fighters had been respons-ible for a few gruesome attacks on key government buildings in which many casualties occurred. They were regarded as a serious threat to national security. Unit Z was ex-pected to monitor and collate all information, and report regularly to the appropriate branch of military intelligence. Different teams of five listeners, spread over eight-hour shifts, were responsible for maintaining constant surveillance.

As the team members were Civil Servants, they were selected for the job on the basis of their scores on traditional Civil Service tests. These tests are fairly comprehensive examinations that assess general world knowledge, general intellectual competence, as well as general reading and comprehension skills. Unfortunately, the traditional Civil Service tests did not seem to address any traits that might be relevant to tasks involved in counter-intelligence, such as loyalty, discretion, and the willingness to engage in deception. Provided that the person had an acceptable level of intellectual compet-ence, and signed the appropriate documents regarding official secrets, they could work at Unit Z, regardless of any other individual characteristics or personality traits they might possess.

BOX 7.13 STANDARDIZED TESTS AND SPECIAL OPERATIONS

The tests used by the Civil Service measure general intellectual abilities, but would not be considered as *psychological*. This is because the tests had no measure of validity or reliability, and were not **stand-ardized tests**. In contrast, the military has made extensive use of standardized psychological tests in selecting those involved in special operations, like counter-insurgency operations. For example, the *Minnesota Multiphasic Personality Inventory* (MMPI) has been used to assess characteristics deemed preferable, or essential, to do a job. These identify such things as propensity to complain about minor aches and pains, and how concerned the person is about right and wrong. The ideal candidate would be someone with high pain thresholds and someone who operated more from pragmatism than from high morals. As outlined by Peter Watson, in his book *War on the Mind* (1980), the use of standardized tests has led to further developments in terms of a 'constellation of reactions', which identify a good agent from a poor agent. These included fear of injury, lack of social responsibility, and uneasiness about the unknown, to name a few.

Over the course of a month's listening sessions, the team pieced together information that the present government was planning to sell arms illegally to the Freedom Fighters, and furthermore was engaged in clandestine talks with those directly responsible for the attacks. The Freedom Fighters, in return, were providing the government with information about a neighbouring nation, suspected by the international community of developing nuclear weapons. The reality of the government's hypocrisy had a significant impact on one of the team, who had lost someone close to them in one of the attacks. After much consideration, the team member decided that her only option was to declare what she knew to the major television networks and national newspapers. A second member of the team, who found the hypocrisy equally difficult to accept, joined her in revealing the contents of the communication.

A highly publicized trial ensued where both were convicted of breaching national security and sentenced to imprisonment. Not surprisingly, the government was concerned on two levels. The first was getting some idea of how many other people currently working in counter-intelligence units would be likely to defect in this manner. The second was putting into place an adequate screening process that would identify applicants who were likely to defect from those who were likely to remain loyal and discrete.

The then head of the bureau of the Civil Service responsible for counter-intelligence units was something of an amateur psychologist and had some knowledge about polygraphs (lie-detector tests). The head decided that all members currently employed in the counter-intelligence units would be required to take an obligatory polygraph test to determine their loyalty to the government. On the basis of the results, the employee could be discharged from duties. Additionally, all new applicants would be required to take a lie-detector test and, if they failed, they would be prohibited from working in counter-intelligence, if not from the Civil Service itself.

The members of the units were appalled at the suggestion. In the first instance, many were aware that polygraph techniques yield mixed results in criminal and forensic cases, and questioned the use of such techniques. Further, unit staff were not allowed union membership in order to prevent them from taking industrial action. This meant that, should any member be unfairly dismissed as a result of an unreliable test, there would be no means for that person to appeal against the management's decision. In essence, unit members could be fired on the basis of a faulty test, and would have no recourse. Faced with these circumstances, teams across different units began to meet and considered their options, which for the first time included the possibility of industrial action. The Civil Service was confronted with a major uprising. Unfortunately, the head was a particularly stubborn woman, and she refused to be persuaded to give up her idea of using the polygraph.

Why was the psychologist involved?

In order to prevent a complete breakdown within the branch, junior ministers convinced the head that she should attempt to find ways of improving the reliability of the polygraph. She agreed and placed one junior minister in charge of finding an expert. The junior minister contacted a national governing body for psychologists and enquired directly about experts in polygraph techniques.

Once an expert psychologist had been contacted, a meeting was arranged between the psychologist, the head, senior members of the branch of the Civil Service in question, and the junior minister who had made the initial enquiries. An agreed agenda was established rapidly. The psychologist's general objective was to address the feasibility of polygraph security screening in the intelligence and security agencies. In particular, the psychologist was charged with providing a summary of the extant literature, including recommendations and conclusions regarding any future work. The psychologist also was asked to address the question of whether any research could be conducted that would highlight how polygraphic techniques could be made more reliable in the detection of deception, especially with reference to screening. Finally, the psychologist was asked to provide some indication of the margin of error in polygraph techniques, and how the techniques could be improved so as to reduce this error.

What psychological concepts are relevant?

Not surprisingly, there are many mainstream psychological concepts that could be applied to this problem. The notion that we can devise a technique that will tell us when someone is lying and when they are telling the truth makes certain basic assumptions about human behaviour. The first, and most obvious, is that psychological states are associated or correlated with physiological and physical symptoms. For example, we when get angry we often experience body heat and our faces turn red. Similarly, in the case of deception, we assume that the psychological state of lying, or deliberately deceiving, is associated with certain changes in our physiological reactions.

The scientific discipline that supports the development of such notions is referred to as *psychophysiology*. Psychophysiology is concerned with the underlying physiological mechanisms that govern human behaviour. In the case of the polygraph, issues surrounded the peripheral indices of activity in the **autonomic nervous system** (ANS), that part of the central nervous system that controls unconscious bodily activity. Autonomic activity can be triggered in at least two ways. Each response has a different pattern. One is triggered by attentional reactions to novel, unexpected, interesting, or meaningful external events. This type of response is generally referred to as an **orienting reaction** (OR), and serves to direct the person's attention to what is happening and what is likely to happen next. A good example of this is when we are engrossed in the act of reading and we hear a sudden, loud noise: generally, we look up in response and orient ourselves in the direction of the sound because the noise is unexpected and surprising. The OR is measurable through virtually all bodily systems, from the humble blinking of an eyelid to patterns of heartbeat and breathing. The same type of response can also be elicited when the person is confronted with painful, emotive, or fear-provoking external events, and serves to prepare the person for either the **fight-or-flight reaction**, also known as the **defence reaction** (DR). A good example, and one often quoted in psychology textbooks, is proffered by William James in his article What is an emotion? (1884), where he cites the defence reaction we might have were we to encounter a bear in the countryside! While both OR and DR share similar properties, there are differences in the patterns of changes that accompany each. This means that when we are surprised we exhibit a different pattern of physiological behaviours than when we are frightened or repulsed.

BOX 7.14 PHYSIOLOGICAL CHANGES AND EMOTION

While there is little disagreement that some form of physiological change accompanies our different emotional states, the question still remains as to whether these physiological changes are unique or specific to the emotional state we are experiencing. William James (1884) was of the view that each emotion could be associated with specific bodily changes. In fact, emotion, according to James, was simply our experience of these different physiological states, so that our emotional reactions were merely bodily changes in blood pressure and so on. While there is some evidence to support James' contention that different classes of emotions are associated with different physiological patterns, there is some doubt as to whether all emotions that we experience can be distinguished on the basis of their unique bodily processes. In contrast to James, modern cognitive approaches put emphasis on the interpretative, or attributional nature of our emotional experiences. For example, according to Teasdale and Barnard (1993) our emotions are, in part, the result of our ability to evaluate our current bodily states in the context of current goals or needs.

Once we accept that a DR is associated with particular pattern of change in the ANS, we can see a theoretical explanation behind how the polygraph might work. Let us assume that the DR, and its particular pattern of physiological change, is in response to fear, or other negative emotions. Let us also assume that the act of deception is stressful and hence negative. Taken together, we see that the polygraph can detect those changes that are related to the person experiencing a frightening or negative event, which lying while being tested would be assumed to fulfil!

For everything to work, we would need some **baseline measurement** of the person's reaction to what we know are negative events, against which to compare the physiological patterns to questions where we suspect the person may be lying. Every polygraphic technique assumes that all of us have *something* to hide. The job of the examiner is to discover these things about the examinee and use them as the basis for control questions. Importantly, this is done with the full agreement of the person, so that certain factors, like surprise, can be ruled out. Control questions will be associated with identifiable changes in the heart, lungs, and electrodermal system; and these serve as the basis to compare the person's reactions to questions where it is suspected that the person is lying.

For example, suppose we want to know whether someone is telling the truth about stealing a car. We would first find out about other known negative events. We might ask the examinee 'is there anything you ever stole, no matter how small?' Once we know these other negative, autobiographical details, we develop control questions. We know that the event occurred and we know that when asked the question, if the person answers 'yes', he is responding truthfully. We would then compare the psychophysiological changes that accompanied the truthful answer with subsequent questions about stealing the car. If the two are similar, we can conclude that the person is telling the truth.

One of the most crucial elements to the polygraph being an accurate assessment tool is that the examinee must believe that the polygraph is infallible. In fact, this is an essential part of the examiner's job—to convince the person that the polygraph is an accurate and reliable way to tell whether someone is lying. If the examinee believes that the test is a reliable index of whether he is being truthful, he is more likely to have detectable physical reactions to lying, as he assumes that the examiner will know anyway! This shows the strong interaction between cognition, in this case our beliefs, and our emotional reactions.

Thus far, we have assumed that people's reactions when lying are uniform, that all of us respond in the same way, with the same set of patterns of ANS responses. In fact, research in the early 1950s and 1960s demonstrated clearly that the various peripheral indices of autonomic activity are poorly correlated (e.g. Lacey et al. 1953; Engel 1960). Further, the indices tend to be arranged in a pattern that is determined more by the constitution and previous experience of the individual examinee than the truthfulness of the replies. Autonomic specificity exists not only between individuals, but also between different situations. This means that the same person might produce a different pattern of responding over different situations.

Related to this is the concept of **habituation.** Habituation refers to the phenomenon where an individual's reactivity to an event becomes lessened through learning. Effectively, the novelty of an event becomes less when the event, or a similar event, is repeated. As the novelty decreases so too does our reaction to the event. The ANS learns that the event is 'old' and is less reactive to it, particularly when the event is associated with neutral, or mildly noxious, consequences. Habituation, which is one of the most basic types of learning, is as subject to individual differences as our initial reactivity to novel, negative stimuli.

Importantly, individual differences in reactivity and habituation seem to be governed by factors that are normally considered to pertain to personality. For example, people who are labelled as neurotic, either by questionnaire or by clinical examination, are more labile and show a different pattern of habituation than people who are not identified as neurotic. Other personality factors known to influence psychophysiological responses include sensation seeking, suggestibility, and gender. In fact, some psychologists have argued that the diversity of electrodermal responses is itself a personality factor.

What did the psychologist do?

The psychologist sought to provide a comprehensive review of all the relevant scientific literature and research, and to determine its viability and the need for further work. The psychologist always kept as his point of reference the application of the polygraph to pre-employment and in-service screening. He first conducted a number of computer searches within the open professional and scientific literature. Eliminating materials that were purely polemical, but retaining commentaries that represented informed opinion, the psychologist derived a literature base of over 370 papers and articles dealing with scientific aspects of polygraphy.

He developed three sections to include in his final report. The first section provided a theoretical and scientific perspective of the field of polygraphy, which was designed to help the naive reader understand the issues involved in evaluation. This included a historical review of the field and outlined guidelines for interpreting any controversial issues that arose regarding evaluation, such as issues of reliability, accuracy, and validity. The second, main section reviewed the literature in sufficient detail so that the reader had a firm appreciation of the types of procedure used in the investigation of the polygraph, and the empirical sources for any controversies or agreements. The final section dealt with the difficult question of how to improve on the reliability and accuracy of polygraphic techniques. The psychologist, by necessity, had to draw on the empirical findings of the scientific literature. However, this final section contained more of the psychologist's own, professional opinion, albeit one that was informed by the scientific literature. This final section also included an overview of the issues that were raised by the scientific literature.

These three sections formed the bulk of the final report that was presented. In addition, the final report contained a summary and recommendations on three separate issues. One regarded whether the government should adopt the polygraph as a reliable and accurate in-service or pre-employment tool. Another considered whether any research might be usefully commissioned to determine the validity of techniques for the detection of deception with specific reference to screening. Finally, a third addressed the extent to which any margins of error inherent in the techniques could be corrected by improving testing procedures.

On the basis of his review, the psychologist concluded that, as an instrument of detection, the polygraph lacked sufficient accuracy, and fell short of the standards set by conventional psychometric tests. He also suggested that any research directed at understanding the causal mechanisms behind the inaccuracy, or individual differences in reactivity or habituation, would not be prudent, as such research would require long-term investments and be unlikely to improve accuracy. However, the psychologist did feel that some efforts could be made in improving current testing procedures, primarily by examining the effectiveness of different examiners. He pointed out that much of the discrepancy between laboratory and field studies seemed to lie in the skill of the examiner.

To this end, the psychologist suggested that research could be usefully applied towards scientifically examining current practice that existed within an established service, such as an US Federal Agency. Through rigorous observation and controlled tests of trained examiners, such studies could throw light on the processes underlying polygraphy, although no research could be expected to provide a precise estimate of the practical efficacy of polygraph techniques. In fact, the psychologist's firm conclusion was that nothing in the polygraph literature led to the expectation that accuracy of detection could be improved substantially.

How was the psychologist's input assessed?

The psychologist delivered his report to the head of the branch, who in turn presented the formal report to the Prime Minister and the Cabinet. The Prime Minister, in turn, reported the conclusions of the study to the House of Commons. The informed decision of the government was that polygraph techniques are not sufficiently reliable to justify their usage in assessing or screening for security risk.

■ **ADDITIONAL READING**

Dixon, N.F. (1976) *On the Psychology of Military Incompetence*. Jonathan Cape, London. This is a serious and searching attempt to explain, in psychological terms, the frequency of disasters in the course of military history. The author served in the military for a number of years before training as a psychologist.

Watson, P. (1980) *War on the Mind: the Military Uses and Abuses of Psychology*. Penguin Books, New York. A careful consideration of the positive and negative aspects of psychology in warfare.

■ **QUESTIONS**

Scenario one

1 Do you think the psychologists had an obligation to report the findings publicly? Why?

2 What specific psychological problems might you expect an air crew to demonstrate after an otherwise avoidable accident had occurred?

Scenario two

1 How did reviewing the literature assist the psychologist in making his recommendations about the polygraph?

2 If you were to build a machine that could reliably detect a lie, what behaviours would you want it to measure?

8

The treatment room

In this chapter, we consider the treatment room, in which psychologists are called upon to deal with a variety of mental and emotional conditions. In the treatment room we find issues that have traditionally been dealt with by clinical psychology, counselling, therapy, and psychotherapy, although many other disciplines of psychology have proved invaluable. The focus of the chapter is to examine the ways in which mental and psychological problems have been understood, and see how modern developments in science and technology have changed the manner in which Western societies treat conditions of mental illness, neuroses, and other psychological problems. We provide a summary of the different major approaches to problems of the human psyche, and show how each approach adopts slightly different assumptions about human nature and what underlies our psychological states. There are a great many approaches to treatment and we cannot consider all of them exhaustively. They fall into two large groups. On the one hand are those methods and techniques that aim to deepen the client's understanding of their situation, believing that greater understanding will lead to greater freedom of action. On the other hand are the methods and techniques that aim directly to change the behaviour, or the attitudes, that trouble the client. The former are often referred to as insight-oriented therapies, whereas the latter are referred to as action-oriented. In this chapter we confine our attention to the insight-oriented therapies, leaving the action-oriented group to be discussed in 'The sport room' (Chapter 9), where they also find application. The two scenarios provide clear examples of how psychologists from diverse disciplines interact with each other to operate in the treatment room. The first scenario deals with the issue of false memories and shows how psychologists from different disciplines clashed over theoretical explanations for recovered memory behaviour, with serious real-world consequences. The second scenario examines the problem of insomnia and illustrates how a modern theory of working memory was applied to develop an effective treatment for sleeplessness.

Introduction

All of us have what we call our good days, or ups, and our bad days, or downs. We associate our good days with positive moods and emotions, such as happiness, interest, creativity, joy, or contentment. We experience a certain physical vitality and our social interactions are satisfying. In contrast, our bad days are associated with darker moods and emotions, such as anxiety, depression, envy, sadness, or fear. Our physical state may reflect uncomfortable restlessness or a lack of vigour; and we may have difficulty in relating to others. Our emotional fluctuations are part of what makes us human, and whether we like it or not, we all have to accept that some days will be better than other days. It is how we come to cope and understand our bad days that forms part of the basis for the treatment room.

While we may accept that we will have the odd bad day, when we have prolonged mood swings, or are so distracted that we cannot live in the manner that is acceptable to us, we want things to change. In fact, many people will enter the treatment room only *after* they have exhausted help from family, friends, general medical practitioners, and pastoral carers. The reason for a person entering the treatment room varies. Some people are referred formally by their medical doctors while others go at the insistence of their spouse or close friends. However, most people will enter the treatment room for the same reason—they want to change so that they can become mentally, emotionally, or spiritually healthier, lead more-productive lives, and learn more-adaptive ways of being.

The late nineteenth century saw the emergence of a technique that served as the basis for most modern psychotherapies—a method used by an Austrian physician Josef Breuer (1842–1925), in his treatment of a young female patient known as Anna O. Anna suffered what Breuer referred to as **conversion hysteria**, which involved a variety of physical symptoms that had no apparent physical cause. These symptoms included paralysis in her arms and legs, and mutism, or the inability to speak. Breuer discovered that when he successfully encouraged Anna to speak of her feelings, at times she would recall what seemed highly painful childhood memories—memories that she had somehow blocked out—and relived painful emotions. Once doing so, her physical symptoms dissipated. Breuer associated the effects of talking with a release of blocked emotional reactions and feelings, and called this emotional release *catharsis*. Breuer shared his story of the success of catharsis to his young friend Sigmund Freud, who, in turn, developed it into a formal system of psychotherapy.

Modern treatment rooms

In this section, we consider modern treatment rooms. We first describe the basic steps usually involved in assessment and identification of the person's problem, and how treatment interventions are selected and reviewed. We then go on to discuss the different major orientations that have emerged from the twentieth century and continue to be dominant today. We identify two major groups, which can be distinguished in terms of the focus of their explanation. One offers explanations of underlying biological and genetic factors, while the other focuses on psychological processes and unresolved conflicts. The first is best described as a medical or biopsychological approach and is characterized by the use of drugs and other physical interventions. Examples of the second group include psychoanalytic models, behavioural and cognitive approaches, and humanistic therapies. Each orientation has different views about mental and emotional health and endorses different techniques in the treatment of dysfunctional behaviours.

The modern treatment room deals with mental, emotional, and behavioural problems; and the explanations offered for these problems rely exclusively on natural causes, be they psychological or physical causes. We distinguish therapies as belonging to two mega-groups. The first can be called the physical or biological group, where explanations of disorders are discussed in terms of neurological, neurochemical, and genetic or physiological problems. This group encompasses *medical models*. Most professionals who adopt the medical model are *psychiatrists*, who have medical training prior to specializing in mental health problems. We will therefore not consider them in detail here.

The second is the psychology group, where explanations focus on disturbances in mental and emotional processes. The psychology group can be further subdivided into two, smaller groups, which some psychologists refer to as the *insight-oriented group* and the *action-oriented group*. The insight-oriented group focuses on the person gaining a better understanding of the underlying causes for the problem by exploring the person's phenomenal experience or *consciousness* (see pp. 174–9). The action-oriented group does not exclude an examination of underlying psychological conflicts; however, their main interest is changing the person's behaviour. Professionals associated with the psychology group include *clinical psychologists, counsellors, counselling psychologists, therapists*, and *psychotherapists*. As noted previously, we discuss the action-oriented approaches in 'The sport room' (Chapter 9).

A psychologist operating within the treatment room may work with major mental health issues, such as **psychoses**; equally, the psychologist may be asked to work with problems like panic attacks, or other types of **neurosis**. The distinction between psychoses and neuroses is not always straightforward, and different authors focus on slightly different features. One clear difference is the extent to which the person has a sense of reality and operates effectively in everyday situations. Generally, people suffering from psychoses have trouble in maintaining a distinction between reality and fantasy, and in extreme cases are incapable of successfully operating in the everyday world. An example would be a person who hears voices coming from their washing machine, ordering them to shave their head. This person has a distorted appreciation of reality; their experience of the world is fragmented, a blur between what is real and what is imagined.

In contrast, a person suffering from a neurotic condition can maintain their grasp of reality and would also be expected to function adequately in everyday situations. For example, a person who suffers from a phobic condition, such as a fear of spiders, can

---

BOX 8.1 THE FRAGMENTED LIFE OF A SCHIZOPHRENIC

Schizophrenia is a psychotic illness, equally likely to occur in men and women, although the most recent research suggests that men develop the illness earlier than women across all cultures (for a detailed analysis of this topic, see Raesaenen et al. 2000). Schizophrenia affects perception, cognition, emotions, and motor behaviour. The person may have sensory experiences without any external, sensory stimulation, called *hallucinations*; for example, hearing voices. Cognition is distorted in schizophrenia primarily through the operation of delusional belief systems. Delusions are irrational, in that the person believes in something that contradicts most of the available evidence, such as a person believing that they are an alien. The emotional symptoms of schizophrenia vary, but often reflect inappropriate reactions, like emotional flatness or outbursts of inappropriate emotional reactions, such as laughing aloud when someone is in need of help. Because of difficulties in processing and reacting to emotional information, the schizophrenic is often socially impaired, and fails to have extensive life experiences, which serves to further ostracize them. Motor symptoms have a similarly negative impact on the schizophrenic's social life, as the symptoms can include unusual eye movements (see Wolff and O'Driscoll 1999).

---

still function in the everyday world, holding down a job and having a family, and does not have a generally fragmented view of reality—except perhaps in relation to spiders. Some authors suggest that neuroses are normal reactions that somehow have become more intense or more exaggerated.

Stages in the treatment room

Regardless of the orientation, the professional will first perform some sort of assessment of the type, extent, or nature of the person's problems—generally referred to as presenting problems or symptoms. The manner in which an assessment is conducted will depend on many factors. For example, some professionals use standardized assessment procedures in order to reach diagnoses of the presenting problems. These diagnoses will be based on clinical observations such as are provided in the diagnostic manuals, the *Diagnostic and Statistical Manual of Mental Disorder* (DSM), and the *International Classification of Diseases* (ICD) of the World Health Organization. Both the DSM and ICD provide a set of discrete categories of mental, emotional, and behavioural problems. Each disorder is described in terms of a set of symptoms that must be present in order for a person to receive a diagnosis. For example, if a person is diagnosed as having **post-traumatic stress disorder** (PTSD), the person must demonstrate a set of symptoms that includes heightened anxiety, intrusive thoughts, avoidance strategies, and emotional re-experiences.

Once an assessment interview has been conducted, the psychologist will identify the intervention techniques that might be used to treat or alleviate the person's difficulties. This can involve some sort of contract with the client or patient, whereby the method of intervention, time of treatment, and area(s) of focus are agreed. It is usual that the

---

BOX 8.2 WHAT CONSTITUTES A DISORDER?

Most experts agree that a disorder has three distinct features. First, the disorder has symptoms that are abnormal, relative to some norm. As this is a statistical concept of average, there are two ways in which symptoms can be abnormal. One is in terms of the type of behaviour, emotions, or thoughts. If most people, on average, do not display similar behaviours under similar situations, then the behaviour is abnormal. An example would be a pedestrian shouting obscenities to passers-by in cars. Most pedestrians do not display that behaviour in most situations. Symptoms can also be abnormal in some quantitative sense. For example, the average person is unlikely to wash their hands forty or fifty times a day, as might happen with some **obsessive compulsive disorders**. Second, the symptoms must disrupt normal, everyday functioning. An example is a *phobia* that prevents a person from leaving her home, significantly disrupting many everyday activities. Third, psychological disorders may have some degree of personal distress associated with them. While the person still has insight into their disorder, they are disturbed and experience other negative emotions. However, obvious exceptions to this exist, as in those individuals who commit criminal offences, and who show little or no remorse for their actions.

---

psychologist and the person coming for treatment will review and assess the progress and success of the intervention programme.

The final stage in the treatment room is, of course, cessation of treatment. When treatment should end is not always easy to define, and what exactly constitutes successful treatment varies with the orientation. Limited research and inconsistent **operational definitions** make it difficult to draw any firm conclusions. However, we note here that most of the evidence suggests that the success of any intervention is entirely unrelated to the orientation used in the treatment room!

An ethical dilemma

Before considering techniques used frequently in modern treatment rooms, there is another highly controversial issue that we need to at least address. It has to do with the relationship between the so-called expert, namely the psychologist, and the person coming for treatment, the layperson. There is a peculiar relationship between the psychologist and the layperson in the treatment room. The psychologist has specialized knowledge and skills, in the same way that the ancient shaman did; and critically the layperson coming into the treatment room is likely to be vulnerable and in need of help. This inequality in knowledge and skill introduces a power imbalance, in favour of the expert.

This power imbalance is associated with an ethical dilemma, as it introduces the possibility for abuse. The potential for abuse is of real concern to governing bodies of today's treatment rooms. In fact, some psychologists, like Jeffrey Masson, argue that any treatment based on *therapy* is inherently unethical, by virtue of the fact that it relies on the inevitable power imbalance between the expert and the client. While Mason argues an extreme view, we believe that any psychologist acting as an expert in the treatment room

---

BOX 8.3 CLIENT CHOICE, A NEW PATH?

By far the most common treatment procedure in busy settings is to assign the patient or client to an available therapist, who chooses a particular treatment. It has often been argued that patients should be free to choose the therapist *and* the therapy that they prefer. The argument advanced against this is that patients and clients do not have sufficient knowledge to make this judgement. Even in private health settings the choice is rarely left to the 'customer'. Recently, two Israeli psychologists, Rachel Lev-Wiesel and Hada Doron, have experimented with programmes in which the patient is offered a choice of therapies and encouraged to choose the one that appeals most, simply on the basis of preference (Lev-Wiesel and Doron 2004). The therapies offered were unconventional non-verbal methods (dance, drama, art, diary-keeping, or bibliotherapy), which are based on the view that self-expression is helpful in resolving personal conflicts. Whether the results would apply across a wider range of therapies remains to be seen, but their findings indicated that choice of the preferable therapy by the patient leads to more-satisfactory outcomes. The ethical problem hopefully disappears! Indeed, some of their patients attributed therapeutic benefits to the mere act of choosing for themselves.

---

must be highly sensitive to the fact that they are powerful and highly influential, especially when working with vulnerable people.

The psychodynamic orientation

In this section we consider the psychodynamic orientation, which includes the insight models of psychoanalysis and other psychodynamic approaches. The psychodynamic orientation is concerned with explaining disorders and psychological problems in terms of conflicts between the different levels of an individual's personality, which largely occur outside of the person's immediate awareness. We briefly consider the common assumptions behind some major models characteristic of this orientation, including Sigmund Freud's theory of consciousness and personality. We touch briefly on some of the modern psychodynamic theories and discuss some of the common humanistic techniques that are used in the treatment room.

All psychodynamic models assume that human behaviour, whether normal or abnormal, is the result of underlying **motivations**, **drives**, or **instincts** associated with different aspects of our personality. Some of our motives are available to our conscious awareness; others are not. Unfortunately, the different bits of our personality, and their respective motives, are not always in agreement and conflicts erupt. Our internal war leads us to experience a breakdown in our insight. The psychodynamic orientation offers a way of better identifying and understanding these conflicts. This is achieved largely through the process of analysis and interpretation, where the *symbolic content* of our behaviours, dreams, thoughts, and language are uncovered, interpreted, and understood.

BOX 8.4 PSYCHIC DETERMINISM AND THE UNDERSTANDING OF BEHAVIOUR

Psychic determinism is one of the major assumptions behind psychodynamic approaches. It argues that every aspect of our behaviour, which includes thoughts, images, feelings, and actions, is influenced by or linked to a related internal state. The term used to describe this internal state differs with different, specific models. Sigmund Freud referred to **drive** or **instinct**, whereas Alfred Adler considered *motivation* to compete. The link between the behaviour and internal state may be direct, and the person may be conscious of the link. For example, you may be aware that you are hungry as you stop off at the food shop to pick up a sandwich. Equally, the links may be indirect and outside the person's awareness or understanding. For example, you may discover that you have eaten a whole bag of peanuts without ever realizing that you were hungry. Importantly because of their emphasis on motivation, psychodynamic models simultaneously consider the nature of personality—which makes them unique among all other orientations. The reason is straightforward: *someone* must have the motivation, and that requires some discussion of the individual, and their personality. In the context of the treatment room, it is the person's inability to have insight or understand the motivation behind their behaviour that results in problems.

Because of the emphasis on analysis, the psychodynamic orientation is an example of insight therapy.

The models of treatment that fall under the psychodynamic heading have in common the following assumptions. The first is that our behaviour is determined by psychological motives, drives, or desires, as we have already said. This is often referred to as **psychic determinism** (see Box 8.4). A second assumption is that our consciousness is along a continuum of awareness to unawareness. Much of what motivates our behaviour is assumed to occur outside of our conscious awareness. Thus we are likely to be aware of only some of the motives behind what we think, feel, and do. Treatments developed from a psychodynamic orientation operate to broaden our awareness, and attempt to bring what is outside our awareness *into* our awareness. A third assumption is that our early personal experiences greatly influence not only our adult personality, but also the habitual ways in which we interact with the world. Consequently, early experiences will often be the focus of therapeutic attention. A fourth assumption is that the therapist, or professional, is the only one, in the first instance, who can help us understand the symbolic content of our behaviour. It is the therapist's interpretation and skills in identifying patterns that serves as the basis for reaching greater insight. Importantly, this introduces the power imbalance that we have already mentioned in the relationship between therapist and the person seeking treatment.

Sigmund Freud and early psychoanalysis

It is beyond the scope of this book to discuss even a minuscule amount of Sigmund Freud's work on the human psyche. We have had difficulty in deciding which of Freud's significant contributions we should highlight, and which we should ignore. We note that Freud had a similarly high regard for himself, expressing on numerous occasions that he was one of the three most important contributors to Western science, along with Copernicus and Darwin! In any eventuality, we cannot do justice to the impact of Freud's work. Instead, we discuss some of his original concepts that have found their place in either colloquial expressions or have been appropriated by professionals from other orientations.

Sigmund Freud (1856–1939) held that all mental behaviour had naturalistic causes, and would eventually be understood in terms of physiological explanations. However, he also realized that medical knowledge was not sufficiently advanced at the time, so he focused on *mental constructs*. Freud's primary interest was to understand *hysterias*, and he already knew of the success of the technique of *hypnosis*, wherein the patient was put in a semi-trance-like state. However, he was particularly fascinated by the work of Breuer (see above, p. 170), as Breuer's work seemed to point to the importance of the *content* of what the patient reported while under hypnosis. Freud reasoned that the positive effects of hypnosis reported by Breuer were the direct result of the patient recalling a traumatic memory, rather than being in a hypnotic state *per se*.

The concept of catharsis allowed Freud to draw a causal link between the mind and the body. Somehow, mental processes were the underlying causes of physical symptoms. To further explore this link, Freud abandoned hypnosis in favour of a new technique, **free association**. In free association, the patient is encouraged to say aloud any thoughts or images that come to mind, without worrying about whether these thoughts or images make sense. Indeed, there would often appear to be no obvious connection between the various thoughts or images that the patient was reporting, and the patient's present-ing symptoms. However, as Freud believed that all behaviour was determined by mental events, the absence of an obvious relationship between the patient's problems and the contents of their free association did not deter him. Quite the contrary; through long and careful analyses, Freud would eventually discover a pattern.

Often, the process of free association would result in the patient recalling a previ-ously forgotten traumatic event, one that the patient seemingly had banished from their conscious awareness. Freud referred to this mechanism as **repression**, where a patient could completely block the memory from consciousness, acting as if they had amnesia for the event. However, after recalling the repressed memory, the patient felt some relief. This led Freud to posit his theory of consciousness and personality, where unpleasant thoughts and experiences are actively pushed away from our conscious awareness, and reside, instead, at hidden, lower levels.

Sources of the Freudian model

Two other factors also greatly biased Freud's thinking. One was his preferred method of study, and the other was the patient population he treated. Although Freud was well educated in experimental methodologies, he was first and foremost a clinician. Because of this, his preferred method for studying human behaviour was the *case study*. As we have shown in Chapter 1, the case study relies on the clinical observations of a single person, which may include in-depth documentation of family and personal history, personal abilities, as well as repeated observations across different time periods, and for varying lengths of time. While the case-study method provides an ideal opportunity to examine specific factors like individual differences to a much greater extent, it can suffer from a lack of generality. This means that conclusions drawn about the relationship between mental problems and personal history may be relevant only to the specific patient being observed, rather than reflecting a general trend that is found in most of the population. We suggest, as do many others, that Freud's conclusions suffer from the fact that they were not based on sufficiently large numbers to make the sweeping generalizations that he wished to proclaim.

The second factor that biased Freud's thinking was the type of cases in which he was involved. Freud mainly treated middle-class women suffering from hysterias, within the historical and cultural context of a sexually repressed society. Importantly, many of Freud's patients recalled childhood memories that were sexual in nature, and in which they implicated family members or family friends as abusers. We discuss the implications of this for Freud below, in scenario one. For the moment we note that because of the sexual nature of many of his patients' recovered memories, Freud assumed that much of what motivates our behaviour is sexual energy. This assumption was abandoned by most of the psychodynamic models that emerged subsequently.

On the basis of his clinical observations and analyses, Freud concluded that human consciousness was divided into the *conscious* and the *subconscious*, the latter of which he further divided into the *pre-conscious* and the *unconscious*. Related to these levels of consciousness were different levels of the personality, including *ego, super-ego*, and *id*. Freud's view of consciousness is topographical, in that some information is *up* in consciousness, while other information is *down* in the unconscious. It is also spatial, in that he assumed that the size of the unconscious was much larger and contained more than either the pre-conscious or conscious.

We discuss all of these concepts at greater length in scenario one. For the moment we note that Freud believed that the contents of the unconscious, and the associated drives of the id, are forcibly kept out of conscious awareness by **defence mechanisms** used by the ego, such as repression. According to Freud, we are constantly in conflict, trying to prevent any of our unconscious thoughts or images from entering our awareness because

---

BOX 8.5 HYSTERIAS AND OTHER MYSTERIES

Hysterias posed a particularly interesting problem for professionals like Freud. Hysterias were defined as disorders where the patient would report physical symptoms for which there would be no physical basis. A good example is that of *glove anaesthesia*. With glove anaesthesia, the patient reports a loss of feeling and sensation in the hand, below the wrist and involving the entire hand, as if they were wearing a glove. While much less was known about the workings of the body, there was sufficient understanding of neurology to know that this condition was essentially impossible from a neurological point of view. Any damage that affected the neural connections in the hand would follow the pattern of nerve distribution in discrete segments. If no such patterned loss of sensation were demonstrated, the professionals could reasonably conclude that glove anaesthesia was not the result of any physical trauma. While common during Freud's time, hysterias are virtually unheard of in modern treatment rooms, reflecting the effects that society's attitudes have on the nature of mental disorders.

BOX 8.6 FREUDIAN SLIPS AND OTHER PARAPRAXES

Freud believed that evidence for the unconscious directly intruding into consciousness came from *parapraxes*, which include everyday errors and slips of the tongue, still known today as Freudian slips. He believed that all behaviour was motivated and that nothing occurred randomly. Thus, when a person did make an error—either in terms of their actions or their speech—Freud assumed that it was the contents of the unconscious slipping through the net of the defence mechanisms into conscious awareness. For example, in a well-known television sitcom, one of the main characters, Ross, is getting married. As he repeats his vows at the church, he says the name of his previous girlfriend, Rachel, rather than saying the bride's name, Emily. This Freudian slip was interpreted as showing that the character still harboured feelings for his old girlfriend, feelings of which he was unaware. Intriguingly, Freud was sometimes reluctant to apply these arguments to his own behaviour. For example, while attending a conference, instead of going to the location where he would be attending lectures, Freud 'found' himself in the red light district. He regarded this as a mere mistake rather than the operation of his unconscious. Even after he had made the same mistake *three times*, Freud still refused to believe that his behaviour was motivated by any underlying drives and described it in his paper as an example of the 'uncanny'!

---

they are too threatening, too dangerous, or too traumatic. When this conflict becomes unmanageable, the ego can no longer prevent unconscious contents from entering consciousness and mental disorders occur.

However, even under normal circumstances, our ego's defence mechanisms are imperfect, and can never completely shut out the contents of the unconscious. Consequently, our unwanted and undesirable thoughts sometimes seep into our conscious awareness. These thoughts can enter our consciousness directly, but more often they will intrude in some converted, symbolical form, as in day and night dreams.

Modern psychodynamic models and treatment techniques

Freud's theories are responsible for the development of many other psychodynamic theories, particularly after the publication of his book, *The Ego and the Id*, in 1923. There are the works of the neo-Freudians, which include the writings of Jung, Anna Freud, and Adler; and then there are the theories of the non-Freudians, which include Horney, Erikson, Winnicott, and Bowlby. We cannot do justice to any of them, any more than we have done justice to Freud's teachings.

All of these subsequent theories share the assumption of psychic determinism and stress the importance of early experiences in influencing the person's development. The major differences occur in terms of what is regarded as the basis for motivation. For example, in Carl Jung's view, the ultimate goal for a person is to achieve **individuation**, whereby the person strives, generally unsuccessfully, for a unification of the conscious with the unconscious. Importantly, Jung believed in the importance of the **collective unconscious**—where we, as human beings, share universal themes and images that are biologically based rather than based on experience. For Adler, another neo-Freudian, love, friendships, and a strong commitment to society motivate a healthy person. In contrast, Karen Horney discusses the child's need for security and the anxiety that is associated with this need; and focuses on early relationships in an effort to understand how the person characteristically deals with other people in intimate relationships.

While the type of treatment technique that is used by different psychodynamic models varies, interpretation is still the most common technique. The professional interprets the symbolic or latent meaning behind the client's behaviours in an effort to enhance the client's insight into the nature of their problems. So, for example, you may be asked to free associate and you suddenly have thoughts about a house you once wanted to buy but did not. The psychodynamic professional will interpret the symbolic meaning of this house, in the context of other images and thoughts that you have reported; for example, how the house represents your unfulfilled desires that you have never realized.

Objections to the psychodynamic model

Psychodynamic models are often criticized on two grounds. First, as interpretation is the major mode of treatment, this introduces the possibility that the same patient can be analysed very differently by different therapists. So, you could go to one therapist and be told that your problems stem from source X, while another therapist will tell you that your problems stem from source Y. Thus, there seems to be an arbitrary nature to the interpretation.

Second, there is the issue of prediction. Few of the psychodynamic models actually provide *predictions about behaviour*, a requisite that is valued in other disciplines of psychology. Thus, while Freud could explain and understand most of human behaviour, he was never able to *predict* whether a certain individual would, or would not, demonstrate a particular type of unhealthy behaviour. However, this criticism is not actually relevant to Freud's contributions, in our opinion. We believe Freud is better viewed as providing a *framework* for understanding the human psyche; a framework, by definition, cannot be falsified.

We conclude our discussion by pointing out that the psychodynamic orientation is fatalistic. From a psychodynamic perspective, our intra-psychic conflict is inevitable and we are all fated to suffer conflict for most of our lives. If that were not bad enough, our past experiences influence the conflicts we have and limit the way in which we can react. Furthermore, most of our conflicts occur outside awareness and we are incapable of explaining our own behaviour—we need an analyst to help us interpret what is going on! The best we can do is to learn how to better cope with our psychic strife, through careful analysis. In part, it was this somewhat pessimistic view of the human condition that led to the development of a different group of insight therapies, known collectively as the humanistic orientation.

The humanistic orientation

In this section, we consider the humanistic orientation, which rejects notions of unconscious drives in favour of more positive views about the psyche. The humanistic orientation is another example of insight therapies, where the goal is to aid the person's understanding of the reasons for their problems. Models under this orientation assume that the human psyche is essentially good and that much of behaviour is under our conscious control, or under our will. While negative, early experiences still have a place in explaining a person's problems, and any blocks resulting from them can be removed and overcome. We review the major proponents of this approach, including Carl Rogers, who is largely responsible for the development of the core conditions of counselling.

Like the psychodynamic orientation, the humanistic orientation is an example of the insight therapies, where the ultimate goal of treatment is to enhance the person's understanding and awareness of, or insight into, their behaviour. However, beyond this similarity, they have very little in common. The humanistic orientation is much more optimistic and positive. It highlights the role of personal choice and heralds the importance of upholding the person's subjective experience. As such, humanism is in direct contrast to the psychodynamic orientation, where treatment is predicated on the assumption that the person's conscious experience reflects the operation of defence mechanisms like repression, and, accordingly, should be discarded.

Basic assumptions

Two assumptions underlie all models associated with the humanist orientation. The first is that the individual's subjective experience of the world, or *phenomenal experience*, is the key to understanding all behaviour. This assumption uniquely distinguishes the humanistic orientation from all others. All of us have their own view of the world, their own way of understanding what is important in life. Humanistic models are concerned with *accepting* our phenomenal experience and personal meaning of the world. This has the immediate effect of making the person who enters the treatment room an equal partner in the therapeutic relationship. Such egalitarianism is reflected in the use of the word *client* rather than *patient*, the latter of which is used in both biopsychological and psychodynamic models.

For the humanist, the client's difficulties arise when they adopt behaviours that are inconsistent or *incongruent* with who they actually are. This distinction has been called the difference between the **ideal self** and the **actual self**. Treatment involves helping the person to value and trust their own experiences and conscious awareness—to be who you *are* rather than who you *should be*. In essence, treatment is about the person having *congruence* between their ideal and actual selves. Not surprisingly, treatment is directed by the client's needs rather than the therapist's interpretations or perceptions.

The second basic assumption is that our behaviour has an element of wilfulness, or choice. We have control over what we do and say, how we react and feel, rather than being enslaved by either past experiences or present drives and instincts. From a humanistic perspective, part of treatment is to help us to regain our free will and choice. Again, this is in direct contrast to both biopsychological and psychodynamic orientations, which assume that our behaviour is governed and programmed by our genetics and physiology, and by our biological and psychological needs, drives and instincts.

Carl Rogers and the person-centred approach

Of all the models that have developed from the humanistic orientation, that proposed by Carl Rogers is one of the most influential. His approach, developed in the 1950s, is known as client-centred or **person-centred therapy**. Rogers considered human behaviour to be motivated by higher-level needs, needs to do with mental, emotional, and spiritual aspects of living. Rogers referred to the source of these higher-level motives as the **actualizing tendency**. According to Rogers, the actualizing tendency enables us to be curious and learn more about our world, and allows us to value things such as beauty, friendship, and love. Rogers believed that the actualizing tendency promotes healthy development and that a person who is sensitive to—'in touch with'—this energy will flourish.

Rogers also believed that each of us has a unique experience, or view, of the world. He referred to this as the person's **phenomenal field**. Importantly, Rogers believed that our phenomenal field was determined not only by what actually *was happening* but also by what we *believed to be happening*. While our perceptions are undoubtedly influenced by the external world, Rogers argued strongly that our perceptions are also based on our own biased interpretations, or values. We have already considered this when we discussed the concept of top-down processing (see Chapter 4, p. 46). Rogers acknowledges the influence of top-down processing when he states, 'We live by a perceptual "map", which is never reality itself' (Rogers 1951, p. 485). For Rogers, when our perceptions are guided more by our past, or by our expectations, rather than by our current needs and our actualizing tendency, things go awry for us.

As no two people will view the same external event in exactly the same way, they will not share the same phenomenal field. However, there may be some overlap. Such overlap might occur if people share similar beliefs about the world, or hold values of the world that are similar. For example, suppose you and another person witness a small puppy being beaten and, simultaneously, you both intervene to protect the defenceless animal. Because of your shared belief that it is unacceptable to beat small animals, you both perceive the situation in a similar fashion and react similarly.

When the phenomenal fields are sufficiently different, difficulties can arise. For example, imagine that you are feeling a bit sensitive about your recent decision to get a startling new haircut. Your friend enters the room and questions your decision to change your image, saying that they are not sure whether they like your new look or not. What

---

BOX 8.7 THE EVER-CHANGING SELF OF THE 1960S

While Rogers maintained his view of a fluid self in the 1950s, the notion that there was stability in personality dominated psychology until the 1960s. The stable self is consistent across situations, which is why we are able to say that we are a caring person, or a fun-loving person. These aspects of our personality do not change over time or, if they do, change only very slowly and after extreme stress. However, Walter Mischel challenged this dominant view (Mischel 1968). According to Mischel, if stable personality traits are the reason why we behave in the way that we do, then there should be strong consistency across behaviours that are supposed to reflect the same trait. For example, if you are an optimistic person, then you should score high on a test that assesses optimism and also have a tendency to behave in an optimistic way, seeing a glass as half full rather than half empty. However, Mischel noted that different behaviours, alleged to reflect the same aspect of the stable self, were at best only modestly correlated, and rarely accounted for more than 10% of the *explanatory variability* in behaviour! This meant that other factors, such as the situation, were responsible in determining why the person behaved in the way that they did. Mischel provided strong evidence to suggest that the importance of a stable self was inadequate at best, and misleading at worst.

---

your friend perceives as showing an interest in your looks is interpreted by you as being critical and just confirming that your decision was a bad one. This shows how a lack of understanding of the other's perceptions can result in problems. Rogers argued that such differences can be minimized if people use *empathy*, and attempt to understand the perceptions and beliefs of others. To this end, he advocated treatment that relies on empathy between therapist and client.

One of the most important aspects of Rogers's thinking was his notion of the self, in which he distinguished the ideal self and the actual self. Rogers regarded the self as something that is constantly changing, and ever developing. In this sense, Rogers is different from other theorists using the concept of self, where the implication is that there is some stable, core aspect to the person that does not change across situations, or across time. For him, the self is constantly changing and, for health, the self needs to be guided by the actualizing tendency, rather than beliefs about what should or should not be.

Treatment in person-centred models

Rogers was responsible for defining what have come to be known as the core conditions of counselling. These are adopted by most humanists, and even find some favour with professionals using other approaches. These conditions are defined in terms of what the client needs in order to achieve congruence between ideal and actual selves, what Rogers called the **conditions of growth** for a healthy individual. As long as the professional in the treatment room ensures conditions of growth, the client will develop in a manner that achieves health and well-being. When these conditions are absent, the client experiences feelings which result in a mismatch between ideal and actual selves.

One of the central conditions for growth is **unconditional positive regard**. Unconditional positive regard is achieved when the professional conveys to the client that they are acceptable just as they are. The professional respects the client, without the client having the need to change, and avoids judging or evaluating the client. Instead, the focus is on accepting and supporting the client. In part, unconditional positive regard means the professional avoids making suggestions or problem-solving, as these would introduce the *therapist's* phenomenal experience and meaning of the world. A second core condition is that the professional is *empathic*, and is willing to adopt the viewpoint and world models of the client. The professional avoids his own interpretation and instead allows the client to act as the guide. This is supported through the technique of reflecting back to the client, where the professional ensures that he has understood the client's meaning by rephrasing or repeating what the client has said.

The third core condition for growth is achieved through the professional being *genuine*, or congruent with their own feelings, and communicating these feelings to the client, be they positive or negative. Whereas this may seem slightly at odds with unconditional positive regard, in practice the two techniques complement each other. For example, if you, the professional, are sad that a client has made the choice to leave his job, you might say, 'I am feeling sad that you have made that choice because I wanted you to stay. And, I support you to make the decision that you want to make.' In this way, you are genuine, or congruent, with your own views, and yet you demonstrate to your client that you are willing to accept the client's choice, unconditionally.

Other humanistic models of treatment

Two other well-known humanistic models are Gestalt therapy and existential psychology. The Gestalt approach was championed primarily through the writings of Fritz and Laura Perls, Ralph Hefferline, and Paul Goodman, with authors like Walter Kempler introducing Gestalt principles into *family therapy*. Gestalt relies on theories of perception advocated by German psychologists like Koehler, who argued that perception is an active process, in which people impose structure on their environment so as to produce a **figure** and **ground**. The figure is something that you are consciously aware of and attending to, that to which you focally attend, such as the words on this page. In contrast, the ground is what is going on outside your focal awareness, which might be your tactile sensations of touching the page. The figure is that which is most related to your current interests, needs, and goals. So, while reading this page, if you heard someone shout 'fire!', the fire exit would become the figure to which you would give your undivided focal attention!

Like other humanistic approaches, Gestaltists believe in the concepts of behaviour being driven by needs, in the importance of the person's genuine or actual self, and in the concept of choice. Gestalt believes that we have needs that direct our behaviour, and that our health is contingent upon us getting our needs fulfilled and interacting with our environment in a way that is good for us. However, when our needs are consistently thwarted or we are prevented from being who we are, we get stuck in a cycle of old behaviours—called *unfinished business*. We are stifled and cannot grow; we develop a false self and suffer from anxieties, depression, and malaise. Our behaviour becomes dysfunctional because we are imposing these old, unfulfilled needs onto the present, thereby preventing us from being in the here and now. Importantly, we do this without awareness, so that it is our unconscious state that is dictating what we are doing. Gestalt treatments involve supporting the client to be aware of when they are imposing old needs onto the present. Like Rogers, the intention is to support the person to be authentic, in the here and now, and base their choices on the present, rather than the past. Gestaltists stress that we are all responsible for our actions, and that, through awareness and choice, we can determine the manner in which live.

The existentialist approach

Existentialism manages to combine the essential pessimism of psychodynamic approaches by asserting that death and suffering are inevitable, with the optimism of Rogers with its emphasis on the importance of finding meaning in one's life. The existential approach in psychotherapy grew out of the popularity of the existential movement in philosophy in Europe after the Second World War. Existentialism as a philosophy had been influential in Europe, especially in France and Germany, for more than a century. Its themes centred on the analysis of being: being-in-itself and being-in-the-world. The latter refers to the state of being fully engaged with the real world in every moment of existence. This was a rather serious and melancholy philosophy that assumed a popular form among students and intellectuals who had experienced the war and its aftermath in Europe. Rollo May, an American psychologist, and his colleagues, introduced these ideas to the English-speaking world as an approach to understanding therapy. (May 1953, 1969, 1983; May et al. 1958) The therapeutic process becomes one of understanding the client's personal situation and the goal of therapy is to 'help the patient recognize and *experience* his own existence' (our italics). Being is defined as the individual's pattern of possibilities; non-being is taken to be the *failure* to realize them. In a later book, May emphasized that existential therapy is not a system of techniques, unlike, for example, Gestalt therapy. Therapy is 'a way of understanding human existence' and the role of the therapist is first to know and understand the client (May 1983).

Viktor Frankl promotes this approach in his 1992 book, *Man's Search for Meaning*. He argues that human malaise is the result of us failing to find meaning in a life that is essentially bound by sorrow and loss. Frankl's emphasis on finding meaning parallels the central importance of subjective meaning in other humanistic approaches. However, unlike Rogers or other humanists, Frankl disputes the existence of any consistent themes in life, as nothing transcends the here and now. Each minute of our lives affords us with a new opportunity to make choices and create whatever it is we want to be, and want the world to be. It will be clear from the foregoing that this form of therapy is not for amateurs. Its concepts are difficult to define and difficult to understand. However, for a group of committed disciples it offers relief from some of the more subtle anxieties of the modern world!

SCENARIO ONE

THE DEBATE OVER RECOVERED MEMORIES

In this scenario we focus on a debate that threatened to tear apart the different disciplines of psychology, the debate over recovered memories. The phenomena of recovered memories involve highly controversial issues, including questions about the nature of consciousness, the relationship between emotions and cognition, and the influence that treatment techniques can have on people undergoing professional help. The modern debate began under the most difficult of circumstances, where adults were accusing their parents of physical and sexual abuse when they were children. The pattern seemed to be that recovery occurred after the person had experienced some form of cathartic experience, resulting in the previously forgotten memories becoming accessible to conscious reporting. This cathartic experience could be the result of some insight gained through therapy, self-help books, or support groups; or through television and media coverage. Clinicians and other professionals with clinical experience could understand easily how such recovery might take place.

Understandably, those parents who believed themselves to be innocent of the charges attempted to enlist support from whatever expert they could, and found experimental psychologists eager to provide their services. In particular, support for parents came from cognitive psychologists, who had no experience of clinical conditions, but thoroughly understood the mechanisms of memory and forgetting from empirical evidence. For them, the nature of the evidence cited by clinicians was dubious. The debate over recovered memories of sexual abuse began.

From the context of the treatment room, the debate over recovered memories of sexual abuse finds early study in the writings of Sigmund Freud. He observed that patients suffering from hysteria often recovered previously forgotten memories of childhood sexual abuse. Importantly, as patients had no memory for these traumatic events prior to this, Freud was able to use his notions of defence mechanisms to account for the prolonged and extended amnesia. Given the number of patients who recovered such memories, Freud initially concluded that sexual abuse of children was far more prominent that anyone had expected, and crossed over boundaries such as socio-economic status. However, he later retracted these ideas and argued instead that recovered memories were not real, but were the fabrications that emerged from the desires of the unconscious, id energy.

It is this point—the truthfulness or accuracy of recovered memories—that really forms the basis for the debate. Unfortunately, the debate instead became distracted and focused on two other questions. One, could someone who experienced childhood sexual abuse have prolonged amnesia for that event, only to later recover it? Two, could someone be led into reporting a detailed account of an event that either did not occur or did not occur in the way it was being reported? The dispute turned into a fierce conflict between two polarized camps of psychologists, each side accusing the other's evidence and methods of study as wrong. Sadly, the debate over recovered memories of sexual abuse resulted in a considerable amount of slandering of professional reputations, and the ruination of many families and lives.

The modern debate over recovered memory started in an inauspicious manner in the USA. A couple, both of whom were well-known and highly respected psychologists, were accused by their adult daughter of sexually abusing her and of colluding to keep the abuse a secret. The daughter, who was also a psychologist, used the opportunity of giving a paper at a large national psychology conference to make her allegations, so the accusations were very public. In her allegations, she claimed that she had recovered these memories after a long period of amnesia. She offered a coherent psychological explanation as to why she had failed to remember the events over the years; and also what had served to trigger their recovery. Not surprisingly, the parents were startled at these allegations, in part because they denied their authenticity.

In the parents' view, their daughter had been misled into remembering traumatic events, which, in fact, were fabrications. These 'false' memories were the result of their daughter's venturing into therapy. The parents argued that somehow their daughter had been exposed to unscrupulous therapeutic techniques that had convinced her that she had experienced abuse. The parents vowed to clear their names. They set up a society for other parents who similarly claimed to have been falsely accused of sexual abuse by their children, calling it the False Memory Syndrome Foundation (FMSF). Many other accused parents reported a similar pattern, where their adult children had never remembered memories of abuse, until coming into contact with therapists, support groups, or media coverage on other cases of recovered memories. By the mid-1990s, the FMSF had received over 7000 enquiries, with hundreds of parents reporting that their children were taking civil and in some cases criminal actions against them.

Given that both sides—the accused and the accuser—were psychologists, it was no surprise that each drafted psychological evidence to support their claims. While overly simplistic, the division was essentially between experimentalists and clinicians. The former argued that memory was fallible and people were gullible, and that no rigorous scientific demonstration of any memory mechanism existed that could account for the prolonged and complete amnesia, and then recovery of traumatic memories. The latter argued that people forgot trauma because they wanted to avoid bad feelings and that some form of repression, albeit not the original Freudian notion, was not only frequently observed, but was also to be expected in cases of trauma and traumatic, sexual abuse. A nasty battle ensued, and the debate escalated to the point where it threatened the unity of psychology as a whole.

While this battle raged in the USA, a similar rift was emerging in the UK. Adult children were alleging that their ageing parents had abused them during childhood and, in response, parents formed a society, called the British False Memory Society (BFMS). Like its American counterpart, the BFMS was designed to support parents who felt that they had been falsely accused, and it soon logged hundreds of enquiries. The founders of the BFMS, in an effort to make some impact on the debate, approached the national governing body for professional psychologists, the British Psychological Society (BPS), and asked the organization to take some action. The BFMS wanted the governing body to provide some guidance regarding professional practice, offer a review of the recent evidence regarding the prevalence of recovered memories, and assess any empirical evidence that might help to support or refute the claim that memory recovery was possible. The BFMS had collected data from the people who contacted them, and the data were offered freely for inspection.

The BPS responded positively, and agreed that a group of professional psychologists, each with expertise in areas that were pertinent to the question of recovered memories, would form as a working party to investigate the phenomena of recovered memories. The BPS appointed a chair for the working party, who, in turn, was responsible for appointing other members of the group. The working party was given the remit to review the empirical evidence, assess the impact that the phenomena of recovered memories was having nationally, identify any therapeutic techniques that were associated with recovered memories, and make general recommendations that could be used to guide professional practice.

What was the situation?

This was a very delicate position for the BPS and, in particular, for the members of the working party. On the one hand, the BPS needed to respond appropriately to the request from the BFMS. Failure to respond would easily be interpreted as suspicious, and understandably so. On the other hand, the governing body itself had not seemed to be interested in initiating a formal inquiry, and with good reason. Everyone knew that the situation in the USA was making enemies out of the different disciplines in psychology. The animosity that had grown between psychologists was something that the BPS wished to avoid. The members of the working party had similar concerns. They were motivated to produce the most objective and accurate report that they could, and yet they were well aware that the topic was highly controversial and that someone, somewhere, would be likely to take umbrage with any conclusions they might draw.

Why were the psychologists involved?

A group of five psychologists were selected by the chair in order to provide a range of expertise that would be relevant to the remit of the working party. It was obvious that the members of the working party should be experts in their fields, and they should also provide a sufficient diversity of interests and breadth of experience and knowledge. As a consequence, the make-up of the working party reflected the necessity to have experts in trauma, and in memory, who understood and could evaluate both experimental and clinical evidence. For example, the working party needed to be able to evaluate empirical investigations into trauma and any research on related concepts like repression. It similarly needed to understand and assess evidence from clinical observations and be able to assess the general treatment techniques that are commonly employed in the treatment of trauma. In addition, an expert in 'normal' adult memory was also important, so that any phenomena that might be evaluated could be done so along some continuum from abnormal to normal. The working party also needed some expertise in memory development, again with the expert having some appreciation of both experimental and clinical methodologies. This was considered essential because the majority of allegations that adults were making were about childhood sexual abuse. As such, it became critical to understand how a child's memory develops and, importantly, how cognitive, emotional, and social development would constrain what an adult would be later able to report.

What concepts are relevant?

Many of the concepts that are relevant involve questions about how people remember traumatic events. Of course, one of the central concepts on which the entire debate is focused is the notion of the defence mechanism, repression. Because repression is so central, we will take some time to discuss how repression first came into the literature. To do this, we need to consider Freud's notions of the different levels of consciousness, and how these relate to different aspects of the personality.

At the uppermost level is what Freud called *consciousness*, or our immediate, focal awareness. Consciousness is associated with that which we can immediately report, such as what we are thinking at a particular moment—what William James called the 'stream of consciousness'. At a lower level is the *subconscious*, which Freud further divided into the *pre-conscious* and the *unconscious*. The pre-conscious is characterized by thoughts, images, and feelings which are not immediately in our awareness, but which we can summon into consciousness, should we so wish. For example, being able to remember something you did yesterday is illustrating how pre-conscious thoughts and memories can be made conscious through the act of intentional remembering. Beneath the pre-conscious is the unconscious. The unconscious harbours our deepest needs and drives, and are generally kept undisclosed as we interact with the world, and for good reason, as we now see.

The different levels of consciousness are associated with different levels of the psyche or personality. At the conscious and pre-conscious levels is the *ego*, that aspect of the personality that is most observable to the outside world, and serves as the person's sense of self. Our ego is responsible for directly dealing with societal demands and everyday experiences and, consequently, is governed by the constraints of the real world.

The ego mediates between two other aspects of the psyche, the *super-ego* and the *id*. The super-ego is the aspect of the psyche that is governed by societal norms and other types of social **introjections** or rules that would be expected to be passed down by one's society, culture, or family. As the super-ego contains motivation for conforming to social norms and social values, it often is referred to as the conscience of the self—that which is responsible for the person knowing the difference between what is right and what is wrong. Freud assumed that the contents of the super-ego were available to the pre-conscious state.

At the other extreme is the id. In contrast to the super-ego, the id recognizes no rules, is unconstrained, and has no regard for right or wrong. The id is motivated entirely by basic innate **drives**, like sexuality and aggression. Freud considered the id and its drives to be the fundamental motives behind all human behaviour. He believed that humans are like any other animal. According to Freud, we have innate drives that direct our behaviour towards that which is pleasurable and direct us away from that which is not pleasurable. Drives are associated with psychic energy, which builds up into tension if not expressed, and the id is motivated to reduce this tension. As children, we are allowed to express our id unhampered and without fear of prejudice. For example, if we are hungry, we are allowed to cry and scream out our demands, until our wish is fulfilled. We do not take into account whether our demands are reasonable or appropriate. As we become older, we are forced by society to thwart he immediate gratification of our basic drives. We are severely constrained by how we should or should not behave—the domain of the super-ego. The demands of our id become less acceptable as we mature into adults. As a consequence, those thoughts, feelings or memories that are strongly linked to our id generally get repressed and are forced to reside in our unconscious.

However, there is a constant, ongoing battle between these different aspects of our psyche. Because our id is only concerned with reducing the tension from our basic drives, it is in direct conflict with our super-ego, which is constantly constraining the expression of any behaviour that might be deemed unsociable, or inappropriate. This conflict is mediated by our ego, which attempts to maintain some type of balance between the two by resolving the conflict, relying on defence mechanisms to prevent most of the contents of the unconscious from ever surfacing.

For example, suppose you are walking along and you find a wallet that is stuffed with cash. Each aspect of your personality will respond differently to that situation. Your id may respond to the situation in a manner that is self-serving, being motivated to take the money as it affords many pleasurable things, such as paying off your longstanding bank loan. In contrast, your super-ego will respond to the situation in terms of whether it is right to take the money, motivating you to act in a manner that would be most acceptable to society—which probably would mean handing the wallet back to its owner. Your ego will respond to the reality of the situation. You become aware that there are people staring at you as you ponder your decision, and that that the chances of someone having seen you pick up the wallet and look through it are very

---

BOX 8.8 THE DEFENCE MECHANISMS AND THE EGO

Freud coined the term defence mechanisms to refer to the ways in which the ego protects itself against the onslaught of the id and the unconscious. The major defence mechanisms include **repression, projection, displacement, identification, regression, sublimation, rationalization, denial**, and **reaction formation**. Projection involves me putting on to you those feelings or thoughts that are too undesirable for me to consciously accept. So I cannot bear to accept that I am angry because I was punished for showing any signs of aggression or anger as a child. When I am feeling unhappy about something you have said to me, I project my anger onto you and accuse you of being unfriendly to me. Projection allows me to experience angry sensations or feelings, but I simply attribute them to you. Denial is a way for us to reduce our anxiety, when our unacceptable thoughts or desires creep into our conscious awareness. While repression is a mechanism that blocks undesirable thoughts from consciousness, denial is a refusal to acknowledge that you have the undesirable characteristic. For example, suppose I am an alcoholic. I deny this and label myself instead as a social drinker. In denial, the undesirable behaviour, my drinking, is still present for all to see; it is me who refuses to acknowledge that my behaviour is undesirable. Thus, I am in denial. All defence mechanisms are designed to help the ego with the intra-psychic conflict.

high. Your ego may decide to resolve the conflict by conforming to the demands of your super-ego, and you return the wallet to its rightful owner.

What is so intriguing is that Freud's arguments can be used both for and against the suggestion that recovered memories are reliable. For example, suppose there is a woman, aged 42 years, who has been feeling very depressed for the last few years. She manages to get enough energy to plan a party for her daughter's twelfth birthday. On the day of the festivities, the woman suddenly has a vivid image of a traumatic sexual assault that occurred when she was 12 years old, which happened after she had blown out the candles on her birthday cake. Importantly, the woman has had absolutely no memory of the event, and can barely believe that what she is remembering is real. Suddenly, fragments of memories start flooding back into her consciousness.

Freud offers an easy explanation as to how this might happen. The concept of repression of trauma, where the painful memory is kept out of consciousness, explains how a person could have amnesia for such an extended period of time. However, the memory might still break through into consciousness, since the defence mechanism of repression cannot always block out the trauma. The person may have been reminiscing, in her pre-conscious, of what happened to her when she was 12 years old, thus thrusting the otherwise forgotten memory closer to consciousness. What eventually triggered her memory was seeing her daughter's birthday cake.

Equally, though, Freud offers an explanation as to why this memory is false. Arguably, the allegations may express unconscious desires, sexual desires that are too threatening to acknowledge, and so have been converted into day dreams or fantasies, which the woman inaccurately believes are true. It seems that both proponents and opponents for the accuracy of recovered memories are able to call upon Freud's views!

Importantly, contemporaries of Freud independently noted the phenomena of recovered memories. Pierre Janet studied hysteria, and, again like Freud, he found that many patients recovered memories of childhood sexual abuse after some period of amnesia. Janet coined the phrase 'phobias of memory' to account for the amnesia (Janet 1892). He argued that people who suffered such trauma developed resultant phobia or anxiety about remembering the event. The person was too frightened to revisit the event, for fear that the act of remembering would reinstate such painful emotions that they would be too overcome. This phobia resulted in the person experiencing a form of amnesia—a classic symptom of avoidance—whereby the memory was made unavailable for recollection. However, it would continue to intrude into the person's consciousness as an invasive thought, due to the unresolved psychic conflict that had been created through the act of repressing it. Janet believed that the only way that the person could rid themselves of the effects of their trauma was to remember the event, for example under hypnosis, thereby releasing the psychic tension.

Importantly, many people since Freud and Janet have documented the occurrence of recovery during treatment. One of the most important contributions has been made by Harvey and Herman in 1994, who illustrated that clients recovering memories of childhood traumas show vastly different phenomenal awareness of the past, and that recovery itself is a highly complicated process. For example, some clients always remember the trauma, but recover some new details that previously they had forgotten. Other clients have some idea that they had experienced abuse, but had no firm memories about any specific incidents. A third group had complete and total amnesia for the traumatic event(s).

Other concepts that are relevant focus on the types of treatments that are used not only in the treatment of trauma but more generally. For example, hypnosis is a technique that is used widely by practitioners following certain orientations, for example psychodynamic, to help the person release feelings or thoughts that are normally repressed and kept outside of our consciousness. However, research points to some negative consequences of hypnosis, and in particular the fact that the technique can increase the susceptibility of the person. Most of us have seen the sort of entertainment where people who have been hypnotized engage in whatever bizarre behaviours the hypnotist suggests. Under hypnosis, the person can be led to believe things that are not true. As a technique, then, hypnosis would be highly dangerous for those individuals who, seeking help from a professional, were in an emotionally vulnerable and suggestible state.

Related to the type of technique used is the extent to which therapists rely on their own interpretation of behaviour in order to draw conclusions about the underlying causes for the client's behaviours. While this need not necessarily pose problems, interpretations are contentious. For example, suppose we have a client who gags every time she brushes her teeth. Importantly, the client wants to know why she gags and she does not have any insight into what is causing her behaviour. We, the therapist, decide that her gagging is the result of her being sexually abused, in this case, being forced to have oral sex. Our client has no memory, whatsoever, of any abuse. We maintain that she has repressed this memory from her consciousness, but that her body, instead, has remembered and this memory comes out in her behaviour. Even if we did not use Freud, there are other theoretical arguments that could support our interpretation. For example, we could argue that our client has an implicit memory for her abuse, but no explicit memory. However, the facts about our client gagging are that she had a fish

---

BOX 8.9 COMBAT TRAUMA AND THE TALKING CURES

Much of what we know about trauma developed from the treatment of combat trauma-a topic that we briefly discussed in 'The war room' (Chapter 7). Abram Kardiner, an American psychiatrist, noted that the use of terms such as hysteria, although an accurate diagnosis of war neurosis, did not provide the soldier with a sympathetic position from which to start treatment (Kardiner and Spiegel 1947). In fact, he considered the use of such terms to be so pejorative that it prevented society, medicine, and the military from seeing how the soldiers were victims of, rather than responsible for, their trauma. His early efforts served as the basis for future clinical analyses of trauma syndromes. Importantly, Kardiner developed the talking cure, which stemmed from his experiences with Freudian analysis. He regarded the symptoms of hysteria as the result of repression of painful memories. In his treatment, soldiers were encouraged to relive traumatic memories, and re-experience all the feelings associated with these memories. It was through this catharsis that the soldier was cured. Kardiner and his colleagues used various techniques, such as hypnosis, to access the traumatic memories. Modern talking cures for the treatment of trauma take their point of departure from these early treatment techniques.

bone stuck in her throat when she was 18 months old. While she did indeed maintain some sort of body, or implicit memory, our interpretation of the causes for her behaviour was wide of the mark. While our example may seem far-fetched, the facts are that some therapists did draw such conclusions, arguing that if someone gagged when brushing their teeth, that was a sign that they had been abused!

Other concepts that needed to be considered are those we have already discussed in an earlier chapter on eyewitness testimony (see 'The crime room', Chapter 4). One of the most relevant here is the effects of misleading information. The early studies of Elizabeth Loftus already conclusively established that people could report false events as well as false details. Ira Hyman and colleagues (Hyman and Billings 1998) provided even further evidence of this more directly, in a wonderful series of experiments. Hyman showed how easily some people are misled into believing that false memories were true. Hyman used certain important conditions to convince people. First, he told the participants that the memory had been confirmed as true by their parents. This meant that participants were already biased to accept the false information as true. Next, Hyman introduced events that had some true elements to them, by finding out some true personal details of the person's life. For example, suppose you had an Aunt Sarah, and you had been to a family wedding where she was present. Hyman would suggest that your mother had said that you spilled a punch bowl over your Aunt Sarah at a family wedding. The misleading, false detail is the action, spilling the punch bowl over Aunt Sarah; the true details are first that you have an Aunt Sarah, and second that you were both at the family wedding. Whereas most participants denied having any experience of the false event the first time the suggestion was made, some proportion gradually began to accept it as true, and began to produce accounts of what had happened!

The significance of Hyman and his colleagues' studies is obvious. The therapist will have some knowledge and accurate details about the client's personal life. The therapist will also have a certain amount of power over the client, to the extent that the client will believe that the therapist is acting in their best interests. Added to this is the fact that the person is likely to want some sort of explanation for their behaviour. With techniques where the therapist requires the client to accept the interpretation, a vulnerable person is highly susceptible to the importation of false information.

The modern debate over recovered memories of sexual abuse also needs to be considered within the context of the social and historical perspectives under which it arose. A good discussion of the socio-historical perspective is provided by Tim Dalgleish and Nicola Morant, in *Representations of Child Sexual Abuse: a Brief Psychosocial History and Commentary* (2001). Not coincidentally, allegations of sexual abuse grew in parallel with the popularity of self-help books regarding survivors of sexual abuse and the simultaneous increase in general media coverage of sexual abuse. In part, the debate was the result of a core shift in societal attitudes regarding sexual abuse. In particular, society and professionals became more willing to acknowledge that sexual abuse occurs. Once society was more able to accept that sexual abuse occurred, the public as well as professionals provided the atmosphere for victims to make their allegations heard. Prior to this, victims were being forced to suffer in silence. Slowly, more and more people were disclosing histories of abuse.

What did the psychologists do?

The members of the working party decided that they would each take some aspect of the remit and provide the major input into that section of the report. For example, one of the remits was to review the available evidence from the empirical and experimental literature. Members of the working party were assigned different topics, such as misleading information or research on trauma, and would provide the chair with draft comments to be circulated to the entire working party.

Other members of the working party were responsible for determining the types of treatment technique that were currently being used and also review evidence from clinical observations of recovered memories. It seemed essential that the practice and beliefs of working practitioners in the BPS were surveyed; to this end, a preliminary questionnaire was devised that addressed some important issues. For example, some questions asked about the frequency that practitioners experienced recovered memories, and also the extent to which the practitioner believed such memories to be true. In addition, the working party sought any evidence that had been brought to bear elsewhere in the world, be it the USA or Europe.

The working party also considered it essential to review any evidence that had been collected by the BFMS. Accordingly, two members asked to visit the then headquarters, and were given complete access to all notes, documentation, correspondence, and tapes that had been submitted to the BFMS. A review of this documentation might shed some light on any patterns and consistencies that emerged across different allegations, and also give an idea as to some of the socio-demographic variables that might be at work, such as gender or age.

The working party eventually prepared and submitted a final report to be published on behalf of the BPS. As was required from the remit, the report included details regarding BPS practitioners' views on recovered memories of sexual abuse, including how frequently clients recovered memories, and the extent to which these memories were viewed as correct. The report provided some arguments regarding how recovered memories might come about, and discussed the memory literature from the standpoint of evidence for and against the concept of repression. The report also concluded that the problem of false memories was not as great as it appeared to be in the USA, although it acknowledged the difficulty and pain for those families in which such allegations had been made. In addition, the report suggested that while the BFMS had indeed some valuable information regarding its members, the quality of the evidence was inconsistent and not suitable for scientific purposes. Finally, recommendations regarding good and bad practice, particularly in the context of sexual abuse, were provided.

Most interestingly, perhaps, is the fact that the report from the BPS working party reached the same conclusions as the report produced by its counterparts in America. One, it is possible, in some cases, for people to recover traumatic childhood memories after prolonged amnesia. Two, memory is malleable and cannot be made fallible, especially if certain techniques are used with vulnerable individuals. Not surprisingly, the same techniques were highlighted as being dangerous.

How was the psychologists' input received?

The report produced completely divided reactions. The BPS felt that the working party had provided an objective and considered report, one that attempted to address the critical issues rather than add fuel to an already overheated debate. Various members of the working party were asked to contribute to debates on radio and provide expert opinion in journalistic reporting.

However, there were some people who did not rate the report quite so highly. Many professionals dismissed the report of the working party, accusing it of being unprofessional, unreliable, inaccurate, and biased. The highly renowned experimental psychologist, Professor L. Weiskrantz, regarded the working party's efforts at addressing the scientific issues as feeble and misguided, concluding that 'The working party ... would have performed a much more useful function ... if it had simply started and stopped with [the professional guidelines]' (Weiskrantz 1995, p. 8). The report was similarly criticized by professional journals such as *The Therapist*, which claimed that 'The British Psychological Society needs its head examined'. Even more disturbing for the members of the working party was the fact that parents and families who had been accused often sent disturbing and in some cases threatening letters. These letters regularly criticized the report of the working party for not giving any consideration to the great distress that is caused when false accusations are made. To these people, the working party was often perceived as engaged in professional negligence at its worst. These conflicting reactions illustrate how divisive and controversial the topic of recovered memories had become!

SCENARIO TWO

APPLYING THE THEORY OF WORKING MEMORY TO INSOMNIA

This next scenario, based on the work of Levey et al. (1991), illustrates how theoretical ideas in cognitive psychology can be applied to a range of important real-world problems in the treatment room. Many times, cognitive theories will have broad application to clinical conditions, particularly when these conditions have a strong cognitive component to them. Not infrequently, psychologists wish to validate some part of their theory by applying it to a real-world clinical problem, since that will enable them to assess the strength of their ideas under circumstances that might be difficult to duplicate in the laboratory. There is a sense in which a theory gains in strength if it can be seen to apply to practical problems in the everyday world. This is as true in psychology as it is in physics and chemistry.

When, as in this scenario, we have a theoretical idea in search of a real-world problem, the driving force behind finding the most appropriate match is the topics that are addressed by the theory. We first identify what the theory addresses and what the major theoretical concepts are; we then look for a real-world problem for which these concepts might be relevant. For example, if we have a theory about how people behave when engaged in communal activities, we might look at the real-world situation of a restaurant, and see whether our theoretical ideas are relevant to any problems that arise.

Such was the case here, where we consider the application of the theory of working memory (WM) to the condition of insomnia. The theory of working memory proposed a new and different way of understanding how we retain information for short periods of time. All of us have had the experience of repeating a telephone number over and over, rehearsing it, until such time as we can write it down and then promptly eject it from our conscious awareness. According to WM theory, we are able to do this because of the operation of a set of systems that help us to keep information central to our current goals, until such time as we no longer need it. As we will see below, laboratory studies have demonstrated how these systems operate and, importantly, for the present purposes, how these systems can be disrupted.

After WM theory had amassed an impressive amount of evidence in its favour, other psychologists, working with clinical conditions, felt that the WM theory had great potential, particularly in its application to problems involving repetitive, intrusive thoughts. One of these conditions is insomnia, where people often report an over-active mind, with thoughts constantly circulating in their heads. The psychologists reasoned that if the findings from laboratory studies were extrapolated, they could produce an important technique that would reduce, if not eliminate, at least some of the cognitive symptoms of insomnia. This scenario illustrates how important experimental research can be in helping to find solutions for a common and disabling problem. It is also an excellent example of how mainstream psychological findings can be successfully translated into effective intervention techniques for the treatment room.

One of the most exciting consequences of working in a research environment is that your colleagues often provide you with ideas about your own work that you would otherwise not consider. Such was the case with the Medical Research Council's then Applied Psychology Unit in Cambridge, UK. A number of psychologists, each specialists in their own field, worked in parallel and in conjunction with each other on developing psychological theories that could be applied to real-world problems. Theoretical ideas and empirical evidence emerging from one line of inquiry could often be directly relevant to another, seemingly unrelated line of inquiry.

A clear example of this productive cross-fertilization of ideas came about through a discussion between colleagues after a theoretical seminar on what was then a new theory of short-term memory. The theory addressed issues that are still of great interest to psychologists—the nature of memory and its differing functions. We give a brief summary of the memory theory first, as it formed the contents of the seminar, and served as the basis for the resulting discussions between psychologists.

Psychologists interested in studying memory prior to the 1960s had exclusively regarded memory as a unitary storage system. Association theory held that the main mechanism for remembering anything is the process of forming mental associations. Temporal contiguity, things co-occurring in time, was regarded as the basis for most learning. Thus, if we are shown A followed by B enough times, we learn and remember that A and B go together. A single memory store served as the container for all our associations.

However, by the 1960s, a change in attitudes was apparent. While memory was still regarded as spatio-temporal, that is something that we put things *into* and get things *out of*, memory was no longer seen as a unitary store. Memory had different stores, and different stages. Richard Atkinson and Richard Shiffrin proposed one of the most influential of these models in 1968.

The Atkinson and Shiffrin model had three memory stores. These stores differed in terms of the length of time they maintained information, the type of information to which they were most sensitive, and their size. The early sensory store—there were two, one for sight and one for sound—maintained relatively unprocessed sensory information only for a very short time. A good example is to look at any object close to you, for a few seconds, then close your eyes. You should be able to see an after-image that lasts only a matter of half a second or so, before it starts to fade. This after-image is held in what Atkinson and Shiffrin called the *iconic store*. The *echoic store*, associated with sound, maintains information for slightly longer, along the order of a few seconds. Through the process of selective attention, sensory information is passed on to a **short-term memory** store, which is sensitive to the auditory modality. short-term memory serves two functions. It supports processes like reasoning and comprehension—both of which are necessary for ongoing communication—y providing some sort of working memory space. It also provides us with a temporary store for information waiting to enter long-term memory. Through rehearsal, we maintain information in short-term memory, although its capacity is limited. George Miller is renowned for coining the phrase, the 'magical number seven, plus or minus two', which is assessed as our **memory span**, in tests such as digit-span tests. After sufficient rehearsal, information gets transferred to our **long-term memory**, which is limitless in its capacity and retains information indefinitely.

However, evidence from research conducted with patients who had brain damage posed problems for multi-stage models. For example, some patients had normal long-term learning but demonstrated an impaired memory span, limited to one of two items. In contrast, other patients had highly impaired abilities to make new associations but had relatively normal performance on other types of short-term memory tasks. If a single, short-term memory was the means through which all information was passed on to the long-term store, then how could a patient with short-term memory problems still show normal long-term learning? Similarly, if short-term memory is responsible for tasks like reasoning and speech comprehension, how could a patient show deficits in learning and not show deficits in other short-term memory tasks, like reasoning tasks? Clearly, multiple stage models were inadequate.

In 1974, Alan Baddeley and Graham Hitch provided a way of addressing such data, challenging the notion of a single short-term memory system. Instead of a single system Baddeley and Hitch (1974) proposed a tripartite system of *working memory* (WM), comprised of a *central executive*, and two slave systems, the *articulatory* or *phonological loop* and the *visuospatial scratchpad*. The central executive operates like the manager of mental attention and energy, prioritizing information in terms of its relevance to current goals, and shunting information to and from the more permanent, long-term memory store. It is also responsible for complex mental operations, such as reasoning and comprehension. The two slave systems are simply responsible for maintaining information that is identified by the central executive as supporting current tasks. The phonological loop keeps speech-based information recycled while the scratchpad keeps visual and imaginal information active.

Research had shown that the slave systems can be disrupted. In the case of the phonological loop, this can be done by articulatory suppression, such as asking a person to repeat the word *'the'* over and over again. This prevents subvocal rehearsal, and impedes any visually presented information from being registered in the phonological store. For example, suppose we ask people to remember a series of numbers −0, 15, 32, 56, 22, 38, 99, 47, 12, 65—and at the same time require them to repeat the word *'the'* three to four times a second. What we find is that people remember less, as they are prevented from rehearsing the numbers.

Now, let us return to the seminar. It was clear that WM theory was relevant to clinical populations with memory problems, such as people with head injuries. However, the psychologists leading the seminar were interested in soliciting opinion from their colleagues as to whether WM theory might be useful in the context of other clinical phenomena. One member of the audience, a classical learning theorist who had extensive experience in clinical settings, suggested that the concept of the phonological loop could be highly useful for clinical conditions that have intrusive, persistent, and unwanted thoughts in their set of symptoms. According to the WM theory, such intrusive thoughts would be recycled in the phonological loop. Anything that could disrupt the loop and block this recycling should similarly be able to disrupt and block the occurrence of the unwanted intrusive thought.

The learning theorist identified several conditions that were of immediate relevance, including obsessive compulsive disorders, depression, general anxiety disorders, bereavement syndrome, and insomnia. While most were unsuitable for study because of their complexity, insomnia had a relatively circumscribed set of symptoms. Additionally, the learning theorist was particularly interested in insomnia, for a number of reasons. For one, insomnia is a serious and common problem, with many people experiencing difficulties in getting to sleep and staying asleep. For another, recycled thoughts are one of the most frequent complaints from people. Sufferers complain that their thoughts 'keep going round and round', that they cannot stop their mind from going over things, in some cases worrying about things. The learning theorist could see how WM would directly link this to the phonological loop, thus highlighting the type of interventions that might be helpful. Last, but certainly not least, the learning theorist had a personal interest in the topic: he, too, was someone who suffered from disturbed sleep patterns. After thorough discussions, the learning theorist and his colleagues agreed that they would extrapolate the theory of WM to discover whether a more cognitive intervention for insomnia might be developed.

What is the situation?

This situation can be described as one where a theory went in search of a problem and, happily, found a good one. However, we must stress that the attempt to translate the WM theory into cognitive interventions for insomnia represented a real departure from typical approaches to insomnia. For example, most interventions for insomnia were behavioural rather than cognitive in nature. Thus, people would be taught to use self-relaxation, such as imaging a peaceful scene, or would be taught to use a form of *stimulus control*. With stimulus control, the person would associate the bed and bedroom exclusively with sleep, so that if they could not sleep, they would get up and go into another room. Some cognitive approaches to the problem of sleepless-ness had been attempted, but these were more concerned with sleep attitudes, such as changing attributions of tiredness to one's current mental state rather than to the lack of a good night's sleep. Importantly, the extrapolation of WM theory represen-ted a new direction, as it focused directly on one of the major cognitive symptoms of insomnia.

What psychological concepts are relevant?

It is obvious that many of the concepts that the psychologists needed to consider involve our understanding of why and how we sleep. Sleep needs to be considered in terms of biological, psychological, environmental, as well as social factors. Like all mammals, we have adapted our cycle of activity and inactivity in what is called a **circadian rhythm**. Our circadian rhythm is based on an approximate twenty-four-hour cycle, where our physiological functions, including body temperature and mental alertness, fluctuate in lows and highs. Our brain, and in particular the *suprachiasmatic nuclei* (SCN), which are located in the hypothalamus, regulates our circadian rhythms. The SCN have a link with the pineal gland, which is responsible for producing the relaxing hormone *melatonin*. During the day, SCN neurons are active and decrease the pineal gland's output of melatonin, resulting in raised body temperature, mental alertness, and physical energy. During the evening, SCN neurons are inactive, allowing levels of melatonin to raise, which promotes us feeling relaxed and sleepy.

While our circadian rhythm is biological, it is sensitive to external stimuli and also subject to individual differences. External stimuli, like the environmental cues of day and night, help keep the SCN on track. In part, this is why people who work night shifts have such difficulty in adjusting their sleep patterns to accommodate their work schedule. Part of the problem is that the artificial light in which most night workers operate is too weak to alter the circadian rhythm. Individual differences are often de-scribed in terms of whether a person is a morning person or early bird, or an evening person or night owl. As their name suggests, those people who are early birds show peaks in body temperature and brain activity at earlier points in the morning than do night owls.

While there are many disorders of our sleep–wake cycle, probably the most common is insomnia. However, insomnia is not all that easy to define. It is one of the few dis-orders where the diagnosis is made by the patient rather than the medical practitioner. So, we go to the doctor complaining that we are not sleeping well; the doctor, in turn, has no evidence to suggest this is, or is not, true apart from our phenomenal reporting. Without the use of experimental techniques, available only in a sleep laboratory, it is often impossible to determine how serious the patient's condition actually is.

While we have all experienced a sleepless night, this does not constitute insomnia. Insomnia is chronic and persistent, and is linked to three aspects of sleep. There is sleep-onset delay, which measures the amount of time it takes for you to fall to sleep. Then there is wakefulness, referring to disturbances in sleep, such as periods of you

BOX 8.10 OUR NATURAL SLEEP–WAKE CYCLE

Suppose that you are living in conditions where you did not have environmental cues like day and night, such as being on a submarine or in a space station. What would happen to your biological clock? Much research has been done on this topic and the findings are consistent. In the absence of any environmental cues, our biological clocks, or circadian rhythms, begin to stretch, falling into what are called *free-running rhythms*. The sleep–wake cycle in free-running rhythms is longer than the average twenty-four-hour cycle. Early studies suggested that people would drift into twenty-five-hour sleep–wake cycles (Webb and Agnew 1974), while more recent studies suggest that the average cycle is only 24.2 hours (Hillman et al. 1994). While this extra time may not seem significant, some authors suggest that, if we followed our free-running rhythms for only a few months, we would rise at noon and not be ready for sleep until midnight! Our natural tendency is to lengthen the sleep–wake cycle, called **phase delay**. This explains why it is easier for most travellers to cope with time differences when travelling west: travelling west stretches the sleep–wake cycle, which is more in line with our free-running rhythm.

BOX 8.11 THE STAGES OF SLEEP

Sleep studies monitor the activity of the cortex in order to identify the different stages of sleep. Although this is technically described as an electrocorticogram, the term, electroencephalograph, or EEG, has instead become the norm. Sleep studies have identified four stages of sleep, which are distinguished by the associated brain patterns. As sleep progresses, our brain waves become slower, as measured by wave frequency, and are greater in height, as measured by amplitude. Stage 1 sleep is associated with a light sleep, from which we can be easily awoken, and we may experience dreams or vivid images and show sudden body jerks. Stage 2 is a deeper sleep, with our muscles and breathing becoming more relaxed. It is much more difficult to wake from Stage 2. Stage 3 is an even deeper sleep, until we reach Stage 4, where we are very relaxed, our brain waves reach their slowest, and activity in some parts of our brain decreases dramatically. Researchers suggest that, within sixty to ninety minutes, we go through a cycle of stages, 1–2–3–4–3–2, followed by what is called *rapid eye movement*, or REM. In REM sleep our brain patterns are very similar to our waking, alert state of consciousness. It is during REM sleep that we have our most vivid dreams.

waking from sleep. Finally, there is sleep length, constituting the amount of time you sleep in a single session. Many insomniacs complain that there have extended sleep-onset delay, fail to stay in a sleep state for long, and get too little sleep overall.

Although sleep undoubtedly performs some significant biological function, the research suggests that sleep deprivation, unless chronic and extended over time, does not affect our body very significantly. Many of our brain functions continue when we are awake or asleep, such as those that support our vital functions like breathing, so any restorative time cannot be contingent on our level of consciousness. In fact, James Horne, in his book *Why we Sleep* (Horne 1988), suggests that only our *cerebral cortex* seems affected by sleep deprivation, with the rest of our body being relatively unperturbed, and even the cerebrum can withstand one sleepless night.

Unfortunately, most insomniacs believe that their sleeplessness *does* affect their physical health. While this belief, in itself, may not be dangerous, it is coupled with the fact that insomniacs are not very accurate in their assessments of their sleep patterns. Horne (1988) summarizes the findings of a study undertaken by the US Institute of Medicine. This study reported that insomniacs get about six hours of sleep a night, with most going to sleep within twenty to thirty minutes, and most having relatively short periods of wakefulness within their sleeping period. This suggests that some insomniacs are actually getting a relatively good night's sleep, and that most have sleeping patterns that *would not* be expected to harm their health. For this reason, sleep workers prefer to use the term sleep dissatisfaction, since the only persons who can decide whether the patients are getting enough sleep are the patients themselves.

Whether insomniacs' descriptions are accurate or not, the fact remains that we expect to get a good night's sleep and when we do not, our health can suffer. This has less to do with the biological need for sleep, and much more to do with beliefs we hold about sleep. As a consequence, sleep researchers are very sensitive to distinguish between sleepiness, which is the result of disturbed sleep, and tiredness, which is generally the result of sleep dissatisfaction.

We have already given quite a bit of background to WM theory, but will briefly focus on the most relevant concept to the current scenario, the phonological loop. Again, the loop is a slave system that maintains information that has been prioritized by the central executive. Because it is sensitive to speech, the loop is easily disturbed, for example, by articulatory suppression in the form of repeating a meaningless sound, such as *the*.

The psychologists reasoned that unwanted thoughts would be recycled in the phonological loop. Importantly, these thoughts would activate the central executive, which, rather than concentrate on the current goal of falling to sleep or getting back to sleep, would become occupied with tasks like deriving meaning from the thoughts. In this way, unwanted thoughts, embodied as inner speech, would pre-empt attention or mental energy, at the expense of sleep. However, if the thoughts were blocked, the central executive would be free to allocate attention towards the onset or return of sleep.

What did the psychologists do?

The psychologists were aware that articulatory suppression should not be too demanding; and that the suppression material also needed to be innocuous so as not to be too arousing. Another serious issue was the rate at which repetition would occur. Suppose we ask a person to repeat the word *the*. Obviously, the rate at which the person repeats *the* needs to be carefully considered. If it is too slow, then the person will easily be able to switch from saying *the* and having a thought. If the rate is too fast, however, the process of suppression is arousing itself, and hence self-defeating. After a series of informal observations, the psychologists developed what they believed to be a practical intervention technique based on articulatory suppression. They then embarked on a single case study in order to provide a preliminary, but controlled and quantitative, investigation of the effectiveness of suppression.

An obvious concern was to select a participant who would be easily recognized as an insomniac. To this end, the psychologists used the six criteria that are commonly regarded in the literature as being necessary for a diagnosis of insomnia. They found Mr X, a 38-year-old translator, who had suffered from insomnia for approximately sixteen years. Mr X suffered from sleep-onset and sleep-maintenance problems, and he had these problems every night. His patterns were variable, sometimes taking twenty minutes to get to sleep and other times taking 120 minutes. Additionally, he woke roughly twice a night, staying awake anywhere between fifteen to sixty minutes. Importantly, the psychologists could not find any reason for being concerned about his diet, any sleep-incompatible activities in the bedroom (like watching television), or other environmental factors. He also made some use of stimulus-control strategies, like not going to bed unless he was ready for sleep.

The psychologists first did a functional analysis of Mr X's sleep patterns in order to get an idea of his unwanted thoughts. For example, they asked Mr X to make a diary of the difficulties he experienced, so that they could assess what types of thoughts intruded and at what point. Sleep-onset difficulties were associated with Mr X first becoming physically restless and then having uncontrollable thoughts and increased mental arousal. The thoughts were usually related to trivial planning, like deciding to buy a record, and were disturbing because he had little control over them. Sleep-maintenance problems were different. Once awake, Mr X reported first having intrusive thoughts, generally taking the form of relatively incoherent worries; these thoughts were then associated with Mr X feeling physically restless.

In order to compare suppression to more established techniques, the psychologists devised a treatment with four phases, with a new component in the treatment being introduced each week. A daily sleep diary was used to measure sleep onset and sleep maintenance. Measures of pre- and post-treatment sleep patterns were also taken. Pre-treatment assessment was a baseline measure of Mr X's sleep patterns, taken one week before any treatment began. Post-treatment measures were assessed for four weeks after treatment had finished.

Treatment consisted of a four-phase design, based on standard treatment procedures used with insomnia. During phase one, sleep-hygiene rules and stimulus-control instructions were given. For example, Mr X was not allowed coffee after a certain time, was to go bed only when sleepy and get out of bed if he could not sleep, was to wake at the same time every morning, and was to keep a sleep diary. Given Mr X had good sleep hygiene prior to the treatment, he was easily able to comply with these rules. Phase two introduced progressive muscular relaxation techniques. For example, Mr X was asked to imagine relaxing his body in a gradual and progressive manner, starting from the fingers on his left hand, then his upper arm, and so on. Phase three, called forward planning, instructed Mr X to set aside a time each evening when he would anticipate and set aside potentially intrusive thoughts. Mr X was asked to identify any potentially intrusive worries, to make any necessary decisions and then to set the thoughts aside. Mr X was told that if any of these thoughts occurred in bed, he should remind himself that they had already been dealt with and that there was no need to think about them further. Phase four introduced articulatory suppression. Mr X was instructed that, if he had any intrusive thoughts, to control the thoughts by repeating the syllable *the* to himself, pacing it in a non-regular manner. The advantage of using the neutral syllable *the* is that it does not lead anywhere. There is no likelihood that the wakeful victim will be led into further disrupting thought streams.

At the end of this phase the psychologists then analysed the sleep diaries. They found that although there was some improvement in sleep onset, the main effect seemed to be in terms of number of awakenings. Mr X reported significantly fewer awakenings as compared to his baseline measure for phases 2, 3, and 4, which showed no difference. This suggested that articulatory suppression was no more effective in maintaining sleep than muscular relaxation or forward planning. However, further analyses showed that there seemed to be an interaction: forward control seemed more effective in promoting shorter sleep onset, whereas articulatory suppression seemed more effective in lengthening sleep maintenance. Interestingly, these analyses were confirmed by Mr X's own observations. When asked, Mr X said that of the four treatment methods he found forward control most effective for getting to sleep; when asked which of the four treatments he found most effective for sleep maintenance, Mr X cited articulatory suppression.

The psychologists explained why articulatory suppression was more effective in sleep maintenance in terms of the difference in the quality of intrusive thoughts. Intrusive thoughts that occur in the middle of the night, during awakenings, are likely to be less coherent than those that disturb sleep onset. This is in part because they occur in a state of drowsiness and greater physical relaxation than those thoughts that intrude before sleep. As such, these thoughts would not demand much attention from the central executive, as they are less focused and less goal-oriented. Because of this, thoughts that occur during awakenings are more likely to be susceptible to the effects of interference from articulatory suppression, in that suppression acts to remove the thoughts from the speech buffer, without placing any extra cognitive load on the person.

How was the psychologists' input assessed?

It was clear that the treatment devised by the psychologists was useful to Mr X. While Mr X had already been aware of sleep hygiene and also had some knowledge of progressive muscular relaxation, he did find that forward planning and articulatory suppression were useful tools. Importantly, the psychologists were able to establish that articulatory suppression provided at least a beneficial, incremental solution to the problems of insomnia. This single case study led to further sleep clinics, where people were instructed in the use of the four treatment phases. Advertisements in local papers invited people suffering from insomnia to take part in experimental treatment sessions. The same procedures were used that had been used with Mr X. However, this was done on a group basis, enabling the participants to discuss their responses and compare notes for the benefit of the psychologists. The principal advantage of this approach, in terms of methodology, was that it enabled the investigators to eliminate any effects of the order of treatment. The final conclusion of the study was that articulatory suppression, by interrupting the unwanted cycle of thoughts typical of insomnia, offers the promise of an effective treatment.

■ ADDITIONAL READING

Seligman, M.E.P. (2002) *Authentic Happiness*. Free Press, New York. This influential book by a well-known theorist is an excellent example of the new positive approach to mental health.

Teasdale, J. and Barnard, P.J. (1993) *Affect Cognition and Change*. Erlbaum, Hove. This pioneering book offers an integrated framework for the application of cognitive principles to the understanding of mental illness.

Williams, J.M.G., Watts, F., MacLeod, C., and Matthews, A. (1997) *Cognitive Psychology and Emotional Disorders*. John Wiley & Sons, Chichester. This is a very popular text highlighting major issues in the practical application of cognitive concepts to emotional problems.

■ QUESTIONS

Scenario one

1 What evidence do you think the working party should have considered, but failed to do so?

2 To what extent should psychologists be used to give expert evidence on recovered memories?

Scenario two

1 What are the advantages of using a psychological approach to the problem, rather than a biological approach?

2 What would be the advantages of combining a biological approach with a psychological one?

9

The sport room

Here we introduce the sport room, in which we consider how psychology has been applied to one of the most essential, and least-studied, aspects of human behaviour: our need for recreational, physical activities. The sport room combines many of the topics and issues that we have already considered in earlier chapters. We discuss some traditional distinctions between different classes of physical activity like exercise and fitness versus athletics and sporting game. We also consider some factors that determine how much and what type of physical activity we choose, and when we choose to do it. We consider questions of motor control and the acquisition of motor skills and we discuss more recent interests in the interaction between mental and physical states. We identify the major themes that emerge in the modern sport room, and highlight links between mainstream psychological theory, for example in explaining complex skill learning. We also highlight the significance of the social aspects of sport, and illustrate how important sport is for group bonding and for developing social cooperation. The two scenarios in this chapter show how mainstream psychological concepts have been appropriated to address common problems in the sport room. The first scenario shows how techniques developed to treat phobias and other anxiety disorders have been modified to help performance anxiety. The second scenario concerns how psychological techniques have been applied successfully to problems of pain management in sporting injuries.

The importance of physical activity

Our enthusiasm for physical, recreational activities has been formally documented since the time of the ancient Greeks, who held the unshakeable belief that a healthy body would lead to a healthy mind. Since the Greeks had no doubt that the state of a person's mind would be reflected in the state of that person's body, and vice versa, it is not surprising that psychological principles were at the core of their attempts to promote excellence in physical ability. For example, they emphasized the importance of mental and emotional control in maintaining a focused attitude. And they used the modern technique of imaging, by which athletes were encouraged to imagine performing physical movements, in order to enhance performance and skill. The ancient Greeks knew that if they wanted to promote health and well-being in their athletes, they would need to incorporate mental—that is, psychological—techniques into their training programmes.

Such was the emphasis on a physically healthy body that the Greeks venerated their athletes. Religious games, which combined athletic competition and festivities, were a dominant feature of the culture. Tradition has it that the first Olympic games were held in 776 BC, and thereafter every four years at the important sanctuaries of Olympia and Delphi. These sporting events—which of course led to our modern Olympic competitions—were held in so much regard that the *plebes*, or common people, would celebrate their athletes' victories as their own personal victories, and be similarly crushed when their athletes were defeated.

Other ancient civilizations also tied physical activity to religion. For example, the Olmec society, one of the greatest ancient civilizations located in the region of Mexico's Gulf Coast, held formal, ritual ballgames as early as 600 BC. These early games were conducted between two teams and played on a rectangular court with a rubber ball. We should point out that Olmec's ball games had more to do with pure ritual than with sport as we have come to know it today. For example, the games required that a team player be sacrificed as the penalty for losing!

Whereas it is obvious that much has changed since the time of these ancient civilizations, our need for recreational, physical activity has remained. Nor has our identification and fascination with athletes waned. We live in modern societies where we are encouraged to take part in physical activity and exercise, and are encouraged to support our athletes and teams in international and national sporting events. The situations and circumstances under which psychologists study such phenomena is the domain of the sport room.

Physical activity and science

The sport room provides opportunities to apply many of the mainstream psychological theories and findings that we have discussed in earlier chapters. Yet, we note that the sport room is not regarded as an important area of study in many general psychology textbooks (the same could be said of the war room!). For example, topics relevant to the sport room are often restricted to a few pages, and under the more general heading of health psychology; for example, the benefits of keeping fit on mental health.

Some psychologists feel that little is gained by integrating topics in the sport room with those of mainstream psychology. They argue instead that the sport room better belongs under the rubric of a sport science. Sport science would combine a number of different disciplines, including medicine, physiology, and psychology. For example, sport scientists would study functional anatomy and biomechanics of sport performance, such

---

BOX 9.1 THE LEGACY OF THE GREEKS

The Olympic games were reputedly modelled on a race run between Hercules and his brothers, under the watchful eyes of the gods in the fields of Olympia. This led to the four-year tradition, or Olympiad, where men from all over the Greek world competed for glory for their region, town, or area. Athletes would train in a gymnasium, in the nude, where they would receive weeks of specialized training. Women were forbidden attendance at the Games, not out of modesty or prudery, but due to the fact that Olympia was dedicated to the honour of the ruler of the gods, Zeus, and was therefore exclusive to men. The arts and sport were inextricably linked in the Games, with poets dedicating work to the newly crowned winners, and sculptors creating statues to commemorate the victors. One of the most interesting stories is how the marathon came to be regarded as the pinnacle of the Olympiad events. It is alleged that in 490 BC a messenger, Phillippides, ran without stopping the forty-one kilometre distance from the city of Marathon to Athens. He brought the news that the Greeks had successfully defeated the Persians, in spite of the fact that the Persian had heavily outnumbered the local forces. The dominance of Greece over her enemies was associated with the marathon thereafter, and it was accorded the highest place at the ancient games. The games were held for over 1100 years, although they were no given no historical significance until the late nineteenth century, when a team of archaeologists from Germany unearthed the remains of the ancient Olympian site.

---

as the analysis of specific muscle groups that are used to perform certain actions. Answers to psychological questions would be expected to address issues raised by the other disciplines within sport science. For example, a psychologist working within this sport science might be prompted to discover how our personality types affect the kinds of physical activity in which we engage. This finding, in turn, would have has serious implications for any medical treatments of cardiac patients that might involve regular, supervised exercise.

The argument is that psychologists working under the rubric of a sport science should develop theoretical questions *specific* to sport science. For example, general personality theories that might be used to explain the effects of personality on choices of social tasks *would not* be considered applicable; only theories that were developed exclusively to consider tasks involving physical routines involving gross exercise would be relevant.

Advocates for this separatist approach also challenge the relevance of empirical investigations in sport psychology to psychology more generally. For example, many sport psychology programmes are aimed at athletes of superior ability. These athletes, by virtue of the amount of practice in which they engage and their degree of commitment, are qualitatively different from the average person. Consequently, any empirical findings regarding the effects of training programmes on physical skills are likely to be applicable only to these very elite and not to the average person. This leads some psychologists to conclude that the empirical answers emerging from the sport room do not inform general psychological theory in any significant way.

Physical activity and psychology

While we can see the logic behind these arguments, we do not agree. For one, many of the major theoretical approaches of general psychology are already successfully applied to the sport room. The behaviourist approach is adopted when basic principles of classical conditioning are used to reduce anxiety before competition, as in progressive relaxation (see 'The treatment room', Chapter 8, scenario two). Social learning theories have been used to explain how children and young people develop attitudes towards physical activity, and physical fitness. They can also explain how cultural attitudes might be successfully modified, through the use of advertisements and changes in school curricula.

Cognitive approaches are reflected in the use of establishing goal-oriented training regimes, and breaking down skills learning into manageable component parts. For example, the higher goal, serving an ace at tennis, can be broken down into smaller, more manageable parts, such as throwing the ball up. Athletes are encouraged to focus on the smaller components until they can perform them with little effort and little variability. Once these lower-level skills are mastered, the person can then build on them. Other techniques that are borrowed from the cognitive approach identify the habitual way in which an athlete perceives the environment, also known as **perceptual type** or perceptual bias. Our perceptual bias will determine what type of training is most effective. For example, some people are vivid visual imagers, and can create, maintain, and even manipulate a visual picture in their head or their mind's eye. If you are a good visual imager, you are better using a training technique that has you *imagine* that you are performing some skill, in addition to physically practising the skill.

Differential psychology, or the study of individual differences, is also well represented. For example, important questions in the sport room include how personality factors and gender differences influence physical activity. One line of research has examined the extent to which women who engage in competitive sports are oriented towards, or away from, traditional feminine sex roles, as defined in standardized tests like the BEM Sex Role Inventory (1974). Thus, general psychological approaches are already underlying much of what we examine in the sport room.

The psychological approach

Another reason for keeping the sport room under the general umbrella of psychology is that the levels of description used in mainstream theories are exactly the same as those operating in the sport room. Levels of description relate to the unit of analysis that we chose to examine and explain. Some authors use the terms molar and molecular, while others prefer macro and micro. Molar or macro levels of explanation include discussions of societal or cultural factors, as well as large-group factors. For example, examining the impact of organizational policies on physical fitness by providing in-house gyms and sporting facilities is looking at the molar level. Included here too could be the effects of smaller groups, such as the effects of team morale on winning or losing in competition.

The molecular or micro level deals with the individual. We can discuss the individual as a biological organism, and talk in terms of physical and neuronal models of motor skill and proprioceptive feedback. For example, simulation of motor schema is one of the

---

BOX 9.2 TRADITIONAL GENDER ROLES AND OTHER SOCIAL CONSTRAINTS

One of the earliest social rules that we learn as children surrounds the differences in gender roles. Gender is more than just being assigned male or female genitalia. Gender encompasses characteristic psychological traits as well as behavioural patterns. For example, we expect little boys in our culture to act in a particularly boisterous manner whereas we expect little girls to be more delicate and social in their interactions. Men, in turn, are said to have difficulty in expressing how they feel, while women traditionally express themselves. Developmental psychologists suggest that our knowledge of gender emerges at roughly 4 or 5 years of age, where we are able to tell the difference between what 'daddies do' and what 'mummies do'. In Western cultures, the gender roles that are traditionally regarded as masculine are acquired sooner than those associated with traditional feminine roles. By the time the child is 6 or 7, she will have gender constancy, be able to answer correctly the question 'will you be a girl when you grow up?' This demonstrates that the child knows that her gender is constant across development. Obviously, social ideologies and rituals largely determine gender roles and traits. However, there are other influences. David Buss (1995, p. 164) believes that men and women 'have faced different adaptive problems over human evolutionary history'. There is also growing evidence that physiological factors, such as hormonal differences, play a large part in gender behaviour (Collear and Hines 1995). Similarly, some studies have suggested that men and women differ in brain development and have different brain structures dominant; for example, differences in hemispheric lateralization (Springer and Deutsch 1998).

---

most exciting areas of study in artificial intelligence and robotics, as in the case in the development of 'intelligent' robots. The molecular level is also represented by psychological theories, for example those of Jean Piaget, a developmental psychologist. Piaget regarded the child's successful acquisition of primitive, early motor schemas, like sucking the thumb, to be the building blocks for all other schematic, mental representations of knowledge.

The sport room also addresses many of the core topics in psychology, such as how we allocate our attention when we perform complicated tasks, what the effects of practice are on our behaviour, and how our emotions and thoughts influence how we behave and perform. For example, the serious problem of aggressive behaviour in sport, and the hostility that can erupt between team members, represents an important area of research, both theoretically as well as practically. For all these reasons, we consider that it is essential to house the sport room in general, mainstream psychological theory and research.

Traditional topics in the sport room

Here we consider topics that have continued to dominate interest in the sport room. We first define the different terms that are used, distinguishing sport from exercise and keep-fit activities, all of which are part of the general category of recreational physical activities. We use empirical findings from studies looking at motor control to illustrate how explanations of motor behaviour can be derived from mainstream hypotheses about attention and consciousness. For example, we show how the notions of automatic and strategic processing provide a description of the effects of practice. We also discuss the relationship between body and mind, and consider the interaction between our physical states and our mental health.

Exercise

Most authors make a distinction between physical activity, exercise, and sport. Physical activity is often defined as bodily movements that are produced by the skeletal muscles which result in some energy being expended, and in which the person is voluntarily engaged. This definition would include both running a twenty-eight-mile marathon and vacuuming the house! In order to distinguish utilitarian activity, like vacuuming, from running the marathon, psychologists further identify habitual physical activity, which is associated with other general, leisure-time activities, like going to the cinema.

Habitual physical activities *include* exercise and sport. Exercise is goal-oriented, structured, and planned. For example, we go to the gym in order to achieve something, be it a better body or improved fitness. This is not restricted to the somewhat rarefied conditions of a gymnasium. Even when we bicycle to work, we are still goal-oriented, although there is an element of utility involved in cycling to work that is not apparent when we get on a stationary bicycle in a gym. Exercise is structured, in that it generally involves us making repetitive body movements, like lifting weights in sets of ten lifts. Finally, exercise is planned: we set aside time to go to the gym, or to go cycling.

Sport

In contrast, the term sport has a clear social component to its execution—some competitor has to be present, somewhere. We note the definition provided by Stuart Biddle and Nanette Mutrie, in their 1991 book, *Psychology of Physical Activity and Exercise*, where sport is 'rule governed, structured and competitive and involves gross motor movement characterized by physical strategy, prowess and chance ...' (Biddle and Mutrie 1991, p. 8). However, we modify this definition so as to include skilled motor movement that is practised.

Modern applications of psychology to the sport room can be traced back to the late nineteenth century and, in particular, to the work of Triplett, although he did not identify himself in any way as a sport psychologist. Triplett observed that cyclists produced faster times when they were paced against either a machine or another cyclist. Triplett reasoned that the pacing machine and the other cyclist provided an incentive to the athlete, the incentive to win. Thus, the presence of another sparked a competitive drive that in turn resulted in better performance. The beneficial effect that spectators, audiences, and other competitors can have on performance is known as *social facilitation*.

Whereas there are a few notable exceptions, such as Coleman Griffith's early work in the USA in the late 1920s and early 1930s, psychologists in North America and Europe showed little interest in the sport room until the late 1960s. This was in direct contrast to the Soviet Union, where formal research was initiated after the end of the Second

---

BOX 9.3 PERSONALITY AND SPORT

The relationship between personality and habitual physical activity has become an important subject of research. For example, why is it that some of us can adhere dedicatedly to an exercise regime, while others of us fail after only a few weeks? Such questions have been addressed through concepts like self-motivation (see Dishman 1982). While the findings have been mixed, there does seem to be some relationship between people who are high in self-motivation and adherence to a long-term exercise regime. This would support the belief that there is a type of person who is more likely to maintain a habit of physical activity. Maehr and Braskamp (1986) have developed what they call personal investment theory to explain individual differences in adherence and drop-out rates for physical exercise. Personal investment theory combines elements that are familiar in mainstream psychological work. For example, physical activities and exercise are said to have some personal meaning to us. Our choice of physical activity, be it judo or pilates, football or tennis, illustrates things about us. This includes our personal incentives or what we hope to gain, our sense of self, or who we believe we are. The choice also reflects our perceptions about our own limitations. More recent research has highlighted the importance of intrinsic motivation—a concept we discussed in 'The work room' (Chapter 6)—in promoting exercise adherence (Ryan et al. 1997).

World War, in such places as the Research Institute of Physical Culture, Leningrad. In fact, many authors suggest that the USA and Europe were relative latecomers in realizing the relationship between mental well-being and physical activity.

Skills acquisition

We include here the topics of motor learning, or how we learn to perform sequences of actions, and motor control, or how we make progressive improvements in performing these sequences. The theories developed to address these questions rely heavily on distinctions that we have made already regarding levels of consciousness and different types of processing. First we define what we mean by skill.

As the name implies, skill represents something more than just an ability to perform a sequence of physical actions. Fortunately, there has been extensive discussion of how skill should be defined and, to this end, we can refer to any number of definitions that have been provided. An often-quoted, early definition is provided by Guthrie (1952): '[skill is] the ability to bring about some end result with maximum certainty and minimum outlay of energy, or of time and energy.' Guthrie's definition focuses on three particular aspects of skill: that it has an identifiable outcome, that it requires minimal energy, and that it requires a minimal expenditure of time.

Sir Frederic Bartlett (1947) emphasized the relaxed nature of a skilled performance: 'What is impressive is the absence of any appearance of hurrying in [performing the constituent movements] . . . . There is not jerkiness or snatching, no obvious racing to catch up on one part and forced sauntering to make up in another.' Bartlett, too, stresses the effortless nature of a skilled performance. A more recent definition provided by Sharp in 1992 focuses on more cognitive features, such as the fact that skills are goal-directed and that they are the product of information processing that combines input from the nervous system and the kinaesthetic system.

Varieties of skill

Psychologists also make distinctions between *closed skills* and *open skills*. The distinction is based on a number of features, including the predictability of the environment. With closed skills, the environmental features are relatively constant and do not change dramatically. Examples of closed skills include diving, gymnastics, and putting the shot. In contrast, open skills have environments that are unpredictable and changing, such as ball sports like football or rugby.

Other features are used to distinguish closed and open skills, such as the nature and role of *feedback* in improving skill. For example, a closed skill like diving is largely concerned with *knowledge of performance*. Knowledge of performance is information about how the dive was conducted; for example, what position the diver's hands were in at the time of contact with the water. In contrast, in an open skill like tennis, *knowledge of outcome* is also vital. Knowledge of outcome includes such information as where the ball landed, or the speed at which the player served the ball to his opponent.

Of course, once we start to examine the different sports, we can see that there are many ways in which sports can differ, and that the differences between closed and open skills are complicated. Take, for example, playing football. Football does not only have an unpredictable environment; it is also performed under pressured conditions, where actions must occur rapidly, and has a certain type of mental effort involved, such as requiring the athlete to 'read the game' and patterns of play. In contrast, diving may be performed under tense conditions, but the actions can be planned and executed at the pace of the performer and, while there is undoubtedly mental effort and focusing of attention, the diver has no game plan to consider.

Skilled performance

Some psychologists contend that there cannot ever be a single, all-encompassing definition of skilled performance. For example, Abernethy et al. (1998) rightly point out why a uniform definition is unlikely. First, the characteristics that distinguish a skilled performance from a less-skilled performance are not the same across different sports. For example, we have already shown that an open skill, like playing football, has different skilled components than a closed skill, like diving. This means that being an expert in one requires a different set of skills than being an expert in the other. Second, perceptual motor skill is very context-specific, just as cognitive skill is context-specific. So, just because you are good at remembering names does not mean that you are good at remembering people's conversations. In the exact same way, just because you are good at cricket does not mean that you will be good at playing baseball.

In fact, there seems to be very little transfer of skill from one sport to another, such that an expert in one sport is likely to be at a beginner's level of skill in another sport. This is true even if the two sports share similar sub-components. For example, suppose you are an expert tennis player; you would not expect to be at the same level of skill if someone asked you for a game of badminton. As Abernethy et al. (1998) so neatly conclude, the most consistent thing about skill is that it defies any attempts at providing a single definition outside a highly constrained and specific context.

Motor learning

When we begin to learn motor movements we go through three distinct phases. Psychologists who explain these phases in terms of information-processing approaches rely heavily on the distinctions between levels of consciousness, and also distinctions in the nature of the knowledge that underlies our performance.

The first phase has been described as the *cognitive phase*. Because the learner is new to the task, they must first understand, learn, and then remember the goals of the activities, and how to perform the actions. Generally, all efforts are highly intentional and deliberate, and the learner relies on **declarative knowledge**. For example, the learner may use sub-vocal reminders, such as 'remember to throw the ball high enough over your head'. This early phase is where more general warm-up effects occur and the extent of improvement in performance is generally the greatest in this first phase.

The second phase is characterized as more of an associative phase, where the learner is now concerned with improving performance, rather than acquiring the rudimentary skills. The knowledge base is now more **procedural**, in that the person knows how to do the skill. Their knowledge about how to hold a racket may no longer be available as a verbal description, but rather is stored in some body memory, and can be recognized by body postures. In the associative phase, the performer is focusing on improving performance in more subtle ways. Some authors suggest that this phase can last for weeks or months. Improvements made during this phase are less dramatic.

The third phase is the autonomous phase. This is characterized by the person being able to perform the physical aspects of the task with little effort, to the extent that the performance is automatic. At this phase, the performer can direct all attention away from the actual motor components, and concentrate instead on other elements, such as artistic interpretation of movement sequences in ice-skating.

The characteristics of skilled performance

Once acquired, our skilled behaviour shows certain characteristics. We refer back to Bartlett's description of the effortlessness of a skilled performance, the fluidity of the movements. We consider this below, when we re-introduce the distinction between automatic versus strategic processing (see Chapter 8, scenario two).

Essentially, effortlessness comes from a combination of appropriate feedback schedules, along with consistent and regular practice. First we consider the effects of feedback. Feedback provides the performer with information about various aspects of their performance. The general consensus is that feedback is a function of sensory information that is related to the execution of movement(s). Feedback can be intrinsic or extrinsic to producing the movement. Intrinsic feedback is what occurs when you actually perform an action, such as the sensations you might have in your hand, arm and shoulder when you hit a ball with a tennis racket. Extrinsic feedback is not contingent upon *producing* the movement, but on its *evaluation*, such as receiving comments from your coach on how you looked as you were completing your dive.

Psychologists highlight how feedback should be viewed in terms of quality, quantity and timing. Quality refers to the level of detail of the feedback, and this must be related to the skill of the performer. For example, knowledge of performance, such as feedback on how to *do* something is more important for the novice. Knowledge of performance influences technical aspects of skill, such as how well someone performs a gymnastic manoeuvre. Knowledge of outcome, such as whether your feet were too close to the edge of the mat, is better used after the novice has learned the rudimentary skill to perform the manoeuvre. Quantity of feedback is essential how much—where you tell someone how poorly they performed on all aspects of the manoeuvre, or whether you focus on one aspect at a time. Timing is when the feedback is given. This varies depending upon many things, but generally it can be classified in terms of whether the feedback is given at the time the performer is executing the action, such as split-times for runners, or at the end of the performance, such as at the end of a dive.

Skill and practice

Explanations of how practice effects our performance reintroduce distinctions among levels of consciousness. Here, we focus on the distinction between having to think about doing something, or strategic processing, versus automatic processing, which requires a minimal amount of our attention and mental energy. We have already considered this extensively in The treatment room, in our discussion of working memory (see Chapter 8, scenario two).

One of the most elegant demonstrations of the effects of practice is discussed by Peter McLeod, Carmel McLaughlin and Ian Nimmo-Smith (1985) in their work on the effects of practice in finely timed actions; for example, hitting a ball with a wooden bat. McLeod *et al.* point out that one of the most adaptive things we do is time our actions to correspond to approaching objects. For example, when we want to cross the road we wish to avoid collision with oncoming traffic, and we time our movements so as to avoid collision. Alternatively, if we wish to pick up an object, such as a cup, or make contact with another object, such as hitting a ball with a bat, we time our actions so that we *do* collide with the object. As we see, McLeod *et al.*'s study of finely timed actions has application to the real world in general, and an obvious application to the sport room.

McLeod *et al.* reasoned that the manner in which we time our actions to coincide with approaching objects is achieved through highly specific operations. They discuss this in terms of information encapsulation, a concept that was first introduced by Fodor

---

BOX 9.4 CONSCIOUSNESS AND PSYCHOLOGICAL THEORY

The concept of consciousness has been one that has come and gone, and come again, into prominence in psychological theories. Early psychologists, such as William James and John Watson, were explicit in their rejection of the concept as a suitable topic of study. James believed that consciousness was a non-entity, 'a mere echo, the faint rumour left behind by the disappearing "soul" upon the air of philosophy' (James 1904, p. 477). Watson was less poetic: 'The time seems to have come when psychology must discard all references to consciousness' (Watson 1913, p. 163). Indeed, even into the 1970s, psychologists seemed to feel that they had to defend consciousness as a construct worthy of study. At that time psychologists did not see the need for a comprehensive theory of mental processing to address consciousness (see Natsoulas 1978). Today, interest is focusing on how we *define* consciousness. Lambie and Marcel (2002), for example, offer an analysis of consciousness that puts at the centre the way in which we experience our own emotions rather than the way we perceive the outside world. This is viewed from two levels: our direct subjective experience, namely *feeling* the emotion, and our *awareness* of that experience. Similarly, developments in brain imaging have extended the study of consciousness to entirely new levels, with findings suggesting that the differential activation of certain brain centres is associated with different levels of our conscious experience. In these days it would be unusual for modern general textbooks on psychology *not* to have a major section devoted to the study of consciousness, if not entire chapters.

---

in his 1983 book, *The Modularity of Mind*. Very simply, Fodor argues that certain types of cognitive process are unfazed by external influences, and these are processes that are informationally encapsulated. Information encapsulation means that some action can be performed on the basis of highly specific input with virtually no recourse to general, cognitive computational resources.

Information encapsulation is very similar to the notions of automatic processing of Atkinson and Shiffrin (1968) that we have discussed previously. Atkinson and Shiffrin argued that when a connection, like the temporal association between a stimulus and a response, is practised sufficiently, the processing that is required to generate the response when the stimulus is presented stops demanding general computational resources. In essence, we do not need to think about executing the motor response, we behave as if the action is second nature to us. For example, a skilled typist can translate the spoken word into motor movements without any effort, such as when a secretary is typing a letter from dictation. This property of being automatic, of not requiring central executive resources, is effectively what Fodor regards as information encapsulation.

McLeod *et al.* suggest that with extensive practice, motor skill becomes automatic, or becomes informationally encapsulated. Admittedly, the suggestion that there is a link between practice and automaticity, or information encapsulation, is not particularly novel. However, what is novel in McLeod *et al.*'s work is how they chose to demonstrate that practice creates information encapsulation. Most other authors choose to examine the effects of practice on motor skill in terms of attentional demands. A classic design used to this end is the dual-task situation. In a dual-task situation, people are asked to perform two tasks simultaneously. With extensive practice there is a noticeable decrease in the extent to which the two tasks interfere with each other. Our example of the skilled typist is shows how, with practice, two separate tasks can be performed without any interference. Other psychologists have tried to explain the effects of practice on average speed, such as how fast it takes someone to execute the task with extensive practice.

What McLeod et al. did instead was to examine more-specific characteristics of task performance and, in particular, variability in producing the response. They argue that the effect of practice is that a particular motor sequence becomes less variable, as assessed by the *standard deviation*, or distribution, of the responses. The standard deviation indicates the average deviation between each response. McLeod *et al.* demonstrated that with practice, the standard deviation—the average difference between responses—becomes significantly less.

Let us take a very simple example to illustrate. Suppose that we ask people to tap after they hear a warning signal, like a bell. Our behavioural measure is how soon after hearing the bell that the person taps. We notice that over the first five times, the person taps quite variably. For example, the first tap is 850 milliseconds after the bell; the second tap is 600 milliseconds; the third tap is 450 milliseconds; the fourth tap is 700 milliseconds; and the fifth tap is 250 milliseconds. We can see that over the five trials, the range of response times is large, between 250 and 800 milliseconds, and that there is at least a 100-millisecond difference between the two closest response times. However, after we give the person one hundred more trials, the range in responses is considerably lower. When we select another five trials, we see that the person's range of response times is between 250 and 275 milliseconds and that there is never more than a 75-millisecond difference between any two responses. We can easily see that, after practice, the person has become less variable in the time it takes them to respond to the bell. According to McLeod et al. this reduced temporal variability is one of the significant results of extensive practice.

The relevance of this to finer sport performance is obvious. With practice, the process of executing a motor response sequence is gradually taken over by more and more specific automatic processes. In this way, practice frees the general mental resources, allowing the athlete to focus on other aspects of their performance. So, once the tennis player has perfected the motor sequence responsible for a return volley, they can direct their mental effort to executing a strategy of proactive, offensive manoeuvres, such as hitting from the front or the back of the court.

Thoughts, feelings, and sport

In this section we focus on the link between our mental and bodily states. The topics that are relevant here have already been discussed in the context of other rooms. For example, we will look at how the concept of motivation is central to a wide range of topics, from exercise adherence to sport performance and training. We illustrate the strong relationship between thoughts and performance; for example, in learned optimism. We also consider the effects that emotions can have on performance; for example, aggression and sport.

We started this chapter by reminding ourselves that the ancient Greeks believed in the relationship between good mental attitudes and producing superior athletic performance. Here we examine further how our mental and emotional states influence our physical performance. We delay the discussion of the effects that negative emotions and thoughts can have on performance until scenario one (pp. 221–9), where we consider in detail the effects of performance anxiety and how relaxation and other mental techniques are used to combat it.

Motivation

The concept of motivation is one of the major themes throughout all of the rooms that we have considered. Because of its complexity, motivation is difficult to define. For example, motivation in some contexts refers to why we act in a particular way; for example, why some people turn to crime and others do not. We have already alluded to the strong possibility that our personality, or individual differences, influences our choice of sport; for example, whether we like tennis or rowing. This definition of motivation is also useful when we consider why some people partake in physical activity, such as exercise, and why other people largely prefer to remain sedentary, and in some instances develop into couch potatoes who have little interest in maintaining any regular form of physical activity. Another definition of motivation is closer to that which

---

BOX 9.5 EXERCISE AND THE HEALTH OF A NATION

One of the most pressing problems that confronts many Western and European societies today is that people are taking less physical exercise as a matter of course in their everyday lives. There is no question that our personal lives—relative to only fifty years ago—are more reliant on machines and automated devices, such as cars, and our work lives have become more reliant on automated devices that require little physical exertion on our part, such as computers and workstations. As a consequence, we are now experiencing, at unprecedented levels, health problems that are directly related to our lack of physical exercise, such as obesity. These health problems are costly, regardless of the public or private nature of health care. People take days off sick when they have health problems and this, in itself, introduces a huge financial burden to the national, regional, and local economy. We have already discussed how psychologists have been useful in helping to identify those people who commit to—and maintain—an exercise regime, and those who do not. Equally important is the research that looks specifically at how exercise improves our overall health. This has been formally addressed by the International Society of Sport Psychology (ISSP) in their 1992 position statement. In their report, the ISSP clearly identify areas where research has consistently shown how exercise benefits psychological functioning. For example, there is a positive relationship between exercise and self-esteem, and there are increases in reports of positive mood following exercise. Importantly, the positive effects of physical activity occur across all time periods of development, from young adulthood to old age. Further, there are indications that physical activity is associated with greater levels of energy in other domains of the person's life, such as a person's economic productivity. From any government's perspective, a fit population of citizens yields wealth and prosperity.

we introduced in 'The war room' (Chapter 7), where we considered the goal-directed nature of behaviour, and the application of energy—both physical and mental—in achieving this goal. Regardless of the particular definition or theoretical explanation, motivation is a serious part of training and coaching.

One of the major problems in coaching and training is to motivate the athlete to perform. Often, the athlete must ignore physical pain (see scenario two, pp. 230–41), as well as other distractions, such as family and social life. From this perspective, we are talking about motivation as if it reflects the athlete's willingness to engage in the physical sport—the extent to which the athlete chooses to approach or avoid the situation. Added to this is some type of intensity or amount: sometimes athletes are very willing and eager, others times they are disinterested and detached.

Another way to consider motivation is developed from looking at what the person hopes to achieve by participating in the sport. Some psychologists refer to this in terms of the person's goal orientation. Some people engage in the sport because they have the desire to learn and become more competent in their skill, and are less concerned with whether they win or lose. These individuals are called task-oriented, as they are primarily concerned with becoming competent in their skill. In contrast, other people participate in sport for the competitive component—whether it be direct, as in a 1000-metre race, or indirect, as in competition diving. For these people, the reason they engage in the sport is that they want to win, to beat someone else. These people are called ego-involved. They are concerned with showing their superior competence relative to another. We can see how these concepts are related to those we discussed in 'The work room' (Chapter 6), and 'The treatment room' (Chapter 8), regarding intrinsic and extrinsic motivation. For example, intrinsic motivation might be more tied to task-oriented individuals, who are more concerned about personal development rather than outcomes relative to others.

Other explanations of motivation focus on the social aspects of sport. Team sports offer us the chance to involve ourselves with a group, and promote our feelings of belonging to the group. As we have already discussed, when we feel we belong to a group, we can experience higher self-esteem. Equally, the group can offer us the possibility of social support in times of emotional need or distress. For people who join in sport for the social interaction, it is neither competence in skill nor achievement relative to another that is their motivation. The motivation is to be with others, and even perhaps to have some fun.

A person's motivation for engaging in sport has very serious implications for training and coaching. For example, suppose someone is motivated to learn, to achieve a greater competence in their skill. If the environment, and particularly the coaching and training environment, fails to provide feedback that monitors and assesses changes and improvements in performance, then this person may become demoralized and demotivated. In contrast, suppose that someone engages in the sporting activity because they want to have fun, or because they enjoy being with other people. Too much emphasis on the outcome—such as overtly demanding people to play to win—may defeat the purpose of engaging in the sport, and result in the person withdrawing.

Thoughts and the body

One of the most interesting questions that has developed from studies in the sport room is why some teams, and some individuals, seem to be winners, while others seem to be unable to break their losing streak. This question is similar, in many ways, to the questions we asked in 'The treatment room' (Chapter 8) regarding why some people never get depressed, and some people regularly do. We have already considered this in terms of attributional style and the development of learned helplessness, which was pioneered by Martin Seligman in the 1970s. Presently, Seligman (1998) has developed the complementary notion to learned help-lessness, *learned optimism*. Because learned optimism is essentially the opposite of learned helplessness, the explanatory style associated with optimism reflects this. Positive attributions and evaluations are used to explain events that happen to the individual, so that the person becomes optimistic in mood, and hence is in a better mental framework for success.

For example, suppose that a team has lost its last two matches. There are a number of ways in which the team might explain and try to understand what is underlying this recent pattern. They could believe that their poor performance is due to the superior abilities of their opponents; and that, they are, in effect, out of their league. Alternatively, the team could believe that their poor performance is due to the fact that they have been less focused and need to practise together on certain aspects of the game. These different explanations will yield different emotional reactions, which in turn will influence performance. According to Seligman, the team's explanatory style will determine whether they successfully win their upcoming game. Seligman believes that the psychologist can teach

---

BOX 9.6 MASCOTS AND OTHER CHARMS

Our irrational beliefs—like our rational ones—influence how we perform, particularly in competition. One of the most peculiar, but endearing, rituals is the function that a mascot serves. While it may not be immediately apparent, our use of mascots can be traced back to the ancient practice of invoking spirits, or good luck, through charms and talismans. The charm, such as the tikis carried by the Maoris, seemed to provide a supernatural advantage to the athlete. They would have the gods' blessing, much in the same way that armies invoked divine support before going into battle. Historians note that the use of charms, like talismans, declined dramatically by the seventeenth century, largely due to the increased formalization of rules regarding sporting events. Nonetheless, the remnants of our ancient beliefs in the importance of external forces is apparent, although not as blatantly. For example, athletes often identify an article, or articles, of clothing that they believe are lucky, such as a pair of shoes, a jersey, or an armband. The athlete may be genuinely disturbed, and their performance affected, if they is prevented from wearing their lucky item. While the athlete is aware, at some level, that the belief is irrational, they are nonetheless unable to relax. Teams use mascots—which are generally animals—as a means of enthusing fans, who in turn motivate the team.

individuals and teams to change their explanations, which will teach them to change their mood.

Cognitive skills

Cognitive psychology has been very successfully applied to the sport room, and no other place demonstrates this as well as in the application of mental skills in training and coaching. In their 1998 chapter, 'Mental skills training in sport', Daniel Gould and Nicole Darmarjian provide an excellent review of the general area of mental skills in training. They cite data from studies where elite athletes and coaches were asked to rate how important different mental skills are in promoting good performance. Mental skills included those that were performance-related as well as non-performance-related. Examples of performance-related skills are arousal regulation, where athletes are instructed how to control their arousal so that they are neither under- nor over-aroused. Another example of performance-related skills is the control of concentration and attention, where the athlete is taught how to focus on a single goal, or aspect of their performance, without any distraction. This type of mental strategy requires the athlete to learn how to silence unrelated thought; for example, how to inhibit disturbing thoughts from the articulatory loop in working memory (see Chapter 8, pp. 195–7). Non-performance-related skills include interpersonal skills and communication, and conflict management such as when there are disputes between team members or athletes and coaching staff.

Gould and Darmarjian (1998) review studies showing that athletes and coaches give similar ratings. According to the empirical research, both groups rate performance-related mental skills as far more important than non-performance-related skills. For example, visualization—where the athlete is required to imagine performing actions—and attention-focusing are rated as among the most important skills. Stress management and relaxation, both of which will be discussed in detail in scenario one, below, are also highly rated by both. When similar studies have been conducted with sport psychologists, the findings are similar. Performance-related skills are always rated as more important, with visualization and stress management being rated as highly valuable.

However, studies that have looked at youth sport coaches and administrators have shown that these groups rate non-performance measures as more important than do elite athletes and coaches. So, for example, youth sport coaches rate communication with team members as more important than visualization techniques. The reason for the difference in ratings may be due to differences in the perceived motivation for en-gaging in sport. For elite athletes and coaches, motivations are likely to reflect desires to win, or personal excellence, particularly given the financial gains that can be accrued. In contrast, youth coaches and administrators are far more likely to appreciate the other benefits of sport, including improvement in interpersonal skills and general problem-solving resources.

BOX 9.7 AROUSAL AND THE ELUSIVE HAPPY MEDIUM

One of the first findings that psychology students are taught is the relationship between arousal levels and performance. One of the earliest theories used to explain the effects that arousal level has on our ability to execute a task is the Yerkes–Dodson Inverted U Theory of Arousal (Yerkes and Dodson 1908). This theory is very simplistic, and asserts that levels of arousal are associated with different levels of performance. At low levels of arousal, performance is sub-average, since the person is not sufficiently driven to achieve. However, at extremely high levels of arousal, the person similarly performs poorly, but this time because their arousal levels are too high, and interfere with the execution of action. Ideally, the athlete should strive to reach moderate levels of arousal, where they are sufficiently energized but not so aroused so as to disrupt performance. This inverted U concept—where too low and too high are suboptimal—has not been supported in subsequent studies. However, it fits with our phenomenal experience in that, if we are too anxious or too aroused, we do not perform well.

Summary and prospect

We have considered some of the more traditional topics that are found in the sport room. In particular, we highlight the fact that many of the concepts that we considered were ones that have been already introduced. These main themes include how we learn, how our behaviour is influenced by our motivation, and how our thoughts and beliefs influence the way we perform. We have argued that because the sport room provides the context for discussing many of the important, mainstream theories in psychology, the sport room is one of the most enriched environments in which a psychologist can operate.

The sport room has been an essential part of human society for millennia. However, our modern societies have resulted in significant changes in our normal levels of physical activity, and, for some of us, these changes have been deleterious to our general physical health. Because of the obvious consequences that lifestyle choices have on the public as a whole, we believe that the sport room is going to continue to grow into a highly popular context in which to apply psychological theories. For example, the significant increase in childhood obesity is likely to prompt further research into the influence that individual differences have on our changing attitudes towards physical, recreational activities. It is also likely to promote research that examines more seriously how to best change the attitudes of a whole generation of people, so that, like the ancient Greeks, we have a nation of healthy minds and bodies.

We also note that, historically, the physical superiority of a nation can be used as a tool for asserting the superiority of a political ideology. Those nations who dominate and excel in physical competitions are somehow regarded as the ideal to which lesser nations should aspire. Because so much is at stake, the use of performance-enhancing drugs has become more and more commonplace. This raises serious ethical questions regarding training regimes as well as the use of drug enhancements, including the excessive use of vitamins and artificially developed performance enhancements. Psychologists must take some responsibility in addressing such issues and directing any debates surrounding their discussion.

Sport scenarios

The following two scenarios highlight problems in the modern sport room that psychologists regularly assist in solving. The first scenario focuses on the problem of performance anxiety in athletes, particularly in the context of competitive sporting events. The scenario shows how techniques used in the treatment of phobias and anxiety related disorders have been easily applied to help athletes overcome setbacks in confidence. Our second scenario illustrates the use of psychological techniques, such as mental re-evaluation and focusing, in the context of pain management and injury. Pain management requires a multi-level approach, primarily because our experience of pain is highly complex. While there is an obvious physical component there is also an equally powerful psychological and subjective component. Rehabilitation techniques must focus on both components to be successful and the scenario amply demonstrates this.

SCENARIO ONE

LOSS OF CONFIDENCE IN A PROFESSIONAL ATHLETE

In this scenario we consider how psychological stress, physical strain, and poor performance can undermine the will and ability of an athlete to compete. Many psychologists who work in the context of the sport room believe that it is not the best athlete who will win a competition, but rather the athlete who is the *best prepared*. Preparation can be thought of in terms of physical and psychological levels. Obviously, the athlete must be physically prepared and must have a certain level of fitness. This would include prior training, in order to ensure appropriate strength and endurance, as well as physical condition on the day of the competition. The characteristics of the athlete, including their general level of fitness, history of injury, and age, will influence the training programme. It is likely that most athletes benefit from strength and power development. However, the nature of the sport will largely determine the relative objectives and perceived value in being strong or fast. This stands to reason, as the skills and abilities necessary to win in a 10,000-metre race are different from those that are necessary to win a 400-metre hurdle race. What is very interesting, however, is that prejudices exist and some myths have been built up surrounding the benefits or disadvantages of different types of training. For example, some athletes believe that over-emphasizing strength will result in a loss of speed, in spite of the fact that there is no empirical evidence to support this belief.

In parallel with one's physical state, an athlete must be prepared psychologically. This mental preparation can take many forms. Part of mental preparation is directing attention and mental resources appropriately. The athlete must be sufficiently flexible so that they can direct their attention to consider factors that are important, but not so flexible for irrelevancies to get in the way of performing. So, a tennis player may need to be able to note certain external features, like the pattern of mistakes that her opponent is showing, but not be distracted by other external features, such as crowd noises. Similarly, the athlete must be sufficiently focused so that she attends to that which is most important at the moment, but not be so focused so that she ignores other critical signals. Again, we use our tennis player as an example. We would want her to be able to attend to features of her performance that are immediately relevant, such as returning a volley, but not be so focused so that she fails to notice that their opponent has changed positions on the court.

One of the most essential ways in which an athlete prepares for competition is through her ability to control nervousness and tension. Competition is always going to be a stressful situation and it would be unnatural if an athlete did not experience some nerves. Indeed, we have already argued that some theories of arousal, like the Yerkes–Dodson theory (see Box 9.7), *require* a moderate level of arousal in order for an athlete to produce a good performance. However, sometimes an athlete's anxiety levels increase so much that her thoughts and emotional reactions start to focus on failure. The ultimate consequence of this is that the athlete underachieves. Her underachievement in performance in turn reinforces negative thoughts and emotions regarding self-ability, and the athlete can become locked in an iterative cycle of negative thoughts, feelings, lowered motivation, and poor performance.

In this scenario, we describe this very situation. A highly accomplished female athlete, Xena, entered a very important international sporting event. She currently held the world record for the two track events in which she would be competing. Xena was in excellent physical condition and had not suffered any injuries. Her practice times were very good and she was consistent in her form and speed. Importantly, the competition was not particularly difficult. The only other athlete who could possibly challenge Xena was not competing, as she had failed a recent drugs test and was disallowed. This meant that Xena was the highest-ranked athlete who was competing, and should win both of her events without too much effort.

Xena's coach knew that this competition was critical in Xena's career, and that the financial consequences for her could be lucrative. The coach did not want to press Xena too much, as this might cause her some unnecessary concern, and yet he saw no reason why he should not encourage her to 'win, win, win!' The media shared her coach's enthusiasm. Everyone, from the crowd to the presenters and her coach assumed that Xena would emerge victorious.

At the start of the first event, the weather was unusually hot, and there had been two incidents of unruly and rude crowd behaviour, which disturbed most of the competitors, including Xena. Whereas Xena made a good start to her race, something seemed to happen suddenly and she stumbled. Xena managed to prevent herself from falling, but she was unable to regain her stride. Minutes later, she appeared to pull a muscle and collapsed in a heap, in tears and in pain. She seemed to be unable physically to raise herself from the ground, and she had to be helped by two onlookers. Xena was devastated by her failure to finish the race. However, Xena decided that she had regained enough composure and confidence to compete in the second event. Shortly after beginning of the second race, Xena stopped and again failed to complete the race.

While some people in the crowd were sympathetic, others were not and felt that Xena had let them down. Similarly many of the media presenters felt that Xena should have tried to finish the second event. Xena's coach was particularly concerned that her failure to complete two races would not only result in a blow to Xena's performance later that season, but also have dire financial consequences. Xena began to complain of general feelings of anxiety and despair, and these symptoms persisted for a few weeks, and prevented Xena from training. In fact, every time that Xena even imagined competing, she began to experience extreme feelings of anxiety and fear, including breathlessness and rapid, pounding heart beats. Both Xena and her coach agreed that she should enlist the support of a psychologist.

Her coach contacted a governing body for psychologists and they were recommended a psychologist. This psychologist had a mixture of backgrounds and experience with different methods of study. The psychologist had experience in mental health settings, in hospitals, and was also an expert in behavioural techniques used to address general anxiety disorders.

What was the situation?

The situation could potentially result in serious consequences, as Xena was a professional athlete, and her career would necessarily be damaged should she be unable to compete. Both Xena and her coach felt that she was would be able to regain her confidence, but needed some psychological techniques that she could use, and which importantly would show results sooner rather than later. This meant that whatever type of psychological input they might receive, it had to be one that demonstrated its effectiveness over the short-term, and could be used again were the problem to re-emerge.

Why was the psychologist involved?

Both Xena and her coach wanted the psychologist to identify the problem and, more importantly, provide them with a way of fixing the problem. As time was short, they also wanted no more than five or six sessions with the psychologist. It is clear that the objectives of Xena and her coach were action-oriented (see Chapter 8). Whereas Xena was interested in why she was experiencing such a breakdown in her performance, she was more interested in correcting her behaviour, rather than discovering any special insight into her personality. The psychologist immediately recognized this and felt that the approach would be compatible with the goals of treatment. It was agreed that Xena would be seen for six sessions, with a view to better understanding what prompted her anxiety attacks and how she might best control them.

What psychological concepts are relevant?

The psychologist obviously needed to consider evidence regarding anxiety and its relationship to behaviour. Anxiety can be defined as the subjective experience of mental apprehension that is accompanied by increased physiological symptoms that include emotional feelings. The psychologist knew that anxiety affects all aspects of behaviour, from physical agility to feelings and thoughts. For example, anxiety can be associated with changes in mental abilities, such as a decreased ability in problem-solving or an inability to concentrate. This would be very deleterious to competition, as the athlete must be able to filter out all irrelevant external and internal thoughts, feelings, and images.

Anxiety also has obvious effects on mood, like increases in feelings of agitation, or feelings of fearfulness. Because of the close interaction between mood and physical agility, increased negative mood is associated with tension and unnecessary muscular activity, like looking around at one's competitors. Equally, anxiety has a strong effect on thoughts, with the thoughts generally being intrusive, in that they are difficult to ignore as well as unwanted and negative. Importantly, intrusive thoughts associated with anxiety are either future-oriented or past-oriented, but they are rarely *present-oriented*. Future-oriented thoughts are those that focus on the future, such as counterfactual thinking; 'if, then...'. For example, the athlete might be thinking, 'if I don't get a good start, then it will be difficult for me to get into my stride ...' Past-oriented thoughts focus on a past event, such as 'if I had only trained more last week, I would not be feeling so nervous now...' It is obvious that the negative tone of these thoughts will impair the athlete's performance: the athlete becomes tenser with negative thoughts; this tension, in turn, serves to support the maintenance of negative thoughts, and so on. Thus, an iterative cycle of mood-thought-mood becomes established. There is another consequence to cognitive distortions such as these. Critically, the athlete is distracted from the present, and cannot appropriately attend and monitor those elements of the environment that are crucial for a good performance. This mental distraction inevitably results in the athlete underachieving.

The psychologist knew that a large part of an athlete's performance is mental preparation. This includes concentration or focusing, visual imaging, arousal control, emotional control, and positive self-talk (see Scenario two, below). All these were

---

BOX 9.8 MOOD PROFILES AND THE ELITE ATHLETE

Whereas it is intuitive that our mood will affect how well we perform, there have been systematic studies that have tried to isolate the type of mood profile, or mood patterns, that are associated with successful sport performance. The work that is cited most regularly is that of Morgan (1985), who identified that successful athletes had more generally positive mental health than the average person, and that a positive mental attitude was closely linked with positive outcomes in performance. He developed what is known as the iceberg profile of mood states for successful athletes. The effect is called this because of the way Morgan chose to depict the data on a graph, and not for any more mysterious reason! Morgan compared athletes with people from the general population on six mood states: tension, depression, anger, vigour, fatigue, and confusion. What he found was that athletes scored lower on all measures, except for vigour, which they scored higher than the general population (the higher scoring on vigour represents the peak of the iceberg). While Morgan found support for his notions, later research has shown that not all successful athletes conform to the iceberg profile.

undoubtedly important to consider. However, the psychologist suspected that the underlying problem was the result of an inappropriate, negative association between some of the aspects of Xena's mental preparation—such as thoughts or images—and her overly aroused, emotional state, most specifically her high levels of anxiety. Proponents of classic association theory have extensively studied how an inappropriate association between an external event and an emotional response might be modified. The psychologist was particularly interested in the work done on **counterconditioning**, as it has been shown to be very effective in breaking inappropriate stimulus–response associations, especially when the person is suffering from either a fear or anxiety response.

Counterconditioning finds its beginnings in the work of Mary Cover Jones (Jones 1924), who was a student of the behaviourist John B. Watson. Jones worked with a young child who had an intense fear of rabbits. She first brought the child and the rabbit (then in a cage) together in a room, while at the same time giving the child some sweets. The first encounter was stressful for the child, and Jones kept the rabbit's cage at a considerably distance from the child. However, over a series of months, Jones would bring the cage slightly closer at each encounter, all the while giving the child sweets. Eventually, the child was not only unafraid of the rabbit but wanted to pet and stroke the animal. This illustrated counterconditioning: the once-feared stimulus, the rabbit, was reconditioned in the presence of a positive stimulus, the sweets. Of course, Jones warned that this procedure needed to be done very slowly, lest the child became fearful of the sweets!

The relevance of classic counterconditioning seemed obvious to the psychologist. Xena had somehow developed an inappropriate association between with her anxiety and her ability to compete. The psychologist would have to use techniques that broke the association, so that Xena did not become anxious when thinking or imaging herself competing. Importantly, such techniques suited Xena's preference for taking an action-oriented approach to her problem, rather than an insight-oriented approach. The techniques advocated by the psychologist did not require Xena to explore any underlying, unconscious processes that might be contributing to her current difficulties.

Related to this is the fact that current memories and thoughts will directly determine the person's current emotional state, which in turn serves to enhance the retrieval and recall of mood congruent memories. This is a very robust experimental finding and is confirmed through clinical observations as well. Mood-congruent effects are very debilitating, and can affect the contents of working memory, misdirect attentional processes, and generally hamper the person's motivation, interest, and activity level. There has been extensive theorizing regarding the re-iterative, negative cycle that can exist between thoughts (images and memories), mood, and physical states, as has been elegantly discussed by John Teasdale and Philip Barnard in their book *Affect and Cognition* (1993). The psychologist was particularly interested in approaches similar to those taken by Teasdale and Barnard, as such multi-level models directly linked cognition, emotion, and bodily states, in an interactive manner.

The psychologist was also interested in reviewing the literature on personality style. While it is virtually impossible to make any predictions about an athlete's performance from their personality type, the available research suggests that most professional athletes are extroverts rather than introverts. This finding seems somewhat intuitive, given the construct of extroversion–introversion. The argument is that introverts experience high levels of arousal, and as a consequence they shy away from those activities that would promote increases in their levels of arousal. As professional competition creates higher arousal levels in all athletes, it is an event that in which introverts would be less inclined to participate voluntarily, as they would find it physically and mentally uncomfortable and distressing. However, personality type is not the only factor in determining an athlete's success, and there are some world-class athletes who are introverts. It may be that these athletes are successful because they have developed adequate mechanisms for controlling any unwanted increases in their arousal levels in sporting-competition environments. Taken together, although the findings were equivocal, the psychologist still felt it important to consider Xena's more general personality traits in the context of standardized tests.

What did the psychologist do?

The psychologist asked Xena to first recount the conditions of the first event, including external and internal factors. External factors would be the weather conditions, as well as any comments made by other people. Internal factors would be whether Xena felt energetic, what kinds of thoughts was she having, and so on. The psychologist realized that something must have precipitated Xena's reaction, and it was important to discover what that was.

The psychologist discovered that Xena had at first been task-oriented. She had not been concerned about winning the competition. Instead, she had wanted to concentrate on her performance, and stay focused on performing as well as she could.

BOX 9.9 PERSONALITY, THE BRAIN, AND SPORT

Hans Eysenck provided an interesting theory that seems well suited to account for the general finding that most professional athletes are extroverts in nature (see Nideffer 1989). Eysenck, like Raymond Cattell (1943), believed that the structure of personality could be described in terms of factors, or features, that in combination produced individual behaviour, attitudes, and feelings. Based on his study of 700 patients suffering from neurotic disorders, Eysenck proposed three major personality dimensions—neuroticism, extroversion, and psychoticism—which he measured in his general personality test, the **Eysenck Personality Inventory** or EPI. Whereas there is a huge literature on the EPI, we focus only on the factors of extroversion and neuroticism, as these have been applied consistently in the context of the sport room. Eysenck suggested that there is a physiological basis underlying scores on the EPI. Specifically, he argued that people who are introverts experience higher average (or chronic) levels of cortical activity than do extroverts. Further he argued that people who score higher on neuroticism also have greater activity in the visceral brain—which includes those brain centres associated with the evaluation of pain (see scenario two). Taken together, Eysenck would predict that successful athletes are likely to be extroverts and score low on neuroticism. This means that these individuals would have lower arousal levels, suitable for the highly charged environment of competition, and would have fewer physiological symptoms associated with injury and general stress, which, again, would render them more suitable for competition.

It became very clear to the psychologist that Xena's coach had been responsible for changing her focus away from the task, and directed her to the outcome of the races. As a consequence, Xena became more concerned about future events and, consequently, less focused on the race itself.

The psychologist knew that he would have to desensitize Xena, in that he needed to break the association of her thoughts of competing with her feelings of anxiety. The psychologist relied on the technique of *systematic desensitization*, as developed from classic association theory. Systematic desensitization is based on the assumption that the person can re-learn how to associate a pleasant, relaxed state with a stimulus that previously was associated with fear, anxiety, or panic. Slowly, and through systematic steps, the feared stimulus is introduced, through what is known as an *anxiety hierarchy*. To establish an anxiety hierarchy, the client is asked to rate how frightening different stimuli are, on a scale from zero to one hundred. For example, if you are frightened of spiders, your anxiety hierarchy might consist of the following: thinking about a spider, an anxiety rating of five; holding a picture of a spider, rating of ten; sitting beside a dead spider, rating of thirty; having a spider walk on your arm, rating of seventy; having a spider crawl on your face, rating of one hundred. The psychologist introduces the lowest level of the hierarchy and does not proceed until you are able to associate your relaxed state with that stimulus. Again, from our example, we would first have you think about a spider; once you were able to maintain your relaxed response, we would then ask you to hold a picture of a spider, and so on. In this way, you would be reconditioned to experience a relaxed response, rather than your phobic one.

The psychologist first established whether Xena had good mental, visual images, or whether she preferred more verbal modes, such as thoughts. Xena had relied

---

BOX 9.10 LEARNING HOW TO RELAX

Most of us have a relatively intuitive understanding of why it is important for us to relax, although there are huge individual differences in how successful we are in doing so. However, our inherent ability to relax can become noticeably impaired after a stressful event(s). This is the same with professional athletes. Psychologists typically rely on three types of relaxation methods: progressive muscle relaxation (PMR), autogenic training, and, biofeedback. PMR requires the person to learn how to focus on individual muscle groups involved in the activity and, importantly, how to distinguish between the build-up and then release of tension. This technique is particularly useful in treating pain (see Scenario two). Autogenic training involves the person using self-suggestions, focusing, and positive imagery. Self-suggestions might be 'I am feeling alright; nothing is wrong with me'. Focusing requires the person to remove all negative thoughts from consciousness, and direct all attention to the feeling of physical relaxation, such as focusing on sensations of warmth and physical solidity (see Gendlin 1978). Positive mental images are those associated with pleasant, soothing reactions, such as quiet parks, still lakes, and so on. Biofeedback is a technique that requires the person to learn how to detect subtle changes in body functions, such as temperature adjustment, heart rate, and breathing. This can be achieved through the use of electromyography or galvanic skin responses (see Chapter 1, pp. 4–5).

BOX 9.11 PAVLOV, DOGS, AND THE IDEA OF ASSOCIATION

Classical conditioning, as developed by the Russian physiologist, Ivan Pavlov, serves as one of the earliest modern theories regarding how we learn. In classical conditioning, an **unconditioned stimulus** (UCS), such as food, elicits a reflexive, or **unconditioned response** (UCR), from an animal, such as salivating. If we repeatedly pair the food with another neutral stimulus, say a light, the neutral stimulus becomes associated to the UCS, so that, when we present just the light alone, the animal will salivate. According to Pavlov, what has happened is that the association between the unconditioned stimulus and the neutral stimulus is learned, so that the animal responds to the neutral stimulus *as if it were the food*. Through conditioning, the once neutral stimulus becomes powerful enough to produce the behaviour. In classical conditioning terms, the neutral stimulus becomes the **conditioned stimulus** (CS) and the animal's response becomes the **conditioned response** (CR).

---

extensively on her good ability to form and manipulate visual images in all of her professional training and so the psychologist ensured that he described the anxiety hierarchy in terms of visual images. The psychologist presented an anxiety hierarchy that involved Xena first imaging herself looking at a calendar at the date of an upcoming competition. He deliberately selected an action that he and Xena knew was easy, giving her not only incentive but also some practice at the task of relaxation. The psychologist knew that it was essential that Xena's performance routines or rituals were included in the hierarchy. Performance rituals and routines are those things that an athlete does before a competition, such as focusing on one's lane, monitoring breathing, totally concentrating on the starting signal, and so on. These performance routines are a critical component of any athlete's performance, and they must be executed almost automatically. The psychologist gradually developed images so that, at the peak of the anxiety hierarchy, he had Xena imaging herself feeling the reaction of her muscles, and her arm and leg movements as she reached the target of finishing the race. The psychologist made sure that Xena could maintain a stable level of relaxation at each phase, before encouraging her to go to the next step in the hierarchy.

The psychologist also felt that Xena could use imagery to create a more positive view of herself and her ability to perform. Psychologists working in the sport room distinguish between different types, such as body rehearsal, mastery rehearsal, coping rehearsal, and time projection. The psychologist had already incorporated body rehearsal in the anxiety hierarchy: he had asked Xena to imagine how specific muscles felt at different points in a race. The psychologist felt that emotive imagery would also be very useful. With emotive imagery, the athlete is asked to imagine (or recall) scenes where she has felt pride, such as the feelings of pride when some past goal had been achieved; for example, remembering a particular race where she reached a new personal best in her finishing time. The goal is to evoke positive feelings that, in turn, support the athlete to maintain a positive self-view. This technique is clearly based on one of the most robust findings from the experimental literature, mood congruent effects (see above).

The psychologist also decided that it would be helpful to determine Xena's more general personality traits; and asked her to complete the Eysenck Personality Inventory (EPI; see Box 9.9). The psychologist hoped that the scores on the EPI would help him to make more general suggestions about how Xena might protect herself from any future occurrences of anxiety, and also how her overall preparation for competition might be improved. Interestingly, Xena did not fit the predicted profile for an athlete, as she scored high on introversion and neuroticism. The psychologist felt that Xena probably needed to re-consider her preparation routines, particularly in light of the fact that she had suffered such extreme anxiety reactions.

While realizing that he might be treading on sensitive areas, the psychologist was also concerned about the level of pressure that Xena was under, not only from the media and general public, but also from her coach. The psychologist felt that Xena had been responding to unrealistic goals and that this needed to be addressed directly. The psychologist believed that Xena needed to reframe her goals and use some cognitive restructuring to regain a more balanced view of competing and the necessity to win. He felt that Xena had problems acquiescing to her own fallibility, and found it very difficult to acknowledge that, sometimes, even the greatest of athletes suffer from emotional trauma and performance anxiety.

How was the psychologist's input assessed?

The use of systematic desensitization had its desired effect in that eight weeks after commencing with her treatment, Xena successfully ran a marathon and came second. In general, Xena felt that the psychologist had certainly helped her overcome her feelings of performance anxiety and she was completely satisfied with that aspect of her treatment. However, neither Xena nor her coach felt that the psychologist's suggestions regarding her preparation routines were useful. There were a number of reasons why they rejected the psychologist's advice. The main reason was that the psychologist based his suggestions on Xena's scoring high on introversion and neuroticism. While the psychologist had attempted to explain the concepts clearly to both Xena and her coach, he had failed to rid either of them of their layperson's view of what introversion and neuroticism was. To them, Xena was *not* neurotic and nor was she particularly shy or overly aroused. As such, the psychologist failed to convince either of them of the need to re-examine Xena's preparation routines. Further, Xena had been a highly successful athlete and, apart from her recent bout of anxiety and panic attacks, she had never failed to do well. Given that, neither Xena nor her coach felt that her preparation routines needed to be altered. The psychologist's suggestions that Xena needed to reconsider her goals, and put less pressure on herself, were similarly greeted with disdain, and were ignored.

SCENARIO TWO

PAIN CONTROL AND THE STORY OF CHUCK

In this scenario, we focus on pain and how we manage it. Not surprisingly, pain is a topic that is well documented in the context of the sport room, as any time we exert ourselves physically we increase the chances of suffering an injury—a **sufficient condition** albeit not **necessary condition** for pain. The psychology of pain has fascinated researchers, and this is not surprising: pain is something that we all feel, regardless of our nationality, racial background, gender, or age. There is a general consensus that our ability to experience pain as a negative state is advantageous to our survival as a species. From an evolutionary perspective, we have two complementary systems involving the **central nervous system** that enable us to respond quickly to threatening or dangerous stimuli. The first is the reflex system, which enables us to move away rapidly from any noxious and potentially dangerous stimulus. Our reflexes are governed nociceptive neurons, which are sensory neurons that transmit information regarding tissue damage (along with heat-sensitive neurons). This information is then sent to *interneurons*, which in turn send information to motor neurons. Motor neurons transmit a signal to the muscle which, once received, enables action to be taken. For example, when we accidentally prick our finger with something sharp, we withdraw our hand without thinking. This is the action of our reflex system. It is relatively local in that all this occurs without recourse to any information being sent to our brain.

Second to the reflex system is the pain system. Nociceptive neurons transmit signals to interneurons that project information up the spinal cord to the brain (or directly to cranial nerves). Our brain is responsible for providing the emotional and motivational components of pain. The hypothalamus and septum, as well as the amygdala, are all likely to be heavily involved in the evaluative components of pain. Information to the amygdala can also arrive via the thalamus, which provides basic information about sensory properties of stimuli—sometimes called the sensory switchboard. Given we experience pain as a negative emotional state, we use pain to learn important lessons about what is, and what is not, safe in our environment. We form memories and use these memories to avoid similar experiences in the future. Pain can also motivate us to take action, as when we change our body posture in response to having the feeling of pins and needles in a leg we have sat on for too long. We might also be motivated to solicit help if we are in enough pain, such as when we go to a chiropractor or physiotherapist for acute or chronic back pain.

From what we have said, we might conclude that pain is the result of the activity of a particular type of neuron—the nociceptive neuron—which itself requires some direct tissue damage. However, things are not that simple. Even with substantial tissue damage, some people will experience little pain, if any. Conversely, some people do feel pain even after their physical injuries have healed. In the same way, surgical techniques used to control pain by severing connections and pathways between neurons do not always work: sometimes the pain returns. These findings serve to highlight the major role that our evaluative, psychological processes have in determining our experiences of pain.

Since there exists this imperfect relationship between neural activity and phenomenal experience of pain, some theory was needed that could integrate the findings. *Gate theory* is one such attempt. A very simplified version of gate theory suggests that nociceptive neurons have synaptic connections with specific cites in the spinal cord, called T-cells. The activation of a T-cell, as when the cell reaches threshold, results in our experiencing pain. However, there is a gate which can block any signals from reaching the T-cell. Thus, even when a nociceptive neuron has sufficient activation to excite the T-cell, if the gate is closed, we do not experience pain. Only when the gate is open can the nociceptive neuron excite a T-cell. Not surprisingly, gate theory postulates that brain processes can influence whether the gate is closed or open. Presumably, this would explain why, under hypnosis, people are able to go through otherwise painful operations without the use of any anaesthetics. Beliefs, such as those imparted through hypnosis, prevent the gate from opening, and hence prevent the person from experiencing any pain.

Without question, our experience of pain is the result of a variety of processes that interact with each other. We need to consider the physical and biological components of pain and injury. We need to question the mental and evaluative components that influence our experience of pain, such as how we label a certain physical sensation as unpleasant or painful. Equally, we must have some idea of the social components behind our experience of pain. We must remember that while pain reflects a universal human condition, how we feel pain and how we express pain is influenced by our culture. The following scenario is a wonderful illustration of how this multi-factor view of pain gets applied into the real world when a psychologist is asked to help someone after an injury.

Chuck, aged 37, had recently divorced after fifteen years of marriage. The break-up of his marriage had been particularly acrimonious and there had been vigorous disputes over custodial rights to his children. He had little enthusiasm or motivation, and was becoming more of a social recluse; his work was suffering as well. Once separated from his wife and family, Chuck got into some bad habits, such as eating fast foods, drinking two or three bottles of wine most evenings, and smoking in excess of twenty cigarettes a day. As a consequence, he was decidedly overweight and unfit. This had the unfortunate effect of making him more depressed, and he experienced very low self-esteem and feelings of hopelessness and despair. Chuck went to his doctor who diagnosed depression and stress. However, rather than prescribing a drug treatment, the doctor was more interested in adopting a *psycho-social model* for Chuck's depression. The doctor first suggested that Chuck might wish to talk to a professional, such as a counsellor or clinical psychologist. However, Chuck's experiences in marriage counselling had soured him against any forms of talking therapy and he refused categorically to take that course of action. The doctor decided that he and Chuck could better approach the problem by finding something that would enhance Chuck's self-esteem, like a hobby or leisure activity.

Chuck had a keen interest in sport as a younger man. In fact, he would have pursued a professional career were it not for a serious injury to his right ankle during a football match. Even though he had refrained from any sports for over ten years, Chuck discussed the possibility of taking up sport again with his doctor, as part of his treatment for his depression. To this end, Chuck joined a fitness club and put his name down on a squash ladder, where each player would knock out another until only one champion remained.

Over the next ten months, Chuck began to get some real enjoyment from his squash games and became an accomplished player. He lost weight, and had more interest in keeping himself healthy. He noticed that the club was advertising for people to take part in a squash competition held by fitness clubs across the region, where members of different clubs were pitted against each other. Chuck decided that entering the competition would be another way of improving his self-image and contribute to his growing self-esteem. He was highly motivated, and was determined that nothing would stop him participating. Chuck began working on a daily basis with a personal trainer from the fitness club. The trainer made a number of suggestions about how Chuck could develop more stamina and strength through weight training; and Chuck had followed the exercise regime meticulously. However, during one session, Chuck turned on his right ankle and suffered a very bad sprain, tearing many ligaments and muscles.

The doctor told Chuck that he would probably not be able to take any rigorous physical exercise for at least twelve weeks. To make matters worse, the doctor said that the recovery from the current sprain would probably be further delayed because of the previous, old injury. It was highly likely that Chuck would need some form of physical therapy in order to gain relatively complete use of his right ankle and foot. The doctor was honest with Chuck that his rehabilitation would be difficult, but essential.

The time frame for Chuck's enforced rest coincided with the squash tournament; however, he refused to succumb to his depression. Although he began to gain weight, Chuck decided he had to maintain a positive approach to things and came to regard his upcoming physiotherapy as a silver lining to the cloud. After six weeks, Chuck started physiotherapy, but discovered that he was experiencing severe pain and began to dread going to the clinic for his treatment sessions. Chuck began to worry that he would not be able to achieve the complete recovery for which he had so hoped. Rather than wait until the situation became unbearable, Chuck visited his doctor, and both agreed that, while he was not nearly as depressed as he was some months ago, he did need to enlist some professional help. Once again, the doctor suggested counselling, and once again Chuck refused categorically to countenance the idea. The doctor suggested that an alternative might be to enlist the support of a psychologist who specialized in rehabilitation after injury; as it happened, the doctor had details of one such psychologist, who worked with professional and amateur athletes. Chuck contacted her and agreed to meet.

What was the situation?

The client, Chuck, was having difficulty in dealing with his pain when completing his physical treatment protocol. This not only represented a daily, distressing situation. His overall, general health, both physical and mental, relied on him being able to continue with his rehabilitation. The link between his current physical state and his emotional state could render him highly vulnerable to depression again. While the client was not in danger of any serious mental-health problems at the moment, he was certainly becoming less able to deal with the amount of stress surrounding his injury. Some specific measures to help him needed to be in place relatively quickly, prior to his next treatment session.

Why was the psychologist involved?

At the initial meeting with the psychologist, Chuck was very clear about the type of help he wanted. He knew that he was injured and he knew he needed to continue with his rehabilitation. He was also very clear that he would only consider certain types of practical and effective ways of dealing with his pain. For example, he had no interest in any talking therapies. For Chuck, the problem was that he was in considerable pain and he wanted practical ways of managing it independently of others. The psychologist agreed that she would provide Chuck with psychological techniques that could better equip him to cope with his pain. During their initial meeting, the psychologist also was able to ask Chuck about vital information about regarding his physical and mental history.

What concepts are relevant?

The psychologist first decided to adopt a version of the model of sports injury that had been suggested by Andersen and Williams in 1988, in an effort to identify theoretical factors that might be important. Andersen and Williams suggested that the occurrence of sports injuries is a function of a core stress response, which itself is affected by the sport situation, history of stressors, personality, coping resources, and any interventions that might be introduced. The psychologist adapted this model and decided that she would consider each of the so-called precursor factors in turn.

One obvious consideration was the history of psychological stressors that the person has experienced. For example, there has been a consistent finding that there is a positive association between major life experiences, like divorce or bereavement, and occurrence of injury. This association is particularly noted in high-contact sports, like rugby or American football, although the same relationship has been shown to exist in other sports as well. Similarly, stressors in daily life, such as difficulties at work or with finances, can also place as great a strain on the person as can their previous history of physical injury. This latter point, namely whether the person has had a physical injury before, was of obvious relevance to this case.

Another general class of factors that the psychologist would have to address was individual differences. One of the most extensively studied is personality type. For example, considerable research has looked at the effects that personality can have in predicting injury occurrence. Unfortunately, the literature has been unable to provide unequivocal, reliable demonstrations of the *specific* personality factors that mediate, and how those factors operate. To further complicate the situation, some psychologists have even suggested that different types of injury, such as sprains versus broken bones, are likely to be associated with different personality variables.

Researchers, using Cattell's 16 PF (Personality Factor) Questionnaire, have shown that scores on some factors are associated with injury occurrence. For example, athletes who are tender-minded and reserved (factors I and A, respectively) are more prone to injury than athletes who score closer to the tougher-minded and outgoing factors. This may be because those who are reserved are perceived as weaker and more aggressively attacked by opponents. Self-esteem has also been implicated, with people who score lower on measures of general self-esteem being more injury prone.

Personality type has also been extensively studied as a mediating variable in understanding pain perception and pain threshold. Research suggests that people who are regarded as high on neuroticism have greater tendency to experience anxiety and depression. Because these people are more sensitive to changes in arousal levels and physical sensations, they are more likely to report higher levels of pain discomfort. This seems to be the case in terms of clinical observations as well as in experimental conditions. In the latter, administrations of painful stimuli such as cold or heat are controlled and the person's rated unpleasantness, or so-called pain experience, is monitored. Under controlled circumstances, people who score higher on neuroticism report more distress and can endure shorter periods of the unpleasant stimuli. This suggests that people who have neurotic tendencies might overreact to an injury and experience greater levels of discomfort and pain.

In contrast, people who can be described as having optimistic dispositions report less pain. This optimistic type of explanatory style is generally associated with internal, stable, and global attributions for positive outcomes and external, unstable, and specific attributions for negative outcomes (see Seligman's book on learned optimism, 1998, for a detailed account). Simply put, people who are optimistic about life—who see the glass as half full—and who believe that they have some control over positive events and outcomes are less likely to suffer pain.

The psychologist also knew that the general beliefs that a person holds about treatment influence the manner and extent to which that person feels pain. A classic demonstration of the effects that beliefs can have on pain perception is known as the placebo effect. Placebos are bogus treatments that have no medicinal value but are nonetheless thought by the patient to be helpful. In an early study on the placebo effect, Henry Beecher, in 1959, showed how powerful beliefs could be on pain perception. Beecher gave either a placebo or a morphine injection to patients who were suffering postoperative pain. Importantly, all the patients believed that they were receiving a painkiller. Whereas more of the patients receiving the morphine injection reported relief (67 per cent), over 40 per cent of the patients receiving the placebo reported comparable levels of relief! Medical evidence has shown that the placebo effect can be even more dramatic, with some studies reporting that 100 per cent of the participants given placebo treatments claim pain relief.

The psychologist also knew that there were important individual differences in the biological factors that influence and mediate the way that people experience pain. She was aware of the research conducted by John-Kar Zubieta and colleagues in 2001, which was a landmark study on the action of brain endorphins on pain perception. Endorphins are internally produced analgesics that act in a similar fashion to opiates: they operate by inhibiting the action of neurotransmitters that are involved in the transmission of pain impulses from the spinal cord to the brain. What Zubieta and colleagues showed was how this action takes place. Participants were given a painful injection and asked to rate their perception of pain every fifteen seconds. Prior to the injection, the participants were given a radioactive form of an endorphin. Brain scans showed that the greatest endorphin activity occurred within several brain areas, including the thalamus, the amygdala, and a sensory area of the cortex. Both the thalamus and amygdala are important in the pain perception. As the endorphins surged, participants reported a decrease in sensory and emotional experiences of pain.

Another of the important findings reported by Zubieta et al. was that people differed in the pain that they experienced, in spite of the fact that they had received exactly the same painful stimulation. The differences in reported pain were associated with two factors. One was the number of opioid receptors that were available for endorphins. Those people with fewer opioid receptors reported more pain. Two, people differed in their ability to release their own endorphins. Not surprisingly, people who produced higher levels of endorphins reported less-painful experiences. Subsequent research has highlighted even further the relationship between psychological and biological factors. For example, work conducted at the Karolinska Institute in Sweden has shown that a positive belief about a placebo treatment results in the brain releasing endorphins to reduce the pain. Such research served to remind the psychologist that some aspects of pain perception would be biologically determined and that these factors needed to be kept in mind.

The psychologist was also aware that there were specific cognitive strategies that had been used to deal with pain, and that these should be considered. Two types of strategy are most often discussed, and these are referred to as dissociative and

---

BOX 9.12 PAIN, SEX, AND CULTURE

Sex is a factor that continuously emerges as significant in influencing all aspects of human behaviour. This is similarly true in the case of our experience of pain. There are differences, and the differences usually indicate that women are more tolerant, have higher thresholds, and deal better with pain than men do. The evidence for this comes from a variety of sources. For example, Professor Mari Botti, Deakin University, Australia, reports on a study where she tested pain thresholds for one hundred men and women who had undergone heart surgery (Botti 2004). The participants had to describe the severity of their pain some three days after they had undergone surgery. From a physical point of view, both men and women would be expected to have roughly the same levels of pain within the first twenty-four hours after surgery. However, there were marked differences in the way that men and women coped with their pain. On average, women needed lower doses of pain killers and took drugs to relieve pain for a shorter period of time than did men. There are a number of explanations that can account this difference. One explanation is that men and women have different perceptions of what is painful. Women may simply have higher thresholds. Alternatively, it could be that men have different ways of expressing their pain than do women; women may have more effective ways of dealing with it. However, there are also important cultural differences. The experience of childbirth is a good example. Whereas this event is generally regarded as a painful experience in western cultures, in other cultures some women show essentially no distress. Indeed, Kroeber (1948) noted that in some cultures the man would get into bed and begin to groan as if in great pain, while the woman calmly gave birth to the child!

associative strategies. As the name implies, dissociative strategies attempt to divert attention away from the painful stimulus, and direct attention instead to aspects of the environment—either internal or external—that are less arousing. A good example is the technique of pinching someone on their hand just before they are to receive an injection. The pinch serves to distract them from the pain of the injection. Alternatively, the act of focusing on a positive visual image can serve to distract attention from the pain. In contrast, associative techniques require the person to focus on the pain in a detached but interested manner, without recourse to any evaluation of good or bad. The person would be asked to direct all focal attention to the painful area, but consider it descriptively rather than evaluating its valence, for example consider whether the pain is sharp or dull, rather than good or bad.

Motivational factors would also be critical to consider, and to this end the psychologist relied on the discussions provided by Heil in his 1993 book, *The Psychology of Sports Injury*. In his book, Heil stipulates the following as important: goal setting, relaxation, imagery, positive self-talk, and social support. Goal setting is concerned with the treatment protocol, and requires the person to set realistic, specific, and measurable goals, both in terms of the short- and longer-term. These goals must be evaluated regularly and reviewed daily by the injured person. Relaxation can be accomplished through progressive muscle relaxation (PMR), autogenic training, and biofeedback (see Box 9.10). Body rehearsal is a type of imaging that is particularly useful in overcoming pain. This, and the more detailed mastery imaging, first requires the person to be given detailed information about the consequence of the internal injuries. In mastery imaging, these detailed are highly graphic and the person is given extensive descriptions regarding how specific muscles, tendons, and bones may actually look. After this, the person is given equally detailed information about the rehabilitation process, and how this is affecting the internal soft tissue, etc. The person is asked to imagine the rehabilitation process as it might happen internally, and is always focused on a positive outcome of rehabilitation—never setbacks or problems. Time projection is another technique that the psychologist considered potentially useful. In this technique, the person is asked to imagine himself in the future, having them picture in their mind's eye themselves in two or four weeks time. This is based on the concept that positive thoughts and images will enhance the person's current mood state, and help to alleviate the painful experience.

Positive self-talk similarly relies on the relationship between cognition, emotions, and physical states. Importantly, positive self-talk is about active problem-solving: this requires the person to consider various situations, or difficulties, and how he might overcome them. This, too, reflects some form of cognitive restructuring, insofar as the person learns how to replace negative, irrational thoughts and images, which are based on the current experiences of pain, with positive action. This further serves to enhance the person's feelings of control, which is another aspect of pain management. The importance of an optimistic explanatory style has already been noted. In this case, empowering the person, through some cognitive restructuring and problem-solving methods, enables the person to fight feelings of helplessness.

In addition to all individual factors, the social support system of the person has also been identified as a mediating factor in pain perception and pain management.

Generally, the research has shown that people who are supported through a strong so-cial network and who are able to turn to others for advice, support and help, report less suffering and manage pain better than those people who are socially isolated. Social co-hesion and social belonging are also positively associated with pain management and the effect seems to occur for both men and women.

While the psychologist had little difficulty in generating possible theoretical con-cepts that might be important, she had some concerns over the limitations of the un-derlying model that she was adopting. The model of sports injury that she was using was essential linear. She was assuming that she could isolate the specific factors that might help her client and address those through different techniques. However, the psychologist knew that recent trends in psychology were suggesting that other explan-atory frameworks might be more fruitful. One such framework is called systems theory.

Systems theory has been advocated by a number of psychologists—among them Norbert Weiner and more recently Robert Jervis—and represents a very different meth-odological approach to the traditional methods associated with experimental psycho-logy. The contrast is best understood in terms of the classic Gestalt premise, that the whole is greater than the sum of its parts. With traditional experimental psychology—and the theories associated with it—psychologists control the environment in an effort to study separately the individual factors that make up a complex behaviour. Through statistical analyses, the different components are reconstituted. Suppose we take a com-plex behaviour, like an athlete's reaction to a sport injury. We can divide this task into a number of different, independent factors, like the type of sport, the athlete's history of stressors, the athlete's personality types, level of experience, and so on. Traditional, empirical methods examine the separate effects of these factors, through controlled ex-periments. So, what we might do is to look at personality types, by asking the athlete to complete a standardized questionnaire and seeing how this might relate to their re-ported experience of pain. Of course, in this experiment we would be controlling—or ignoring—many of the other factors that would be expected to influence our athlete's pain perception, such as current levels of fatigue, recent life events, and so on. We would conduct experiments for each of the factors believed to be important and then integrate our findings, generally through our theoretical hypotheses. In this way, psy-chologists reduce the real world to its constituent parts, and then somehow put all the parts back together again.

In contrast, a systems-theory approach suggests that there are emerging properties that come from the interaction of all these factors—and these are not the same as combining the factors. The whole does not equal the sum of its parts; the whole is something entirely different altogether. Thus, according to systems theory, psycholo-gists *cannot* put all the parts back again—much in the same way as Humpty Dumpty! Certainly, personality type might be associated with history of stressors. However, they combine in an entirely novel way once placed in the context of the entire system. The psychologist knew that, from a systems-theory approach, her attempt to explain her client's perception of pain, and consequently her attempts to alleviate it, might be misguided.

BOX 9.13 POSITIVE AND NEGATIVE FEEDBACK IN THE SYSTEM

Because the emphasis is on the emerging, or emergent, properties of the system, the systems-theory approach is less likely to predict how the system will act, and more likely to describe the relative relationships amongst the various factors. Nonetheless, there are a few concepts on which there is general consensus. For example, most theorists agree that the system—which in the case of human beings means the person—is able to operate through two processes of feedback, *negative feedback* and *positive feedback*. Negative feedback serves to keep the system stable, and is used to maintain the current state. Generally, negative feedback involves minor but consistent adjustments. For example, suppose we want to kick a ball in the direction of a goal post, between two points A and B. We use negative feedback to keep the ball on its trajectory, such as making small adjustments for uneven surfaces or objects that need to be avoided. Positive feedback serves to upset the system and introduces change, by amplifying disturbances. For example, in response to an unforeseen challenge from our opponent, we may kick the ball in the opposite direction to the one we had been pursuing. We may overreact, though, and kick the ball too far away for our team mate to intercept. This unanticipated consequence illustrates how positive feedback can result in an outcome that is *not* predictable from our original action or intention. For a systems-theory perspective, a complex behaviour, like pain, is beyond our scope to anticipate. All we can hope to achieve is a better understanding of those factors that are important to address and how they might act relative to each other.

What did the psychologist do?

There were two general ways the psychologist felt that she could help Chuck. One was to provide Chuck with information about his injury and his rehabilitation. The other was to help with motivational aspects of his rehabilitation. Motivational components included setting appropriate goals, imagery, and relaxation techniques, and positive self-talk, as in self instructions for dealing with his pain during his rehabilitation treatment.

As a first step, the psychologist found out how much information the doctor had given Chuck regarding the injury and the rehabilitation process. While the doctor had provided Chuck with some information, the psychologist felt that Chuck would benefit from more highly detailed information. To this end, the psychologist relied on a list of factors stipulated by Heil in 1993 as being effective in promoting a comprehensive injury-management programme, and provided Chuck with some injury guidelines. These included describing the injured area anatomically, any changes caused by the injury, and differentiation of benign pain from dangerous pain. These guidelines also included information about anticipated timetables for treatment and any plateaus in improvement, methods of assessing readiness to play, and how to maintain and support the rehabilitation process so as to reduce the possibility of a future occurrence of injury.

As a further support to the injury guidelines, the psychologist also suggested that Chuck might need to speak to someone who is professionally trained as a counsellor, if his levels of depression worsened. The psychologist took great care in explaining to Chuck that injury and rehabilitation were emotional processes, and that it was essential that Chuck air his negative feelings and views. While the psychologist was a good listener, and was prepared to support Chuck to maintain a positive attitude during rehabilitation, she was concerned that Chuck may have depressive tendencies. In the event that his depression became acute, Chuck would be advised to see a professional who had the adequate experience or training to support him in dealing directly with his depression.

The psychologist anticipated that motivational techniques would be very important in helping Chuck manage his pain. This was particularly true, as it appeared that Chuck was an independent type of person, who had little daily social support from others. The psychologist decided to focus particularly on positive-self talk, and developed a self-instruction training to deal for Chuck's visits to the clinic for treatment. The training involved four phases. The first supported any negative thoughts or sensations that Chuck might have before he went to the clinic. This could be called the preparation for the stressor, where the stressor is the treatment. The psychologist suggested how Chuck might combat any negative feelings or sensations with more positive thoughts on preparing for the treatment. For example, any negative thinking could be replaced by a more positive, preparative thought: 'In order to get better, I have to go through this'; or, 'I know that this treatment isn't going to be easy, but I know I have to learn how to cope with it.' The next stage involved experiencing the stressor, namely having the treatment. This stage was most likely to be the one associated with pain, so it was important that Chuck focus on thoughts and feelings that were associated with his well-being and relaxation. The psychologists reminded Chuck to restructure his evaluation of the pain, and consider the pain as something constructive to his rehabilitation process. She also encouraged him to create a positive, internal dialogue, where he reminded himself that he was in control and to continue to take deep, relaxing breaths.

The psychologist taught Chuck the difference between dissociative and associative techniques. She further suggested that Chuck might use dissociative techniques if his pain was not too intense; for example, he could image a pleasant scene and distract himself away from his pain. However, should his pain get too extreme, he was to use associative techniques; for example, focus on the pain more objectively, as something that involved the stretching and lengthening of certain tendons and ligaments.

The psychologist knew that, even with the best techniques possible, Chuck's pain during treatment might still be overwhelming. The psychologist provided Chuck with ways in which he could encourage himself to keep his concentration and stay on track. She suggested that he might first decide how great his pain was, on a scale from one to ten, where one is as low as he has ever felt, and ten is as high as he has ever felt. In this way, Chuck could establish how painful his experiences were in the context of the history of his injury. Next, he could tell himself that, while the pain might be high, he has felt this bad before and importantly, has methods of dealing with it, such as breathing deeply and relaxing his body by dropping his shoulders.

The final stage involved Chuck reflecting on what had happened during treatment and how he dealt with his pain. The point here would be to allow Chuck to evaluate his efforts objectively. This would mean identifying what did and did not work for him; and, associating any positive techniques to his own efforts and achievements. For example, if he remembered that a particular dissociative technique was useful in reducing his pain perception, he would note that for future use. This would enable Chuck to build up schematic memories of positive techniques, and importantly, more specific memories in terms of when and how the techniques were most successfully used. Equally, techniques that were unsuccessful should be similarly evaluated, although the psychologist warned Chuck against being critical and negative about his failures. For example, if he was unable to use a breathing technique successfully, Chuck should examine what precisely went wrong, and how he could learn from his unfruitful attempt.

The psychologist also felt that she needed to address Chuck's emotional problems, and the fact that his social support system may be contributing to the difficulties he was experiencing. In particular, she stressed how major life stressors, like divorce, have a negative influence on people's experience of pain, and how important social support was in helping the person to manage their pain. The psychologist suggested that Chuck might consider going to a counsellor, even if for a short time, to make sure that he did not have unresolved, underlying feelings that might be contributing to his overall stress levels.

How was the psychologist's input assessed?

Chuck was very happy with both the injury guidelines and the self-instruction techniques that the psychologist had given him. He felt that he could get more control over his pain, and also began to believe that he would regain full use of his ankle, and return to sport. He decided that he would did not need any further help from the psychologist, and also felt optimistic that even if he could not avoid another injury in the future, he certainly knew of ways of dealing with any pain, and subsequent treatment he might need. He did not agree with the psychologist's suggestions about seeking counselling, and did not pursue that course of action.

■ ADDITIONAL READING

Biddle, S. and Mutrie, N. (1991) *Psychology of Physical Exercise and Activity: a Health-Related Perspective.* Springer-Verlag, London. A good review of how and why people undertake difficult physical activities.

Elliott, B. and Mester, J. (eds) (1998) *Training in Sport: Applying Sport Science.* John Wiley & Sons, Chichester. This is a very useful collection of articles focusing on the important issues in sport and athletics.

■ QUESTIONS

Scenario one

1 Is it healthy to have the extensive public and media pressure on athletes to perform well in competition? Why?

2 Suppose there were a treatment that would enable you to erase all of Xena's negative memories about competing and completely eliminate her anxiety. Do you think this treatment is ethical?

Scenario two

1 Do you think that the psychologist needed to address the underlying psychological problems that Chuck was showing?

2 If there was a treatment that could offer a pain-free existence, would you advocate using the treatment in all cases that someone had pain? Why?

GLOSSARY

A-B, A-Br paradigm A technique used in paired-associate learning, where the stimuli from one list are re-paired with responses from the same list. For example, cat–hat and dog–bowl would be repaired to form cat–bowl and dog–hat.

actual self A term used in Rogerian therapy to denote the real, genuine self, which is dynamic and changing. *See also* ideal self.

actualizing tendency A concept from the Rogerian approach to psychotherapy, which reflects the person's innate desire and drive to grow, develop, and enhance their potential.

analysis of covariance A family of statistical techniques enabling the user to partial out, or cancel, the effects of a correlated variable in assessing the significance of differences in group or sub-group means.

association A concept used in learning theory to denote the manner in which two events that are proximal become linked together as a unit.

autonomic nervous system (ANS) The part of the nervous system that is responsible for regulating and controlling the body's internal environment, through involuntary smooth muscle and glandular activity.

baseline measurement An assessment of some behaviour prior to the introduction of any variables or interventions.

behavioural psychology The study of human behaviour that focuses on observable outcomes, and relies on concepts from conditioning theories.

bottom-up processing A type of information processing that relies on lower-level analyses to send information to higher-level centres; for example, retinal information.

central nervous system (CNS) The brain and spinal cord.

circadian rhythm Biological functions that occur within an approximately twenty-four-hour cycle, such as sleep.

collective unconscious A concept developed by Carl Jung to denote primal drives, images, and desires that are outside our conscious awareness and that are universal and innate to the species of *Homo sapiens*.

combat trauma Anxiety and other related trauma reactions that are in direct response to being exposed to or participating in military action.

conditioned response (CR) A concept used in classical conditioning whereby a previously unrelated response becomes associated with a stimulus; for example, salivating to a bell.

conditioned stimulus (CS) A concept used in classical conditioning whereby a previously unrelated stimulus can be used to evoke a response; for example, a bell eliciting a salivation response.

conditions of growth A concept from the Rogerian approach to therapy that represents those environmental features that enable the person to grow healthily; these include unconditional positive regard, openness, and empathy.

conversion hysteria A term used to denote disorders whereby the person experiences neurological symptoms, such as paralysis or blindness, that may have a sudden onset, but no physical basis.

conversion symptoms *See* conversion hysteria.

counterconditioning The process derived from classical learning theory, whereby a maladaptive response to a stimulus, such as anxiety when seeing a spider, is replaced by an incompatible, more adaptive response, such as relaxation.

covariability When two measures are correlated they are said to covary; that is, scores on one reflect, in some degree, scores on the other. For example, age and height would be expected to covary in a sample of children.

cued recall A memory technique that reinstates some aspects of the to-be-remembered event at the time of retrieval. For example, a stimulus is presented and the person is asked to recall the response to which it was paired.

decibels (dB) A logarithmic measure of sound intensity.

declarative knowledge (or declarative memory) A term used to describe knowledge that can be verbalized by the person. This would include personal, autobiographical information, such as events and facts; and semantic or abstract information about the world and language.

defence mechanisms Theoretical processes originally derived from Sigmund Freud's work on the id, ego, and super-ego, which enable the ego to prevent unwanted and threatening thoughts, images, and actions from entering conscious awareness, or help to modify the drives into more socially acceptable forms. These are processes that occur outside awareness, and include repression, identification, regression, displacement, sublimation, rationalization, denial, projection, and reaction formation.

defence reaction (DR) Innate physiological reaction to intense stimuli. It may prepare for action. *See also* orienting reaction (OR).

denial An example of a defence mechanism developed from Freudian theory, whereby the person refuses to acknowledge their behaviour, feelings, etc. and denies their existence; for example, someone who has a drug problem referring to themselves as a casual user.

discourse analysis A general term for a set of qualitative techniques that examine discourse and focus on the subjective experiences of the person, rather than quantifiable measurements of behaviour. These techniques consider thematic content, topic development, and the use of metaphors and other images to understand the underlying psychological processes.

displacement An example of a defence mechanism derived from Freudian theory whereby the person directs feelings to a substitute object; for example, being angry with your partner and yelling at your friend instead.

distributed practice A method of training where the person is asked to perform the task with practice trials being more dispersed across a longer period; for example studying all term for an exam, one day a week, is distributed practice; cramming for the exam the night before is massed practice. Distributed practice is known to yield superior learning and skill.

dizygotic twins Non-identical twins, where each foetus develops from its own individual egg.

drive A theoretical concept that reflects a state of psychological tension, or imbalance, in response to some need; a drive is assumed to motivate the organism to reduce the tension or redress the imbalance.

ecological validity The extent to which a set of theoretical ideas or empirical findings can be transferred to other settings, such as real-world situations.

episodic memory A term used by spatio-temporal models of memory to denote our ability to recollect or retain knowledge over long periods of time, about specific events that occurred at specific times and places.

ethology A method of studying animal behaviour where observations are made without intervention of the animal(s) in their natural habitat or environment.

event memory *See* episodic memory.

existential approach A general framework for understanding the human psyche where emotional problems and difficulties are the result of the person failing to find meaning in a life filled with pain and suffering. This general approach supports people to discover their own meaning of life to promote inner health.

experimental methodology A research technique where the person, the experimenter, examines a particular aspect of behaviour by manipulating some features of the environment and holding other features constant. The behaviour that is measured is called the dependent variable; the features of the environment that the experimenter manipulates are called the independent variables.

experiment-wise error rates A statistical measure of the likelihood of incorrectly identifying differences across all analyses conducted within a particular experiment.

explicit knowledge Knowledge or skills intentionally gained and accessible to immediate awareness; for example, knowing that Paris is the capital of France is explicit knowledge. *See also* implicit knowledge.

explicit memory A psychological state where the person is consciously aware that they are engaged in the act of remembering a past event or knowledge. This is in contrast to implicit memory. *See also* implicit memory.

Eysenck Personality Inventory (EPI) A standardized personality test developed by Hans Eysenck that relies on three general factors: extraversion, neuroticism, and psychoticism.

face validity A term used in psychometric testing to identify tests that can be seen to measure what they purport to measure, hence engender confidence in their use.

factor analysis A statistical technique that relies on correlations between different measures of different tasks to identify larger and common underlying characteristics, referred to as factors.

fight-or-flight reaction A state of physiological arousal in response to sudden threat or danger, which enables us to flee from the situation, or confront and challenge the threat.

figure Along with **ground**, concepts used in Gestalt theories of perception to distinguish those elements of the world to which we give our focal attention (figure) from those elements of the world that are outside our focal attention (ground). The figure has form, meaning and appears more salient than ground.

frequency The number of times that a sound wave is repeated in one second, measured in cycles per second. This determines the pitch of the sound: high frequency means high pitch. *See also* Hertz (Hz).

functional magnetic resonance imaging (fMRI) Use of the magnetic resonance imaging (MRI) scanning technique during active responding, in order to identify the structures involved in the response. *See also* magnetic resonance imaging (MRI).

focused attention Directing one's current awareness and conscious efforts towards one element in the environment, at the expense of other elements. This is in contrast to divided attention, where the person is allocating mental energy and awareness to more than one element in the environment.

formal knowledge A term used to denote knowledge that can be expressed either through words, or abstract symbols, such as formulae.

free association A technique most commonly used in psychoanalytic therapies, where the person is asked to report on the content of their consciousness, without monitoring or censuring.

galvanic skin response (GSR) In response to emotional or attentional demand, the sweat glands on the palms of the hands and fingers increase their activity. This is measured as an increase in skin conductance or a decrease in resistance, monitored by electrodes attached to the fingers. Also known as the electrodermal response (EDR).

Gestalt A school of psychology that focuses on our innate response to complete a whole, based on incomplete fragments. Gestalt theories of perception hold that the brain automatically organizes perceptual information into whole objects; Gestalt therapies assume that the person has a habitual response to re-enact old patterns of behaviour that can symbolically re-appear in later life.

ground See *figure*.

group norm A term used to denote the average performance, or behaviour of a large number of individuals, for example, norm reading behaviour for 13-year-old boys. The norms are often used as a control or comparison for groups in which some intervention has been given, or which are a special sub-group, such as clinical disorders.

habituation A general decline in the organism's capacity to respond to an innocuous stimulus that has been repeated. At the neural level this is reflected in a reduction in responsiveness to continued stimulation.

Hertz (Hz) The technical term for wave frequency in cycles per second; named after Heinrich Hertz, a German physicist who discovered radio waves.

hot cognitions A term used to denote beliefs or thoughts that have personal significance and emotive power for the person, such as ardent religious beliefs. This is in contrast to cold cognitions, which reflect facts and information that have no personal significance or importance.

hysterical disorder *See* conversion hysteria.

ideal self In Rogerian therapy, a dynamic set of characteristics, goals, or aspirations that the person would most like to have. *See also* actual self.

identification An example of a defence mechanism whereby the person does not express a drive or need, but rather mimics or adopts characteristics of a drive object, which is generally someone who is the focus of that drive; for example, a young girl wants to dress like a pop star; similar to introjection, which refers to the person adopting the values and beliefs of the drive object.

implicit knowledge A concept that reflects knowledge that can be demonstrated, but it is expressed without the person's awareness; for example, amnesiac patients who can show evidence of learning but have no explicit awareness. *See also* explicit knowledge.

implicit memory A state where the person shows evidence of using past information or knowledge, but has no conscious awareness that they are engaging in the act of remembering. *See also* explicit memory.

individual differences A general term used to denote long-term factors that help to explain the variability in behaviour of different people; for example, gender or intelligence.

individuation Introduced by Carl Jung to describe the goal of personal development, where the ego or conscious self become integrated with the unconscious aspects of self through expansion.

information processing A general framework that regards the environment in terms of units of knowledge, or information, and attempts to explain how this information becomes analysed and understood; typically involves stages of analyses, including encoding, storage, and retrieval.

instinct A complex behavioural pattern that is inherited by members of the same species, for example, an automatic specific response to a specific stimulus.

introjection *See* identification.

learning schedule Description of the methods used to introduce the organism to new information, which vary in terms of time, frequency, and regularity; for example, interval reinforcement schedules will reinforce a response within a certain time interval. *See also* distributed practice *and* massed practice.

learning to learn A description of improvement in knowing how to perform a task through repeated practice trials.

limited processing capacity A concept widely used in discussing attention and short-term memory, which refers to our restricted ability to analyse more than a certain amount and type of information at any given time.

long-term memory One component of spatio-temporal models of memory where information is stored and retained for a long period of time, over months and years.

magnetic resonance imaging (MRI) A technique that uses strong magnetic fields to construct accurate, three-dimensional, computer-generated images of the brain or other body areas. Unlike X-rays, it can image soft tissue.

massed practice A method of learning where the person is repeatedly exposed to the information with short or no temporal breaks in between different presentations; for example, showing the same word four times in a row. Known to produce superior learning and memory over short time periods, this is in contrast to distributed practice.

means-steps analyses A method of problem-solving in which characteristics of the current state of affairs are compared with characteristics of the desired final state of affairs (solution) and adjusted repeatedly to achieve an optimum match.

memory span The limited amount of information that can be held within short-term memory, suggested by George Miller to be seven plus or minus two bits of information.

monozygotic twins Identical twins, produced from the same egg.

motivation The term used to identify all the internal factors that initiate and maintain goal-directed behaviours. These include both biological and social factors; for example, hunger, thirst, the need for approval, the need for security, etc.

multi-modal A description of the type of information considered, using the different modalities of sight, hearing, touch, smell, and thought.

multiple regression A statistical technique for combining several measures into a single best predictor of some criterion.

multi-task situation A description of an environment where there is more than one goal operating at a time and where the person is required to perform more than one set of actions at a time to achieve these goals; for example, driving a car is a multi-task setting, involving many component actions.

necessary condition A description of a state that must be present for a particular behaviour to occur, but that, by itself, is not sufficient to produce that behaviour.

neuropsychology A general area of psychological interest that uses medical models to explain behavioural patterns particularly in those populations with neurological damage.

neurosis A term introduced by Freud to refer to maladaptive anxiety responses. Now commonly used to describe mental disorders that are affective in nature but do not involve serious distortions of reality. *See also* psychosis.

obsessive compulsive disorder (OCD) An anxiety disorder that has two components; an obsessive component reflected in thoughts and concerns, and a compulsive component which is reflected in habitual, stereotypical behaviours.

occupational psychology The study of how individuals behave within the work place. *See also* organizational psychology.

offender profiling A general class of analyses of criminal behaviour where the offender's personality traits and personal history are used to explain the motives for and reasons for the specific ways in which the crime is committed.

operant conditioning A type of learning where an organism's behaviour is shaped and modified through the use of positive or negative reinforcements, which serve to increase or lessen a behaviour in response to specific stimuli or sets of stimuli. First introduced by B.F. Skinner.

operational definition A term referring to a psychological construct, behaviour, or variable whose meaning is defined by the processes used to elicit or measure it.

organizational psychology The study of the behaviour of groups of individuals and the impact of organizational structure within a working environment. *See also* occupational psychology.

orienting reaction (OR) The initial reaction that an organism shows to a newly introduced stimulus, usually associated with initial attentional responses. Pavlov referred to it as the 'what is this?' reaction. *See also* defence reaction (DR).

paired-associate learning A learning procedure whereby two items appear contiguously in time, or simultaneously, and are learned as a unit of stimulus-response pairs.

parallel processing A description referring to the state of performing multiple analyses or processes simultaneously, in contrast to serial processing, where only one analysis can occur at one time. Commonly used in the context of parallel distributed processing models of G. Hinton and D. Rumelhart.

perceptual type A concept that refers to the variability that people show in the way they attend to and perceive the environment, based on expectations, feelings, motives, and beliefs; similar to perceptual set.

person-centred therapy A humanistic therapy first advanced by Carl Rogers, which supports the person to take responsibility for their own change and stresses the importance of the person's subjective experience.

phase delay A change in the circadian rhythm where the length of the sleep–wake cycle is extended, such as when flying from east to west across time zones. This is in contrast to phase advance, where the sleep–wake cycle is shortened.

phenomenal field A term from humanistic therapies that refers to the person's own, subjective experience of the world; used in Rogerian therapy to denote the client's unique perception of the world.

post-traumatic-stress-disorder (PTSD) A clinical anxiety disorder that is associated with physical symptoms of hyper-vigilance and over arousal, feelings of anxiety and apprehension, and mental disturbances such as intrusive thoughts.

proactive interference A concept developed from verbal learning theories to explain the negative impact of prior learning on later learning; for example, learning a first list, A, will slow down learning and impair memory for a second list, B.

procedural knowledge A term which refers to information that cannot be reproduced through verbal descriptions; for example, often linked with *how to do things*, as well as other motor-related skills and actions.

projection An example of a defence mechanism introduced by Sigmund Freud, where the person disowns the dangerous, threatening, or unacceptable parts of the id by attributing them to someone else; for example, a woman who is attracted to another man cannot own her feelings and so accuses her husband of wanting to have an affair.

psychic determinism A core assumption in psychodynamic theories first suggested by Sigmund Freud that all behavioural responses are caused by some form of mental activity or process.

psychoacoustics The psychology of hearing processes.

psychosis A broad classification of serious mental disorders where the person's ability to maintain an accurate sense of reality is severely disturbed, often demonstrated in irrational belief systems and erratic behaviours. *See also* neurosis.

qualitative data Behavioural responses that reflect the participant's subjective experience of the world, and are analysed so as to identify any major themes that emerge for the person; non-numerical commonly used for analyses such as interpretative phenomenal analysis, and other discourse analyses, for example, conversations between dyads.

quantitative data Behavioural responses that reflect the amount or extent of a participant's response, and are analysed using parametric and nonparametric statistics; for example, numerical data, like means, used for *t*-tests.

rationalization As used by Sigmund Freud, an example of a defence mechanism where the ego cannot acknowledge the true motives behind the behaviour, so a more reasonable explanation is constructed instead; for example, a child fails to clean their room, saying that there was a spider which stopped them. As used by Frederick Bartlett, a process through which the cultural expectations of the person are reflected in the errors that they produce when remembering a story, such as *The War of the Ghosts*.

reaction formation An example of a defence mechanism introduced by Sigmund Freud where the person does the opposite of their true, unconscious impulses or desires; for example, being in love with someone and ignoring them every time you see them.

recognition memory Conditions where the to-be-remembered information is presented and the person is required to make a familiarity judgement; for example, old/new, multiple choice, and yes/no judgements rely on recognition memory.

recovered memories A general term used to refer to the recollection of events for which the person previously had little or no conscious awareness; for example, amnesia for traumatic life events.

regression An example of a defence mechanism introduced by Sigmund Freud, where the ego cannot cope with the demands of a current situation and the person retreats to an earlier, younger stage of development; for example, when an 18-year-old girl begins to suck her thumb during her exams.

rehearsal A concept used in memory research to denote the repetition of information; generally distinguished between rote rehearsal, where information is simply repeated; the term is linked with discussions of short-term memory, as in the working memory model of memory.

reinforcement A concept used in operant learning theory, as developed by B.F. Skinner, which denotes an outcome to an organism's response that is intended to motivate the organism to continue or discontinue producing that response; the outcome can be positive, as in positive reinforcement, or negative, as in negative reinforcement.

reinforcement theories A general class of theories, first developed by B.F. Skinner, that rely on the notion that reinforcement acts as a motivator for, or against, the production of responses to a stimulus.

reliability An estimate of the degree to which a psychometric test measures some variable consistently. It is assessed by comparing scores on the same test, repeated on the same subjects, or dividing the test items into two halves and comparing them. A perfectly reliable test (there is no such thing!) would yield identical scores. A number of mathematical procedures is available to measure degrees of agreement.

repression An example of a defence mechanism first postulated by Sigmund Freud, whereby unpleasant or negative thoughts, desires or memories are relegated to the person's unconscious, and are effectively banished from conscious awareness; the term is commonly used without reference to Freud's psychoanalytic model of the ego.

schema A concept first put forward (in its modern sense) by Bartlett, and widely used in many contexts to denote an organizing constellation of thoughts or cognitions that direct perception, comprehension, and memory on the basis of information already gained, serving to organize them in such a way that they make sense to the individual in terms of past experience (plural, schemas).

serial processing Commonly associated with limited capacity models of memory, which stipulate that the analyses of information is restricted to one input, modality, or source at a time and that further analyses occur in a sequential fashion.

shaping A process used in operant conditioning, whereby the acquisition of a desired response is achieved by reinforcing successive approximations of the response; the process begins with a response that the organism already knows and can perform, such as a dog being taught to sit on verbal command.

short-term memory One component of multi-storage models of memory that represents our ability to retain a limited amount of information over short-periods of time, for example twenty seconds, without rehearsal.

signal-detection theory An information processing theory of perception which conceptualizes perception as detecting an external stimulus, or signal amidst a background of noise; the detection of the signal is a function of the distinctive perceptual properties of the signal and the psychological, motivational, and physical state of the individual.

Skinner box An apparatus used in the operant conditioning of small mammals and birds, with a bar or lever; upon pressing the bar or lever, the animal can obtain food, water, or change some aspect of the environment, like a light on or off, as a reward.

social learning theory A general theory that argues that a person's development is influenced by those people who surround them, and that these social influences teach the person about all aspects of behaviour, including their personality, attitudes, beliefs feelings, how to behave, etc.

spectral characteristics The pattern of multiple frequencies that determine the quality or timbre of a sound. A pure sound, such as that made by a flute, has few frequencies. A raucous sound, such as by a trombone, has many. Sounds heard as noise have random frequency components.

standardized psychological test A psychometric test that has been administered to a large cross-section of individuals, to determine the range of normal responses, is said to be standardized.

state anxiety A concept used to denote a temporary condition of heightened arousal, worrisome thoughts, and agitation; it is considered along a continuum of high to low.

sublimation An example of a defence mechanism first introduced by Sigmund Freud that refers to the person redirecting unwanted or unacceptable thoughts or drives into socially acceptable behaviours, or constructive or creative goals, such as a man who is sexually frustrated collecting great works of art with nudity.

sufficient condition A description of a state that can be present in order for a particular behaviour to occur, but is not required for that behaviour to be demonstrated; for example, being a bird is a sufficient condition for flying, but not a necessary one.

systems theory An approach which disputes traditional experimental methods that control and manipulate variables in the environment, and suggests that there are emerging properties from the whole that cannot be deduced by combining the separate components making up that whole; this approach does not proffer any predictions regarding overall outcomes, but looks instead to patterns of relationships between the different component parts.

tacit knowledge Information about the world, actions, and self that is not available to explicit description or conscious awareness; often used to describe knowing *how to do* something.

task analyses A technique developed from the human-relations movement that breaks down a goal-directed behaviour, or task, into its component parts—for example, sub-actions; used to determine ways of improving the match between job and worker, and also to teach workers how to perform sub-actions more efficiently and effectively.

temperament A term used to describe behavioural tendencies and personality characteristics that are believed to be the result of heredity; for example, adaptability, sociability, synchronicity of sleep and eating patterns, and emotionality.

top-down processing A description of information analyses where processing is initiated at more abstract, higher levels, in contrast to more peripheral levels; for example, the effects of expectations on object recognition.

total-time hypothesis The view that the amount of time spent in rehearsing an item in memory determines the strength of that memory.

trait anxiety A concept used to denote behavioural patterns associated with anxiety symptoms that occur consistently across a range of situations and time; a specific personality characteristic that is considered along a continuum of high to low.

unconditional positive regard A term used in Rogerian therapy to denote one of the core conditions for the healthy development of personality; acceptance and care that is given to an individual without imposing any restrictions on how the person must be, act, or feel.

unconditioned response (UCR) A term used in classical conditioning denoting a reflexive response to a particular stimulus, such as blinking in response to a puff of air to the eye.

unconditioned stimulus (UCS) A term used in classical conditioning denoting a stimulus that elicits a reflexive, or unconditioned response, such as a puff of air to the eye.

validity A measure of the degree to which a psychometric test measures what it is supposed to measure. It is assessed by comparing scores on another test that is known to be valid. The potential circularity of this procedure is well known. *See also* reliability.

verbal learning A school of experimental psychology that devoted its study to how we acquire and remember abstract, verbal materials, such as nonsense syllables, words, and numbers; stimuli like pictures and objects were also considered under verbal learning theories.

vicarious learning Acquiring information or knowledge about something through watching or observing others; a concept often used in social learning theory

vicarious observation *See* vicarious learning.

warm-up The general, positive transfer of non-specific motor components to a task which results from practice trials.

BIBLIOGRAPHY

Abandinsky, H. and Winfree, L. (1992) *Crime and Justice: an Introduction*, 2nd edn. Nelson-Hall, Chicago.

Abernethy, B., Wann, J., and Parks, S. (1998) Training perceptual-motor skills for sport. In B. Elliott and J. Mester (eds), *Training in Sport: Applying Sport Science*. John Wiley & Sons, Chichester.

Aghajanian, G. and Marek, G. (2000) Serotonin model of schizophrenia: emerging role of glutamate mechanisms. *Brain Research Reviews* 31, 302–312.

Agnew, N.M. and Pyke, S.W. (2004) *Science Game: an Introduction to Research Methods in the Behavioural Sciences*, 7th edn. Oxford University Press, Toronto.

Anderson, J.R. (1983) *The Architecture of Cognition*. Harvard University Press, Cambridge, MA.

Andersen, M.B. and Williams, J.M. (1988) A model of stress and athletic injury: prediction and prevention. *Journal of Sport and Exercise Psychology* 10, 294–306.

Andrade, J. (1995) Learning during anaesthesia: a review. *British Journal of Psychology* 86, 449–506.

Andrews, B., Morton, J., Bekerian. D., Brewin, C., Davies, G., and Mollon, P. (1995) The recovery of memories in clinical practice: experiences and beliefs of British Psychological Society Practitioners. *The Psychologist* May 1995.

Arnold, J., Cooper, C.L., and Robertson, I. (1995) *Work Psychology: Understanding Work Behaviour in the Workplace*. Pitman Publishing, London.

Arrigo, B.A. (2000) *Introduction to Forensic Psychology: Issues and Consequences in Crime and Justice*. Academic Press, London.

Asch, S.E. (1956) Studies of independence and conformity: a minority of one against a unanimous majority. *Psychological Monographs* 70.

Atkinson, R.C. and Shiffrin, R.M. (1968) Human memory: a proposed system and its control processes. In K. Spence and J. Spence (eds), *The Psychology of Learning and Motivation*, vol. 2. Academic Press, New York.

Baddeley, A. (2001) Remembering memory research. In G.D. Dunn, A.D. Lovie, and G.D. Richards (eds) *Psychology in Britain*. BPS Books, Leicester.

Baddeley, A.D. and Warrington, E.K. (1970) Amnesia and the distinction between long- and short-term memory. *Journal of Verbal Learning and Verbal Behavior* 9, 176–189.

Baddeley, A.D. and Hitch, G. (1974) *The Psychology of Learning and Motivation*. Academic Press, New York.

Bandura, A. (1969) *Principles of Behaviour Modification*. Holt, Rhinehart and Winston, New York.

Banks, J.P. (1989) *Psychological Factors in Sports Injuries among Elite Hockey Players*. Master's thesis, University of Western Australia, Perth.

Barber, T. (2000) A deeper understanding of hypnosis: its secrets, its nature, its essence. *American Journal of Clinical Hypnosis* 42, 208–272.

Barling, J. (1990) *Employment, Stress and Family Life*. John Wiley & Sons, Chichester.

Barnard, P.J. and Marcel, A.J. (1979) Paragraphs of pictographs: the use of non-verbal instructions for equipment. In P.A. Kolers, M. Wrolstad, and H. Bourma (eds), *Processing of Visible Language 1*. Plenum Publishing, New York.

Barnard, P.J. and Grudin, J. (1988) Command names. In M. Helander (ed.), *Handbook of Human–Computer Interaction*. North Holland Press, Amsterdam.

Barnard, P.J. and Teasdale, J. (1991) A systemic approach to cognitive-affective interaction and change. *Cognition and Emotion* 5, 1–39.

Barnes. P. (ed.) (1998) *Personal Social and Emotional Development of Children*. Blackwell Publishing, Milton Keynes.

Bartlett, F.C. (1927) *Psychology and the Soldier*. Cambridge University Press, London.

Bartlett, F.C. (1932) *Remembering: a Study in Experimental and Social Psychology*. Cambridge University Press, Cambridge.

Bartlett, F.C. (1947) The measurement of human skill. *British Medical Journal* 4, 835–838; 877–880.

Beecher, H.K. (1959) Generalisation of pain from various types and diverse origins. *Science* 130, 267–268.

Bekerian, D.A. and Baddeley, A.D. (1980) Saturation advertising and the repetition effect. *Journal of Verbal Learning and Verbal Behaviour* 19, 17–25.

Bekerian, D.A. and Dennett, J.L. (1990) Spoken and written recall of visual narratives. *Applied Cognitive Psychology* 4, 175–187.

Bekerian, D.A. and Dennett, J.L. (1993) The truth in content analyses. *Experimental Psychology: Learning, Memory and Cognition* 13, 501–518.

Bekerian, D.A. and Dennett, J.L. (1996) *The Child's Account: Evidential Interviews with Children*. Cambridgeshire County Council Publication, Cambridge.

Bekerian, D.A., Conway, M., and Dennett, J.L. (1986) Improving jurors' understanding and memory for evidence by pre and post evidence summaries. In *MRCAPU (Medical Research Council Applied Psychology Unit) Improving the Presentation of Information to Juries in Fraud Trials*, part IV. HMSO, London.

Biddle, S. and Mutrie, N. (1991) *Psychology of Physical Activity and Exercise; a Health-Related Perspective*. Springer-Verlag, London.

Bidwell, S. (1973) *Modern Warfare: a Study of Men, Weapons and Theory*. Allen Lane, London.

Binet, A. and Henry, V. (1966) *On the Psychology of Individual Differences*, 1895. In R.J. Herrnstein and E.G. Boring (eds), *A Source Book in the History of Psychology*. Harvard University Press, Cambridge, MA, pp. 428–493.

Black, A. (1986) The effect of glossaries on jurors' comprehension in fraud trials. In *MRCAPU (Medical Research Council Applied Psychology Unit) Improving the Presentation of Information to Juries in Fraud Trials*, part I. HMSO, London.

Botti, M. (2004) Men, it's time to face the painful truth. *Daily Mail*, Monday 22 November 2004, p. 5.

Bray, C.W. (1948) *Psychology and Military Proficiency: a History of the Applied Psychology Panel of the National Defence Board Research Committee*. Princeton University Press, Princeton, NJ.

Bretherton, I. and Main, M. (2000) Mary Dinsmore Saltworthy Ainsworth (1913–1999): obituary. *American Psychologist* 55, 1148–1149.

Brewin, C.R. (1988) *Cognitive Foundations of Clinical Psychology*. Laurence Erlbaum Associates, Hove.

Broadbent, D. (1958) *Perception and Communication*. Pergamon Press, Oxford.

Buchholz, R.A. (1978) An empirical study of contemporary beliefs about work in American society. *Journal of Applied Psychology* 63, 219–227.

Burnham, J. (1942) *The Managerial Revolution*. Penguin Books, Harmondsworth, Middx.

Buss, D.M. (1995) Psychological sex differences: origins through sexual selection. *American Psychologist* 50, 164–168.

Canter, D. (2000) Offender profiling and criminal identification. *Journal of Legal and Criminal Psychology* 5, 23–46.

Carmak, M.A. and Martens, R. (1979) Measuing commitment to running: a survey of runners' attitudes and mental states. *Journal of Sport Psychology* 1, 25–42.

Catell, R.B. (1943) The description of personality: basic traits resolved into clusters. *Journal of Abnormal and Social Psychology* 38, 476–506.

Ceci, S.J. and Bruck, M. (1993) Suggestibility of the child witness: a historical review and synthesis. *Psychological Bulletin* 113, 403–439.

Cermak, L., Verfaillie, M., and Chase, K. (1995) Implicit and explicit memory in amnesia: an analysis of data-driven and conceptually-driven processes. *Neuropyschology* 9, 281–290.

Chapman, P.D. (1988) *Schools as Sorters*. New York University Press, New York.

Cherry, E.C. (1953) Some experiments on the recognition of speech with one and two ears. *Journal of the Acoustical Society of America* 25, 974–979.

Christianson, S.A. and Loftus, E. (1987) Memory for traumatic events. *Applied Cognitive Psychology* 1, 225–239.

Clark, R. (1953) *Analysing the Group Structures of Rifle Squads in Combat*. Paper presented to the American Psychological Association Convention, Cleveland, OH.

Clifford, B.R. and Bull, R. (1978) *The Psychology of Person Identification*. Routledge and Kegan, Boston.

Cloninger, C.R., Sigvardsson, S., Bohman, M., and von Knorring, A.L. (1982) Predisposition to petty criminality in Swedish adoptess, II, Cross-fostering analysis of gene-environment interaction. *Archives of General Psychiatry 39*, 1242–1249.

Collaer, M.L. and Hines, M. (1995) Human behavioural sex differences: A role for gonadal hormones during early development? *Psychological Bulletin* 118, 55–107.

Coolican, H., Cassidy, T., Cherchar, A, Harrower, J., Penny, G., Sharp, R., Walley, W., and Westbury, T. (1996) *Applied Psychology.* Hodder & Stoughton Educational, London.

Cooper C.L. and Marshall, J. (1988) Sources of managerial and white collar stress. C.L. Cooper and R. Payne (eds), *Causes and Consequences of Coping with Stress at Work.* John Wiley & Sons, Chichester, pp. 219–227.

Craigshead, W.E. and Nemeroff, C.B. (2001) *Corsini Encyclopedia of Psychology and the Behavioural Sciences*, 3rd edn, vols 1–4. John Wiley & Sons, New York.

Craik, F.I.M. and Lockhart, R.S. (1972) Levels of processing: a framework for memory research. *Journal of Verbal Learning and Verbal Behaviour* 11, 671–684.

Dalgleish, T. and Morant, N. (2001) Representations of child sexual abuse: a brief psychosocial history and commentary. In T. Dalgleish and G. Davies (eds) *Recovered Memories: Seeking the Middle Ground.* John Wiley & Sons, Chichester.

Davies, G., Wilson, C., Mitchell, R., and Milsom, J. (1995) *Videotaping Children's Evidence: an Evaluation.* Home Office, London.

Descartes, R. (1972) *The Treatise of Man*, T.S. Hall (ed.). Harvard University Press, Cambridge, MA.

Diamond, S. and Casper, J. (1992) Blindfolding the jury to verdict consequences: damages, experts, and the civil jury. *Law and Society Review* 26, 513–563.

Dishman, R.K. (1982) Compliance/adherence in health-related exercise. *Health Psychology* 1, 237–267.

Donnelly, J. (2003) Blot on the landscape? *The Psychologist* 16, 246–249.

Ecclestone, C. Williams, A.C.C., and Stainton-Rogers, W. (1997) Patients' and professionals' understanding of the causes of

chronic pain. *Social Science and Medicine* 45, 699–709.

Eldridge, M., Barnard, P. and Bekerian, D. (1994) Autobiographical memory and daily schemas at work. *Memory* 2, 51–74.

Ellis, A. (1962) *Reason and Emotion in Psychotherapy.* Lyle Stuart, New York.

Ellis, A. (1999) Why rational-emotive therapy to rational emotive behaviour therapy? *Psychotherapy* 3, 23–33.

Engel, B. (1960) Stimulus-response and individual response specificity. *Archives of General Psychiatry* 2, 305–313.

Fairbanks, J.C. and Roland, M. (2001) The Roland-Morris Disability Questionnaire and the Oswestry Disability Questionnaire. *Spine* 26, 874.

Fairbanks, J.C., Couper, J., Davies, J.B., and O'Brien, J.P. (1980) The Oswestry Low Back Pain Disability Questionnaire. *Physiotherapy* 66, 271–273.

Farede. L. (1997) Brain imaging of schizophrenia: the dopamine hypothesis. *Schizophrenia Research* 28, 157–162.

Fivush, R., Hammond, C., and Reese, E. (1996) Remembering, recounting and reminiscing: the development of autobiographical memory in social context. In D. Rubin (ed.), *Remembering Our Past: Studies in Autobiographical Memory.* Cambridge University Press, Cambridge.

Foa, E., Dancu, C., Hembree, E., Jaycox, L., Meadows, E., and Street, G. (1999) A comparison of exposure therapy, stress inoculation training, and their combination for reducing posttraumatic stress disorder in female assault victims. *Journal of Consulting and Clinical Psychology* 67, 194–200.

Fodor, J. (1983) *The Modularity of Mind: an Essay on Faculty Psychology.* MIT Press, Cambridge, MA.

Forman, M. (1975) *One Flew Over the Cuckoo's Nest.* United Artists, Hollywood.

Frank, L.K. (1948) *Projective Methods.* Thomas, Springfield.

Frankl, V.E. (1992) *Man's Search for Meaning.* Beacon Press, Boston.

Freud, S. (1923) The ego and the id. In J. Strachey (ed.) *The Standard Edition of the Complete Psychological Works of Sigmund Freud,* vols 1–24. Hogarth Press, London.

Gacono, C.B. and Meloy, J.R. (1994) *Rorschach Assessment of Aggressive and Psychopathic Personalities*. Erlbaum, Hillsdale, NJ.

Geisleman, E., Fisher, R., MacKinnon, D., and Holland, H. (1985) Eyewitness memory enhancement in the police interview: cognitive retrieval mnemonics versus hypnosis. *Journal of Applied Psychology* 70, 401–412.

Gendlin, E.T. (1978) *Focusing*. Bantam Books, New York.

Gibson, J.J. (1966) *The Senses Considered as Perceptual Systems*. Houghton Mifflin, Boston.

Gilbreth, F.B. (1911) *Motion Study*. Van Nostrand, New York.

Gill, S.P. (1995) *Dialogue and Tacit Knowledge to Knowledge Transfer*. Doctoral dissertation, University of Cambridge, Cambridge.

Gill, S.P. and Borchers, J. (2003) Knowledge in co-action: social intelligence in collaborative design activity. *AI and Society* 17, 322–339.

Godden, D. and Baddeley, A.D. (1975) Context dependent memory in two natural environments: on land and under water. *British Journal of Psychology* 66, 325–331.

Goldmann, L., Ogg, T.W., and Levey, A.B. (1988) Hypnosis and daycase anaesthesia. *Anaesthesia* 43, 466–469.

Gould, D. and Darmarjian, N. (1998) Mental skills training in sport. In B. Elliott and J. Mester (eds), *Training in Sport: Applying Sport Science*. John Wiley & Sons, Chichester.

Gudjonsson, G. (1992) *Psychology of Interrogations, Confessions and Testimony*. John Wiley & Sons, Chichester.

Gudjonsson, G. and Haward, L. (1981) *Forensic Psychology: a Guide to Practice*. Routledge, London.

Guthrie, E.R. (1952) *The Psychology of Learning*. Harper & Row, New York.

Haney, C. (1980) Psychological and legal change: on the limits of a factual jurisprudence. *Law and Human Behaviour* 4, 147–200.

Harvey, M. and Herman, J. (1994) Amnesia, partial amnesia and delayed recall among adult survivors of childhood trauma. *Consciousness and Cognition* 3, 295–301.

Haward, L.R.C. (1981) *Forensic Psychology*. Batsford Academic and Educational, London.

Heidl, Jr, R.D. (1967) *Dictionary of Military and Naval Quotations*. U.S. Naval Institute, Annapolis, MD.

Heil, J. (1993) *The Psychology of Sports Injury*. Human Kinetics Publishers, Champaign, IL.

Herman, J. (1994) *Trauma and Recovery*. Pandora Books, London.

Herzberg, F. (1966) *Work and the Nature of Man*. World Publishing, Cleveland.

Hillman, D.C., Siffre, M., Milano, G. and Halberg, F. (1994) Free-running psycho-physiological circadian rhythms and three month pattern in a woman isolated in a cave. *New Trends in Experimental and Clinical Psychiatry* 10, 127–133.

Hinton, G.E. and Anderson, J.A. (eds) (1981) *Parallel Models of Associative Memory*. Erlbaum, Hillsdale.

Hoffman, B.F. and Spiegel, H. (1989) Legal principles in the psychiatric assessment of personal injury litigants. *American Journal of Psychiatry* 146, 304–310.

Hofstede, G. (1980) *Culture's Consequences: International Differences in Work Related Values*. Sage Publications, Beverly Hills.

Hollingsworth, L.S. (1916) Social devices for impelling women to bear and rear children. *American Journal of Sociology* 22, 19–29.

Hollingsworth, L.S. (1922) Differential action upon the sexes of forces which tend to segregate the feebleminded. *Journal of Abnormal Psychology and Social Psychology* 17, 35–57.

Hollway, W. (1991) *Work Psychology and Organisational Behaviour*. Sage Publications, London.

Holub, R.J. (1992) *Forensic Psychological Testing: a Survey of Practices and Beliefs*. Unpublished manuscript. Minnesota School of Professional Psychology, Bloomington.

Horne, J. (1988) *Why We Sleep: the Functions of Sleep in Humans and Other Mammals*. Oxford University Press, Oxford.

Howe, M.L. and Courage, M.L. (1997) The emergence and early development of autobiographical memory. *Psychological Review* 104, 499–523.

Hull, C.L. (1943) *Principles of Behaviour*. Appleton-Century-Crofts, New York.

Hyman, Jr, I.E. and Billings, F.J. (1998) Individual differences in the creation of false childhood memories. *Memory* 6, 1–20.

Inman, M. (1981) The admissibility of confessions. *The Criminal Law Review* July, 469–481.

International Society of Sport Psychology (1992) Physical activity and psychological benefits: A position statement from the International Society of Sport Psychology. *Journal of Applied Sport Psychology* 4, 94–98.

Jackson, J.A. and Bekerian, D.A. (eds) (1997) *Offender Profiling: Theory, Research and Practice.* John Wiley & Sons, Chichester.

Jackson, J.A., van de Eshof, P., and de Klever, E. (1998) Offender profiles in the Netherlands. In J.A. Jackson and D.A. Bekerian (eds), *Offender Profiling: Theory, Research & Practice.* John Wiley & Sons, Chichester.

Jacoby, L. (1984) Incidental versus intentional retrieval: remembering and awareness as separate issues. In L. Squire and N. Butters (eds), *Neuropsychology of Memory.* Guilford Press, New York.

James, W. (1884) What is an emotion? *Mind* 9, 188–205.

James, W. (1904) Does 'consciousness' exist? *Journal of Philosophy, Psychology and Scientific Methods* 1, 477–491.

Janet, P. (1892) *L'etat Mental des Hysteriques* [English translation: The Mental State of Hystericals: a Study of Mental Stigmata and Mental Accidents (1901)]. Putnam and Sons, New York.

Janoff-Bullman, R. (1992) *Shattered Assumptions: Towards a New Psychology of Trauma.* Free Press, New York.

Johnson, M. and Hasher, L. (1987) Human learning and memory. *Annual Review of Psychology* 38, 631–638.

Johnson, M. and Wiggins, E. (1994) Drawing on the experiences of alternative decision makers: can we preserve the jury in complex civil litigation? *Behavioural Sciences and the Law* 12, 161–179.

Jones, M.C. (1924) A laboratory study of fear: the case of Peter. *Pedagogical Seminary* 38, 308–315.

Jung, C.G. (1963) *Memories, Dreams and Reflections* (recorded and edited by Aniela Jaffe). Collins and Routledge & Kegan Paul, London.

Kahneman, D. and Tversky, A. (eds) (2000) *Choices, Values and Frames.* Cambridge University Press, Cambridge.

Kardiner, A. and Spiegel, H. (1947) *War, Stress and Neurotic Illness.* Hoeber, New York.

Karon, B.P. and Widener, A. (1998) Repressed memories: The true story. *Professional Psychology: Research and Practice* 29, 482–487.

Kassin, S.M., Ellsworth, P., and Smith, V. (1989) The 'general acceptance' of psychological research on eyewitness testimony. *American Psychologist* 44, 1089–1098.

Katzell, R.A. and Thomson, D.E. (1990) Work motivation. *American Psychologist* 45, 144–153.

Kellett, A. (1982) *Combat Motivation: the Behaviour of Soldiers in Battle.* Kluwer Academic, Dordrecht.

Koper, J.A., Esdaile, J.M., Abrahamowicz, S., Lamping, D.L., and Williams, J.L. (1996) The Quebec Back Pain Disability Scale: conceptualisation and development. *Journal of Clinical Epidemiology* 49, 151–161.

Kosslyn, S.M. (1980) *Image and Mind.* Harvard University Press, Cambridge, MA.

Kroeber, A.L. (1948) *Anthropology.* Harcourt Brace Jovanovich, New York.

Kubrick, S. (1971) *A Clockwork Orange.* Warner Bros, Hollywood.

Kuhn, T.S. (1970) *Structure of Scientific Revolutions.* Cambridge University Press, London.

Kurleycheck, R.T. (1984) The contributions of forensic neuropsychology. *American Journal of Forensic Psychology* 2, 147–152.

Lacey, J., Bateman, D., and Van Lehn, R. (1953) Autonomic response specificity: an experimental study. *Psychosomatic Medicine* 15, 8–21.

Ladd, G.T. (1894) Is psychology a science? *Psychological Review* 1, 392–395.

Lambie, J.A. and Marcel, A.J. (2002) Consciousness and the varieties of emotional experience: a theoretical framework. *Psychological Review* 109, 219–259.

Laufer, M. and Laufer, E.M. (1995) *Adolescence and Adolescent Breakdown.* Yale University Press, New Haven, CN.

Lee, D. (1980) Visuo-motor co-ordination in space-time. In G.E. Stelmach and J. Requin (eds), *Tutorials in Motor Behaviour*. North-Holland, Amsterdam.

Levey, A.B. and Goldmann, L. (1986) Orienting under anaesthesia. *Anaesthesia* 44, 1056–1057.

Levey, A.B., Aldaz, J.A., Watts, F.N., and Coyle, K (1991) Articulatory suppression and the treatment of insomnia. *Behavioural Research and Therapy* 29, 85–89.

Lev-Wiesel, R. and Doron, H.(2004) Allowing clients to choose their preferable nonverbal therapeutic modality. *The Arts in Psychotherapy* 31, 261–269.

Ley, R. (1978) Memory for medical information. In M. Gruneberg, P. Morris, and R Sykes (eds) *Practical Aspects of Memory*. Academic Press, London, pp. 120–127.

Locke, E.A. (1990) What is job satisfaction? *Organisational Behaviour and Human Performance* 4, 309–336.

Loftus, E. (1979) *Eyewitness Testimony*. Harvard University Press, Cambridge, MA.

Loftus, E. and Burns, T. (1982) Mental shock can produce retrograde amnesia. *Memory and Learning* 10, 318–323.

Logie, R., Duncan, J., and Baddeley, A.J. (1986) Difficulties in listening to complex information. In *MRCAPU (Medical Research Council Applied Psychology Unit) Improving the Presentation of Information to Juries in Fraud Trials*, part III. HMSO, London.

Maehr, M.L. and Braskamp, L.A. (1986) *The Motivation Factor: a Theory of Personal Investment*. Lexington Books, Lexington, MA.

Malpass, R.S. and Devine, P.G. (1981) Guided memory in eyewitness identification research. *Journal of Applied Psychology* 66, 343–350.

Marr, D. (1982) *Vision: a Computational Investigation into the Human Representation and Processing of Visual Information*. W.H. Freeman & Company, New York.

Marshall, S.L.A. (1950) *Men Against Fire*. Infantry Journal Press, William Morrow and Co, Washington DC.

Masson, J. (1989) *Against Therapy*. Collins, Glasgow.

May, R. (1953) *Man's Search for Himself*. George Allen and Unwin, London.

May, R. (1969) *Existential Psychology*. Random House, New York.

May, R. (1983) *The Discovery of Being*. W.W. Norton and Co, New York.

May, R., Ellenberg, H.F., and Angel, E. (eds) (1958) *Existence: a New Dimension in Psychiatry and Psychology*. Simon & Shuster, New York.

Mayo, E. (1933) *The Human Problems of an Industrial Civilisation*. Appleton-Century-Crofts, New York.

McClelland, D.C., Atkinson, J.W., Clark R.A., and Lowell, E.L. (1953) *The Achievement Motive*. Appleton-Century-Crofts, New York.

McLeod, P., McLaughlin, C., and Nimmo-Smith, I. (1985) Information encapsulation and automaticity: evidence from the visual control of finely timed actions. In M.I. Posner and O.M. Marin (eds), *Attention and Performance XI*. Lawrence Erlbaum Associates, London.

Melton, G., Petrila, J., Poythress, N., and Slobgin, C. (1997) *Psychological Evaluations for the Court: a Handbook for Mental Health Professionals and Lawyers*. Guilford Press, New York.

Mischel, W. (1968) *Personality and Assessment*. John Wiley & Sons, New York.

Morgan, W.P. (1985) Selected psychological factors limiting performance: a mental health model. In D. Clarke and H. Eckert (eds), *Limits of Human Performance*, Academy Paper, No. 18. Human Kinetics Publishers, Champaign, IL.

Morton, J., Andrews, B., Bekerian, D., Brewin, C., Davies, G., and Mollon, P. (1995) *Recovered Memories: the Report of the Working Party of the British Psychological Society*. British Psychology Society Publications, London.

Munsterberg, H. (1908) *On the Witness Stand: Essays on Psychology and Crime*. Doubleday, New York.

Munsterberg, H. (1913) (reprinted 1933) *Psychology and Industrial Efficiency*. Hive Publishing Company, Easton.

Natsoulas, T. (1978) Consciousness. *American Psychologist* 33, 906–914.

Neisser, U. (1967) *Cognitive Psychology*. Appleton-Century-Crofts, New York.

Neisser, U. (1976) *Cognition and Reality*. Freeman Press, San Francisco.

Neisser, U. (1978) Memory: what are the important questions? In M. Gruneberg, P. Morris, and R. Sykes (eds), *Practical Aspects of Memory*. Academic Press, London, pp. 3–20.

Neisser, U. (1981) John Dean's memory: a case study, *Cognition* 9, 1–22.

Neisser, U. (1984) Interpreting Harry Bahrick's discovery: what confers immunity against forgetting? *Journal of Experimental Psychology: General* 113, 32–35.

Neitzel, M., McCarthy, D., and Kerr, M. (1999) Juries: the current state of the empirical literature. In R. Roesch, S. Hart, and J. Ogloff (eds), *Psychology and Law: the State of the Discipline*. Kluwer, New York, pp. 25–52.

Nideffer, R.N. (1989) Predicting human behaviour: a theory and test of attentional and interpersonal style. Enhanced Performance Services, Oakland, CA.

Osofsky, J. (1995) The effects of exposure to violence on young children. *American Psychologist* 50, 782–788.

Palmer, S. (1975) The effects of contextual scenes on the perception of objects. *Memory and Cognition* 3, 519–526.

Patterson, R.D. (1990) Auditory warning sounds in the work environment. *Philosophical Transactions of the Royal Society Series B* 327, 485–492.

Pavlov, I.P. (1932) The reply of a physiologist to psychologists. *Psychological Review* 39, 91–127.

Petrovic, P., Kalso, E., Petersson, M., and Ingvar, M. (2002) Placebo and opioid analgesia: imaging a shared neuronal network. *Science Express Reports* February, 17–22.

Porteus, M. (1997) *Occupational Psychology*. Prentice-Hall, London.

Postman, L. and Underwood, B.J. (1973) Critical issues in interference theory. *Memory and Cognition* 1, 19–40.

Prichard, J.C. (1845) *The Natural History of Man*. Hippolyte Balliere, London.

Raesaenen, S., Pakaslahti, A., Syvaelahti, E., Hones, P., and Isohanni, M. (2000) Sex differences in schizophrenia: a review. *Nordic Journal of Psychiatry* 54, 37–45.

Richardson, R. (1978) *Fighting Spirit: a Study of Psychological Factors in War*. Leo Cooper, London.

Riggio, R.E. (2000) *Introduction to Industrial/Organisational Psychology*. Prentice-Hall, London.

Roediger, H. and McDermott, K. (1993) Implicit memory in normal human subjects. In J. Foster and M. Jelic (eds), *Handbook of Neuropsychology*. Elsevier, Amsterdam.

Roesch, R., Hart, S., and Ogloff, J. (eds) (1999) *Psychology and Law: State of the Discipline*. Kluwer Academic, New York.

Rogers, C. (1951) *Client Centred Therapy*. Houghton-Mifflin, Boston, MA.

Rogers, W.S. (2001) Explaining illness as a discursive strategy. *Health Psychology Update* 10, 29–32.

Rozenberg, J. (2003) Why juries could soon be retiring for good. *Daily Telegraph* 22 May 2003, p. 23.

Ryan, R.M., Frederick, C.M., Lepes, D., Rubio, N., and Sheldon, K.M. (1997) Intrinsic motivation and exercise adherence. *International Journal of Sport Psychology*. 28, 335–354.

Schein, E.H. (1988) *Organisational Psychology*, 3rd edn. Prentice-Hall, Englewood Cliffs, NJ.

Schneider, R.M. and Shiffrin, W. (1977) Controlled and automatic human information processing II: perceptual learning, automatic attending and a general theory. *Psychological Review* 84, 127–190.

Seligman, M.E.P. (1978) Comment and integration. *Journal of Abnormal Psychology* 87, 165–179.

Seligman, M.E.P. (1998) *Learned Optimism*. Pocket Books, New York.

Semeneoff, B. (1976) *Projective Techniques*. John Wiley & Sons, Chichester.

Shallice, T. and Warrington, E.K. (1970) Independent functioning of verbal memory stores: a neuropsychological study. *Quarterly Journal of Experimental Psychology* 22, 261–273.

Sherrington, C.S. (1933) *The Brain and Its Mechanisms*. Cambridge University Press, Cambridge.

Shiffrin, R.M. and Schneider, W. (1977) Controlled and automatic human information processing I: detection search and attention. *Psychological Review* 84, 1–66.

Sharp, B. (1992) *Acquiring Skills in Sport*. Sports Dynamics, Eastbourne.

Springer, S.P. and Deutsch, G. (1998) *Left Brain, Right Brain*, 5th edn. Freeman Press, New York.

Stevens, J. (1998) Standard investigatory tools and offender profiling. In J.A. Jackson and D.A. Bekerian (eds), *Offender Profiling: Theory, Research and Practice*. John Wiley & Sons, Chichester.

Sun Tzu (1997) *The Art of Strategy* (translated by R.L. Wing). Thorsons, London.

Sweet, J.J., Moberg, P.J., and Westergaard, C.F. (1996) Five year follow-up of practices and beliefs of clinical neuropsychologists. *The Clinical Neuropsychologist* 10, 202–221.

Tateyama, M., Asai, M., Kamisad, M., and Hasimoto, M. (1993) Comparison of schizophrenic delusions between Japan and Germany. *Psychopathology* 26, 151–158.

Taulbee, P. (1983) Solving the mystery of anxiety. *Science News* 124, 45.

Taylor, F.W. (1911) *The Principles of Scientific Management*. Harper, New York.

Teasdale, J. and Barnard, P.J. (1993) *Affect Cognition and Change*. Erlbaum, Hove.

Tredgold, A. (1920) *Mental Deficiency*. Wm. Wood and Co, New York.

Tuckman, B. (1965) Developmental sequences in small groups. *Psychological Bulletin* 63, 384–399.

Tulving, E. and Thomson, D. (1973) Encoding specificity and retrieval processes in episodic memory. *Psychological Review* 80, 352–373.

Turner, J.A., Deyo, R.A., and Loeser, J.D. (1994) The importance of placebo effects in pain treatment and research. *Journal of the American Medical Association* 271, 1609–1614.

Undevtsch, U. (1982) Statement reality analysis. In A. Trankell (ed.), *Reconstructing the Past*. Law and Taxation Publishers, Deventer.

Van der Ver, A. (1980) *Introduction to Scaling*. John Wiley & Sons, Chichester.

Wagenaar, W.A. (1978) Memory for public broadcasts. In M. Gruneberg, P. Morris, and R. Sykes (eds), *Practical Aspects of Memory*. Academic Press, London.

Wagenaar, W.A. (1988) *Identifying Ivan*. Harvester-Wheatsheaf, Hemel Hempstead.

Wagstaff, G., Vella, M., and Perfect, T. (1992) The effect of hypnotically elicited testimony on jurors' judgement of guilt and innocence. *Journal of Social Psychology* 132, 591–595.

Watson, J. (1913) Psychology as the behaviorist views it. *Psychological Review* 20, 158–177.

Watson, P. (1980) *War on the Mind: the Military Uses and Abuses of Psychology*. Penguin Books, New York.

Webb, W.B. and Agnew, Jr, H.W. (1974) Sleeping and waking in a time free environment. *Aerospace Medicine* 45, 617–622.

Weekes, J., Lynn, S., Green, J., and Brentar, J. (1992) Psuedomemory in hypnotised and task motivated subjects. *Journal of Abnormal Psychology* 10, 356–360.

Weiskrantz, L. (1995) Comments on the Report of the Working Party of the British Psychological Society on 'Recovered Memories'. In *Recovered Memories: the Report of the Working Party of the British Psychological Society*. British Psychological Society Publications, London.

Weissman, H.N. (1985) Psycholegal standards and the role of psychological assessment in personal injury litigation. *Behavioral Sciences and the Law* 3, 135–147.

Wells, G. (1978) Applied eyewitness testimony research: system variables and estimator variables. *Journal of Personality and Social Psychology* 36, 1546–1557.

Wells, G. (1988) *Eyewitness Identification: a Systems Handbook*. Carswell Legal Publications, Toronto.

Wells, G. and Lindsay, R.C.L. (1985) Methodological notes on the confidence accuracy relationship in eyewitness identifications. *Journal of Applied Psychology* 70, 413–419.

Whelton, W.J. (2004) Emotional processes in psychotherapy: evidence across therapeutic modalities. *Clinical Psychology and Psychotherapy* 11, 58–71 (published online).

Wigmore, J. (1909) Professor Munsterberg and the psychology of testimony. *Illinois Law Review* 3, 399–445.

Wing, R.L. (1997) Art of Strategy: The Lending Modern Translation of Tzu's Classic. *The Art of War*. Thorsons, London.

Wolff, A. and O'Driscoll, G. (1999) Motor deficits and schizophrenia: The evidence from neuroleptic-naive patients and populations at risk. *Journal of Psychiatry and Neuroscience* 24, 304–314.

Wong, D.F., Wagner, H.N. and Tune, L.E. (1986) Positron emission tomography reveals elevated D2 receptors in drug naïve schizophrenics. *Science* 234, 1558–1563.

Wright, P., Lickorish, A., and Hull, A. (1985) Presenting numerical information to fraud jurors. In *MRCAPU (Medical Research Council Applied Psychology Unit) Improving the Presentation of Information to Juries in Fraud Trials*, part II. HMSO, London.

Yerkes, R. and Dodson, J. (1908) The relation of strength of stimulus to rapidity of habit-formation. *Journal of Comparative Neurology and Psychology* 18, 459–482.

Zigmond, A.S. and Snaith, R.P. (1983) The Hospital Anxiety and Depression Scale. *Acta Psychiatrica Scandanavica* 67, 361–370.

Zubieta, J.K., Smith, Y.R., and Bueller, J.A. (2001) Regional mu opioid receptor regulation of sensory and affective dimensions of pain. *Science* 293, 311–315.

■ SUBJECT INDEX

■ INDEX OF NAMES